DUE PROCESS OF LAWMAKING

With nuanced perspective and detailed case studies, *Due Process of Lawmaking* explores the law of lawmaking in the United States, South Africa, Germany, and the European Union. This comparative work deals broadly with public policymaking in the legislative and executive branches. It frames the inquiry through three principles of legitimacy: democracy, rights, and competence. Drawing on the insights of positive political economy, the authors explicate the ways courts uphold these principles in the different systems. Judicial review in the American presidential system suggests lessons for the parliamentary systems in Germany and South Africa, while the experience of parliamentary government yields potential insights into the reform of the American law of lawmaking. Taken together, the national experiences shed light on the special case of the European Union. In dialogue with each other, the case studies demonstrate the interplay between constitutional principles and political imperatives under a range of different conditions.

Susan Rose-Ackerman is the Henry R. Luce Professor of Jurisprudence (Law and Political Science) at Yale University. She has published widely on administrative law, corruption, federalism, and law and economics. She is the author of *From Elections to Democracy: Building Accountable Government in Hungary and Poland* (2005) and *Corruption and Government: Causes, Consequences, and Reform* (1999) (translated into seventeen languages; second edition, with Bonnie Palifka, forthcoming). Her current research and teaching interests are the comparative study of administrative law and public policy analysis, with a focus on the United States and Western Europe, and the political economy of corruption and its control. She directs the program in comparative administrative law at Yale Law School.

Stefanie Egidy studied law and European law at the universities of Würzburg, Germany, and Bergen, Norway. She obtained an LL.M. degree at Yale Law School with scholarships from the German National Academic Foundation and the German Academic Exchange Service. She worked as a research and teaching assistant at the University of Würzburg and as a research assistant for Aharon Barak. Egidy is currently completing her doctoral dissertation on the constitutional problems of financial market stabilization in financial crises at the University of Würzburg under the supervision of Helmuth Schulze-Fielitz, while working as a research fellow at the Max Planck Institute for Research on Collective Goods in Bonn, Germany.

James Fowkes obtained a law degree from the University of the Witwatersrand, South Africa, and an LL.M. from Yale Law School as a Fulbright Scholar. He completed his JSD at Yale under the supervision of Bruce Ackerman. Fowkes clerked at the South African Constitutional Court in 2008 and has held research fellowships at the Max Planck Institute for Comparative and International Private Law, Hamburg and the Max Planck Institute for Comparative Public Law and International Law, Heidelberg, Germany. He is currently Senior Researcher at the Institute for International and Comparative Law in Africa at the University of Pretoria, South Africa. He has published articles in the *South African Journal on Human Rights*, the *Constitutional Court Review*, and the *Cambridge Journal of International and Public Law.*

CAMBRIDGE
UNIVERSITY PRESS

32 Avenue of the Americas, New York, NY 10013-2473, USA

Cambridge University Press is part of the University of Cambridge.

It furthers the University's mission by disseminating knowledge in the pursuit of education, learning, and research at the highest international levels of excellence.

www.cambridge.org
Information on this title: www.cambridge.org/9781107043671

First published 2015

A catalog record for this publication is available from the British Library.

Library of Congress Cataloging in Publication data
Rose-Ackerman, Susan, author.
Due process of lawmaking : the United States, South Africa, Germany, and the European Union / Susan Rose-Ackerman, Yale University, Ct.; Stefanie Egidy, Max Planck Institute for Research on Collective Goods, Bonn, Germany; James Fowkes, University of Pretoria, South Africa
pages cm
ISBN 978-1-107-04367-1 (hbk.)
1. Due process of law – United States. 2. Due process of law. I. Egidy, Stefanie, 1984– author. II. Fowkes, James, 1984– author. III. Title.
KF4765.R67 2015
342.73′052–dc23 2014020986

ISBN 978-1-107-04367-1 Hardback

Contents

Preface

This project began with a conversation among the three authors at Yale Law School about our joint interest in comparative public law, especially administrative law and the law of lawmaking. Over time it developed into a book manuscript as we shared drafts and discussed new issues. Our book's title is borrowed from the title of a seminal article by Hans Linde that was one inspiration for our project. That article, *Due Process of Lawmaking*, published in 1975, focused on judicial review of the legislative process at the federal and state levels in the United States. We build on his analysis to contrast the legislative with the administrative process and to compare the United States with Germany, South Africa, and the European Union.

One of us, Rose-Ackerman, has been interested in comparative administrative law and public policymaking since 1991–2 when she spent a year in Berlin under Fulbright and Guggenheim fellowships. The result was a book, *Controlling Environmental Policy: The Limits of Public Law in Germany and the United States* (1995), that combines legal and social science analyses to contrast executive branch policymaking processes in the two countries. Ten years later she lived in Budapest and wrote a companion book on executive policymaking in Eastern Europe entitled *From Elections to Democracy: Building Accountable Government in Hungary and Poland* (2005). With this background, she has developed a broader interest in comparative policymaking processes in the executive and in independent agencies, but the legislative process is, for her, a new topic.

Stefanie Egidy's and James Fowkes's comparative law interests were fuelled by their studies at Yale Law School combined with their research in their home countries of Germany and South Africa, respectively. Both have carried out research that complements the present study. Egidy's doctoral research analyzes German and U.S. policy during the financial crisis in 2008/2009. Government responses to that crisis raise fundamental questions about the constitutional requirements of the legislative process in urgent, multidimensional situations where legislative and executive powers interact. It reflects her deeper interest in the ways procedure can help safeguard constitutional values. Fowkes's doctoral thesis, *Building the Constitution: The Practice of Constitutional Interpretation in Post-Apartheid South Africa* (J.S.D., Yale Law School, 2014), draws on both legal and political theory to understand the work done by the South African Constitutional Court since its creation in 1995 as well as the vital, underacknowledged role of the African National Congress government in constructing the country's celebrated constitutionalism.

Our conversations on the law of lawmaking were motivated by two constitutional law cases, one from Germany and one from South Africa, that are striking to an American scholar of public law. In the South African case, *Doctors for Life*, the Constitutional Court struck down two statutes because there was insufficient consultation before passage. In the German case, *Hartz IV*, the Constitutional Court voided part of a statute because the legislature did not articulate the factual basis of key provisions. These decisions contrast with the American case, where legislative procedures and reasons are seldom subject to court review. Of course, as we examined these cases and the legal landscape further, we discovered much nuance and complexity in all three legal regimes, a complexity that is also reflected in the experience of the European Union, a case that we added for contrast and because the German case operates with the European Union as a background.

We began with the goal of writing a law review article, but the project soon developed a logic of its own and grew to book length as we moved beyond our initial interest in judicial review of the legislative process. We saw that we also needed to draw on our interests in administrative law to compare democratic accountability, technical competence, and the protection of rights in both the legislative and the rulemaking processes in the executive and the independent agencies. The result, we hope, will provide insights not only to public lawyers and policymaking in our case study countries, but also to those in other polities seeking ways to enhance the democratic accountability of both the legislature and the executive without sacrificing competence or the protection of rights.

Several people commented on portions of the draft within their areas of expertise. We wish to thank Bruce Ackerman, Tom Ginsburg, Michaela Hailbronner, Jonathan Klaaren, Patrick Luff, Jud Matthews, Joana Mendes, Nicholas Parrillo, Matthias Rossbach, Ewold Sakkers, Johannes Saurer, Kevin Stack, Peter Strauss, and the Cambridge University Press referees for their essential help as the manuscript developed. We are also very grateful to Cathy Orcutt for her excellent work on the index and her other assistance in preparing the manuscript and to the Yale Law School librarians for their expert help. The financial support of the Yale Law School is gratefully acknowledged.

Introduction

Laws are like sausages. It is better not to see them being made.[1]

If this republic is remembered in the distant history of law, it is likely to be for its enduring adherence to legitimate institutions and processes, not for its perfection of unique principles of justice and certainly not for the rationality of its laws.

Hans Linde[2]

Our topic is the law of lawmaking – both in the legislature and in the executive. Combining knowledge and insights from the United States, South Africa, Germany, and the European Union, we illustrate the distinctive value of comparative work.[3] We strive for a middle ground between particularism and universalism. By comparing different responses to similar problems, observers in different countries can learn something about the strengths and weaknesses of their own legal systems. We show how fundamental differences in institutional design shape the very nature of due process of lawmaking in both the legislative and the executive branches. Most notably, we stress the way presidential and parliamentary forms of government influence the lawmaking process, and we show how fundamental

1 Remark attributed to Otto von Bismarck. According to Fred Shapiro of the Yale Law Library, the earliest attribution to Bismarck occurred in CLAUDIUS O. JOHNSON, GOVERNMENT IN THE UNITED STATES (1933). Shapiro's search of online newspaper archives points to a lawyer-poet named John Godfrey Saxe as the originator of the quip. Saxe is quoted in the DAILY CLEVELAND HERALD, Mar. 29, 1869 as saying: "Laws, like sausages, cease to inspire respect in proportion as we know how they are made." Saxe was the attorney general of Vermont, a two-time Democratic candidate for governor of New York, and eventually the editor of the NEW YORK EVENING JOURNAL. Fred Shapiro, *You Can Quote Them*, YALE ALUMNI MAGAZINE, July/August 2009.

2 Hans Linde, *Due Process of Lawmaking*, **55** NEBRASKA LAW REV. 197, 255 (1975–6).

3 *See also* SUSAN ROSE-ACKERMAN & PETER LINDSETH, EDS. COMPARATIVE ADMINISTRATIVE LAW (2010).

constitutional structures and values influence constitutional court review. In contrast, particularism stresses the deeply contingent nature of law and sees it as an outgrowth of the unique history of each society. Under that view, comparisons are touristic exercises that detail the exotic practices of strange places. We reject the strong form of that claim. History does matter, but it is not destiny. We also differ from those universalists who stress the intrinsic value of "the rule of law" or of human rights as expressed in the UN Universal Declaration of Human Rights, the European Convention on Human Rights, and similar texts.[4] We do not try to adjudicate debates over the meaning of the rule of law, and we do not seek to assess the proper content of rights or take a stand on which rights ought to be universally recognized. We take the differing contents of rights across our cases as given, and focus instead on democratic legitimacy.

We study the law of government policymaking – in the legislature, in the executive, and in the courts. Most constitutions contain little guidance on the substance of policy beyond the protection of rights. Rather, the legitimacy of the state to its citizens derives from the acceptability of its institutions and the procedures they follow. We show that in polities with basically democratic structures, there is room for a range of institutional choices, both in fact and in principle.

The closest cousin of our effort is the project on Global Administrative Law (GAL). That project began as a collaboration between a professor of American administrative law and two colleagues who specialized in international law; it has expanded to involve many scholars worldwide. Its protagonists have produced a casebook that frames the project.[5] At its core GAL studies international bodies with policymaking authority that are

[4] United Nations General Assembly, Universal Declaration of Human Rights, adopted December 10, 1948, http://www.un.org/en/documents/udhr/; Council of Europe, The European Convention on Human Rights (ECHR), adopted Rome, November 4, 1950 as amended, http://www.hri.org/docs/ECHR50.html. There is considerable overlap in the basic rights, but the UN Universal Declaration includes a number of substantive rights not included in the ECHR. The Universal Declaration is not directly enforceable. The ECHR is enforced by the European Court of Human Rights, although its remedies are limited and its caseload is overwhelming. For a strong statement on the priority of rights, *see* Ronald Dworkin, Taking Rights Seriously (1978).

[5] Benedict Kingsbury, Nico Krisch, & Richard B. Stewart, *The Emergence of Global Administrative Law*, **68** Law and Contemporary Problems 15 (2005); Benedict Kingsbury, *The Concept of "Law" in Global Administrative Law*, **20** European J. Int. Law 23 (2009). The GAL casebook is: S. Cassese, B. Carotti, L. Casini, E. Cavalieri, & E. MacDonald, eds., Global Administrative Law: The Casebook (3rd edition, 2012), available at: http://www.amazon.it/Global-Administrative-Law-Casebook-ebook/dp/B009JDN33U/ref=sr_1_3?ie=UTF8&qid=1349039229&sr=8-3

distinct from national polities. Many of them are free-standing administrations, not checked by legislatures, courts, or even quasi-constitutional texts. GAL's normative stance borrows the basic framework of the American rulemaking process with its focus on transparency, outside access, and reason-giving based on a rational connection between means and ends. We share GAL's interest in the public legitimacy of policymaking, but our focus is somewhat different. Like GAL, we study process; unlike GAL, we concentrate on well-developed polities responsible to a defined citizenry and containing legislatures and courts as well as administrative policymaking bodies. We seek both to provide a positive political economy argument for the cross-national differences we see and to argue for productive cross-country learning.

We hope to show that comparative public law is a two-way street. American law has lessons for the parliamentary systems in Germany and South Africa. Conversely, the parliamentary systems suggest potential reforms of the U.S. law of lawmaking. The European Union is special, but our other cases provide some lessons as the European Union struggles to balance the competing demands of the Parliament, the Council, the Commission, and of its Member States.

We argue that constitutional courts should review the democratic legitimacy of procedures *both* when they are deployed by the legislature in making laws *and* by the executive in making rules that have the force of law. But this is not an unproblematic enterprise. Courts that insist on "due process of lawmaking" must do so in ways that respect the underlying realities of each nation's constitutional structure and acknowledge the limited competence of the judiciary.

The basic empirical differences are clear and striking. Under the U.S. presidential system, the federal courts do not review internal legislative processes to check their democratic efficacy. Rather, legislative deliberations only enter the picture, if at all, as part of efforts to convince the *courts* that a statute has a valid substantive justification. In contrast, review of executive rulemaking is fundamentally concerned with the *public* accountability of rulemaking in agencies and cabinet departments.

The German Federal Constitutional Court is more likely than the U.S. Supreme Court to scrutinize the factual bases of statutes – an enterprise that can lead it to review the legislative process as well. The German Basic Law's list of constitutional rights covers many more substantive policy areas than does the U.S. document; hence, the German Constitutional Court can review the legislative reasoning behind a broader range of statutes than the U.S. Supreme Court. In contrast to the United States, however,

discuss the traditional due process or rule of law concerns that focus on the state's treatment of particular individuals.[9] We use the insights of positive political economy to explicate the role of courts in the review of policy-making procedures in the legislative and in the executive. We then consider our four cases and ask if existing legal patterns are sufficient to uphold democratic values in these polities with their rather different constitutional structures.

The three principles of legitimacy – democracy, rights, and competence – overlap and conflict in practice, and modern constitutions deal with the tensions in different ways. One route to legitimacy is through process, but the appropriate response is not always obvious. Procedures that further one type of legitimacy – say, individual rights – may limit others – for instance, democratic legitimacy or competence. The judiciary plays a role in policing these tensions and conflicts, and we study its role in monitoring and controlling legislative and administrative procedures. Our study puts the courts front and center as they confront the paradoxes of their role in reviewing how the rest of the state goes about its work.[10] As unelected bodies, how can they legitimately monitor other institutions that are more closely tied to the electorate and its elected representatives?

A key feature of judicial review is the link between the separation of powers and checks and balances. The separation of powers requires each branch to stay within certain boundaries to avoid interfering with the others. It counsels courts to show restraint, especially when dealing with politically sensitive issues. The doctrine of checks and balances holds that, in exercising its own particular powers, each branch should constrain the others' potential abuses. Some scholars stress that the separation of powers permits independent action by each branch; others see institutional separation

SOCIAL TRUST IN POST-SOVIET TRANSITION 13 (János Kornai, Bo Rothstein, & Susan Rose-Ackerman, eds., 2004). The connection that Rothstein posits may well be an important determinant of government legitimacy, but it is not our object of study. It might be necessary, but it can hardly be sufficient – for example, if the basic legal texts are themselves irrational and unconnected to citizen demands.

9 We also do not study the law of torts, contracts, and property that provides a framework for private activity. The literature on due process and the rule of law that covers these senses of the term is vast. For an overview, which incorporates our topic as a subset, see Jeremy Waldron, *The Concept of the Rule of Law*, **43** GEORGIA LAW REV. 1 (2008–9). For a general overview in the context of fragile states, see Susan Rose-Ackerman, *Establishing the Rule of Law*, in WHEN STATES FAIL: CAUSES AND CONSEQUENCES (Robert Rotberg, ed., 2004).

10 We leave to one side the role of higher-level courts in reviewing the procedures used by the courts themselves.

as a route to oversight without direct hierarchical supervision.[11] We will be exploring the complex ways courts check both the legislature and the executive in our cases.

Constitutional and statutory provisions frequently restrict the jurisdiction of the courts to cases involving the violation of rights. But other texts enable judges to impose procedural and structural constraints on both the executive and the legislature. These "process controls" can be quite aggressive and can merge with substance. For example, if the law requires the executive to give reasons before issuing a rule, is that a procedural requirement or a means for the courts to review substance? In all our case studies, courts exercise one or another kind of process control, but there are many differences in legal provisions. We will be exploring how interstate textual differences might be explained through a mixture of constitutional and democratic principles, on the one hand, and political self-interest, on the other.

Written texts only take us part way to an adequate understanding. Courts also play an independent role in defining their mandate in more or less aggressive fashion. Judges have different understandings of the restraints imposed by the separation of powers under their constitutions, and they also differ on the need to maintain the judiciary's reputation with the public and with the rest of government. They sometimes test the boundaries of their role through constitutional and statutory interpretations that challenge the political choices of the executive and the legislature.

To elaborate these tensions, we compare the U.S. presidential system with two parliamentary democracies, South Africa and Germany, and with the European Union. In each case, we place the judiciary in the broader constitutional and governmental structure of our case studies. We then ask some basic normative questions: Have the courts usefully contributed to the functioning of the political/policymaking system? Can the experience of one system contribute lessons to aid in the improvement of others? The

[11] *See, e.g.*, Torsten Persson, Gérard Roland, & Guido Tabellini, *Separation of Powers and Political Accountability* **112** Quarterly J. of Economics 1163 (1997). *See* Bruce Ackerman, *The New Separation of Powers*, **113** Harvard Law Rev. 633 (2000) for an overview of the debate and proposals for constitutional reform. In presidential systems chief executives have sometimes asserted that the separation of powers implies that the other branches cannot legitimately check their actions. *See, e.g.*, Susan Rose-Ackerman, Diane A. Desierto, & Natalia Volosin, *Hyper-Presidentialism: Separation of Powers without Checks and Balances in Argentina and the Philippines*, **29** Berkeley J. of International Law 101 (2011), http://www.boalt.org/bjil/documents/Rose-Ackerman.pdf

first chapter outlines our basic framework. We then focus sequentially on the United States, South Africa, Germany, and the European Union. We conclude by summarizing our findings and reflecting on the relationship between judicial review and the values of democratic legitimacy and policymaking competence.

1

Political Economy and Constitutional Law

Broad differences in judicial review motivate our inquiry. At one end, the U.S. courts provide much more review of executive policymaking processes than those in the other systems. The U.S. judiciary seldom reviews the democratic character or competence of the legislative process. Our other cases make less of a distinction between statutes and executive rules; both are subject to limited judicial review.

The U.S. Constitution is silent on policymaking inside government departments and agencies. However, statutes fill the gap. Review in the United States derives not just from constitutional and judge-made law, but also from the rulemaking and judicial review provisions of the Administrative Procedure Act (APA) and of substantive statutes.[1] Courts in South Africa and Germany could legally review rulemaking procedures, but they seldom do so because they lack explicit legal mandates that would provide a framework for review and set standards of oversight.[2] Courts in both countries

1 The terminology is not standardized across legal systems. We will use the term *rulemaking* to refer to government policy documents issued by any executive body or independent agency that have external legal force. They are legally equivalent to statutes, although if a statute conflicts with a rule, the statute dominates. Another umbrella term, which we also use, is *secondary legislation*. Thus, we seek to distinguish this category of policymaking both from policy built up through a multitude of adjudications and from *guidelines* or *policy statements* that merely create a framework for implementation without creating legal rights or duties. We also recognize that in Germany the term *agency* is sometimes used only to refer to independent or quasi-independent bodies that regulate particular sectors or provide oversight of the government itself. However, we use the term in the looser American sense also to cover core executive branch bodies, such as the Environmental Protection Agency. If the distinction between independent agencies and other public bodies is important to our argument, we clarify our meaning in the text.

2 In South Africa it remains unclear if the term *administrative acts* in the Promotion of Administrative Justice Act includes rulemaking. If the South African Constitutional Court reads rulemaking into the Act, as seems likely, then rulemaking will be subject to an array of procedural standards and duties. *See* Chapter 3.

review adjudicatory processes but provide little review of executive policy-making processes unless they violate rights.[3] When it comes to legislation, the South African Constitutional Court has enforced procedural requirements, and the German Constitutional Court has struck down a statute because the underlying statistical analysis was inadequate. Such reasons for voiding a rule are familiar in U.S. administrative law, but not in the review of U.S. statutes. Just as review in the United States only examines legislative processes insofar as they may violate rights or undermine the federal structure of government, so in Germany and South Africa review of rulemaking processes occurs mainly as a side effect of substantive review. A debate is in progress in the United States about the role of "legislative findings," but it concerns the standard of federal court review, not the democratic accountability of lawmaking.

The European Union is a hybrid body that is not clearly either a federal state or an association of sovereign states. It has many distinctive features, but it resembles the parliamentary cases in blurring the line between statutes and rules when it comes to judicial review. A growing trend toward procedural values is visible not only in the Lisbon Treaty, but also in EU soft law, mainly inside the Commission. Nevertheless, the nonbinding nature of these procedures paired with limited access to the courts means that these developments have not been subject to judicial review. Citizens and businesses that object to the procedures used or the transparency of decision-making are rarely successful if they go to court to seek more access to EU processes. Rather, cases that challenge the authority of one or another EU institution are usually brought by Member States or EU institutions themselves.

What might explain the differences? A number of factors matter based on positive political economy, constitutional rights and structures, and institutional and political history. Different structures create different incentives and expectations in relation to judicial review. Constitutional rights and values both affect and are affected by these structural patterns. Before introducing our cases, this section spells out these possible explanations in more detail.

I. POSITIVE POLITICAL ECONOMY

Positive political economy takes some aspects of the institutional structure as given and explores the behavior of political and economic actors within

[3] *See* Ittai Bar-Siman-Tov, *Semiprocedural Judicial Review* **6** Legisprudence 271 (2012).

that structure. We assume fixed constitutional structures and ask how they affect the behavior of politicians, bureaucrats, and judges as they enact statutes and rules, make policy, and resolve issues in court.[4] We focus on the statutes and constitutional provisions that govern policymaking procedures inside the legislature and the executive.[5]

We do not assume that members of the legislature, political appointees, and civil servants are necessarily concerned only with their own narrow self-interest. They may have public-regarding motives, endorse a particular theory of constitutional law, aim to be faithful agents of the voters, or seek to further a political agenda. We do assume, however, that politicians seek to preserve their own freedom of action tempered only by the collective action problems that dog the legislature – a multimember decision-making body that persists over time. We also assume that politicians and political parties seek to claim credit for benefits to their constituents and to society at large and to avoid blame for imposing costs.[6]

Our analysis leaves the motivations of judges open. We do not follow early work in positive political economy where judges' motivations were placed on the same single-policy dimension as those of officials and

[4] Some research in the positive political economy tradition considers the incentives facing those who draft constitutions. For a collection of reprinted essays dealing with these issues, *see* Stefan Voigt, ed., Design of Constitutions (2013). In particular, *see* Jon Elster, *Forces and Mechanisms in the Constitution-Making Process* **45** Duke Law J. 364 (1995), and Tom Ginsburg, Zachary Elkins, & Justin Blount, *Does the Process of Constitution-Making Matter?* **5** Annual Rev. of Law and Social Science 201 (2009).

[5] We recognize that, in practice, the constitutional amendment process in some polities is similar to the process for passing statutes. Some constitutions require only an absolute supermajority of the lower house and assent by the upper house, if one exists. Hence, conditional on the need for a larger majority, the passage of amendments in such systems is subject to the same political incentives that we outline in this chapter. In both South Africa and Germany the legislature can amend the constitution subject to certain conditions and supermajority rules. According to the German Basic Law, constitutional amendments are inadmissible that affect the core principles of federalism and of certain fundamental rights, such as the due process clause and human dignity, and South Africa requires a period for public comment. We assume, however, that the basic parliamentary structure of these polities is not realistically open to change through these procedures. *See* German Basic Law art. 79; South African Constitution, art. 74.

[6] The classic works are David R. Mayhew, Congress: the Electoral Connection (1974, 2004); David R. Mayhew, Parties and Policies: How the American Government Works (2008); Morris Fiorina, Congress: Keystone of the Washington Establishment (1977, 1989). The connection to judicial review is developed in Philip P. Frickey & Steven S. Smith, *Judicial Review, the Congressional Process and the Federalism Cases: An Interdisciplinary Critique* **111** Yale Law J. 1707, 1728–31 (2002). On blame avoidance, *see* Christopher Hood, The Blame Game: Spin, Bureaucracy, and Self-Preservation (2011).

politicians in the executive and the legislature. In those models, based on the U.S. framework, judges rule strategically to avoid being overturned by the legislature.[7] In contrast, we follow William N. Eskridge Jr. and John Ferejohn in supposing that judges may be driven by constitutional and legal principles that do not easily translate into the rubric of day-to-day politics.[8] Although they are likely to temper their decisions in the light of political reality, they do not flout clear legal mandates. They may bend the interpretation of open-ended texts toward preferred policies, but they are committed to "the rule of law," even if it leads them to rule against their own policy preferences in particular cases. We suppose that judges are sensitive to their status as unelected officials who should not interfere too aggressively with political processes.[9] This sensitivity constrains them from imposing doctrines that are deeply at odds with the practical operation of the political system. Such behavior is both principled and strategic.[10] It derives from a normative commitment to a particular judicial

[7] *See*, *for* example, John Ferejohn & Charles Shipan, *Congressional Influence on the Bureaucracy* **6** J. of Law, Economics and Organization (special issue) 1, 9–12–20 (1990). The model is developed further in William N. Eskridge Jr. & John Ferejohn, *Making the Deal Stick: Enforcing the Original Constitutional Structure of Lawmaking in the Modern Regulatory State* **8** J. of Law, Economics and Organization 165 (1992). For critiques, *see* Susan Rose-Ackerman, *Comment on Ferejohn and Shipan's "Congressional Influence on Bureaucracy,"* **6** J. of Law, Economics and Organization 21 (1990), and Peter L. Strauss & Andrew R. Rutten, *The Game of Politics and Law: A Response to Eskridge and Ferejohn* **8** J. of Law, Economics and Organization 205 (1992).

[8] William N. Eskridge Jr. & John Ferejohn, A Republic of Statutes: The New American Constitution, 22–8 (2010) (arguing that judges should seek to promote deliberation in the administration and in Congress). Their detailed analyses of administrative policymaking are in chapters 6–9.

[9] In the United States some state judges are elected. It is an open question whether such judges act as if they have a mandate from the public to oppose other political actors. *See* Ethan Leib & Aaron-Andrew Bruhl, *Elected Judges and Statutory Interpretation* **79** University of Chicago Law Rev. 1215 (2012). Statistical evidence supports the view that judges who run in contested, partisan elections favor in-state plaintiffs in tort cases and impose stricter penalties on convicted criminals as election dates approach. The former results are reported in Alexander Tabarrok & Eric Helland, *Court Politics: The Political Economy of Tort Awards* **42** J. of Law and Economics 157 (1999); Eric Helland & Alexander Tabarrok, *Exporting Tort Awards* **23** Regulation 21 (2000). The latter are in Sanford C. Gordon & Gregory A. Huber, *Accountability and Coercion: Is Justice Blind When It Runs for Office?* **48** American J. of Political Science (2004), 247–63; Sanford C. Gordon & Gregory A. Huber, *The Effect of Electoral Competitiveness on Incumbent Behavior* **2** Quarterly J. of Political Science, 107 (2007).

[10] Understanding judges' motivations has proved a contested issue in positive political economy. "Ideology" has explanatory power, but it may be trumped by purely legal factors or by judges' understanding of their role in particular cases. *See* Frank B. Cross, *The Judiciary and Public Choice* **50** Hastings Law J. 355 (1999); Frank B. Cross & Emerson H. Tiller, *Judicial Partisanship and Obedience to Legal Doctrine: Whistleblowing on the*

role, but it also acknowledges that the judiciary cannot enforce controversial decisions without political and popular support.

We begin by discussing the incentives for legislatures in presidential and parliamentary democracies to delegate policymaking to the executive while constraining executive power through judicial oversight. We then ask whether the legislature will ever have an incentive to limit its own behavior by statute, enforced by judicial review.

A. Administrative Rulemaking Processes

Legislators have neither the time nor the expertise to solve all policy problems – delegation to the executive is inevitable. They may also want a regulatory system that can respond quickly to changes in underlying conditions without requiring statutory amendment. These motives are expressed differently, however, in presidential and parliamentary systems.

First, consider a presidential system. Here the legislature has an additional reason to support delegation beyond expertise, time constraints, and the need for flexibility. It can shift hard choices onto the shoulders of cabinet departments and agencies while taking credit for the benefits a statute provides.[11] However, even if the executive bears the burden of implementation, legislators will seldom want to be completely isolated from executive actions. They will want to be informed, even if only to better criticize the president and his top officials. Members will get involved by holding hearings, demanding reports, controlling agency budgets, and threatening to repeal or amend statutes.[12] Some might prefer formal statutory pathways to review executive rulemaking ex post, but only if these mechanisms do

Federal Courts of Appeals **107** Yale Law J. 2155 (1998); Richard L. Revesz, *Environmental Regulation, Ideology, and the D.C. Circuit* **83** Virginia Law Rev. 1717 (1997).

11 The classic reference is James Q. Wilson, The Politics of Regulation (1980); formalized by Morris Fiorina, *Legislative Choice of Regulatory Forms: Legal Process or Administrative Process* **39** Public Choice 33 (1982).

12 Mathew D. McCubbins, Roger G. Noll, & Barry Weingast, *Administrative Procedures as Instruments of Political Control* **3** J. of Law, Economics and Organization 243 (1987) [hereinafter *Administrative Procedures*]; Mathew D. McCubbins, Roger G. Noll, & Barry Weingast, *Structure and Process, Politics and Policy: Administrative Arrangements and the Political Control of Agencies* **75** Virginia Law Rev. **431** (1989) [hereinafter *Structure and Process*]. Congress may also seek to design regulatory institutions that are relatively independent of presidential control. Its ability to do this, however, depends on its bargaining power vis-à-vis the president and the party of the president compared to the parties that control the houses of Congress. For a study of these institutional choices, *see* David E. Lewis, Presidents and the Politics of Agency Decisions: Political Insulation in the United States Government Bureaucracy, 1946–1997 (2003).

not implicate them in unpopular decisions. Furthermore, ex post legislative approval or disapproval of rules undermines many of the incentives for delegation in the first place; it fills up the legislative agenda and diverts members from other business.

Even those legislators who support ex post review face an uphill battle in a presidential system. The president is unlikely to favor such review unless, in a particular case, it is part of a broader deal. The U.S. experience suggests that such situations do occur.[13] However, as a practical matter, they are a rather blunt tool that demands an up or down vote, not a nuanced review of a range of policy options.

But there is an alternative to ex post legislative review of rules. The legislature can exercise indirect policy control by requiring procedures such as notice, an open hearing, and reason-giving before the executive announces its final rule. Such requirements further the goals of transparency, openness to outside input, and justification in ways that help the general public and affected interests to learn about and to influence the policymaking process.[14] In addition, they aid the legislature. Interested legislators can find out what rules are in the pipeline and seek to affect their development. Hence, a law covering rulemaking procedures may gain the support even of legislators with no strong commitment to the public accountability of the executive per se. Once again, however, one can ask why a president would support such a law. It raises fewer separation of powers concerns than does a legislative vote on rules, but it still constrains the executive. In our U.S. case study we cite literature outlining the rather special political alignment that led to the passage of the U.S. APA with provisions for notice and comment rulemaking.[15]

An administrative procedure law may or may not include provisions for judicial oversight of the rulemaking process. The incentives and bottlenecks of a presidential system suggest that the legislature may support court review. Legislators opposed to an executive policymaking initiative cannot change the law without surmounting numerous veto gates.[16] Legislative control of agency budgets and its oversight activities may not be effective. Hence, legislators may wish to give courts the job of enforcing procedural

[13] *See* Chapter 2.

[14] Jerry L. Mashaw, *Reasoned Administration: The European Union, the United States, and the Project of Democratic Governance* **76** George Washington Law Rev. 99, 111 (2007–8). Mashaw argues that reason-giving enhances the public legitimacy of policies because it "treats persons as rational moral agents who are entitled to evaluate and participate in a dialogue about official policies on the basis of reasoned discussion" (*id.* at 118).

[15] *See* Chapter 2.

[16] George Tsebelis, Veto Players: How Political Institutions Work (2002).

constraints on executive policymaking.[17] Statutes that permit judicial review of executive policymaking processes are a rational response to the separation of powers between the president and legislature. Once again, the president may accept such constraints, not with enthusiasm, but as part of a political compromise. Of course, as we will see in the U.S. case, the courts themselves may interpret their mandate in a way that gives an expansive reading to the statutory language, but they are ultimately constrained by the possibility of statutory amendments to the APA and to provisions in substantive statutes.

Second, consider an archetypal parliamentary system, where the same party coalition controls both the legislature and the cabinet.[18] In that case, the distinction between statutes and executive rules is less clear-cut than in a presidential system. One political coalition is behind both forms of policymaking. So long as the constitution's non-delegation principle is not too stringent, the government can decide how much detail to include in the statute and how much rulemaking authority to keep inside the cabinet.[19] This decision can be made on technical grounds based on the relative expertise of government officials inside and outside the legislature. Ministerial drafts will often be enacted into law with little or no input from the legislature after their submission.[20] There is no delegation at all in political terms. Delegation is not a way for the legislative majority to avoid blame for hard choices.

In a parliamentary system the legislature is the prime locus of political legitimacy, and there is no independent executive with its own political power base. This might imply that the legislature ought not to delegate its lawmaking authority, even if there are strong functional reasons for doing so. Such a strong anti-delegation position is, however, unrealistic in the modern regulatory welfare state. One compromise, illustrated by the

17 William M. Landes & Richard Posner, *The Independent Judiciary in an Interest Group Perspective*, **18** J. OF LAW AND ECONOMICS 875 (1975), McCubbins, Noll, & Weingast, *Administrative Procedures*; McCubbins, Noll, & Weingast, *Structure and Process*, both *supra* note 12.

18 Here, we ignore some special features of the German and South African cases to be discussed later. We also leave aside the complications introduced by minority or coalition governments.

19 Germany's delegation doctrine is expressed in Basic Law *(Grundgesetz)*, art. 80 (1). The content, purpose, and scope of the authority must be stated in the statute that delegates authority to issue secondary legislation.

20 SUSAN ROSE-ACKERMAN, CONTROLLING ENVIRONMENTAL POLICY: THE LIMITS OF PUBLIC LAW IN GERMANY AND THE UNITED STATES, 7–17 (1995) [hereinafter CONTROLLING] provides some German examples in the environmental field.

German case, is to permit the legislature to review and possibly veto certain types of particularly sensitive rules. Such provisions preserve the form of legislative dominance without substantially constraining executive rule-making. Unlike the United States, the same political grouping controls both branches, unless there is a minority government or a fractious coalition. Hence, rules will seldom be vetoed.

However, in politically controversial cases, the coalition controlling the legislature may benefit from delaying issuance of the detailed rules needed to put a policy into practice. Just as the legislature in a presidential system might seek to shift politically vexing issues onto the shoulders of the executive, a parliamentary majority might support delegation that pushes hard choices into the future, when the members may hope that other events will obscure the executive's choices. Of course, the prime minister and cabinet must also agree with this strategy. Delegation is not a way for the government to avoid formal responsibility, but it may limit the political fallout.[21]

Another reason laws may be rather general in a parliamentary system is that clear and detailed laws need not bind future governments. If a new coalition comes into power, it can modify existing laws relatively easily. It may be in the government's interest to bind its own hands – perhaps in response to popular demands or external pressure from domestic business and international investors. But it cannot be sure that its actions will carry over to a new government, which can simply repeal the act.

Opposition parties in the legislature do have a strong incentive to complain about the government's lack of transparency. Opposition leaders sometimes chair important committees – South Africa and Germany are examples.[22] This gives opponents a forum to voice complaints or oversee inquiries, but not to enact statutes. However, the possibility of a contested debate in the parliament can lead the government to propose barebones, framework statutes, with little specific policy content, that can be filled in through government rulemaking after passage.[23] Such statutes might be

[21] We are grateful to Kevin Stack for suggesting this possibility.

[22] On Public Accounts Committees in Westminster systems, *see* SUSAN ROSE-ACKERMAN, CORRUPTION AND GOVERNMENT: CAUSES, CONSEQUENCES AND REFORM, 163–4 (1999); Alan Doig, *Politics and Public Sector Ethics: The Impact of Change in the United Kingdom*, in POLITICAL CORRUPTION IN EUROPE AND LATIN AMERICA 173 (Walter Little & Eduardo Posada-Carb, eds., 1996).

[23] In France some commentators argue that the legislature passes too many laws. They advocate for broad, framework laws that the professional bureaucracy will implement. The argument is a principled one based on an understanding of the proper division of responsibilities, but to political leaders in the cabinet it could also be a way to enact their agendas with a minimum of controversy. The counterargument is the claim that cabinet officials

coupled with legislative vetoes that only permit an up or down vote on rules. The cabinet can craft a rule assured that it will not be struck down so long as it stays within rather broad bounds.

Of course, if a coalition controls the legislature, it may not always present a unified front, and disputes can occur even in single-party governments. In such circumstances, even members of parliament inside the governing coalition may want to constrain and monitor policymaking by the cabinet. This could lead them to insist on clear and limited statutory language and on future consultation with parliamentary committees or even formal ex post review when the cabinet makes policy.[24]

Votes of no confidence are an important way the legislature controls the executive in parliamentary systems – an option not available in a presidential system. If members of coalition governments or disgruntled backbenchers join with the opposition, oversight and the veto of individual rules might morph into an effort to bring down the government. For example, the Canadian government fell in spring 2011 after the parliament held it in contempt for failing to provide information to parliament on the cost of certain programs.[25] Unlike a presidential system with fixed terms, members of the governing coalition must balance the benefits and costs of actions that may cause the government to fall, triggering elections.

Because the same coalition controls both the executive and the legislature in a parliamentary system, the legislative majority has little incentive to give courts a mandate to review secondary legislation promulgated inside the executive.[26] Even if some parts of the governing coalition seek to control other parts, they will be unlikely to obtain majority support for formal judicial oversight. An APA, if one exists, will govern official dealings with

support too many laws because they enhance their own reputations by having their names attached to statutes. *See* Susan Rose-Ackerman & Thomas Perroud, *Policymaking and Public Law in France: Public Participation, Agency Independence, and Impact Assessment* **19** Columbia J. of European Law 223 (2013).

24 We discuss the German case in Chapter 4. The British Parliament established a Regulatory Reform Committee under the Legislative and Regulatory Reform Act of 2006 with a purely advisory role. Dawn Oliver, *Regulation, Democracy, and Democratic Oversight in the UK*, in The Regulatory State: Constitutional Implications 243, 258 (Dawn Oliver, Tony Prosser, & Richard Rawlings, eds., 2010).

25 House of Commons, Canada, Questions of Privilege Relating to the Failure of the Government to Fully Provide the Documents as Ordered by the House, 40th Parliament, 3rd Session, March 2011. The same party was returned to power after the election with a stronger mandate.

26 *See* Christian B. Jensen & Robert J. McGarth, *Making Rules about Rulemaking: A Comparison of Presidential and Parliamentary Systems*, **20** Political Research Q. 1 (2010). On the German case, *see* Rose-Ackerman, Controlling, *supra* note 20.

individual citizens and businesses seeking to obtain benefits or avoid costs. The APA will not cover secondary legislation. As we will see, this difference in political incentives helps explain the APA's reviewable rulemaking procedures in the United States and their absence in Germany; it also is consistent with the South African legislature's restrictive attitude during the drafting of its administrative procedures statute, including its decision not to provide explicitly for rulemaking in that statute.

B. The Law of the Legislative Process

As a general rule, democratic legislatures want to control their own procedures. They will avoid giving either the executive or the courts a role in overseeing their internal deliberations and drafting practices.[27] Judicial review of legislative procedures, nevertheless, does occur. But it generally arises from constitutional texts and fundamental legal principles – for example, the strong focus on democratic inclusiveness inherent in South Africa's postapartheid constitution. Popular discontent with legislative operations has sometimes triggered constitutional provisions that tie the hands of legislatures. This happened in many American states during the nineteenth century.[28]

In a parliamentary system the work of the legislature is generally less important than in a presidential system. Hence, its internal procedures may not seem as fundamental, even if it is nominally the site of democratic legitimacy under the constitution. Instead, the legitimacy of the governing coalition that controls both the legislature and executive is a high priority for democratic functioning. In Germany, the main constraint on the government in the constitutional text is the constructive vote of no confidence.[29] Parliament can bring down a government, but only if it also approves a new

[27] Early disputes over legislatures' freedom to determine their own procedures involved, not courts, but monarchs. In Germany before 1848 many state constitutions included detailed procedural requirements and could only be changed by the monarch or by the monarch and the parliament together. Fabian Wittreck, *Parliamentary Law: The German Experience*, in Constitutionalism and the Role of Parliaments 55, 61–7 (Katja S. Ziegler, Denis Baranger, & Anthony W. Bradley, eds., 2007).

[28] The most pervasive reforms in the U.S. state constitutions are single-subject rules for statutes combined with a requirement that the title of the bill accurately express its content. *See* Brannon P. Denning & Brooks R. Smith, *Uneasy Riders: The Case for a Truth-in Legislation Amendment*, **1999** Utah L. Rev. 957, 1005–24; Appendices A and B (1999) list the forty-three states with at least one of these provisions, most added during the nineteenth century. The states with no such provisions are the New England states and North Carolina.

[29] Basic Law, art. 67.

government to take its place. However, the German Constitutional Court's efforts to protect rights have had a marked impact on both legislative and executive lawmaking processes.[30] These effects result from the text of the German Constitution, not the activities of the legislature to control its own procedures.

There is one important exception to our broad claim of legislative resistance to procedural controls by outsiders. Collective action problems can lead a legislature to tie its own hands – and those of future legislatures.[31] This option is more plausible in a presidential system because it is harder for later political coalitions to amend statutes. The legislature may support a hands-tying statute that will benefit most legislators or that is arguably in the public interest. It will, however, be reluctant to invite judicial involvement.[32] If these provisions were merely internal legislative rules, a majority could overcome them at any time. If the president has signed them into law, repeal is more difficult, and simply ignoring the constraint may be politically costly. Judicial review is another matter. Even legislatures in presidential systems will be very reluctant to give the courts a role in overseeing their internal procedures – even if it would make their commitments more credible.[33] The president's signature is all the commitment they want.

In short, the legislative majority in parliamentary systems has little incentive to enact procedural statutes that govern either administrative rulemaking or statutory drafting. Oversight of the administration by opposition parties, coalition partners, and back benchers is likely, but passage of a judicially enforceable statute governing rulemaking seems unlikely absent acute external pressure. The parliament might create "independent" agencies for other purposes outside the cabinet structure, such as bodies to regulate privatized utilities or to protect personal data, but these are special

[30] *See* Chapter 4 and Pascale Cancik, *Making Parliamentary Rights Effective: The Role of the Constitutional Courts in Germany*, in Constitutionalism and the Role of Parliaments 239 (Katja S. Ziegler, Denis Baranger, & Anthony W. Bradley, eds., 2007).

[31] *See* Adrian Vermeule, Mechanisms of Democracy, 229–44 (2007) (recognizing that Congress is a collection of individuals whose members face collective action problems and recommending several reforms).

[32] Many examples exist in the United States, although some contest the constitutionality of strong forms of hands tying. *See* Chapter 2.

[33] As John Martinez states: "Given that a rational legislating requirement would hold state legislators and members of Congress to a higher standard than occurs under current practice, it seems unlikely that either would adopt a rational legislating requirement on its own impetus" [John Martinez, *Rational Legislating*, **34** Stetson L. Rev. 547, 590 (2005). He recommends passage of a statute by referendum that would require a legislative record (*id.* at 612–20)].

cases that challenge conventional understandings of parliamentary regimes in the interest of furthering other goals.[34]

In contrast, presidential systems face a somewhat more complex situation. As in parliamentary systems, the legislature is unlikely to enact statutes that permit judicial review of its own internal procedures. However, so long as one party does not control both the executive and the legislature, the legislature has an incentive to mandate procedures for executive policy-making and to make them subject to judicial review. These procedures help keep both the legislature and the citizenry engaged in and informed about policy. Court review is a complement to direct legislative oversight, provided that the courts are competent and are not dominated by the executive or by the political opposition.

II. CONSTITUTIONAL RIGHTS AND CONSTITUTIONAL STRUCTURES

Constitutional doctrines, as interpreted by high courts, trump statutory language. Individual rights and the distribution of power between levels of government are central constitutional concerns in all our cases. However, except in South Africa, direct appeals to the democratic values of dialogue, public participation, and transparency are uncommon. This is perhaps surprising because the nation-states that we study are all democracies.[35]

A. Constitutional Rights

Constitutional courts use the language of rights to review legislative and administrative procedures. The scope of review turns on the definition of rights. We demonstrate the limitations of rights-based judicial review in South Africa and Germany. In South Africa, however, this framework is less restrictive than in Germany because courts link rights to democratic values, and because the South African constitution treats procedurally fair administrative action as a fundamental right. If more traditional rights were the only basis for review, it would be hard for judges to consider explicitly whether government processes promote democratic legitimacy.

[34] *See* Lorne Sossin, *The Puzzle of Administrative Independence and Parliamentary Democracy in the Common Law World: A Canadian Perspective*, in COMPARATIVE ADMINISTRATIVE LAW 205 (Susan Rose-Ackerman & Peter Lindseth, eds., 2010).

[35] There is much controversy over exactly how to characterize the European Union. PETER LINDSETH, POWER AND LEGITIMACY: RECONCILING EUROPE AND THE NATION-STATE 4–14 (2010) summarizes the debate.

All courts recognize that most rights are not absolute. They carry out proportionality analyses to see if there are countervailing reasons for permitting restrictions. Even in the United States, where proportionality is a less familiar concept, balancing tests are common in the courts.[36] If the legislature anticipates this type of review, it has an incentive to do the balancing at the time of the law's passage to try to preempt subsequent judicial intervention. This balancing can also shape statutes that implicate other constitutional principles, such as federalism. Of course, as our case studies show, the high court need not accept the legislature's exercise in deliberation and reason-giving. But, at least, legislative balancing can set the stage for judicial review.

We do not attempt to summarize the vast scholarship on constitutional rights. We seek, instead, to understand how the language of rights intersects with legislative and administrative processes in our case studies. Do constitutional or supreme courts recognize procedural rights that further democratic values, or do they only consider the process that is due to individuals seeking to protect themselves against state overreaching? In parliamentary systems, does the jurisprudence of rights substitute in part for the lack of statutes that specify legislative procedures and administrative policymaking processes? If so, how do these constraints differ from the American presidential system? In the United States, where there are incentives for the legislature to require open and participatory procedures inside the executive and to mandate reason-giving, how do these incentives interact with constitutional mandates grounded in individual rights? In the legislature itself, does judicial protection of rights and federalism conflict with the legislature's own interest in politically efficacious procedures?

B. Constitutional Structures

Given a constitutional court willing to examine the legislative process, how does the structure of government affect judicial oversight of the rationality and coherence of legislation? Part of the answer rests on empirical claims about the real-world nature of statutory drafting. In a parliamentary government with a stable parliamentary majority, statutory drafting can be more coherent and logical than in the United States.[37] Parliaments generally have

[36] Jud Mathews & Alec Stone Sweet, *All Things in Proportion? American Rights Review and the Problem of Balancing*, **60** Emory L. J. 797 (2011).

[37] Terry M. Moe & Michael Caldwell, *The Institutional Foundations of Democratic Government: A Comparison of Presidential and Parliamentary Systems*, **150** J. of Institutional and Theoretical Economics 171 (1994).

quite limited staff, and most statutes are drafted in the executive. Given this fact, it may not seem to violate the separation of powers for courts to review legislative texts for consistency and the use of state-of-the-art data, and to review the legislative process for transparency and inclusiveness. Of course, heated disputes do sometimes mark parliamentary debates that can lead to textual revisions. However, if party discipline ordinarily prevails, our basic claim still holds. As a practical matter, if courts review statutes for coherence and adequate reasoning, they will intrude less on democratic prerogatives in parliamentary than in presidential systems.[38] In the United States, the Supreme Court has sometimes required Congress to produce "findings," a mandate that flies in the face of the process of compromise and horse trading that lies behind any important statute in a presidential system. "One of the most basic legislative facts is that insistence on statutory clarity of ends and means requires a reduction in the role of politics."[39] Nevertheless, even if statutes can be competently drafted, court review in parliamentary systems raises exactly the same concerns for judicial overreaching as arise in critiques of U.S. administrative law.

If constitutional courts in parliamentary systems do review legislative and administrative rulemaking procedures under their mandate to protect rights, they may not make a sharp distinction between statutes and rules. The traditional hierarchy of legal norms does not speak to the courts' review of process. Such a unified approach may seem unproblematic to courts in parliamentary systems because there is, in fact, less difference between lawmaking and rulemaking. The same observation applies to the European Union's distinctive structure, where the legislative process is complicated and where both the executive (the Commission) and the legislatures (the Council and the Parliament) produce legally binding texts together and, sometimes, separately. However, the growth in the number and influence of EU agencies raises a new set of questions involving institutional competence and public accountability.[40]

[38] One contrasting tendency, however, raises separation of powers issues similar to those that pervade American public law. Many parliamentary systems have created new regulatory agencies to oversee privatized utilities; these agencies are an anomaly, and their special status could open up a space for greater judicial oversight. On independent agencies in parliamentary systems *see* Lorne Sossin, *supra* note 34; Daniel Halberstam, *The Promise of Comparative Administrative Law: A Constitutional Perspective on Independent Agencies*, in COMPARATIVE ADMINISTRATIVE LAW 185 (Susan Rose-Ackerman & Peter Lindseth, eds., 2010).

[39] Frickey & Smith, *supra* note 6 at 1742. Their general argument (*id.* at 1740–52) is made in the context of recent Supreme Court cases striking down laws on federalism grounds. *See* our discussion in Chapter 2.

[40] *See* Chapter 5.

In short, looking across parliamentary systems, constitutional doctrines play a large role in explaining inter-country differences. If there is no constitutional mandate, courts will not review process in either branch. The clearest example here is the United Kingdom's Westminster democracy with its principle of parliamentary sovereignty. At present, however, the United Kingdom's position in Europe is prompting change. The European Court of Human Rights' intervention led Parliament to pass the Human Rights Act,[41] and EU environmental directives, which mandate participatory processes, have given domestic civil society groups access to the courts.[42]

Once given a constitutional green light, courts in parliamentary systems may engage in more searching review of legislation than in presidential systems. This may seem less at odds with the separation of powers between courts and the rest of the state because a unitary parliamentary system is, at least in principle, capable of producing more coherent statutes than a presidential system – especially under divided government. As a consequence, review for consistency and competence will be less at odds with the real world of parliamentary lawmaking. Nevertheless, courts will be reluctant to go too far, recognizing that even in a parliamentary system, statutory language is the product of political compromise and that courts should not "supervise the internal proceedings of the national legislature, at least in the absence of the breach of a constitutional guarantee."[43]

Federalism also has an impact in some of our case studies, especially the United States and the European Union. Some federal states, such as the United States, have a presumption in favor of lower-level state governments that must be overcome by the national legislature. If judges favor the states, as in recent U.S. Supreme Court cases, national statutes that impinge on their power bear a relatively strong burden of proof.[44] In imposing this standard, the Court's goal is not to improve the legitimacy of Congress's legislative process, but to force Congress to create a stronger record to help the Court itself to strike the balance between national interests and federalism values. Heavy fact-finding requirements of this type may place unrealistic burdens on the bargaining process required for successful legislation in a

41 United Kingdom, Human Rights Act, 1998 chapter 42; Robert Carnwath, *Tribunal Justice – A New Start*, 2009 United Kingdom Public L. 48 (2009).

42 The UK Supreme Court has grappled with the procedural implications of an EU directive that requires public participation in executive branch decisions concerning the environment but that exempts decisions adopted by a specific act of the national legislature. (R on the application of HS2 Action Alliance Ltd. v. Secretary of State for Transport, Hilary Term, [2014] UKSC 3, 22 January 2014).

43 *Id.* para. 112.

44 The recent cases are discussed in Chapter 2.

presidential system.[45] In South Africa, in contrast, the federal government is presumed to have the power to enact statutes subject to exceptions granted to state and local governments. Federal/state relations are not currently a subject of substantial legal contention among judges in that country.

In the United States, judicial review of notice and comment rulemaking recognizes the importance of democratic accountability and participation. However, whether the focus is on individual rights, federalism, or the separation of powers, concern for democratic legitimacy is generally lacking in the review of statutes in the United States, Germany, and the European Union and in the review of secondary legislation outside the United States. If judicial review leads to greater deliberation and reason-giving, the motivation is most often to inform the judges so they can evaluate the constitutionality of some action. With the sole exception of South Africa, procedural requirements are seldom justified in terms of accountability to the citizenry even if they, in practice, have that effect. In fact, just the opposite result is possible. Because of judicial strictures, the legislature may be unable to respond to certain strong citizen demands for policy. One's judgment of these constraints will depend not only on the substantive balance between public demands and constitutional principles, but also on one's view of the way the separation of powers ought to constrain courts in their review of the legislative process.

In considering the judicial role in reviewing process, the South African Constitutional Court provides an instructive exception. It is robustly engaged in assuring the democratic legitimacy of legislative procedures, and although it has not gone as far in its review of administrative rulemaking, a future move in that direction would be consistent with its jurisprudence. Its attempt to uphold democratic values without overstepping its limited mandate can, we argue, provide lessons for other constitutional courts.[46] As Eskridge and Ferejohn argue in the U.S. context, constitutional courts ought to act in ways that respect and enhance deliberation over policy.[47]

III. INSTITUTIONS AND POLITICAL HISTORY

Other features of constitutional design affect the way courts review both primary and secondary legislation. Some of them have deep historical roots while others respond to recent events. We will outline these structural

[45] Frickey & Smith, *supra* note 6 at 740–52 (arguing for that interpretation of the federalism cases). *See* Chapter 2.

[46] *See* Chapter 3.

[47] Eskridge & Ferejohn, *supra* note 8 at 446–68.

differences in the context of each individual case. For example, the South African constitution is particularly sensitive to democratic participation and inclusiveness because it was written against the background of the old apartheid regime. The German Basic Law, written after the Second World War, emphasizes the protection of rights in contrast to the recent Nazi past.

Older patterns also matter. German public law traditions based on an expert, professional bureaucracy create a presumption against public participation and open procedures. This traditional respect for the bureaucracy appears to have influenced the development of administrative law as applied to the policymaking process. South African administrative law – historically drawn from England – was isolated from English reforms during apartheid. Postapartheid law reform started from an old English baseline historically focused on the judicial review of small-scale decisions affecting individuals, and it was cautious about extending judicial review to mass decisions or rulemaking.

In the United States, in spite of a professional civil service with considerable expertise and professionalism, the bureaucracy has a large overlay of political appointees, and faith in apolitical policymaking in the executive is not widespread. Furthermore, the separation of powers has produced a much stronger professional policy staff inside Congress than in the parliamentary legislatures.[48] This is both an effect and a cause of Congress's greater policy independence. Because the legislative process inside the U.S. Congress quite simply matters more than in the parliamentary systems, there will be more at stake as the legislature debates its own procedures. This is true even though the practical politics of legislative drafting makes tight textual drafting standards unrealistic.

Outside the United States, some presidential systems have a dominant president who overshadows a fractious and divided legislature that does not have much professional competence. This has been the experience in some Latin American democracies with legislatures chosen by proportional representation and in present-day Russia and some of the other republics created after the fall of the Soviet Union.[49] Hence, our case study of the United States will not apply to the legislative/court relations in such polities.

[48] On the U.S. Congress, *see* Frickey & Smith, *supra* note 6 at 1736–40.

[49] *See* Juan J. Linz, *The Perils of Presidentialism*, **1** J. Democracy 51 (1990); Susan Rose-Ackerman, Diane A. Desierto, & Natalia Volosin, *Hyper-Presidentialism: Separation of Powers without Checks and Balances in Argentina and the Philippines*, **29** Berkeley J. of International Law 101 (2011); Mariana Mota Prado, *Presidential Dominance from a Comparative Perspective: The Relationship between the Executive Branch and Regulatory*

Turning to the formal law, clear rules or standards facilitate judicial review, but even in the absence of established legal principles, courts may engage in aggressive review. As our case studies demonstrate, the level of review depends on local circumstances, legal culture, constitutional values, and the institutional position of the courts. Our cases illustrate the range of possibilities. For example, in Germany the Constitutional Court, a respected institution, has shaped substantive constitutional provisions into indirect procedural duties. In South Africa the Constitutional Court, eager to uphold democratic values, reads the constitutional provisions that support legislative consultation aggressively, but it has been much less willing to reach out to fill gaps in administrative rulemaking law, perhaps because the formal law lacks clear standards.

The notice and comment provisions of the American APA along with its judicial review sections set the stage for the U.S. courts' proactive review of executive branch rulemaking. These provisions lay out the bare bones of the rulemaking process: public notice, an open-ended hearing, and reason-giving.[50] The federal courts review both process and substance. They are supposed to check if the APA rulemaking process has been followed properly. This statutory language helps guide the court, which seldom considers regulatory decisions de novo. Rather, it asks if officials followed the proper procedures and remands the rule to the agency if they did not. Of course, this short description does not do justice to the way the courts have expanded on the few short sentences of the APA, which are full of ambiguous language, and it ignores the intersection between the preservation of constitutional rights and administrative procedure. Nevertheless, it captures the important point that courts that are constrained by statute can engage in judicial review and can defend themselves from claims of overreaching by the very limits embedded in the law.

In parliamentary systems that lack a rulemaking statute, the courts have no legal provisions to enforce outside of the constitutional text with its focus on the preservation of rights, the separation of powers, and the structure of government. In Germany, whose APA has no analogue to U.S. notice and comment rulemaking, courts may be cautious because they have

Agencies in Brazil, in Comparative Administrative Law 225 (Susan Rose-Ackerman & Peter Lindseth, eds., 2010).

50 The procedures are outlined in USAPA §553. It is called "informal" rulemaking to contrast it with "formal" rulemaking governed by more court-like procedures under §§556, 557. However, informal rulemaking has a certain formality in that it is legally required and has accumulated more detailed requirements through the development of case law. *See* Chapter 2.

no framework to guide their judgments. The lack of statutory provisions governing rulemaking processes means that there are few hooks for either constitutional or administrative courts to latch on to. Even in South Africa, whose APA does make explicit provision for U.S.-style notice and comment procedures, both legislatures and courts have moved slowly to overcome administrative law's traditional focus on small-scale administrative actions – a tradition inherited from the British colonial past.

Constitutional court justices face a tension between their limited role and their desire to have an impact on legal developments. Overly vague standards of review may make them cautious so as to avoid criticism, but one response may be to develop their own judge-made criteria or "canons" of interpretation. We are interested in the feedback that judicial opinions provide to legislators and executive branch officials as they craft statutes and decrees.[51] If the courts impose a stronger burden of proof on some textual provisions than on others, the drafters may focus on those sections and perhaps modify their procedures to satisfy the courts. Alternatively, lawmakers may simply avoid policy areas subject to enhanced scrutiny. Judges may review substance, but the legislative and administrative response may be partly procedural.

Some justices may have strong theories of statutory interpretation that are not tied to particular constitutional clauses such as federalism or rights. However, neither the majority of the U.S. Supreme Court nor the other high courts that we consider have a clear, deterministic set of interpretative principles. In Europe, for example, the proportionality principle serves an interpretive role, but it is open to a range of interpretations depending on the specifics of individual cases.[52]

IV. DEMOCRACY AND COMPETENCE – A ROLE FOR THE COURTS?

There are three parts to our claims about judicial review of lawmaking – one based on political economy, a second on constitutional drafting, and a third on the role of constitutional courts operating under a given constitutional framework.

First, especially in times of divided government, legislative majorities in presidential systems have an incentive to impose procedural constraints on executive branch policymaking and to enforce them through judicial

[51] *See* Chapter 2 for the U.S. case.
[52] Mathews & Stone Sweet, *supra* note 36.

review. They will resist judicial review of their own internal processes, unless they seek to solve collective action problems through statutes that tie the hands of future legislatures. They will seldom endorse statutes that constrain their own procedures because they are harder to modify than internal rules. In parliamentary systems where the executive and the legislature are controlled by the same political coalition, there is little incentive for the government (or its accompanying parliamentary majority) to support statutes that constrain the process of policymaking in either the executive or the legislature. Opposition parties and disgruntled coalition members, along with outside pressure groups and citizen complainants, might force the government's hand – for example, in the aftermath of a scandal – but the government's actions will be purely defensive. It may face the same coordination and time inconsistency problems as a presidential system, but it has fewer tools to combat them in a credible manner.

Second, modern constitutions sometimes contain explicit provisions dealing with the democratic legitimacy of policymaking in the legislature and in the executive. These arise out of the particular conditions that framed the debate over the creation of a new polity. In our cases only South Africa falls into that category and only for legislation, not executive rulemaking. The legacy of apartheid produced a strong desire to assure representative, participatory government, and that desire is reflected in the text. In Germany, in contrast, popular sovereignty was not seen as an unambiguously good thing. The European Union was initially a treaty signed by Member States; it was not the result of a popular movement. The United States with its old and difficult to amend written constitutional text is particularly dependent on the case law of its Supreme Court although, as Bruce Ackerman argues, the U.S. constitutional framework has evolved, without formal amendments and often outside of the judiciary, in the legislature and the executive.[53]

Third, unless the constitution contains explicit requirements, constitutional courts seldom directly further democratic accountability in our cases. They may regulate policymaking procedures indirectly through the protection of individual rights and through the enforcement of other constitutional provisions, such as federalism. Sometimes the protection of rights trumps democratically accountable procedures. In other cases, they are complements. Constitutions may give rights holders access to policymaking processes.[54] In such cases, those with protected rights are not guaranteed substantive

[53] Bruce Ackerman, We the People, vol. 1 Foundations (1991); vol. 2 Transformations (2000); vol. 3 The Civil Rights Revolution (2014). *See also* Eskridge & Ferejohn, *supra* note 8, on super-statutes.

[54] Daryl Levinson, *Rights versus Votes*, **121** Yale Law J. 1286 (2012).

results, but they must be part of the debate. Court enforcement of other constitutional provisions can spur certain kinds of procedural responses as policymakers try to satisfy the courts' burden of proof. However, except in South Africa, the justices have crafted procedural requirements to satisfy their own demands for information and justification, not to improve democratic accountability. If that happens as well, it is a by-product. In contrast, the South African Constitutional Court has built on the text to implement the postapartheid emphasis on openness and inclusion and has positioned itself as a conscious promoter of participatory democracy.

There are two structural issues here. On the one hand, holding constitutional provisions constant, high courts can be expected to be more willing to provide review of the internal coherence and evidentiary basis of statutes in parliamentary compared to presidential systems. Even recognizing that compromise is a feature of all systems, parliaments can reasonably be held to workable standards because the same coalition or political party controls the government and the legislature. Judges do not obviously overstep their role as apolitical monitors if they demand consistency and factual justification. On the other hand, once again holding the constitutional text constant, a statute providing for review of administrative policymaking is more likely in a presidential system because the legislature has an incentive to maintain oversight by specifying the nature of the policymaking process. It may support constrained judicial review as a second-best alternative because direct legislative oversight is beyond its capacity.

Finally, the third prong of legitimacy – technical competence and effectiveness – raises vexed problems in all polities. Few judges will be knowledgeable about science, social science, or public administration. This puts them at a disadvantage in reviewing many modern statutes and rules. Their reluctance to base decisions on nonlegal expertise is consistent with the separation of powers as an institutional constraint. Thus, if the courts are reluctant to provide substantive review of technical matters, both the legislature and the executive have greater freedom to act in such areas than in other fields. This seems to be true for all constitutional arrangements that lack highly specialized "science" courts.[55] However, science and data quality frequently interact with claims based on either democratic legitimacy or the protection of rights, and they push the courts into the awkward position

[55] The U.S. Court of Appeals for the Federal Circuit is an exception – a specialized court that hears patent appeals from all the district courts as well as from the Patent and Trademark Office. It also has jurisdiction over trademark challenges, international trade cases, and a range of other suits against the government. In 2012, 45 percent of its caseload involved patents. *See* http://www.cafc.uscourts.gov/the-court/statistics.html

of judging mixed questions of fact and law with important implications for state legitimacy and respect for the judiciary.

We now turn to our case studies. After presenting the cases, we conclude by arguing for limited judicial review of legislative and administrative processes that is grounded in the preservation of democratic values and competence, not just the preservation of rights or of other constitutional provisions. Courts should be cautious in checking other branches, but they can and should move beyond an exclusive focus on individual rights. This is true, even and perhaps especially in the European Union and South Africa, where democratic institutions have only recently been established. Nevertheless, even in the United States and Germany, there is room for broader but well-focused judicial oversight of procedures that avoids judgments on substance. In the United States that would involve legislative processes; in Germany it would involve executive rulemaking.

2

The United States

Legislatures in presidential systems have an incentive both to delegate to the executive and to constrain that delegation through judicial review. In the United States these incentives have generated a statutory response – one that does not build on the constitutional text. Under these statutes, U.S. public law has a stronger focus on rulemaking procedures inside the executive and the independent agencies compared to the other advanced democracies that we study.[1]

The U.S. Constitution does not constrain the legislative process as a whole beyond certain framework provisions. Until recently, the Supreme Court's interpretation of the separation of powers led it to refuse to review the legislative process absent a violation of rights, of the separation of powers, or of the most basic features of the legislative process (quorum rules, passage by both chambers with presentment to the president).[2] The Court sometimes explains its deference by saying that the legislature is better equipped to judge the facts and make trade-offs than the courts, or that, because Congress must make compromises, the Court ought to expect and accept vague statutes and not judge internal deliberative processes.

Traditionally, the separation of powers dominates checks and balances. The Constitution establishes the basic parameters, but periodic elections,

1 This argument was first made by one of us in a study comparing the United States and Germany. SUSAN ROSE-ACKERMAN, CONTROLLING ENVIRONMENTAL POLICY: THE LIMITS OF PUBLIC LAW IN GERMANY AND THE UNITED STATES (2005).

2 For an overview of these provisions, *see* Adrian Vermeule, *The Constitutional Law of Congressional Procedure*, **71** U. OF CHICAGO LAW REV. 361 (2004) (stressing their importance). As we show later in this chapter, they have attracted little in the way of judicial enforcement, both because they are mostly uncontroversial within Congress itself, and because of the federal courts' limits on standing and jurisdiction. They do not deal with the adequacy of consultation or the quality of the text. We discuss some of his specific claims later in this chapter.

media scrutiny, and presidential or gubernatorial pressure are the primary loci of legislative oversight. Occasionally, plaintiffs challenge the constitutionality of a statute on procedural grounds, but courts at all levels are reluctant to interfere explicitly with the internal operation of legislatures except in particularly obvious or egregious cases. In the United States, the "law of lawmaking" by the legislature is very thin.

Once one moves beyond the Constitution, few enforceable statutes govern legislative procedures.[3] The U.S. Constitution gives Congress the power to enact its own rules,[4] and this power is central to its status as an independent branch of government. As one would expect, the congressional majority has not made its internal rules reviewable by courts. The few legal cases that review the legislative process are linked to constitutional questions. The Supreme Court has held that it can review legislative procedures for constitutionality, but in the classic case where it asserted this principle, it upheld the legislature's rule.[5] Furthermore, when members of Congress have sought access to the federal courts to challenge internal Congressional processes, they are seldom granted standing. Under the separation of powers, the courts are reluctant to permit members of the minority to go to court to seek review of the rules of Congress.[6] In one case where the Senate did seek review of a rule, it did so to counter the president's contrary interpretation.[7]

In a narrow range of cases, the congressional majority does try to constrain both itself and future Congresses through a statute governing its internal operation.[8] These efforts suffer from an obvious time-inconsistency

[3] As Peter Strauss states, "members of Congress are under no procedural obligations whatever to the outside world in what they may choose to introduce as legislative business." Peter L. Strauss, *Rulemaking in the Ages of Globalization and Information: What America Can Learn from Europe and Vice Versa*, **12** Columbia J. of European Law 645, 654–5 (2005–6).

[4] U.S. Const. art. I, §5 cl. 2.

[5] U.S. v. Ballin, 144 U.S. 1 (1891).

[6] In *Ballin* the plaintiff was an importer of cloth who objected to the duty levied on his imports. In Raines v. Byrd, 521 U.S. 811 (1997), the first challenge to the Line Item Veto Act, the Supreme Court refused to grant members of Congress standing to sue on the ground that they had not been individually injured.

[7] U.S. v. Smith, 286 U.S. 6, 26 (1932). Note that the plaintiff is the United States, not the Senate. The Department of Justice took the case in deference to the desire of the Senate.

[8] Examples are: Balanced Budget and Emergency Deficit Control Act of 1985 (Gramm-Rudman-Hollings), PL 99–177, December 12, 1985, 99 Stat 1037; Statutory Pay-as-You-Go Act of 2010, Public Law 111–139 (2010); Bipartisan Trade Promotion Authority Act (Fast Track), B Trade Act of 2002, Pub. L. No. 107–210, 116 Stat. 933, division B (2002); Defense Authorization Amendments and Base Closure and Realignment Act (Base Closure Act), PL 100–526, October 24, 1988, 102 Stat 2623; Unfunded Mandates Act, Pub. L. No. 104–4,

problem. If they start to bind, Congress can seek to amend or repeal them, or it may simply ignore them.[9] Even though formal amendments may not be possible because they require either a presidential signature or a supermajority vote, the legal constraints are rather weak. Judicial review could help assure that future Congresses follow these constraints; however, few statutes provide for review. Some statutes contain waivers, and judicial review is either explicitly excluded or not mentioned.[10] Access to the courts is limited not only by the statute itself but also by rules of standing and jurisdiction.[11]

109 Stat. 48. *See* Kevin M. Stack & Michael P. Vandenbergh, *The One Percent Problem*, **111** Columbia Law Rev. 1385, 1425–9, 1436–7 (discussing hands-tying internal rules and statutes); Jerry Brito, *Running for Cover: The BRAC Commission as a Model for Federal Spending Reform*, **9** Georgetown J. of Law & Public Policy 131 (2011); and Jon D. Michaels, *The (Willingly) Fettered Executive: Presidential Spinoffs in National Security Domains and Beyond*, **97** Virginia Law Rev. 801, 893–4 (2011).

9 For example, the Gramm-Rudman-Hollings statute, which sought to bind future Congresses and presidents to reduce the deficit, was routinely amended when its strictures started to bite. Balanced Budget and Emergency Deficit Control Act of 1985, Pub. L. No. 99–177. *See* Stack & Vandenbergh, *supra* note 8 at 1436–9 (comparing failures to meet targets under that statute with recent Pay-as-You-Go rules).

10 Aaron-Andrew Bruhl, *Using Statutes to Set Legislative Rules Entrenchment, Separation of Powers, and the Rules of Proceedings Clause*, **29** J. of Law and Politics 345 (2003) (pointing out that many seemingly hands-tying statutes include opt-out clauses). Neither Fast Track nor the Base Closure Act has any general mention of judicial review; the Unfunded Mandates Act applies to both Congress and federal agencies. However, judicial review is only explicitly available for the portions of the Act that apply to agencies [sec. 401], and there has, in fact, been no review of the congressional sections. Even the Act's application to agencies is not enforced. *See* Connor Raso, *Agency Avoidance of Rulemaking Procedures* Administrative Law Rev. (forthcoming 2015). Gramm-Rudman-Hollings, sect. 274, includes expedited provisions for judicial review, but only because of concerns for its constitutionality. *See* Bowsher v. Synar, 478 U.S. 714 (1986). However, sect. 274 (h) states: "The economic data, assumptions, and methodologies used by the Comptroller General in computing the base levels of total revenues and total budget outlays, … shall not be subject to review in any judicial or administrative proceeding." Bruhl argues that a statute that fully binds the hands of Congress would be unconstitutional, and he points out that many seemingly hands-tying statutes include opt-out clauses. Vermeule, *supra* note 2, at 429–31, also worries that such statutes might be unconstitutional on separation of powers grounds, but he argues that if so, that is an unfortunate result.

11 *See* Bruhl, *supra* note 10, at 370, n. 102: "In 1981, for example, the House deviated from the Alaskan Natural Gas Transportation Act's rule, 15 U.S.C. §719f(d)(5)(B), that no resolution approving a presidential recommendation to waive regulatory requirements could be considered within sixty days of another resolution concerning the same presidential recommendation. In debate, Representative Long referred to the disclaimer clause to justify circumventing the rule. *See* Metzenbaum v. Fed. Energy Regulatory Comm'n, 675 F. 2d 1282, 1284–86 (D.C. Cir. 1982) (describing the incident). In the subsequent suit challenging the propriety of the House's consideration of the waiver resolution, the D.C.

Substantive review of statutes for constitutional violations sometimes has indirect procedural implications. In a number of cases the Court tests the factual basis of statutes, but it does so to aid its own deliberations, not to enhance democratic values. However, such review gives Congress an incentive to prepare a better record and to engage in more hearings and background research. The claimed constitutional violations involve due process and equal protection for individuals, and, recently, the Commerce Clause and federalism.[12] The federalism cases, decided by a closely divided Court, raise troubling questions about the Court's role in checking the legislative activity of Congress.[13] The Court asks if Congress has issued "findings" that comply with a burden of proof established by the Court itself; review does not consider legislative accountability to the citizenry. This seemingly substantive standard sits at the overlap between substance and procedure. Reason-giving is both an aspect of process and a way to articulate a statute's substance, over and above the formal text. The Court's newly aggressive review is selective; it makes a prior judgment that the issue fits into a category subject to scrutiny.[14] However, if the Court continues to expand the

Circuit ruled that it lacked jurisdiction because the case presented a political question (*id.* at 1286–88)."

12 In 2012 the taxation provisions in the Constitution entered the picture with the Court upholding the individual mandate in the Patient Protection and Affordable Care Act in National Federation of Independent Business v. Sebelius, 132 S. Ct. 2566 (2012). Five members of the Court found that the individual mandate could not be upheld under the Commerce Clause. These five justices found that the choice *not* to purchase health insurance is properly classified as inactivity, and inactivity is not commerce. *See* Chief Justice Roberts' opinion, *id.* at 2585, and Justice Scalia's opinion, *id.* at 2647–8. Conversely, five justices upheld the mandate as a proper exercise of Congress's taxing power on the grounds that individuals cannot avoid taxes through inactivity. *See* Chief Justice Roberts' opinion, *id.* at 2599–601, and Justice Ginsburg's opinion, *id.* at 2629.

13 With respect to the federalism cases, *see* Philip P. Frickey & Steven S. Smith, *Judicial Review, the Congressional Process, and the Federalism Cases: An Interdisciplinary Critique*, **111** Yale Law J. 1707, 1746 (2002). They distinguish between the Court's protection of "substantive values, free speech, equality, Indian rights, and the like … [where it] may very well consider itself well situated to force Congress … to articulate clearly an institutional rationale for all the public to see." They then critique the federalism cases, at 1747–8, because there "the Court seems to insist that Congress must provide a formal record [to the Court] providing a strong factual basis for reasoned judgment."

14 *See* Ittai Bar-Siman-Tov, *Semiprocedural Judicial Review*, **6** Legisprudence 271 (2012). Alberto Alemanno, *The Emergence of the Evidence-based Judicial Reflex: A Response to Bar-Siman-Tov's Semiprocedural Review*, **1**(2) Theory and Practice of Legislation (2013), argues, consistently with our claim, that the phenomenon that Bar-Siman-Tov observes is a way for courts to articulate what the law means. Alemanno sees this as a largely positive development that reflects the heightened importance of evidence in the lawmaking process. We question that optimistic conclusion, at least in the U.S. case, but agree with his description of its origins.

range of statutes open to challenge, it may affect the operation of Congress in ways inconsistent with the democratic and representative character of the U.S. system of government. Its jurisprudence risks imposing procedures that are not only intrusive but are also unresponsive to the democratic deficit that does exist within Congress.

In Chapters 3 and 4 we compare these developments with South Africa and Germany. Germany's constitutional court also scrutinizes the factual basis of statutes that may violate rights, but it has a much longer list of rights to work with. The South African constitution is the only one of our cases where democratic procedural values are explicitly mandated, and its constitutional court has enforced these values in recent cases.

If the democratic legitimacy of lawmaking has constitutional status, U.S. judicial oversight is misdirected. Democratic accountability may be weak because of collective action problems. Individual members of Congress represent particular districts or states. They can appeal to their constituents by position taking and "bringing home the bacon." They may also attach riders to omnibus statutes to benefit their financial supporters. Preserving and enhancing the quality of the deliberative process in the legislature could provide broad public benefits but will be unlikely to further the reelection chances of particular legislators.[15] However, the recent spate of Supreme Court cases that strike down statutes that lack adequate "findings" does not respond to the question of democratic accountability. At present, either the Court's majority has a poor understanding of the way Congress operates, or it affirmatively seeks to limit legislation in areas that a bare majority of the justices view as questionable.

Turning to executive branch policymaking, the courts are deeply involved in review of both substance and process. They frequently evaluate the democratic legitimacy of agency procedures so long as someone has standing to bring a case;[16] here checks and balances dominate concerns

[15] On the motivations of legislatures *see* David R. Mayhew, Congress: The Electoral Connection (1974); Morris P. Fiorina, Congress; Keystone of the Washington Establishment (2nd ed., 1989); Keith Krehbiel, Information and Legislative Organization (1991); Victoria Nourse, *Misunderstanding Congress: Statutory Interpretation, the Supermajoritarian Difficulty, and the Separation of Powers*, **99** Geo. Law J. 1119 (2011).

[16] The U.S. Administrative Procedure Act (APA), 5 U.S. C., §702 states that review is open to "[a] person suffering a legal wrong because of agency action, or adversely affected or aggrieved by agency action within the meaning of the relevant statute." The courts have read that phrase generously but have also read the Constitution to limit both jurisdiction and standing under the clause that limits the courts to hearing "cases and controversies" (U.S. Const. art. III, §2). In Lujan v. Defenders of Wildlife, 504 U.S. 555, 560–1 (1992),

for judicial overreaching. The Constitution says little about administrative procedure, but statutes codify the courts' oversight role. The U.S. Administrative Procedure Act (APA) is the primary legal route to bureaucratic control.[17] Bruce Ackerman designates the APA a "landmark" statute and gives it quasi-constitutional status. It could be repealed like any other statute, but, in practice, it has become part of the structure of government.[18] Even if the APA did not have de facto landmark status, however, its repeal would be unlikely. It fits well with the incentives of Congress under divided government to create such oversight mechanisms.[19] The main legislative challenges to the present APA are proposals by Republican lawmakers to impose more procedural constraints on rulemaking inside the administration, not fewer.[20] Such an amended statute might be enacted by a deregulatory Congress backed by a Republican president.

The asymmetric legal framework governing statutes and administrative rules is consistent with the positive political economy perspective outlined in Chapter 1, and it has normative aspects as well. The legislature is ultimately responsible to the voters; if it behaves too irresponsibly, the voters will select new representatives. Although the same is ultimately true of the president, the sheer volume and complexity of the executive's regulatory

the Court stated that the standing requirement is an "essential and unchanging part of the case-or-controversy requirement." The Court defined standing in terms of a three-part test: (1) Plaintiffs must have suffered an "injury in fact"; (2) there must be a "causal connection" between the defendant's actions and the injury; and (3) it must be "likely ... that the injury will be 'redressed by a favorable decision.'" *Id.* (citing Simon v. E. Kentucky Welfare Rights Org., 426 U.S. 26, 38 (1976). *See also* Evan Tsen Lee & Josephine Mason Ellis, *The Standing Doctrine's Dirty Little Secret*, **107** Northwestern U. Law Rev. 169, 170 (2012). Of particular importance for our study is the debate between the justices in *Lujan* over the status of procedural injuries.

17 APA, 5 U.S.C. §§551–9, 701–6 (1946).

18 Bruce Ackerman, *The Living Constitution*, **120** Harvard Law Rev. 1727 (2007). On the APA, in particular, *see* Peter Strauss, *Statutes that Are Not Static: The Case of the APA*, **14** J. Contemporary Legislative Issues 767 (2005). William Eskridge and John Ferejohn develop a broader category called "super statutes," but they do not explicitly discuss the APA. *See* William Eskridge & John Ferejohn, A Republic of Statutes: The New American Constitution (2010).

19 Of course, one can ask why the APA was passed in 1946 and not earlier or later. *See* the sources cited *infra* note 194 putting its passage in the historical context of the rise of executive rulemaking and the administrative state during the New Deal and World War II.

20 Regulatory Accountability Act of 2011, H.R. 3010 (112th Congress, 1st session), passed by the House, December 2, 2011, http://www.gpo.gov/fdsys/pkg/BILLS-112hr3010eh/pdf/BILLS-112hr3010eh.pdf. It would impose more restrictions on agency rulemaking and guidance documents, some similar to a cost/benefit test, and would require the courts to defer less to agency rules. A somewhat less restrictive Regulatory Accountability Act of 2013, S. 1029, was introduced in the Senate.

tasks mean that the electoral link is weak for any particular piece of secondary legislation. Administrative rulemaking processes that require public input and reason-giving can enhance democratic legitimacy. They can also preserve rights and help assure that policy is technically competent, for example, through impact assessment or cost/benefit analysis. However, the Republican-backed proposals for more restrictive rulemaking processes demonstrate that procedural constraints need not necessarily further the democratic legitimacy of executive rulemaking. Taken to extremes they could undermine, rather than help, fulfill public values.[21]

We proceed as follows. Section I examines judicial review of the legislative process, isolated from substantive review. Section II shows how reason-giving mandates can indirectly affect the legislative process. We pay particular attention to recent cases that have struck down statutory texts, at least in part, for lacking sufficient "findings." Then, in Section III we turn to the administrative process, where judicial review of process is entrenched, and contrast review of the legislative process with the review of executive and agency rules. Section IV concludes with our policy reflections.

I. THE LEGISLATIVE PROCESS

The U.S. Constitution allows each House to determine its own rules of procedure so long as a quorum, constituting a majority of the members of that House, is present to do business.[22] If asked to review legislative procedures, the courts struggle with the tension between the separation of powers and checks and balances. In practice, they seldom rule against Congress purely on procedural grounds. The few cases that challenge technical aspects of the legislative process do not raise fundamental objections to the democratic

[21] Some argue that U.S. rulemaking procedures have already "ossified" in ways that undermine the values expressed in the text. The usual explanation, however, is overly aggressive judicial review, not restrictive statutory language. *See* Thomas McGarity, *Some Thoughts on "Deossifying" the Rulemaking Process*, **1992** Duke Law J. 1385, Richard Pierce, *Seven Ways to Deossify Agency Rulemaking*, **47** Administrative Law Rev. 59 (1995).

[22] *U.S. Const. art. I, §5, cls. 1, 2.* The Constitution does not state the voting rule for the initial passage of statutes, but under current rules a bill passes if supported by a majority of those both present and voting, so long as at least a quorum is present. A Member who is present and abstains counts toward the quorum but not as part of the base for calculating the number needed to pass a measure. Rules of the House of Representatives, Rule XX, cl. 6(b) (113th Congress); Standing Rules of the Senate, Rules VI, XII (113th Congress). Other provisions dealing with the operation of Congress state that Congress shall meet at least once a year (*U.S. Const. art. 1, §4, cl. 2*) and must keep a Journal (*art. 1, §5, cl. 3*). Each House chooses its own officers, except that the vice president is the president of the Senate but votes only in the case of a tie (*U.S. Const. art. 1, §2, cl. 2; §3, cls. 4, 5*).

or representative legitimacy of congressional practices. One case that did pit Congress against the voters involved the House's refusal to seat one of its members – a case that did not implicate the legislative drafting process. Other cases, not involving elections, were challenges where particular individuals claimed injury from congressional practices.[23]

The arguments over judicial review of legislative processes are mostly couched in separation of powers terms between the legislature and the courts. Article I, section 5 sets up a presumption in favor of Congress that few judges or scholars are willing to challenge. Nevertheless, there are a few cases at the interface between majoritarian requirements and internal procedural rules. We begin with structural issues: the non-delegation doctrine and other inter-branch controversies, then consider the Court's willingness to hear cases dealing with the legislature (i.e., issues of jurisdiction and standing), followed by cases that directly confront aspects of the legislative process.

A. Structural Issues: The Separation of Powers

If the Supreme Court puts constitutional limits on legislative choices, its decisions usually turn on the separation of powers between the legislature, the executive, and the judiciary, not on the quality of the lawmaking process inside Congress. The non-delegation doctrine imposes very weak constraints, but a few structural limits do exist.

1. The Non-Delegation Doctrine

A judicially generated non-delegation doctrine imposes weak conditions on delegation to the executive or to independent agencies.[24] Justice William Rehnquist tried to breathe some life into the doctrine in his concurrence in *Industrial Union v. American Petroleum Inst. (The Benzene*

[23] The Supreme Court has been much more active in ruling on the design of electoral districts on equal protection grounds. In Baker v. Carr, 369 U.S. 186 (1962) it required districts to have approximately equal numbers of eligible voters, and in the subsequent gerrymandering cases the Court ruled on the distribution of political power. The Court first held that partisan gerrymandering at the state level was justiciable in Davis v. Bandemer, 478 U.S. 109 (1986). For a history of the gerrymandering cases after *Bandemer*, *see* Laughlin Mcdonald, *The Looming 2010 Census: A Proposed Judicially Manageable Standard and Other Reform Options for Partisan Gerrymandering*, **46** HARVARD J. ON LEGISLATION 248–52 (2009).

[24] A. L. A. Schechter Poultry Corp. v. U.S., 294 U.S. 495 (1935); Panama Refining v. Ryan, 293 U.S. 388 (1935).

Case).[25] However, he was unable to attract any other justices to his view. He finds the term "feasibility" in the Occupational Safety and Health Act "largely, if not entirely, precatory" and writes that:

> Congress was faced with a clear, if difficult, choice between balancing statistical lives and industrial resources or authorizing the Secretary to elevate human life above all concerns save massive dislocation in an affected industry.... That Congress chose, intentionally or unintentionally, to pass this difficult choice on to the Secretary is evident from the spectral quality of the standard it selected.[26]

Rehnquist argued that the Act violated the non-delegation doctrine; he believed that the Court should "reshoulder the burden of ensuring that Congress itself makes the critical policy decisions." To him, the statutory language was an "obvious example of Congress simply avoiding a choice which was both fundamental ... and yet so politically divisive that the necessary decision or compromise was difficult, if not impossible, to hammer out in the legislative forge."[27] Hence, he acknowledged that if the court followed his lead, Congress would simply fail to enact statutes in certain controversial areas.

Judge Stephen Williams tried to revive the doctrine in *American Trucking v. EPA*, but the Supreme Court was not interested. The D.C. Circuit per curiam decision found that the Environmental Protection Agency (EPA) had not articulated an "intelligible principle" and that none was apparent from the Clean Air Act (CAA) under which it was acting. That court would have remanded to the EPA to see if it could come up with an intelligible principle.[28] The decision invited the Supreme Court to hold that the CAA violated the non-delegation doctrine. However, the Supreme Court in *Whitman v. American Trucking* held that the CAA set out guidelines that were clear enough to survive constitutional scrutiny.[29] The doctrine is not likely to be given teeth anytime soon. The Supreme Court seems to recognize that the realities of the American lawmaking process will often produce vague language that reflects political compromise and expediency.[30]

25 Industrial Union Department, AFL-CIO v. American Petroleum Inst., 448 U.S. 607 (1980).

26 *Id.* at 685.

27 *Id.* at 687.

28 American Trucking Ass'n, Inc. v. Environmental Protection Agency, 175 F. 3d 1027 (D.C. Cir. 1999).

29 Whitman v. American Trucking Ass'n, Inc., 531 U.S. 457 (2001).

30 *But see* Ass'n of American Railroads v. U.S. Dept. of Transportation, 721 F. 3d 666 (D.C. Cir. 2013 (rehearing en banc denied, Oct. 11, 2013) (finding delegation of rulemaking authority to Amtrak unconstitutional because it holds that it is a private corporation with

The courts justify their acceptance of delegation on the ground that judicial review of the executive limits the mischief that Congress can do. As Judge Harold Leventhal states in his famous concurrence in *Ethyl Corp. v. EPA*:

> In the case of agency decision-making, the courts have an additional responsibility set by Congress. Congress has been willing to delegate its legislative powers broadly – and courts have upheld such delegation because there is court review to assure that the agency exercises the delegated power within statutory limits, and that it fleshes out objectives within those limits by an administration that is not irrational or discriminatory [footnotes omitted].[31]

2. Structural Limits

The Court has disapproved certain structural provisions on the ground that they give the legislature too much executive authority and vice versa for some executive mandates. It has accepted others as pragmatic responses to policy problems.[32] So long as Congress does not assign executive or judicial power to itself or violate other constitutional provisions that we discuss later in this chapter, Congress can do as it likes when it drafts statutes.

The justices are reluctant to interfere in inter-branch disputes, but they do not have a unified view of their role in mediating such controversies. *Goldwater v. Carter* illustrates their differing views.[33] President Carter terminated a treaty with Taiwan as part of the process of recognizing mainland China. Several members of Congress complained that the president could not constitutionally abrogate a treaty that the Senate had ratified.

respect to Congress's power to delegate)). The delegations in the 1935 cases of *Schechter* and *Panama Refining* also were held unconstitutional, in part, because of the involvement of private entities in regulatory policymaking. Amtrak is, however, "a curious entity that occupies the twilight between the public and the private sectors" (*id.* at 668). The court, however, finds that because the statute requires Amtrak to be operated like a for-profit corporation, that is sufficient to overturn the delegation, even though Amtrak was treated as a public entity in a 1995 Supreme Court decision dealing with a different type of constitutional challenge (*id.* at 676–7).

31 Ethyl Corp. v. EPA, 541 F. 2d 1, 68 (1976). As we discuss later in this chapter, Leventhal's statement here is a response to Judge Bazelon's claim that the courts should not become immersed in the technical matters behind regulations (*id.* at 66–7).

32 Bowsher v. Synar, 478 U.S. 714 [involvement of the Comptroller General in executive decision unconstitutional because he heads the General Accounting Office (now the Government Accountability Office) that is an arm of Congress]; Metropolitan Washington Airports Auth. v. Citizens for the Abatement of Airport Noise, 501 U.S. 252 (1992) (striking down Board of Review with veto power over airport policy because it has executive power and consisted of nine members of Congress). The Court upheld the structure of the Sentencing Commission in Mistretta v. United States, 488 U.S. 361 (1989) and the independent counsel statute in Morrison v. Olsen, 487 U.S. 654 (1988).

33 Goldwater v. Carter, 444 U.S. 996 (1979).

Thus, the case presented a fairly straightforward issue of constitutional interpretation. Six justices joined or concurred in a one-paragraph opinion that granted certiorari, vacated the lower court's judgment, and remanded the case with directions to dismiss the complaint. However, two concurrences stated quite different rationales.

Justice Rehnquist recognized an independent role for the president in foreign affairs. According to him, the controversy was a nonjusticiable political dispute.[34] He argued that each of the coequal branches has the resources to defend its own interests and does not need the Court's help.[35] In contrast, Justice Lewis Powell argued that differences between the president and Congress "should, and almost invariably do, turn on political rather than legal considerations.... [The Judiciary should not intervene] until the political branches reach a constitutional impasse."[36] To him, the issue raised by the members was not a nonjusticiable political question. He cited the three questions listed in *Baker v. Carr*, ultimately answering "no" to the first two, but finding it prudent to refrain from review:

> (i) Does the issue involve resolution of questions committed by the text of the Constitution to a coordinate branch of Government? (ii) Would resolution of the question demand that a court move beyond areas of judicial expertise? (iii) Do prudential considerations counsel against judicial intervention?[37]

He would have supported review if the case were ripe.[38] His justification for review is fundamentally tied to the lawmaking process in a presidential system with separation of powers. In a parliamentary system one could ask the same questions about an executive action, but the first question would have less practical relevance. A related issue could arise in such a system, however, if a treaty must be approved by a supermajority, and the government only controls a majority of parliamentary seats.

B. Jurisdiction and Standing

Before reaching the merits, courts must decide if the litigants have standing and if the courts have jurisdiction.[39] These preliminary questions balance

[34] *Id.* at 1003–5.

[35] *Id.* at 1004.

[36] *Id.* at 997.

[37] *Id.* at 998 [citing Baker v. Carr, 369 U.S. at 217].

[38] *Id.* at 1001.

[39] In some cases the federal courts distinguish between subject matter jurisdiction and justiciability. The former concerns whether the plaintiff has a claim under federal law and the latter asks whether the court can legitimately resolve the dispute without, for example, violating the separation of powers. *See* Powell v. McCormack, 395 U.S. 486, 512 ff (1969).

the separation of powers and the courts' role as a check on the legislature. This interplay is evident in the jurisprudence of the Supreme Court and the District of Columbia Circuit.[40] Accepting jurisdiction presumably implies that the Court might in some cases hold for the plaintiff. The lawsuit is not, by definition, futile.

An important early case, *United States v. Ballin*, illustrates this mixture of jurisdiction and the merits.[41] The plaintiff, an importer of cloth, claimed that a law passed under the House of Representatives' newly enacted quorum rule was constitutionally invalid. Rule XV, promulgated in 1890, counted toward the quorum any members in the chamber, whether or not they cast a ballot. Opponents had defeated bills by showing up and then not voting; the rule eliminated this possibility. However, as a consequence, the recorded votes might be less than a majority of the members. The Court stated that, although the House can determine its own rules of procedure, it may not promulgate unconstitutional rules, and the Court has the power to make that judgment. It reviewed the rule and judged it constitutional. The relevant language is:

> [T]he advantages or disadvantages, the wisdom or folly, of such a rule [do not] present any matters for judicial consideration. With the courts, the question is only one of power. The Constitution empowers each house to determine its rules of proceedings. It may not by its rules ignore constitutional restraints or violate fundamental rights, and there should be a reasonable relation between the mode or method of proceeding established by the rule and the result which is sought to be attained. But within these limitations, all matters of method are open to the determination of the house, and it is no impeachment of the rule to say that some other way would be better, more accurate, or even more just. It is no objection to the validity of a rule that a different one has been prescribed and in force for a length of time. The power to make rules is not one which once exercised is exhausted. It is a continuous power, always subject to be exercised by the house, and, within the limitations suggested, absolute and beyond the challenge of any other body or tribunal.[42]

[40] *See* Frederick van Tatenhove, *A Question of Power: Judicial Review of Congressional Rules of Procedure*, **76** Kentucky Law J. 597 (1987), and Stephen Raher, *Judicial Review of Legislative Procedure; Determining Who Determines the Rules of Proceedings*, ExpressO (2008), available at http://works.bepress.com/stephen_raher/1. See also Michael B. Miller, *The Justiciability of Legislative Rules and the "Political" Political Question Doctrine*, **78** California L. Rev. 1341 (1990) (summarizing the case law up to 1990 and arguing that standing should only be given to private plaintiffs to avoid judicializing the political process).

[41] U.S. v. Ballin, 144 U.S. 1 (1891).

[42] *Id.* at 5. For discussions *see* Van Tatenhove, *supra* note 40, at 605–8; Raher, *supra* note 40, at 12–14.

In 1932 Justice Louis Brandeis went further in asserting the Court's jurisdiction. In *United States v. Smith* the Court sided with the president and struck down a Senate interpretation of its own rule. It claimed the right to reject a presidential nominee to the Federal Power Commission (FPC), George Otis Smith, after it had communicated a positive decision to the president.[43] The Court did not view the issue as primarily a constitutional one, but, quoting the paragraph excerpted above from *Ballin*, it, nevertheless, accepted jurisdiction:

> As the construction to be given to the [Senate's] rules affects persons other than members of the Senate, the question presented is of *necessity* a judicial one. Smith asserts that he was duly appointed to office in the manner prescribed by the Constitution.... The Senate disputes the claim. In deciding the issue, the Court must give great weight to the Senate's present construction of its own rules; but, so far, at least, as that construction was arrived at subsequent to the events in controversy, we are not concluded by it [emphasis added].[44]

The affected persons are, of course, both the president and Smith himself. The Court is willing to consider the rules of Congress if they have external effect, either on a coordinate branch of government and more generally as well. Brandeis justifies this position as a generic feature of the jurisdiction of courts, not based on the constitutional text. The Court reviewed the rule on the ground that the Senate was interpreting its own rules in a way that differed from their meaning when the president signed his commission. The president was justified in keeping Smith at the FPC, as was Smith in taking up his position. The Court is confident in its holding because the Senate in subsequent actions appears to support the Court. The decision apparently did not foment controversy at the time it was decided:

> To place upon the standing rules of the Senate a construction different from that adopted by the Senate itself when the present case was under debate is a serious and delicate exercise of judicial power. The Constitution commits to the Senate the power to make its own rules, and it is not the function of the Court to say that another rule would be better. A rule designed to insure due deliberation in the performance of the vital function of advising and consenting to nominations for public office, moreover, should receive from the Court the most sympathetic consideration. But the reasons, above stated, against the Senate's construction seem to us compelling. We are confirmed in

[43] U.S. v. Smith, 286 U.S. 6 (1932). *See also* Van Tatenhove, *supra* note 40, at 608–10; Raher *supra* note 40, at 14. The plaintiff is only nominally the United States. The attorney general took the case under an agreement with the Senate to provide its own lawyers to argue the case.

[44] U.S. v. Smith, 286 U.S. at 33.

> the view we have taken by the fact that, since the attempted reconsideration of Smith's confirmation, the Senate itself seems uniformly to have treated the ordering of immediate notification to the President as tantamount to authorizing him to proceed to perfect the appointment [footnote omitted].[45]

The Smith case has not led to a flood of legislation challenging congressional rules. *Powell v. McCormack* is the most high-profile subsequent case that resolved a jurisdictional issue in favor of review.[46] The case stemmed from a vote by the House of Representatives to bar Adam Clayton Powell from taking his seat on the grounds that he had committed various financial improprieties connected with his past tenure in the House. The Court of Appeals found that it had jurisdiction but dismissed the case because it was not "justiciable" on separation of powers and political question grounds. The Supreme Court disagreed, holding that it could rule on the matter. Once it decided to resolve the case, the Court held that Congress could only exclude a duly elected person if he or she failed the requirements of age, citizenship, and residence grounded in the Constitution. Although the case dealt with an action of the House of Representatives, it did not deal with the content of legislation. The Court did not consider charges against Powell that involved misuse of his position as committee chair with possible implications for the integrity of the legislative drafting process. The decision simply limited the adjudicatory powers of Congress vis-à-vis its own members.

Occasionally, the federal courts consider the impact of congressional rules that govern committee behavior. However, the relevant cases only concern individuals who claim to have been harmed, not the validity of statutes enacted under these rules. *Christoffel v. United States*[47] is a challenge to a quorum requirement for committee hearings. A quorum was not present when the witness allegedly committed perjury. The plaintiff argued that the committee had violated House rules, and hence, he had not testified before a "competent tribunal" under the District of Columbia's perjury statute. The majority accepted that argument, but a strong three-judge dissent argued that "this Court has the duty to presume that the conduct of a Congressional Committee, in its usual course of business, conforms to both the written and unwritten rules of the House which created it."[48] Another challenge to a committee's investigatory practice arose in *Yellin v. United States*.[49] In that case the Court required the House Committee on

[45] *Id.* at 48–9.
[46] Powell v. McCormack, 395 U.S. 486 (1969).
[47] Christoffel v. United States, 338 U.S. 84 (1978).
[48] *Id.* at 91. *See* Van Tatenhove, *supra* note 40, at 611–12; Raher, *supra* note 40, at 15–16.
[49] Yellin v. United States, 374 U.S. 109 (1963).

Un-American Activities (HUAC) to follow its own rules, as interpreted by the Court.[50] Chief Justice Warren Burger, writing for the majority, stated that "[i]t has long been settled, of course, that rules of Congress and its committees are judicially cognizable."[51]

At the appellate level, the District of Columbia Circuit deals with any challenges to congressional procedures. In one case, the judicial panel rejected a challenge to a House rule, but only after stating that "this circuit has previously expressed its reluctance to review congressional operating rules, though it has never denied its power to do so." It went on to state that, although it could not mandate rules, it could strike down constitutionally invalid ones.[52] However, it dismisses suits brought by legislators "[w]here a congressional plaintiff could obtain substantial relief from his fellow legislators through the enactment, repeal or amendment of a statute."[53] In a second case, not dealing with the legislative process, the appellant complained that the chaplain of the House and Senate, following the chambers' rules, refused his request to deliver secular remarks during morning prayers. The D.C. Circuit concluded that the appellant lacked standing, citing the separation of powers.[54] Judge Ruth Bader Ginsberg, in dissent, gave the decision a jurisdictional spin: "the majority – notwithstanding its use of a 'standing' label – is deciding not *who* may sue, but an anterior question, *viz, what issues* are legitimately open to third branch resolution."[55]

A similar blending of standing and jurisdiction is evident in *David E. Skaggs v. Robin H. Carle*, a D.C. Circuit case that challenged two House rules.[56] In one of the few provisions dealing with the operation of Congress, the Constitution requires that all revenue bills originate in the House.[57] The House enacted a rule requiring that any bill to raise income tax rates must

50 Van Tatenhove, *supra* note 40, at 612–61; Raher, *supra* note 40, at 16–17. Raher sees this case as anomalous, perhaps because it arose in the context of a HUAC investigation.

51 Yellin v. United States, 374 U.S. at 114.

52 Van der Jagt v. O'Neil, 699 F. 2d 1166, 1171–3 (D.C. Cir. 1983), *cert. denied*, 464 U.S. 823 (1983).

53 Riegle v. Federal Open Market Committee, 656 F. 2d 873 (D.C. Cir. 1981) *cert. denied* 454 U.S. 1082 (1981). *See* Van Tatenhove, *supra* note 40, at 617–18.

54 Kurtz v. Baker, 829 F. 2d 1133 (D.C. Cir. 1987).

55 *Id.* at 1138. *See also* Morgan v. United States, 801 F. 2d 445, 449 (D.C. Cir. 1986); *cert, denied* 480 U.S. 449 (1987) (Rulemaking Clause not an absolute bar to judicial review of House rules).

56 David E. Skaggs v. Robin H. Carle, 110 F. 3d 831 (D.C. Cir. 1997).

57 U.S. Const. art. 1, §7, cl. 1. *See* Vermeule, *supra* note 2, at 426–7 (justifying this provision). Note, however, that at the time the Constitution was written only the House was directly elected – a reason for the clause that is no longer valid, although its representative character is still superior to the Senate.

pass by at least three-fifths of the Members voting. The plaintiffs – twenty-seven Members of the House, six of their constituents, and the League of Women Voters – claimed that the rule was unconstitutional.[58] The majority opinion by Judge Douglas Ginsburg found that the Members had not suffered an injury essentially because they could vote to repeal the rule.[59] A dissent by Judge Harry Edwards would have found that the Members suffered vote dilution and given them standing. He objected to the majority's use of the concept of "remedial discretion" to dismiss the suit. As he writes: "It permits the court to decline to hear a case even when it has Article III jurisdiction over the controversy."[60] He goes on to reach the merits and argues that the three-fifths voting rule is unconstitutional. To him, the judges' worry about violating the separation of powers led them to ignore the importance of checks and balances.[61]

The case law has not developed toward a more general review of legislative rules that might affect, say, the time for floor debate, or the identity of interest groups invited to testify before congressional committees. The Court uses deferential language at the same time as it asserts that judges can police the external effect of congressional procedures. We are left with a split between the claim that the federal courts have no jurisdiction to review legislative procedures and the argument that courts do have jurisdiction but ought to limit the scope of review either to clearly unconstitutional processes or to those that have external effect on individuals or other branches of government. Within the latter group, there is a further split between a faction that believes that courts should dismiss most suits given the possibility of remedial action by the legislature and others who would have courts reach the merits of rules that are suspect on constitutional grounds or because they have effects outside the legislative body.

C. The Legislative Veto, the Speech and Debate Clause, and the Enrolled Bill Rule

A statute that has passed both houses of Congress and been signed by the president seldom faces procedural challenges. When the Court has struck

58 An open letter from seventeen professors of constitutional law to Newt Gingrich, the incoming Republican Speaker, supported this position. Bruce Ackerman, *An Open Letter to Congressman Gingrich*, **104** YALE LAW J. 1539 (1995).

59 Rules are, in fact, seldom changed during a session. However, in November 2013 the Senate majority voted 52 to 48 to change the filibuster rule for executive nominees and lower court judges from three-fifths to a majority. *See* Jeremy W. Peters, *In Landmark Vote, Senate Limits Use of the Filibuster*, NEW YORK TIMES, November 21, 2013.

60 *Skaggs v. Carle*, 110 F. 3d at 840.

61 *Id.* at 841–7.

down violations of these basic requirements, it often uses rather mechanical language that suggests its unwillingness to examine underlying rationales. Absent violation of these procedures, the Speech and Debate Clause and the "enrolled bill rule" limit judicial oversight to the enacted text of a statute.

1. The Legislative Veto and the Line-Item Veto

The main cases dealing with the nature of a "statute" outlawed both legislative vetoes and presidential line-item vetoes as unconstitutional. These vetoes both challenge the principle of the separation of powers between the legislature and the executive. The Supreme Court judged that each went too far although, of course, there are many remaining ways each branch seeks to influence the other outside of formal statutory texts. Both opinions build on a rather mechanical view of the constitutional requirements.

Legislative vetoes of executive branch rules were found unconstitutional in *I.N.S. v. Chadha* because they did not follow the constitutional requirement of presentment to the president.[62] A dissent by Justice Byron White worries that the case will cast doubt on delegation of rulemaking authority to the executive, but that has not been the result. White supplies an appendix listing fifty-five statutes that included vetoes.[63] In spite of the clarity of the *Chadha* opinion, a recent review found that Congress still exercises vetoes at the committee and subcommittee levels.[64] In our other

[62] I.N.S. v. Chadha, 462 U.S. 919 (1983). Subsequently Congress passed the Congressional Review Act, 5 U.S. C. §§ 801–8 [U.S. 417 (1998)] that requires major rules to be submitted to the Government Accountability Office for review. The statute provides for expedited congressional passage of a joint resolution to overturn a major rule, but, of course, it cannot go into effect unless the president signs it. Thus, the law plays no role except for rules promulgated at the end of a president's term before a president of a different party takes office. The Act was only used once – to repeal a workplace rule dealing with ergonomics after President George W. Bush took office. *See* Pub. L. 107–5, March 20, 2001.

[63] Justice White's dissent in I.N.S. v. Chadha, 462 U.S. at 967. The appendix begins at 1004 ff. *See also* Peter L. Strauss, *Was There a Baby in the Bathwater? A Comment on the Supreme Court's Legislative Veto Decision* **1983** Duke. Law J. 789, 791–2 (citing a Congressional Research Service study showing that the veto was used only 230 times between 1930 and 1983 with only thirty falling into the residual category of "foreign relations, international affairs, and regulatory matters." Almost half involved the immigration status of particular individuals, as in *Chadha*.

[64] Louis Fisher, Committee Control of Agency Decisions, CRS Report to Congress, RL33151 (November 16, 2005). Fisher argues that such controls play a useful role and are unlikely to be litigated because no one will have standing to sue. President Obama, in a signing statement in December 2011, stated that he found a committee veto in a budget bill to be unconstitutional. Fisher provides a critique in *Obama's Objections to Committee Veto Misguided*, Roll Call, Jan. 19, 2012, pp. 14–15, available at: http://www.loufisher.org/lv.html. Peter Strauss argues that existing uses of the veto are mostly in his "baby"

case studies legislative vetoes are acceptable. In Germany, South Africa, and the European Union legislative bodies can be given the power to veto rules promulgated by the executive. In Germany, however, such actions are uncommon; in South Africa parliamentary oversight of delegated power, in general, remains limited, and its courts have not yet squarely evaluated the legality of the legislative veto.[65]

The Supreme Court also struck down a statute giving the president limited line-item veto power for appropriations' statutes. Along the same lines as the *Chadha* opinion, the majority found that the provisions violated formal lawmaking requirements. Justice John Paul Stevens' opinion argued that if the line-item veto were used, then the act that went into force was not the one passed by Congress, a violation of the Constitution.[66] Justices Stephen Breyer, Antonin Scalia, and Sandra Day O'Connor, in partial dissent, argued that the statute did not actually permit a line-item veto.[67] Rather the president signs an act into law and then announces an intention not to enforce certain provisions. To Breyer, such actions, because they were expressly permitted by the statute, are no different from other provisions under which Congress gives discretion to the president to set priorities. Such delegations of policymaking authority have long been accepted by the Supreme Court. To him, the Act was wrongly titled from the point of view of constitutional law; it is equivalent to other acceptable delegations of policymaking authority to the executive.

2. The Speech and Debate Clause

The legislative veto and the line-item veto cases dealt with the constitutionality of statutes that affect the link between legislative and presidential actions. The Speech and Debate Clause, in contrast, limits challenges to congressional rules themselves. It states that "for any Speech or Debate in either House, they [Senators and Representatives] shall not be questioned

category (budget adjustments, reorganizations) that gives the president flexibility subject to this check [e-mail from Peter Strauss, February 15, 2014].

65 *See* Chapters 3, 4 and 5.

66 Clinton v. N.Y., 524 U.S. 417 (1998). For general discussions of statutory constraints on legislative action *see* Bruhl, *supra* note 10, and Aaron-Andrew P. Bruhl, *Return of the Line Item Veto? Legalities, Practicalities, and Some Puzzles*, **10** J. of Constitutional Law 447 (2008).

67 Clinton v. N.Y., 524 U.S. at 473. Justice Breyer joined the Court in accepting the standing of both plaintiffs. Justice Scalia and Justice O'Connor would have denied one of the plaintiffs standing (*id.* at 453).

in any other Place."[68] According to *Gravel v. United States*, to be covered, actions must be:

> an integral part of the deliberative and communicative processes by which Members participate in committee and House proceedings with respect to the consideration and passage or rejection of proposed legislation or with respect to other matters which the Constitution places within the jurisdiction of either House.[69]

Thus, it covers not only floor speeches but also Committee reports, resolutions, and votes, as well as "things done in a session of the House by one of its members in relation to the business before it."[70] The Court rejected as nonjusticiable the challenge in *Gravel* and subsequent challenges to congressional actions.[71] None of these cases involves attempts to evaluate deliberations in committees or on the floor, but one can assume that the Court would dismiss for lack of jurisdiction any attempt to bring a court challenge to the quality or comprehensiveness of debate in Congress.

3. The Enrolled Bill Rule

Beyond these constitutional conditions, an old legal doctrine helps the courts resolve certain disputes. Under the "enrolled bill rule" the courts will not entertain suits that challenge the wording of a bill that has been officially accepted as the definitive text by the presiding officers of each House.[72] This seems a pragmatic response to the worry that those who are harmed by a piece of legislation will look for technical glitches of little substantive importance, thus casting doubt on many enactments. Even if the

[68] U.S. Const. art. I, §6.

[69] Gravel v. United States, 408 U.S. 606, 625 (1972). The case dealt with Senator Gravel's decision to read into the Congressional Record large portions of the Pentagon Papers released by Daniel Ellsberg dealing with the conduct of the Vietnam War. Congress has seldom directly leaked information under this clause, however. *See* David E. Pozen, *The Leaky Leviathan: Why Government Condemns and Condones Unlawful Disclosures of Information*, **127** Harvard Law Rev. (2013).

[70] Kilbourn v. Thompson, 103 U.S. 168 (1881).

[71] *See also* Consumers Union v. Periodical Correspondents Ass'n, 515 F. 2d 1341 (D.C. Cir. 1975), *cert. denied*, 423 U.S. 1051 (1976); Eastland v. United States Servicemen's Fund, 421 U.S. 491 (1975); Cable News Network v. Anderson, 723 F. Supp. 835 (D.D.C. 1989) (all rejecting claims as nonjusticiable under the Speech and Debate Clause to protect the independence of the legislature).

[72] The rule is "a common-law doctrine which has historical origins in the Anglo-Saxon rule prohibiting impeachment of documents representing the king's word. American courts have substituted legislative deference for regnal deference, often citing separation-of-powers doctrine" (Raher, *supra* note 40, at 61).

plaintiffs have standing and the courts accept jurisdiction, the courts are likely to reject the claim.

The federal courts applied the enrolled bill rule in a strong form beginning with *Marshall Field & Co. v. Clark*, an 1892 case on the separation of powers:

> [B]etter, far better that a provision should occasionally find its way into the statute through mistake, or even fraud, then that every act, state and national, should at any and all times be liable to be put in issue and impeached by the journals, loose papers of the legislature, and parole evidence. Such a state of uncertainty in the statute laws of the land would lead to mischiefs absolutely intolerable.[73]

This precedent still holds.[74] Judges have invoked the enrolled bill rule not just to prevent trivial challenges to minor wording discrepancies but also to prevent the courts from considering the legislative process that produced the bill. Although this reading is not the only plausible one,[75] if it is adopted, only the enrolled text is subject to judicial review even if there is substantial evidence of procedural violations or even corruption.[76] Combined with Congress's power to make its own rules and the Speech and Debate Clause, it insulates both the rules and their application from review on

[73] Field v. Clark, 143 U.S. 649, 675 (1892) [quoting Sherman v. Story, 30 Cal. 253, 275 (1866)].

[74] *See* OneSimpleLoan v. U.S. Secretary of Education, 496 F. 3d 197, 202–3 (2nd Cir. 2007); *cert. denied* OneSimpleLoan v. Spellings, 128 S. Ct. 1220 (2008). There, the Second Circuit held that a statute was valid and did not look beyond the version of the bill authenticated by the presiding officers of the House and Senate. The court refused to reassess the rule in spite of "technological and political developments since Marshall Field was decided" (at 198). *See also* Baker v. Carr, 369 U.S. at 214–15; Public Citizen v. United States District Court for the District of Columbia, 486 F. 3d 1342 (D.C. Cir. 2007). The act in question was the massive Deficit Reduction Act of 2005, and all agreed that, through a clerical error in a time limit in one clause of the law, the versions passed were not identical. The error was corrected before the bill was enrolled, but the corrected version was not repassed by both houses.

[75] *See* Robert F. Williams, *State Constitutional Limits on Legislative Procedure: Legislative Compliance and Judicial Enforcement*, **48** University. of Pittsburgh Law Rev. 797, 822–3 (1987) (citing a state case refusing to apply the rule where the court inquired if a statute passed by majority vote).

[76] Michael E. Libonati, *Congress in Comparative Perspective: State Constitutions and Legislative Process; The Road Not Taken*, **89** Boston University Law Rev. 863, 867–8 (2009) claims that state courts often refuse to enforce constitutional constraints on the legislative process under this rule, arguing that the rule prevents them from considering any evidence outside the text of the statute. *See also* Williams, *supra* note 75, at 816–18. Nineteenth-century courts in some states refused to consider cases claiming that legislators had been bribed. *See* Caleb Nelson, *Judicial Review of Legislative Purpose*, **83** New York University Law Rev. 1784, 1792, note 42 (2008).

constitutional or other grounds. However, the Supreme Court has left itself some space to inquire into the legislative process in exceptional cases. Thus in *Baker v. Carr*, after quoting *Field v. Clark*, Justice William Brennan goes on to add that: "it is not true that courts will never delve into a legislature's records … The political question doctrine, a tool of government order, will not be applied as to promote only disorder."[77] This is dicta, but it states a limiting principle, not only for the enrolled bill rule but also for the role of the Court generally in its dealings with the other branches.

Steven Raher argues that, at the state level, the rule is often applied too strictly to exclude relevant evidence.[78] Raher favors limited judicial review of the legislative process and argues for such review in cases brought by citizens to defend democratic values. He cites New Jersey as a model of how courts might judge procedural violations while avoiding separation of powers concerns and discouraging a flood of frivolous lawsuits.[79] The New Jersey statute, passed in 1873, allows the governor or any two New Jersey citizens to challenge a bill or joint resolution based on procedural violations.[80] The New Jersey law has not led to a flood of lawsuits, both because the legislature seems to have been diligent in complying with the required procedures and because the courts impose a strong burden of proof on petitioners and a *de minimus* exception.[81] The law permits abstract review, not anchored in adversary litigation. The New Jersey Supreme Court upheld the statutory provision as a permissible exercise of legislative power and stated that:

> we see no reason for concluding that it is beyond the power of the Legislature to create a method of judicial procedure in which the sole and only question … is whether or not a given statute was enacted in conformity to constitutional requirements … In no other way can the people of the state be informed whether a given law which appears upon the statute book is one which they are obliged to obey.[82]

77 Baker v. Carr, at 214–15.

78 Raher, *supra* note 40, at 61–81.

79 *Id.* at 77–82.

80 N.J. Rev. Stat. §§1:7–1, 1:7–4. The passage of this legislation is in tension with our claim that legislatures will seldom act to give outsiders the ability to police their actions. However, the date of passage, 1873, was in the midst of a period of heightened public concern for legislative corruption and a lack of representation in state legislatures. *See* Williams, *supra* note 75, at 798.

81 In re Application of Reilly, 364 N.J. Super. 519 (App. Div. 2003), *cert. denied*, 179 N.J. 369 (2003). The court upheld the legality of a statute passed and signed by the governor that was almost identical to one that had been provisionally vetoed by the former governor.

82 In re An Act to Amend an Act Entitled "An Act Concerning Public Utilities," 84 A. 706 (N.J. 1912), quoted in Raher, *supra* note 40, at 78.

This kind of abstract review is common in countries, such as Germany, with specialized constitutional tribunals. Presidents and certain other state organs can refer statutes for constitutional review before they have been applied to concrete cases. In the United States the federal courts would likely refuse such a referral.[83]

Timely review of the legislative process seems a particularly appropriate arena for abstract review because the challenge is to the legislative process, not the application of the law in practice. It permits a rapid resolution of procedural or constitutional challenges when information on legislative behavior is easy to find, and it can resolve any doubts about legality. However, the U.S. federal courts do not provide abstract review of statutes, and, of course, there is no federal law comparable to the New Jersey statute. Something like the German concept of "abstract review" does, however, occur in administrative law where pre-enforcement review of rules is common, and enforcement of rules may be stayed until judicial review is completed.[84]

Because the constitution gives Congress the power to make its own rules, review of legislative processes would raise separation of powers issues in a particularly stark and paradoxical form. If a statute gives jurisdiction to the courts to evaluate legislative procedures, can the courts refuse jurisdiction on constitutional grounds? Separation of powers cuts both ways and creates a dilemma. On the one hand, the courts should defer to the choices of the legislature and accept their new role. On the other hand, they should avoid interfering in the legislative process and reject their new role.

At the federal level the enrolled bill rule is usually accepted by commentators, but one scholar, Ittai Bar-Siman-Tov, has been on something of a campaign to limit its use.[85] He locates recent cases where the enrolled bill

[83] See, for example, the original line-item veto case denying standing to congressional plaintiffs, Raines v. Byrd, 521 U.S. 811. In addition, a federal court dropped the Government Accountability Office (GAO) from a case seeking documents from the Executive Office of the President, Walker v. Cheney, 230 F. Supp. 51 (D.D. C. 2002). The GAO decided not to appeal the ruling. *See* Bruce Montgomery, *Congressional Oversight: Vice President Richard B. Cheney's Executive Branch Triumph*, **120** POLITICAL SCIENCE Q. 581 (2005–6). The Supreme Court opinion did not address this issue because the GAO was no longer a plaintiff; *see* Cheney v. U.S. District Court, 124 S. Ct. 2576 (2004).

[84] Compare Abbott Laboratories v. Gardner, 387 U.S. 136 (1967) (allowing pre-enforcement review) with Toilet Goods Assn. v. Gardner, 387 U.S. 158 (1967) (finding dispute not ripe for review).

[85] Ittai Bar-Siman-Tov, *Legislative Supremacy in the United States: Rethinking the "Enrolled Bill" Doctrine*, **97** GEORGETOWN LAW J. 323 (2009) [hereinafter, *Legislative Supremacy*]. *See also* Ittai Bar-Siman-Tov, *Lawmakers as Lawbreakers*, **52** WILLIAM & MARY LAW REV. 805 (2010) [hereinafter, *Lawmakers as Lawbreakers*]; Ittai Bar-Siman-Tov, *The Puzzling*

was clearly defective.[86] The version of the Deficit Reduction Act of 2005 passed by the House omitted a section included in the Senate's version. A clerk in the Senate "corrected" the discrepancy before the bill was sent to the president for signature. The 2008 Farm Bill submitted to President Bush lacked a section passed by both houses of Congress. The omission was discovered only after the president vetoed the bill and Congress passed it over his veto. These two cases look like pure carelessness that resulted from the size and complexity of the legislation. In a third case the chair refused to promptly close the time for voting on the 2003 Medicare Bill; this was a strategic effort to assure passage. Bar-Siman-Tov also cites cases from state courts that were not simply careless errors, and he points out that improved record keeping today compared with the 1890s makes the worry about "loose papers" less salient.[87]

D. Conclusions

The federal judiciary's reluctance to examine the legislative process was on display during oral argument in *Nevada Commission on Ethics v. Carrigan*, a 2011 First Amendment challenge to a Nevada law governing conflicts of interest.[88] Justice Scalia, in response to the claim of dire consequences if the constitutional challenge were denied, asks: "If that's what it means, you would think the legislature would change it, wouldn't you?"[89] This confidence in the legislature to police its own processes seems to be the baseline hurdle that any challenge must overcome. It downplays collective action problems and time constraints, and reflects a general concern

Resistance to Judicial Review, **91** Boston Univ. Law Rev. 1915 (2011) [hereinafter, *Puzzling Resistance*]. Similar arguments are made by Victor Goldfeld, *Legislative Due Process and Simple Interest Group Politics: Ensuring Minimal Deliberation Through Judicial Review of Congressional Processes*, **79** N. Y. U. Law Rev. 367 (2004). But Bar-Siman-Tov, *supra* note 14, documents and advocates limiting procedural review to cases where constitutional courts review statutes for substantive constitutional violations.

86 These cases are outlined in Bar-Siman-Tov, *Lawmakers as Lawbreakers*, *supra* note 85, at 820–6.

87 Bar-Siman-Tov, *Legislative Supremacy*, *supra* note 85, at 334–44.

88 The case involved a First Amendment challenge to an application of the Nevada Ethics in Government Law, Nev. Rev. Stat. §281A.160 (2009), that found a local councilman in violation of the law for not recusing himself from a vote on conflict of interest grounds. The statute applies to state executive branch officials and to elected local governments, but not to the state legislators, who are covered by their own rules of procedure [§281A 420(7)]. The Supreme Court unanimously upheld the statute in Nevada Commission on Ethics v. Carrigan, 131 S. Ct. 2343 (2011).

89 Transcript of Oral Argument at 36, Nevada Comm'n on Ethics v. Carrigan (No. 10–568).

with maintaining the separation of powers between courts and the rest of government.[90]

The federal courts have rejected constitutional challenges to legislative procedures on jurisdictional or standing grounds, and even when they have accepted cases for review, the plaintiffs seldom win. If they do, the complaints are almost always based on violations of individual rights, not defects in the democratic legitimacy of the legislative process. Except for violations of the explicit constitutional text, as in *Chadha*, *Clinton*, and *Powell*, or cases where someone's rights have been violated, the federal courts either will decline jurisdictions or will hold in favor of the legislative practice. The federal courts seldom act as a check on the legislative process in spite of some judges' acceptance of jurisdiction. The one exception, *Powell v. McCormack*, did concern a House procedure, but not a legislative enactment. Once the Supreme Court decided to resolve the dispute, it gave a straightforward reading of the constitutional text to limit congressional power to deny seats to elected representatives.

Several legal scholars build on the positive political economy literature to highlight democratic deficits present in the U.S. legislative process. Bar-Siman-Tov argues that the legislature has insufficient incentives to police itself, and he argues that judicial review is warranted. His critique of the quality of the legislative process leads him to support more aggressive judicial review of that process, and he attempts to show that this would be consistent with U.S. constitutional principles and history.[91] Victor Goldfeld is particularly concerned with riders added to omnibus bills that benefit particular members and their constituents but that would not obtain majority support.[92] Logrolling, in which legislators support each others' proposed

[90] *See* Nixon v. U.S., 506 U.S. 224 (1993), dealing with the Senate trial of a judge who had been impeached by the House. The Supreme Court found the dispute nonjusticiable for many different reasons, but the separation of powers claim seems most persuasive.

[91] *See* especially, Bar-Siman-Tov, *Puzzling Resistance*, *supra* note 85.

[92] Goldfeld, *supra* note 85. *See also* Brannon P. Denning & Brooks R. Smith, *Uneasy Riders: The Case for a Truth-in Legislation Amendment*, **1999** Utah Law Rev. 957 (1999); Brannon P. Denning & Brooks R. Smith, *Proposed Amendment: The Truth-in Legislation Amendment; An Idea Whose Time Has Come*, **78** Tenn. Law Rev. 831, 834–6 (2011) [hereinafter, *Truth-in-Lending*] (proposing a U.S. constitutional amendment enshrining the single-subject rule); and Libonati, *supra* note 76, at 864–6. The state constitutional law provisions grew out of the Jacksonian Democrats' distrust of the legislature and were an effort to limit special interest legislation. *See* G. Alan Tarr, Understanding State Constitutions (1998), chapters 4 and 5. Tarr (at 118–19) mentions other limitations requiring: supra-majorities for some types of laws, drafting in plain English, recorded votes for taxing and spending matters, and that no special law be permitted when a general law is possible.

provisions as part of a compromise, presents special problems for Goldfeld. He recognizes the need for compromise, but he would require legislators to show that they have considered the merits of all bills that they support.[93] As recognized in the political science literature, logrolling is not inherently undesirable. Hence, Michael Gilbert would make a sharp distinction between a logrolled deal that obtains majority support and a rider that is only voted through as part of a larger measure but is not part of a quid pro quo deal. However, asking courts actually to make such a distinction looks extremely difficult.[94]

Richard Lazarus's critique of lawmaking in the environmental area echoes Goldfeld's concern with the democratic deficiencies of the legislative process.[95] As he explains, under the current appropriations process, Congress combines many areas of spending together in large omnibus bills. These are vulnerable to special interest add-ons, and, at least in the environmental area, the appropriations committees have largely taken over from the authorization committees where the real policy expertise lies. These criticisms lead Lazarus to argue for more judicial review of the legislative process to further democratic values, but he also worries about judicial overreaching. Congress is unlikely to impose such restraints on itself. Nevertheless, many U.S. state constitutions include checks on legislative processes and statutory drafting; hence, the idea is not deeply unfamiliar in the American context. There is a tension between narrow interest group influence and legislators' ignorance of statutory details, on the one hand, and critiques of judicial review's efficacy, on the other. We agree with Lazarus but would not limit our recommendations to the environmental area. Limited abstract review of legislative deliberations could enhance democracy without tipping over to the review of substance characteristic of the pre-New Deal era. Review would focus on process, not on the legislative language. However, as we argue later in this chapter, the Court's current opinions voiding statutes on constitutional grounds could have just the opposite effect – undermining Congress's ability to act in a range of important policy areas.

[93] Goldfeld, *supra* note 85, at 385, n. 51.

[94] Michael D. Gilbert, *Single Subject Rules and the Legislative Process*, **67** UNIVERSITY. OF PITTSBURGH LAW REV. 803 (2006). His argument is discussed with some skepticism by Denning & Smith, *Truth-in-Lending*, *supra* note 92, at 834–6 (2011).

[95] Richard J. Lazarus, *Congressional Descent: The Demise of Deliberative Democracy in Environmental Law*, **94** GEORGETOWN LAW REV. 619 (2006).

II. GIVING REASONS: SUBSTANCE AND PROCESS

Review of legislative substance has traditionally been deferential except where constitutional rights are at stake. A very permissive rational basis test is the only generic constraint. However, the Rehnquist and Roberts courts have been signaling a more aggressive attitude, not toward protecting rights, but toward limiting federal power. These developments, although nominally substantive, could have implications for the legislative process. They impose a reason-giving requirement that places a strong burden of proof on Congress if it legislates in certain areas. The expansion of review could end up applying the same standards to the review of legislation as the APA applies to the review of rules. To the extent that the Supreme Court extends its reach to a wider range of statutes, it risks undermining the democratic character of the modern American state. After reviewing these developments, we ask if there is a middle way that could support democratic deliberation without overstepping the Court's role.

A. Means/End Rationality

Since its shift during the New Deal, the Supreme Court has imposed few substantive constraints on state or federal legislatures under the Due Process and Equal Protection Clauses of the Constitution. The iconic case is the 1955 case of *Williamson v. Lee Optical*, which upheld an Oklahoma law against a due process challenge, saying that "[t]he Oklahoma law may exact a needless, wasteful requirement in many cases. But it is for the legislature, not the courts, to balance the advantages and disadvantages of the new requirement."[96] Justice William O. Douglas imagines various legitimate justifications for the law that the legislature "might" have had, without considering whether members did, in fact, invoke those reasons. He concludes that:

> a law need not be in every respect logically consistent with its aims to be constitutional. It is enough that there is an evil at hand for correction and that it might be thought that the particular legislative measure was a rational way to correct it.[97]

[96] Williamson v. Lee Optical, 348 U.S. 483, 487 (1955). During the *Lochner* era through the early New Deal period, the Supreme Court did review substance quite aggressively. Lochner v. New York, 198 U.S. 45 (1905). On the shift in the Court's opinions during the New Deal period *see* Bruce Ackerman, We the People, Vol. II: Transformations (2000).

[97] Williamson v. Lee Optical, 348 U.S. at 487–8.

The indefinite form – "it might be thought" – implies that the justices do not necessarily agree with any of the justifications that they list, only that it is at least possible that someone might find them convincing. Although stated in terms of "process," these cases do not concern legislative procedures, but instead they ask whether the substance of statutes is consistent with constitutional rights.[98] The means are the statutory provisions designed to further the law's ends.[99] As we will see, this judicial stance contrasts with that of the South African Constitutional Court where deference to hypothetical possibilities is uncommon. There, the justices themselves have to be convinced that a valid purpose exists.

If a statutory scheme depends on technical data, the U.S. federal courts have not generally required legislatures to justify their use of scientific information or to judge its reliability.[100] The cases go back at least to the 1905 case of *Jacobson v. Massachusetts*,[101] concerning mandatory smallpox vaccinations. The Supreme Court stated: "We assume that when the statute in question was passed, the legislature of Massachusetts was not unaware of these opposing theories [as to the vaccine's safety], and was compelled, of necessity, to choose between them."[102] However, the Court did double check the evidence, and stated that it was enough that the legislature viewed the law as promoting the general welfare "whether it does in fact or not."[103]

The Court defers because: "The Constitution presumes that, absent some reason to infer antipathy, even improvident decisions will eventually be rectified by the democratic process."[104] Other cases acknowledge the imperfections of the legislative process from the point of view of logic or scientific accuracy, but accept these weaknesses as a response to legislative realities. Even if errors are not "eventually" corrected, courts should defer because it would be too much to expect clarity and precision from the legislature. "The problems of government are practical ones and may justify, if they do not

[98] Hans Linde, *Due Process of Lawmaking*, **55** Nebraska Law Rev. 197, 254 (1975–6) says, "the misdirection of due process to the substance of enactments diverts it from testing the process of enactment itself."

[99] *See e.g.*, Gerald Gunther, *Foreword: In Search of Evolving Doctrines on a Changing Court: A Model for a Newer Equal Protection*, **86** Harvard Law Rev. 1 (1972).

[100] Emily Hammond Meazell, *Scientific Avoidance: Toward a More Principled Judicial Review of Legislative Science*, **84** Indiana Law J. 239, 260 (2009). Her note 107 cites: Gammoh v. City of La Jabra, 395 F. 3d 1114, 1127 (9th Cir. 2005); G. M. Enters., Inc. v. Town of St. Joseph, 350 F. 3d 631, 640 (7th Cir. 2003); UFO Chuting of Haw, Inc. v. Young, 380 F. Supp. 2d 1160, 1163 (D. Haw. 2005).

[101] Jacobson v. Massachusetts, 197 U.S. 11 (1905).

[102] *Id.* at 30.

[103] *Id.* at 35.

[104] Vance v. Bradley, 440 U.S. 93, 97 (1979).

require, rough accommodations – illogical, it may be, and unscientific."[105] In some cases the judges expressly accept the fact that legislation will represent a compromise that cannot always be expressed in consistent terms, and many justices refuse to investigate the internal operation of the legislature.[106] Justice Joseph Story, writing in 1833, recognized that the mindsets of individual legislators might be "opposite to, or wholly independent of each other."[107] In 1960, Chief Justice Earl Warren said much the same thing:

> What motivates one legislator to make a speech about a statute is not necessarily what motivates scores of others to enact it, and the stakes are sufficiently high for us to eschew guesswork.[108]

In a comprehensive review, Emily Meazell lists numerous examples of judicial deference involving fluoridation of drinking water, smoking bans, environmental zoning, and laws designed to protect the public health.[109]

Under this view of the separation of powers, courts refrain from judging the merits of legislative enactments, including the validity of the underlying scientific evidence, unless the plaintiffs claim a violation of their rights. It embodies a realistic view of the procedures that generate laws. American legislative procedures may not produce substantive laws that are logical, internally consistent, and an effective means to an end. Hence, courts should not require laws to conform to these values. Hans Linde says it well:

> [T]he search for a goal beyond the enacted policy itself will be illusory because a policy often results from the accommodation of competing and mutually inconsistent values, or because it simply intends to favor one interest at the expense of another.[110]

[105] Metropolis Theatre C. v. City of Chicago, 228 U.S. 61, 69–70 (1913), cited by Meazell, *supra* note 100, at 265, n. 133.

[106] Nelson, *supra* note 76, at 1836, 1857.

[107] Joseph Story, Commentaries on the Constitution of the United States, vol. 2, 533 (1833); quoted by Nelson *supra* note 76, at 1808.

[108] Flemming v. Nestor, 363 U.S. 603, 617 (1960). Discussed in Nelson, *supra* note 76, at 1841.

[109] Meazell, *supra* note 100, at 265.

[110] Linde, *supra* note 98, at 212. *See also* Richard A. Posner, *The De Funis Case and the Constitutionality of Preferential Treatment of Racial Minorities*, 1974 Supreme Court Rev. 1, at 27–9 (viewing the political process as a power struggle among interest groups so that a rationality requirement does not make sense); Robert W. Bennett, *"Mere" Rationality in Constitutional Law: Judicial Review and Democratic Theory*, **67** California Law Rev. 1049, 1072 (1979) (many purposes may be behind a law when different groups vote for the law for different purposes).

As we will see in discussing recent cases, however, this realistic understanding of the legislative process seems to be breaking down at least for some areas of judicial review.

B. Heightened Scrutiny: Liberal and Conservative Versions

Although the federal courts generally do not probe the logic or the data behind statutes, they do subject some enactments to "heightened scrutiny" because of claims that the statute violates constitutional provisions unrelated to the legislative process per se. They may still defer to technical experts on the facts, but review is otherwise quite stringent. Statutes dealing with race are obvious candidates for heightened scrutiny, but the list has expanded and contracted over time.[111] That scrutiny reflects a special solicitude for the particular right at stake.[112] The Supreme Court essentially imposes a burden of proof on lawmakers when it checks to be sure that the legislature has articulated valid reasons.[113]

Although the leading cases seldom mention democratic legitimacy, one prominent scholar justified heightened scrutiny on that ground. Gerald Gunther, in urging "a greater burden on the state to come forth with explanations about the contributions of its means to its ends," writes:

> It does indeed follow from the political process theme that legislative value choices warrant judicial deference so long as the people can have their say in the public forum and at the ballot box.... [But means scrutiny by the courts] can improve the quality of the political process – without second guessing the substantive validity of its results – by encouraging a fuller airing in the political arena of the grounds for legislative action. Examination of means in light of asserted state purposes would directly promote public considerations of the benefits assertedly sought by the proposed legislation; indirectly, it would stimulate fuller political examination, in relation to those benefits, of the costs that would be incurred if the proposed means were adopted.[114]

Here, Gunther suggests that heightened scrutiny is an aid to the democratic process. Review of substance may improve procedures. His argument, however, would seem to apply to all statutes, not just to those now accorded

[111] *See* Gunther, *supra* note 99; Nelson *supra* note 76, at 1850–9.

[112] Exxon Corporation v. Federal Trade Commission, 589 F. 2d 582, 590 (D.C. Cir. 1978) (holding that "when constitutional rights are not violated, the judiciary ought not to interfere with the internal procedures of Congress"), *cert. denied* 441 U.S. 943 (1979).

[113] *Cf.* Jud Mathews & Alec Stone Sweet, *All Things in Proportion? American Rights Review and the Problem of Balancing*, **60** Emory Law J. 797 (2011).

[114] Gunther, *supra* note 99, at 44.

"heightened scrutiny." There is no logical reason that review of means/end rationality as an aid to democratic legitimacy ought to be limited to situations where rights are at stake.[115] The worry, of course, is that broader review would risk judicial overreaching.[116]

To illustrate the Court's approach, we consider cases decided under the Due Process and Equal Protection Clauses and a church/state dispute involving the nature of science. We conclude this section with the Supreme Court's newly aggressive review of cases dealing with federalism. We highlight aspects of these cases that seem troubling in light of U.S. political realities and the separation of powers. It is one thing for judicial review to further democratic values; it is quite another for it to impose stringent burdens on Congress designed to convince the judiciary itself of a law's validity.

1. Due Process

The Due Process Clause of the Constitution does not apply when the government makes general policy. An individual may claim due process to contest a targeted decision within the administration, but broad-based policy choices and targeted statutes do not trigger due process protections.

The famous cases of *Londoner v. Denver* and *Bi-Metallic v. State Board of Equalization* illustrate the limits of procedural protections under the Constitution.[117] *Londoner v. Denver* requires a hearing on constitutional due process grounds when a city levies taxes based on individual property assessments. The hearing need not be "strictly judicial," but "he who is entitled to it shall have the right to support his allegations by argument however brief, and, if need be, by proof however informal."[118]

In contrast, when the Colorado State Board of Equalization and its Tax Commission raised the assessed value of all Denver property by 40 percent, *Bi-Metallic* held that the Constitution does not provide due process protections for property owners who are "all equally concerned." Even though this was not a decision by the legislature, the Court stated that it "must assume that the proper state machinery has been used," and it held that there "must be a limit to individual argument in such matters if government is to go on." It would be "impracticable that everyone should have a direct voice" in the adoption of the taxation formula. The rights of the complainants "are

[115] Linde, *supra* note 98, at 201–6.

[116] For example, reinstating the aggressive review of substance in *Lochner* 198 U.S. 45.

[117] Londoner v. Denver, 210 U.S. 373 (1908); Bi-Metallic Investment Co. v. State Board of Equalization, 239 U.S. 441 (1915).

[118] Londoner v. Denver, 210 U.S. at 386.

protected by the only way that they can be in a complex society, by their power, immediate or remote, over those who make the rule."[119] However, although all property owners were concerned about the tax increases, in fact, they are not all *equally* affected. Since the last assessment, the market values of some properties would have risen, and others would have fallen, even if the average increase was 40 percent. The Court does not consider this variation in the decision's effect. For the Court, the key aspects of the formula are its nominal uniformity and its comprehensive coverage.

In both these cases the plaintiffs invoked their property rights as the reason for demanding process; they did not appeal to democratic values. In *Bi-Metallic* the Court itself argues that the comprehensive nature of the decision *exempts* Colorado from due process obligations.[120] In its opinion the Court makes no distinction between a statute and an executive policy decision. Neither is subject to due process protections, which focus on individual rights – to property, in these cases.

Individuals who claim that a statute deprives them of due process rights are not challenging the democratic legitimacy of the statute, but rather the law's failure to permit them to defend their individual claims. This is essentially Justice Powell's argument in his concurring opinion in *Chadha*.[121] He argued that Congress's use of the veto to deny permanent residency to Chadha was an adjudicatory decision that violated the separation of powers and was a prohibited bill of attainder.[122] Because his fate was decided by Congress, Chadha had no due process protections, and that made the congressional action unconstitutional.

If the Supreme Court holds that a legislative action is a bill of attainder, it simply finds the action unconstitutional. It does not order the legislature itself to provide due process protections to the complainants. Thus, in *U.S. v. Brown* the Supreme Court voided a statute that made it a crime for members of the Communist Party to serve on the executive board of a labor organization.[123] The Court did not suggest that the law would have been

[119] Bi-Metallic v. State Board of Equalization, 239 U.S. at 445.

[120] *See also* Interport Pilots Agency v. Sammis, 14 F. 3d 133 (2d Cir. 1994) (holding that a "policy statement" issued by a state agency is not subject to due process requirements).

[121] *Chadha*, 464 U.S. (Powell, J. concurring) at 959–67.

[122] U.S. Const. art. 1 §9, cl. 3.

[123] U.S. v. Brown, 391 U.S. 437, 442 (1965): "The Bill of Attainder Clause was intended not as a narrow technical … prohibition, but rather as an implementation of the separation of powers, a general safeguard against legislative exercise of the judicial function, or more simply – trial by legislature." The same clause also outlaws ex post facto laws that would apply retroactively. Of course, that condition limits the substantive choices of the legislature, but it does not affect procedures except to the extent that Congress organizes its drafting procedures to avoid this result.

constitutional if only Congress itself had given due process protections to its potential addressees. In other words, certain kinds of legislative actions are simply forbidden. A more accountable legislative process would not fix the problem. Rather, providing due process to individuals is the responsibility of courts and executive branch adjudicators.

If the federal courts uphold a statute in spite of due process claims from individuals, they do not condition their holdings on legislative procedures. For example, in *McMurtray v. Holladay* state employees in Mississippi challenged a statute that suspended their job protections for one year and led them to lose their jobs.[124] The Fifth Circuit dismissed their claim that they had been deprived of property without due process of law. Because the statute affects a general class of people, the legislative process is all the process that is due. Similarly, Judge Richard Posner in *Coniston Corp. v. Village of Hoffman Estates* found that a village governing body did not violate due process when it acted in executive session and gave no reasons in denying a land development permit.[125] He held that the decision was not adjudicative in nature, so due process was not required. In a village with little separation of powers between the legislature and the executive, denial of a permit was not adjudicative because it depended on "potential criteria and considerations [that] are too open-ended and ill-defined." In a subsequent case, decided under the Administrative Procedure Act, which we discuss later in this chapter, he relied on a similar characterization of a decision by a federal department to insist on notice and comment rulemaking – more process, not less.[126]

Hence, shortcomings in the due process accorded to individuals sometimes remove actions entirely from the legislative arena, but if the courts accept them as valid legislative actions, the judges will not demand individualized due process protections inside the legislature. Contrary to cases dealing with the administrative process, the courts will not void a law and remand it to a legislature to carry out procedures that provide individual addressees with due process. In contrast, as we discuss later in this chapter, they do sometimes demand better justified "findings" from Congress in particularly contested legislative areas.

To summarize this difference, under U.S. law, due process requirements only apply to administrative adjudications affecting an individual (and, of course, to the courts themselves). Congress can pass legislation governing

[124] McMurtray v. Holladay, 11 F. 3d 499 (5th Cir. 1993).

[125] Coniston Corp. v. Village of Hoffman Estates, 844 F. 2d 461 (7th Cir. 1988).

[126] Hoctor v. U.S. Department of Agriculture, 82 F. 3d 165 (7th Cir. 1996) discussed *infra*.

"a legitimate class of one,"[127] although, as we have seen, some targeted laws are voided as bills of attainder. A statute can be struck down if it does not include due process protections for those individually affected by its administration.[128] However, in voiding the statute, the Court does not critique the legislative process itself, only the result as applied. The famous constitutional cases dealing with due process, *Goldberg v. Kelly* and *Mathew v. Eldridge* and their progeny, are not concerned with the legislative process. Rather they focus on the process due when the government administers existing programs. They concern individual beneficiaries and, in other cases, employees or contractors.[129] These decisions, of course, are likely to have feedback effects on the design of programs, but they do not directly constrain the legislature.

Supreme Court opinions based on the Due Process Clause do not examine the legislative process, as distinct from the substance of the law, even though they sometimes recognize an historical precedent for doing so.[130] Thus, in *Planned Parenthood v. Casey* the Court examines the legislative history but only to determine what the legislators wanted to accomplish.[131] The Court may order a remand to the legislature to come up with alternative justifications or to rewrite the law to avoid the offending provisions. However, just as in the rational basis cases, heightened scrutiny does not lead the Court to condemn statutes because congressional hearings were inadequate or committee reports too short. Critics of this approach concentrate on the difficulty of figuring out legislative purpose, not on the lack of procedural review.[132] The legislative process is only indirectly at issue.[133]

In providing heightened review, the Supreme Court sometimes evaluates how the legislature used science to justify restrictions on individual rights. To illustrate the justices' differing approaches, consider two due process cases challenging statutes banning "partial birth abortion." The first, *Stenberg v. Carhart (Carhart I)*, struck down a Nebraska law banning the

[127] Nixon v. Administrator of General Services, 433 U.S. 425, 472 (1977). See also Biodiversity Associates v. Cables, 357 F. 3d 1152, 1162 (10th Cir. 2004).

[128] *See* Southern Railway v. Virginia, 290 U.S. 190 (1933) discussed *infra*.

[129] Goldberg v. Kelly, 397 U.S. 254 (1970); Mathews v. Eldridge, 424 U.S. 319 (1976).

[130] Dan T. Coenen, *A Constitution of Collaboration: Protecting Fundamental Values with Second-Look Rules of Interbranch Dialogue*, **42** William & Mary Law Rev. 1575, 1755–72 (2001).

[131] Planned Parenthood of Southeastern Pennsylvania v. Casey, 505 U.S. 833 (1992).

[132] Coenen, *supra* note 130, at 1756–8.

[133] See the discussion of *Shelby County infra* where the dissent does mention the number of hearings and the volume of supporting material, but only to rebut the majority claim that as a matter of fact the contested provision of the Voting Rights Act is no longer needed.

practice.[134] Seven years later, it upheld a similar federal statute in *Gonzales v. Carhart (Carhart II)*.[135] The Nebraska law had no exception for preserving the health of the mother. Given debate in the medical profession over whether the procedure would ever be necessary to preserve a woman's health, the majority held that an exception was required.[136] Thus, the Court looked at the conflicting medical evidence and concluded that the Nebraska legislature was not constitutionally permitted to ignore that evidence, even if it was not absolutely conclusive. Conversely, the dissent by Justice Anthony Kennedy used the medical debate as a *reason* to defer, arguing that, even if fundamental rights are at stake, legislatures are better fact finders than courts.[137]

The United States passed a statute, the U.S. Partial-Birth Abortion Ban Act of 2003, in light of *Carhart I*. The statute contained unusually detailed findings that claimed "a moral, medical and ethical consensus."[138] Justice Kennedy, in the majority in *Carhart II*, continued to cite medical disagreements, and he deferred to Congress in the face of "medical and scientific uncertainty."[139] The justices all acknowledged that Congress had gotten the science wrong; they just differed on whether that should matter to their own review.[140]

Justice Ruth Bader Ginsburg, in dissent, argued that the courts should rule on whether the procedure would ever be medically necessary; she argued that such a ruling was appropriate because the courts are neutral fora, and the adversary process gives incentives to the parties to present their best evidence.[141] The problem with Ginsburg's view is that it does not always hold. Meazell recommends, instead, that the courts ask if the legislature actually considered the scientific issue. If not, they should stay enforcement of the law and remand to the legislature for more fact-finding.[142] This is a procedural response to a substantive concern. By requiring the legislature to engage in more thorough deliberation ex post, the courts would give the legislature an incentive to do so ex ante.

[134] Stenberg v. Carhart, 530 U.S. 914 (2000) (Carhart I).
[135] Gonzales v. Carhart, 127 S. Ct. 1610 (2007) (Carhart II).
[136] *Carhart I*, 530 U.S., at 938.
[137] *Id.*, Kennedy, J., dissenting, at 968.
[138] Meazell, *supra* note 100, at 277–8.
[139] *Carhart II*, 127 S. Ct., at 1636.
[140] *Id.* at 1637–8, 1643; Meazell *supra* note 100, at 279.
[141] *Carhart II*, 127 S. Ct. at 1644–6.
[142] Meazell, *supra* note 100, at 282–3. Note the similarity to hard look review in administrative law discussed *infra*.

2. Equal Protection

Turning to equal protection, the Court's decisions often hinge on the political powerlessness of the affected groups. The Court sometimes articulates substantive concerns by pointing to unrepresentative legislative processes. The famous *Carolene Products* footnote expresses a special solicitude for "discrete and insular" minorities.[143] However, even when the Court seems to favor the powerless, it does not evince a sophisticated or realistic understanding of the legislative process or consider how procedural changes might remedy the situation. The opinions are mostly exhortations to politicians to consider interests beyond the most politically salient. Bruce Ackerman argues that if the Court really had been concerned with politically ineffective citizens in *Carolene Products*, it would have focused on diffuse minorities that face particularly troublesome problems of political organization.[144]

Perhaps because of an unwillingness to intrude further into the legislative process, the federal courts are cautious in accepting equal protection challenges. To illustrate, consider *FCC v. Beach Communications, Inc.*[145] The law distinguished between cable television suppliers that serve separately owned and managed facilities and those that serve buildings under common ownership or management. The statute exempted the latter from regulation so long as they did not use public rights of way.[146] The Court of Appeals found that the distinction violated equal protection because "the court saw no rational basis 'on the record,' and was 'unable to imagine' any conceivable basis" for the distinction.[147] When the case reached the Supreme Court, it asserted a strong presumption of legislative validity and reiterated its limited willingness to review the rational basis of legislation, whether or not rights are at stake. The opinion states that "equal protection is not a license for courts to judge the wisdom, fairness, or logic of legislative choices.... [T]he absence of 'legislative facts' explaining the distinction 'on the record'... has no significance in rational-basis analysis"; hence, the legislature need not articulate a purpose or rationale.[148] This hands-off attitude is justified "to preserve to the legislative branch its rightful independence and its ability to function."[149] "The Constitution presumes that, absent some

[143] U.S. v. Carolene Products, 304 U.S. 144 (1938).

[144] Bruce Ackerman, *Beyond Carolene Products*, **98** HARVARD LAW REV. 713 (1985).

[145] FCC v. Beach Communications, Inc., 508 U.S. 307 (1993).

[146] *Id.* at 309–10.

[147] *Id.* at 312.

[148] *Id.* at 315.

[149] The last quote is from Carmichael v. Southern Coal & Coke Co., 301 U.S. 495, 510 (1937).

reasons to infer antipathy, even improvident decisions will eventually be rectified by the democratic process and that judicial intervention is generally unwarranted no matter how unwisely one may think a political branch has acted."[150]

3. Separation of Church and State: What Is Science?

In spite of the courts' generally deferential approach, extreme cases can trigger a response. A recent example involved a local school board's interpretation of the nature of scientific truth. The U.S. District Court scrutinized the board's actions under the Establishment Clause of the First Amendment. Creationists proposed "intelligent design" as a supposed scientific alternative to evolution. In doing so, they hoped to avoid running afoul of the Establishment Clause.

The case arose when a school district in Pennsylvania required teachers to read a statement to ninth grade biology students that referenced Intelligent Design (ID) as if it were an alternative scientific theory. Judge John E. Jones II in *Kitzmiller v. Dover Area School District*[151] went to great pains to hold that the policy violated the Establishment Clause and to enjoin the school board from carrying it out. In a comprehensive and wide-ranging decision, Judge Jones dealt with the question of whether ID is a science and concluded that it fails on three levels.

> (1) ID violates the centuries-old ground rules of science by invoking and permitting supernatural causation; (2) the argument of irreducible complexity, central to ID, employs the same flawed and illogical contrived dualism that doomed creation science in the 1980's; and (3) ID's negative attacks on evolution have been refuted by the scientific community.... [In addition,] ID has failed to gain acceptance in the scientific community, it has not generated peer-reviewed publications, nor has it been the subject of testing and research.[152]

The decision is unusually comprehensive, but it is based on the simple premise that political decision makers cannot claim the mantle of science as a way to shield policies that have a religious purpose. The judge concludes:

> [T]his case came to us as the result of the activism of an ill-informed faction on the school board, aided by a national public interest law firm eager to

[150] Vance v. Bradley, 440 U.S. at 97, quoted in FCC v. Beach Comm., 508 U.S. at 314. However, that opinion then goes on to undercut itself. It suggests "at least two possible bases for the distinction" in the law that are "arguably" plausible (*id.* at 317).

[151] Kitzmiller v. Dover Area School District, 400 F. Supp. 2d 707 (M.D. Pa. 2005).

[152] *Id.* at 735–46.

> find a constitutional test case on ID, who in combination drove the Board to adopt an imprudent and ultimately unconstitutional policy. The breathtaking inanity of the Board's decision is evident when considered against the factual backdrop which has now been fully revealed through this trial. The students, parents, and teachers of the Dover Area School District deserved better than to be dragged into this legal maelstrom, with its resulting utter waste of monetary and personal resources.[153]

The case involved the Establishment Clause as applied to the public schools, not the general uses and abuses of scientific arguments in lawmaking. Other equally suspect "science" avoids judicial scrutiny, as we have seen in the *Carhart II* case. Few cases are likely to raise the issue of the very nature of science in quite as stark a form as *Kitzmiller*. Generally, the nature of science is not in doubt, but rather the plaintiff questions the probity of the evidence in a particular case.

4. Limits on Federal Power

In spite of the courts' reluctance to examine means/end rationality except in extreme cases, such judicial scrutiny has taken on new meaning in the Rehnquist and Roberts Courts. Majorities have examined the evidentiary basis of legislation and struck down statutes that would extend federal power.[154] Some commentators argue that these decisions show that the Court has a very poor understanding of the nature of the legislative process compared with administrative and judicial processes.[155] We agree that this line of cases demonstrates that "the intrusion into congressional processes is not simply too rigorous, but institutionally wrongheaded … [It is] contrary to any plausible scholarly understanding of Congress as an institution."[156] One aim of our comparative exercise is to emphasize the way legislative/judicial interactions ought to vary with constitutional structures. Philip Frickey and Steven Smith conclude that "Congress is capable of meeting the Court's fact-finding requirements, but cannot satisfy the Court's requirement of due deliberation and rational, articulated

[153] *Id.* at 765.

[154] A. Christopher Bryant & Timothy J. Simeone, *Remanding to Congress: The Supreme Court's New "On the Record" Constitutional Review of Federal Statutes*, **86** Cornell Law Rev. 328 (2001). *See also* Ruth Colker & James J. Brudney, *Dissing Congress*, **100** Michigan Law Rev. 80 (2001) (arguing that the Court is diminishing the proper role of Congress and treating it like an administrative agency or a lower court).

[155] Bryant & Simeone, *supra* note 154; Frickey & Smith, *supra* note 13, at 1708, William W. Buzbee & Robert A. Schapiro, *Legislative Record Review*, **54** Stanford Law Rev. 87 (2001).

[156] Frickey & Smith, *supra* note 13, at 1708.

decision."[157] Christopher Bryant and Timothy Simeone go somewhat farther, critiquing the Court's approach because:

> First, Congress is simply not an administrative agency, and the reasons that justify "on-the-record" review in the administrative context, where it arose, do not apply to the legislative branch. Second, the Court's imposition of new procedural conditions on Congress's exercise of its legislative authority raises substantial separation-of-powers questions. Third, the Court's new approach is inconsistent with the realities of congressional fact-finding. Consequently, the Court's recent rulings threaten to divert scarce congressional time and resources to creating a legislative record that satisfies judicial needs at the expense of legitimate legislative ones.[158]

Most of the recent cases striking down statutory provisions were decided by narrow majorities. Nevertheless, they have important implications for congressional operations.[159] We focus on several key cases that involve federalism challenges under the Commerce Clause. Begin with *United States v. Lopez* striking down the Gun Free School Zone Act of 1990.[160] The five-judge majority found the Act's link to interstate commerce to be too weak. The opinion, however, seemed to leave it open to Congress to buttress future laws with careful drafting and formal or informal findings. It left unclear exactly how much evidence would be enough, but a subsequent case cited the Voting Rights Act (VRA) of 1965 as a model for future drafters of acts that might otherwise violate the Constitution.[161] The issue for the majority

[157] *Id.* at 1709.

[158] Bryant & Simone, *supra* note 154, at 331.

[159] The Court's shift toward more intrusive review of the congressional record as part of a review for constitutionality began with Turner Broad. Sys., Inc. v. FCC, 512 U.S. 622 (1994) (Turner I), and Turner Broad. Sys., Inc. v. FCC, 520 U.S. 180 (1997). The 1994 decision remanded to the district court a dispute over the constitutionality of a statute regulating cable television. The 1997 decision upheld the law in a 5 to 4 decision. The majority found that there was sufficient evidence to support the statute against a First Amendment challenge. The minority disagreed, and it was their more rigorous standard that has narrowly prevailed in the cases discussed in the text. For an overview of the Turner cases *see* Bryant & Simeone, *supra* note 154, at 323–39.

[160] United States v. Lopez, 514 U.S. 549 (1995). Lopez was superseded by statute. See United States v. Danks, 221 F. 3d 1037 (8th Cir. 1999). For background and discussion of related cases *see* Frickey & Smith, *supra* note 13, at 1720–3. The cases were mostly decided under section 5 of the Fourteenth Amendment. Eskridge & Ferejohn, *supra* note 18, at 442–3, see *Lopez* "as an example of deliberation-inducing review." They point to *Lopez* 514 U.S. at 562 (finding that neither "the statute nor its legislative history contain[ed] express congressional findings regarding the effects upon interstate commerce of gun possession in a school zone"). However, we read the case not as seeking to further broad-based deliberative values, but only as requiring Congress to convince *the Court* that it has fully aired the issue.

[161] City of Boerne v. Flores, 521 U.S. 507, 530–6 (1997). Frickey & Smith, *supra* note 13, at 1721, point out that the VRA sets a high bar with its "thorough and well-documented

in *Lopez* was whether the justices themselves had enough information to judge the Act's constitutionality. The opinion is not concerned with the democratic legitimacy of congressional processes. Justice David Souter's dissent worries about judicial overreaching. To him, judicial "review for deliberateness [in the legislative process] would be as patently unconstitutional as an Act of Congress mandating long opinions from this Court."[162] Review of the legislative process, for him, interferes with the constitutional position of Congress.

Five years later, *United States v. Morrison* struck down the civil remedy portion of the Violence against Women Act as a violation of the Commerce Clause and an unwarranted application of the Equal Protection Clause.[163] The decision was 5 to 4. Both the majority opinion by Chief Justice Rehnquist and Justice Breyer's dissent highlight the information available to Congress at the time of the law's passage, but they disagree sharply on its probity. Neither justice, however, referenced the democratic legitimacy of the process. Rather, each asked whether Congress had accumulated sufficient data to show the Court that the statute was consistent with the Constitution.[164] Heightened scrutiny, used in the past to defend individual rights against legislative overreaching or to defend federal laws against state challenges, now limits congressional power to protect those very rights. Over sharp dissents, the case further shifted the constitutional ground toward skepticism about legislative efforts to extend the regulatory power of the federal government to states and localities. As Frickey and Smith argue, legislation is a messy process, and the courts need to accommodate the reality of American lawmaking processes.[165]

One year later, *University of Alabama v. Garrett* struck down provisions of the Americans with Disabilities Act (ADA) on federalism grounds with five justices again in the majority.[166] The ADA was backed up by an extensive legislative history that the Court undermined with claims that it had

record of a pattern of the denial of constitutional rights." BRUCE ACKERMAN, WE THE PEOPLE VOL. III: THE CIVIL RIGHTS REVOLUTION (2014) documents just how high a bar is set by the VRA, an extremely contested piece of legislation passed in the midst of a national debate over the role of race in politics and society.

162 *Lopez*, 514 U.S. at 613–14.

163 United States v. Morrison, 529 U.S. 598 (2000).

164 Frickey & Smith, *supra* note 13, at 1724–5. ESKRIDGE & FEREJOHN, *supra* note 18, at 43, critique this opinion because the statute was passed after four years of hearings and consultations. The opinion was based on substantive, not procedural grounds.

165 Frickey & Smith, *supra* note 13, at 1744–5.

166 Board of Trustees of the University of Alabama v. Garrett, 531 U.S. 356 (2001). For background *see* Buzbee & Schapiro, *supra* note 155; Frickey & Smith, *supra* note 13, at 1725. *See also* Kimel v. Fla. Bd. of Regents, 120 S. Ct. 631 (2000) and Florida Prepaid Postsecondary

not actually affected the drafters or that it was irrelevant to the ADA's passage. Justice Breyer in dissent criticized the majority both for "reviewing the congressional record as if it were an administrative agency record" and for applying standards appropriate for a court of law, not a legislature.[167] To him, the Court violated the separation of powers. It ought to have understood and accepted the way Congress evaluates policy issues:

> Unlike courts, Congress can readily gather facts from across the Nation, assess the magnitude of a problem, and more easily find an appropriate remedy. Unlike courts, Congress directly reflects public attitudes and beliefs, enabling Congress better to understand where, and to what extent, refusals to accommodate a disability amount to behavior that is callous or unreasonable to the point of lacking constitutional justification. Unlike judges, members of Congress can directly obtain information from constituents who have first-hand experience with discrimination and related issues.[168]

Against this background, the role of legislative "findings" was recently on view in *Shelby County v. Holder* that struck down a key provision of the Voting Rights Act as unconstitutional.[169] The Act was designed to enforce the Fifteenth Amendment to the Constitution giving African Americans the right to vote; subsequent amendments extended the Act to cover non-English speakers. The majority found unconstitutional the provisions that required the Department of Justice to pre-clear voting law and policy changes in a selected group of jurisdictions. Both the five-member majority and the four justices in dissent considered the nature of the evidence before Congress in 2006 when it renewed the Act. Both cited other types of evidence, including some from the post-enactment period, but for us, the key issue is how the justices viewed the legislative process. The majority opinion by Chief Justice John Roberts emphasized that the law treats different states differently. He asserted that any statute that has unequal impacts on the states must carry a high burden of proof.[170] As a result, he criticized Congress for mechanically extending the law based on historical data. Thus, the opinion is strongly interventionist; it required Congress to demonstrate to the Court that it had good current data to support unequal treatment of the states, but it does not evaluate the material before

Education Expense Board v. College Savings Bank, 527 U.S. 627 (1999). Bryant & Simeone, *supra* note 154, at 329–54, discuss these and other relevant cases.

[167] *Garrett*, 531 U.S. at 376–7, 379–80 (Breyer dissenting).

[168] *Id.* at 384 (citations omitted).

[169] Shelby County, Ala. v. Holder, 133 S. Ct. 2612 (2013).

[170] *Id.* for a critique of Roberts's position as a matter of constitutional law *see* Bruce Ackerman, *supra* note 161.

Congress in 2006 that was designed to show the continued need for federal pre-clearance.

The dissent by Justice Ginsburg notes that the Constitution explicitly empowers Congress to implement the Fifteenth Amendment, and hence she would defer to Congress. To counter the opinion's dismissive characterization of the legislative process, she cites the number of hearings and the presence of supportive background papers:

> In the long course of the legislative process, Congress "amassed a sizable record." ... The House and Senate Judiciary Committees held 21 hearings, heard from scores of witnesses, received a number of investigative reports and other written documentation of continuing discrimination in covered jurisdictions. In all, the legislative record Congress compiled filled more than 15,000 pages.
>
> The compilation presents countless "examples of flagrant racial discrimination" since the last reauthorization; Congress also brought to light systematic evidence that "intentional racial discrimination in voting remains so serious and widespread in covered jurisdictions that section 5 preclearance is still needed."
>
> ... The overall record demonstrated to the federal lawmakers that, "without the continuation of the Voting Rights Act of 1965 protections, racial and language minority citizens will be deprived of the opportunity to exercise their right to vote, or will have their votes diluted, undermining the significant gains made by minorities in the last 40 years." Based on these findings, Congress reauthorized preclearance for another 25 years [citations omitted].[171]

The majority accorded little deference to Congress and went out of its way to stress the aspects of the VRA that it found problematic. Chief Justice Roberts reanalyzed the issue on his own terms without taking account of the congressional record except to claim that the drafters relied on outdated historical evidence.[172] To the dissenters, the main justifications were not historical, and the Act easily satisfied the rational basis test.[173]

In the future, if the constitutionality of other statutes is brought into question, the justices, whether in the majority or in dissent, may look closely at the legislative process and at the nature of the evidence before Congress. However, if they follow the reasoning in *Shelby County*, this will not be done to uphold democratic values internal to the legislative process, but rather to judge the constitutionality of statutes on other grounds. Democracy enters here only as part of a separation of powers inquiry. Should the courts defer

[171] *Shelby County*, 133 S. Ct., Ginsberg dissent at 2635–6.

[172] *Id.* at 2628–9.

[173] *Id.* at 2638.

to Congress when the case deals with constitutional principles or rights? How much will its degree of deference depend on the thoroughness with which Congress considered the matter? Alternatively, will the Court decide the issue de novo using the data supplied by the legislative process and other sources?

C. Conclusions

In general, the Supreme Court does not ask if Congress went to the trouble to gather state-of-the-art information or if committees held hearings that fairly reflected the interests at stake. It does not ask if one or another interest group had too large a role in the enactment of a statute or if the majority permitted the minority party to have its say. It examines legislative history to find out what Congress intended, not to judge the quality of deliberations.[174] If individuals claim due process violations, the Court's response is either to reject the claim or, in extreme cases, to hold that the statute is an unconstitutional bill of attainder.

Recently, the Supreme Court has begun to examine the evidentiary base of statutes that extend rights protections, especially if they preempt state and local law. This revived interest in the limits of the Bill of Rights, the Commerce Clause, and the Equal Protection Clause may signal a shift in emphasis that could indirectly affect the legislative process. Recent Court rulings have depended on the factual justifications provided in congressional testimony and committee reports. There is no general requirement for the legislature to give reasons when it votes on bills, but if legislators seek to justify their actions in constitutional terms, the Court sometimes requires them to amass justificatory information. Failure to do so can be a sufficient condition to strike down a law as a violation of the Constitution. This heightened review in particular areas may affect the legislative process writ large; in particular, it may affect the legislative agenda. As Matthew Stephenson argues, the Court's enhanced scrutiny of the evidence in some areas may deter Congress from legislating in fields that require more time and trouble at the drafting stage.[175] To Stephenson, heightened scrutiny

[174] On the general issue of the relationship between the courts' evaluation of statutory language using the "canons" of interpretation and the congressional response *see* Abbe Gluck & Lisa Bressman, *Statutory Interpretation from the Inside – An Empirical Study of Congressional Drafting, Delegation, and the Canons*, Part I, **65** Stanford Law Rev. 901 (2013); Part II, 66 Stanford Law Rev. 725(2014).

[175] Matthew C. Stephenson, *The Price of Public Action: Constitutional Doctrine and the Judicial Manipulation of Legislative Enactment Costs*, **118** Yale Law J. 2, 42–55 (2008). Conversely,

filters out "decisions that have low benefits relative to their constitutional costs."[176] That is, of course, only a benefit if one agrees with the Court majority's interpretations. Raising costs on the margin should be distinguished from decisions that deeply misunderstand or seek to undermine established legislative practices and institutions. Stephenson's sanguine view of the Court's selective imposition of burdens also neglects the fact that the Court can only review statutes that have been passed and that provoke a court challenge. It cannot order Congress to pass a law that could enhance the protection of a right or further other values. It has sticks but no carrots; it cannot push Congress to pass constitutionally beneficial laws.

Shelby County illustrates the limits of process as a defense. The majority gave little consideration to the evidence available to Congress and to the Court itself on the continuing need for the challenged provisions of the Voting Rights Act. It did not mention the legislative process except to critique the failure to update the formula that determined which jurisdictions are subject to pre-clearance. Justice Ginsburg, in dissent, demonstrated the care that Congress took to hold hearings and consider evidence when it extended the law. She was doing this essentially to counter the arguments of the majority, not to introduce a direct concern for process detached from the substance of the act. Recall her dissent in *Carhart II* where she extolls the comparative advantage of the courts as factfinders insulated from the political pressures of the legislature.

The Supreme Court is unlikely to extend its scrutiny of the evidentiary basis of statutes beyond those that may run afoul of constitutional rights or the federal structure of government. The Court does not evaluate the whole range of legislative enactments. As in the case of Germany,[177] the Court asks for evidence to aid its own decision making, not to enhance democratic accountability. In contrast, South African constitutional law, which we examine in the next chapter, emphasizes the democratic legitimacy of open procedures and reason-giving. Some U.S. judges and legal scholars

if Congress, nevertheless, does seek to legislate in one of the areas of heightened review of the record, other legislative work may be slighted (Colker & Brudney, *supra* note 154, at 120–1). In any case, some legislative business will not get done.

[176] Stephenson, *supra* note 175, at 44.

[177] *See* 125 Bundesverfassungsgericht (BVerfG) 175, 145 (2010) (*Hartz IV* decision); "In order to facilitate this constitutional review, there is an obligation for the legislature to disclose the methods and calculations used to determine the subsistence minimum in the legislative procedure." The decision is available in English at http://www.bverfg.de/entscheidungen/ls20100209_1bvl000109en.html. *See also* Stefanie Egidy, *Casenote – The Fundamental Right to the Guarantee of a Subsistence Minimum in the Hartz IV Decision of the German Federal Constitutional Court*, 12 GERMAN L.J. 1961 (2011).

link substance and legislative procedures, and they argue that scrutiny of substance can be a route to a more robust democratic lawmaking process.[178] However, at present that link only applies if individual rights or constitutional principles are at stake.

The basic problem with the Supreme Court's willingness to examine the factual basis of certain statutes – to require "findings" – concerns the separation of powers. Five-person majorities are asserting constitutional meanings that are at odds with settled precedents and that cannot command broad support even on the Court.[179] Armed with a narrow majority, they may deeply interfere with the lawmaking activities of Congress. This is a problematic assertion of power especially because it ignores the functioning of Congress as a democratic institution. As several critical commentators and justices have pointed out, Congress is neither a lower court nor an administrative agency. It has considerable resources at its disposal both to assess technical material and to determine public sentiment.[180] However, the process by which policy initiatives result in legislative drafts is political and multifaceted. In spite of a multitude of reports and extensive testimony, the end result cannot realistically be held to the standards of a reasoned judicial opinion or a technocratic agency rule.[181] Nevertheless, judicial review could play a limited role if it concentrates on democratic legitimacy and is consistent with political science research documenting the bargaining and compromise behind most legislation.

III. JUDICIAL REVIEW OF THE ADMINISTRATIVE PROCESS

The U.S. courts' selective review of the legislative process and the burden of proof they place on Congress for some statutes contrasts sharply with the role of the judiciary in administrative law.[182] Review of the administration is mostly derived from statutes, notably the Administrative Procedure Act. Constitutional law plays a limited role in the review of executive

[178] Gunther, *supra* note 99; ESKRIDGE & FEREJOHN, *supra* note 18.

[179] In overruling its own precedents, a Supreme Court majority has stated that a precedent is more vulnerable to an override if it was decided by "the narrowest of margins" [Payne v. Tennessee, 501 U.S. 808, 828–9 (1991)]. A strong dissent by Justice Marshall challenges that view (*id.* at 850–1). That case, however, dealt only with the Court's fidelity to its own precedents, not with the external impact of its decisions on another branch of government. We are grateful to Adrian Vermeule for pointing us to this case.

[180] Colker & Brudney, *supra* note 154, at 117–20.

[181] Frickey & Smith, *supra* note 13; Bryant & Simeone, *supra* note 154.

[182] *See* Linde *supra* note 98, at 225.

policymaking. The Supreme Court invokes the Constitution's Due Process and Equal Protection Clauses to review executive branch and agency actions, but the courts do not interpret them to require broad public input into executive branch or independent agency rulemaking. The constitutional provisions apply to individualized adjudications, not delegated policymaking. We begin by providing the constitutional law background and then discuss the role of the judiciary under the APA.

A. The Constitution and the Administrative Process

In the early cases of *Londoner* and *Bi-Metallic*, the Court distinguished between administrative adjudications and general policy. It did not distinguish between policy made in a representative legislature and that made in an executive department. In 1933, with the further development of the modern administrative state, the Court recognized that administrative and legislative procedures might require different levels of scrutiny, but only with respect to individual violations of rights. The context was property rights, not democratic deficits. In *Southern Railway v. Virginia*, the Court held that a Virginia statute violated the Due Process Clause.[183] The act permitted an administrator to require railroad companies to pay for the elimination of particular grade crossings that he determined to be unsafe; he did not provide any due process to the railroads. The possibility of going to court to challenge an order was not a sufficient protection for the railroad companies' property interests because the courts could not make a sensible judgment without information. The opinion distinguishes between a (permissible) direct act of the legislature that orders the railroads to bear the costs of eliminating a crossing, on the one hand, and delegation of such decisions to an administrator, on the other. In both cases there has been a taking of private property.

> But, if we assume that a state legislature may determine what public welfare demands and by direct command require a railway to act accordingly, it by no means follows that an administrative officer may be empowered, without notice and a hearing, to act with finality upon his own opinion and ordain the taking of private property. There is an obvious difference between legislative determination and the finding of an administrative official not supported by evidence. In theory, at least, the legislature acts upon adequate knowledge after full consideration and through members who represent the entire public.[184]

[183] *Southern Railway v. Virginia*, 290 U.S. 190.

[184] *Id.* at 197.

The caveat "in theory, at least" suggests that, as in *Williamson*, the Court has some doubts about the truth of this claim but views its own role as limited. It is not appropriate on separation of powers grounds for it to inquire further. In contrast, the opinion seems to leave the way open for the Court to impose due process requirements on a range of executive actions from adjudications to rulemaking – procedures that not only could protect individual rights, but also might enhance public accountability. However, the Court did not take that route. Rather, it focuses on the process due to individual persons or businesses if a government action threatens their rights, especially their property rights. Administrators must provide due process when they take individualized actions that violate rights; the legislature need not do so. So long as the legislative action is not an unconstitutional bill of attainder or is otherwise unconstitutional, the courts will not interfere with the legislative process.

Plaintiffs in a more recent case sought another constitutional route to participate in administrative policymaking. A group of college professors sued a state board based on free speech. However, *Minnesota Bd. for Community Colleges v. Knight* holds that college professors do not have a First Amendment right to present their views to the academic administrators who make policy.[185] Justice O'Connor wrote for the Court that:

> The Constitution does not grant to members of the public generally a right to be heard by public bodies making decisions of policy.... Absent statutory restrictions, the State must be free to consult or not to consult whomever it pleases.... In *Bi-Metallic* the Court rejected due process as a source of an obligation to listen.... [The First Amendment also does not] require government policy-makers to listen or respond to individuals' communications on public issues....Nor, finally can the structure of government established and approved by the Constitution provide the source. It is inherent in a republican form of government that direct public participation in government policymaking is limited.... Disagreement with public policy and disapproval of officials' responsiveness ... is to be registered principally at the polls.[186]

The Court was unwilling to use the First Amendment to bootstrap an individual right to participate in policymaking into the Constitution.[187] Hence,

[185] Minnesota Bd. for Community Colleges v. Knight, 465 U.S. 271 (1984).

[186] *Id.* at 283–5.

[187] In Erik O. Autor, et al., v. Rebecca Blank, et al., 892 F. Supp. 2d 264 (D.D.C. 2012), lobbyists requested membership on Industry Trade Advisory Committees (ITACs) that excluded registered lobbyists under a 2009 presidential policy that implemented a statute. In one part of her holding, the district judge quoted from the paragraph in the text to find that the plaintiffs had no legal entitlement to ITAC membership. *See also* Foster v. Hughes, 979 F. 2d 130, 132 (8th Cir. 1992) ("[p]ersons are entitled to due process, in the form of an

neither a claim of injury nor a claimed right to speak requires a public agency to establish a process to hear the concerned public when it makes a general policy. The Constitution requires certain due process protections when the state acts against individuals or businesses through individualized decisions that may violate their rights.[188] These cases, taken together, leave it to statutory law to govern the policymaking processes of government outside the legislature. The opinions refuse to find a constitutional right for the public to participate in policymaking, whether made through statutes or executive rules.

B. The Administrative Procedure Act

Although the Constitution does not constrain the production of rules and regulations inside the executive and the independent agencies, statutory law influences those processes in accord with our positive political economy arguments. However, the United States had no general law governing administrative procedures until passage of the Administrative Procedure Act (APA) in 1946.[189] Individual statutes set out the authority of government departments and agencies in particular areas, but there was no overall requirement for notice, consultation, or reason-giving. Instead, inter-branch checks were used. The early Interstate Commerce Commission could not act without a court order, a cumbersome requirement that was soon repealed.[190] Congress added legislative vetoes to numerous statutes beginning during the administration of Franklin Delano Roosevelt. These permitted one or two houses of Congress, or even a key committee, to veto an executive decision if it wished, but did not require congressional review. Vetoes were exercised at the discretion of the current Congress. As we noted earlier, such vetoes were declared unconstitutional in the *Chadha* decision,

individual opportunity to be heard, only when the government makes an individualized determination, not when the government commits a legislative act [here, a regulatory act by the prison authorities] equally affecting all those similarly situated").

188 The classic cases are *Goldberg v. Kelly*, 397 U.S. 254, and *Mathews v. Eldridge*, 424 U.S. 319 and the subsequent development of the case law. We do not analyze adjudicatory procedures because our focus is on the quasi-legislative activities of executive departments and agencies. Of course, policy can be built up through a series of individual cases, as it is under the antitrust laws and in some other regulatory areas. The possible tension between the norms of case-by-case adjudication and rulemaking procedures is an important topic for research, but we leave it to one side here to focus on the contrast between administrative rules and congressional statutes.

189 Administrative Procedure Act, 5 U.S.C. §§551–9, 701–6.

190 Thomas W. Merrill, "The Origins of American-Style Judicial Review," in Comparative Administrative Law 389 (Susan Rose-Ackerman & Peter L. Lindseth, eds., 2010).

but even when they had legal force, their impact on executive action appears to have been limited, although, of course, their mere existence may have influenced executive action.[191] They were frequently enacted as part of a deal between the president and Congress that allowed a president's favored policy to go into effect. For example, a legislative veto permitted Roosevelt to reorganize the cabinet structure of government subject to congressional disapproval.[192] Congressional veto provisions were common in the United States before they were declared unconstitutional in 1983, and Congress continues to enact them, even though they are not enforceable.[193] However, they were never a general requirement, and their prevalence did not prevent the passage of the APA in 1946.

The APA's passage was surely related to the growth of the administrative state; it depended on the joint efforts of Republicans seeking to constrain the exercise of delegated power and of New Deal Democrats seeking to entrench the accomplishments of their fragile political coalition. President Roosevelt vetoed an earlier more restrictive bill. President Harry S. Truman signed the 1946 bill in spite of the limits it placed on the presidency.[194] The

[191] Kevin M. Stack, *The Irony of Oversight: Delegated Acts and the Political Economy of the European Union's Legislative Veto under the Treaty of Lisbon* 2 THEORY AND PRACTICE OF LEGISLATION 61 (2014).

[192] The 1933 Legislative Appropriations Act for Fiscal Year 1933 permitted the president to reorganize the government by executive order, but the orders had to be submitted to Congress. If neither House passed a resolution of disapproval, the reorganization would go into effect. For U.S. examples *see* I.N.S. v. Chadha, 464 U.S., at 969 (J. White, dissenting), and Strauss, *supra* note 63 (putting these in the "baby" category that serves a valid purpose).

[193] Strauss, *supra* note 63; Louis Fisher, *The Legislative Veto: Invalidated, It Survives*, **56** LAW & CONTEMPORARY PROBLEMS 273 (1993).

[194] President Truman may well have also sought to maintain New Deal accomplishments. Studies of the passage of the APA in 1946 contrast its fate with the earlier Walter-Logan bill of 1939–40. The latter, supported by conservative Republican opponents of the president, was vetoed by President Roosevelt. The APA passed by a voice vote. McNollgast, *The Political Origins of the Administrative Procedure Act*, **15** J. OF LAW, ECONOMICS & ORGANIZATION. 180 (1999), argues that the APA obtained broad support because both Republicans and Democrats obtained part of what they wanted. The Democrats' concerns were borne out later in 1946 when they lost control of the House, and by Truman's narrow victory in 1948. For histories of the passage of the APA *see* Reuel E. Schiller, *Reining in the Administrative State: World War II and the Decline of Expert Administration*, in TOTAL WAR AND THE LAW: THE AMERICAN HOME FRONT IN WORLD WAR II 185 (Daniel R. Ernst & Victor Jew, eds., 2002); Martin Shapiro, *APA: Past, Present, and Future*, **76** VIRGINIAN LAW REV. 447 (1986); George Shepherd, *Fierce Compromise: The Administrative Procedure Act Emerges from New Deal Politics*, **90** NORTHWESTERN LAW REV. 1557 (1996); and Joanna Grisinger, *Law in Action: The Attorney General's Committee on Administrative Procedure* **20** J. OF POLICY HISTORY 379 (2012). Grisinger argues that the AG's Committee found many of the practices eventually codified in the APA in use in various parts of the bureaucracy,

law included judicial review provisions. Given that American statutes are quite difficult to amend or repeal, Congress had reason to constrain executive power through the judiciary, even though it could not perfectly control the judges' behavior. One reason the New Dealers supported the judicial review provisions in 1946 was that by then the courts were largely sympathetic to New Deal legislation.[195] Reuel Schiller claims, in addition, that observers across the political spectrum had become skeptical of unchecked administrative power because of the rise of fascism and the experience of intrusive wartime administration.[196]

The Act governs both rulemaking and adjudication, but we focus on so-called notice and comment or informal rulemaking. Under the APA §553, such rulemaking requires public notice in the Federal Register, a hearing open to all interested persons, and a published rule accompanied by a statement of reasons. Article 553 fills less than a page of the U.S. Code, but it is of central importance to U.S. administrative law; it applies both to agencies in executive departments and to independent agencies.[197] The rulemaking process has three features.

First, a public notice must be put in the Federal Register that includes a proposed rule or "a description of the subjects and issues involved."[198] In practice, agencies routinely post proposed rules; and some begin with an Advanced Notice of Proposed Rulemaking that will produce two rounds of comments.[199] The Act says nothing about how an agency sets its agenda.[200] The APA provisions only start to operate once the agency decides to issue a rule in a particular area. Some statutes set deadlines or include "hammers"

but, of course, rulemaking practices were not reliably subject to judicial review before the passage of the APA.

195 McNollgast, *supra* note 194.

196 Schiller, *supra* note 194.

197 "Agency" is defined in the APA as "each authority of the Government of the United States, whether or not it is within or subject to the review of another agency" but with certain exceptions such as Congress and the courts. APA §551(1).

198 APA §553(b)(3).

199 *See* examples in Wendy Wagner, *Participation in the US Administrative Process*, in Research Handbook on Comparative Law and Regulation (Francesca Bignami & David Zaring, eds., forthcoming 2015).

200 Agencies frequently engage in some form of consultation before the APA notice and comment process begins, but these are not subject to judicial review. Steven J. Balla, *Between Commenting and Negotiating*, 1 J. of Law and Policy for the Information Society 59 (2004/2005) (documenting the various forms of commenting on Department of Transportation rules between 2001 and 2003). Since the passage of the Negotiated Rulemaking Act, 5 U.S. C., §§561–70 (1990), agencies can carry out a negotiation process under that act's guidelines, but this is a voluntary process that must be followed by an APA notice and comment process. It has been infrequently used, Balla, at 65–6.

that penalize delay or set agendas, but these provisions are specific to particular statutes.[201]

Second, the agency must organize a process to hear from "interested persons." This need not involve an oral hearing, but the agency must accept "written data, views, or arguments."[202] The open-ended nature of the agency hearing is a key aspect of the U.S. process; there is no mention of "stakeholders," and the agency cannot issue a closed list of those allowed to submit comments. On the down side, the agency is not required either to engage in outreach beyond public notice or to help overcome financial barriers to participation.[203]

Finally, the agency must publish rules and provide "a concise general statement of their basis and purpose."[204] The APA does not require that comments be made public, but this has become the general practice with

[201] *See, e.g.*, the 1984 amendments to the Resource Conservation and Recovery Act (RCRA): 42 U.S.C. §6924(d)(1) ("Effective 32 months after November 8, 1984 … the land disposal of the hazardous wastes … is prohibited unless the Administrator determines the prohibition on one or more methods of land disposal of such waste is not required in order to protect human health and the environment for as long as the waste remains hazardous"); *id.* §6924(e) ("Effective twenty-four months after November 8, 1984 … the land disposal of [solvents and dioxins] is prohibited unless the Administrator determines the prohibition of one or more methods of land disposal of such waste is not required in order to protect human health and the environment for as long as the waste remains hazardous"); *id.* §6924(f)(3) (prohibiting waste disposal into deep injection wells if the administrator fails to make a determination for those wastes within forty-five months of November 8, 1984). *See also* Asbestos Hazard Emergency Response Act of 1986, Pub. L. No 99–519, 100 Stat. 2970 (codified at 15 U.S.C. §2644) (directing local agencies to carry out requirements if the EPA fails to promulgate final regulations within a specific amount of time); Sidney A. Shapiro & Robert L. Glicksman, *Congress, the Supreme Court, and the Quiet Revolution in Administrative Law*, **1988** Duke Law J. 819, 839–40 (discussing hammers and other action-forcing provisions).

[202] APA §553(c). "Person" is defined as "an individual, partnership, corporation, association, or public or private organization other than the agency." This broad definition distinguishes a person from a "party," which is close to the legal definition of a party involved in a lawsuit and is used in the sections on adjudication. APA §§551(3), 554(c).

[203] *See* Wagner, *supra* note 199: "Much like market processes, U.S. administrative process is structured in a way to make opportunities available, but it does not require that all significant stakeholders be actually represented in the decision-making. If the advocates for important sets of affected interests … do not participate due to lack of resources, for example, the agency is not required or even expected to solicit their views, nor is their absence noted officially in the agency's administrative record." Some agencies have programs of outreach, and intervenor funding is sometimes available, but not as a result of APA requirements. In the 1970s both statutes and agency practice provided intervenor funding in some regulatory areas, but these were subject to criticism and have fallen into disuse or been explicitly outlawed. *See* Steven Croley, *Theories of Regulation: Incorporating the Administrative Process*, **98** Columbia Law Rev. 1, 124 (1998).

[204] APA §553(c), (d).

few exceptions. The agency can supplement the provisions of §553 with a formal on-the-record hearing, but agencies seldom use this more court-like process for rulemaking unless explicitly required by statute;[205] agencies have wide discretion to choose the rulemaking format.[206] They also negotiate with affected parties before and even after the final rule is issued, especially if a lawsuit is imminent.[207]

The procedural requirements of §553 do not apply to "interpretive rules, general statements of policy, or rules of agency organization procedure, or practice" or if the agency finds the process "impractical, unnecessary, or contrary to the public interest." In the latter case, it must supply "a brief statement of reasons" for not engaging in notice and comment.[208] Some types of government activity are exempt – for example, those dealing with military and foreign affairs and benefit programs,[209] but some agencies that provide benefits voluntarily follow APA rulemaking procedures.[210] Even though such agencies could discontinue these practices by an order from the agency head, the courts have upheld their notice and comment processes in a number of instances.[211]

[205] Based on a sample of federal government rulemakings, the Government Accountability Office (GAO) estimated that less than 2 percent of all rules used formal rulemaking procedures in 2003–10, that is, 587 out of a total of 30,583. General Accountability Office, Federal Rulemaking: Agencies Could Take Additional Steps to Respond to Public Comments, GAO-13–21 (December 2012) table 3, 32–3.

[206] National Petroleum Refiners Ass'n v. FTC, 482 F. 2d 672 (D.C. Cir. 1973).

[207] Balla, *supra* note 200.

[208] APA §553(b)(3).

[209] APA §553(a).

[210] In 1970, the U.S. Administrative Conference, an official government advisory body, recommended that agencies that allocate "grants, benefits, and contracts" should, when feasible, comply with the APA's notice and comment rulemaking procedures. Recommendation No. 16, U.S. Administrative Conference, Recommendations and Reports 29–30 (1970). Several cabinet departments then issued directives that waived their exemption for a broad range of their otherwise exempt activities. These included the Departments of Agriculture, Health, Education and Welfare (HEW), Housing and Urban Development, and Labor. When HEW became Health and Human Services, the directive remained in effect and now also applies to the Social Security Administration as well under the statute that spun it off from HHS [42 U.S. C. §902a(5)]. It would be interesting to study the pattern of voluntary acceptance further. Why did these key spending agencies impose procedural constraints on themselves? Did they realize that courts would enforce their choices? These questions are especially salient at present because the Department of Agriculture revoked its waiver in 2013 citing procedural delays, 78 Fed. Reg. 64194 (2013).

[211] Department of Agriculture cases are: Rodway v. U.S. Dept. of Agric., 514 F. 2d 809 (D.C. Cir. 1975); National Women, Infants, and Children Grocers Ass'n v. Food and Nutrition Service, 416 F. Supp. 2d 92 (D.D.C. 2006); but see Rainbow Valley Citrus Corp v. Federal Crop. Ins. Corp., 406 F. 2d 467 (9th Cir. 1974) (upholding the exemption for contracts). Cases enforcing the HEW/HHS waiver are: Humana of South Carolina v. Mathews, 419 F.

The Act provides for judicial review of both the substance of rules and the adequacy of agency processes, whether or not the agency used the notice and comment process. The federal courts have the authority to review the final rules for conformity with statute, for conformity with the APA and other required procedures, and to be sure they are not "arbitrary and capricious."[212] Review is almost never de novo, and the remedy for a defective rule is generally a remand to the agency. The court seldom tries to craft a legally acceptable rule itself, and it cannot award money damages in cases brought under the APA.[213]

The courts understand that agencies are better able to evaluate technical evidence compared to courts, and that broad-ranging public input can help to further the public legitimacy of executive branch policymaking. Thus, the courts play a legally mandated, but limited role in monitoring the competence and democratic accountability of executive policymaking, while not interfering too much in substantive policy, where they have little competence. The relationships between the courts and agencies and between the Supreme Court and the lower courts have, however, not always been smooth. The history of administrative law since the passage of the APA has turned on the courts' shifting levels of oversight of both process and substance. The growing importance of rulemaking as an executive policymaking tool has influenced the nature of judicial review under relatively open-ended statutes. The APA forms the background for judicial review, and its passage is consistent with our political economy view of congressional incentives.

Supp. 253, 260 (D.D.C. 1976), aff'd Humana of South Carolina v. Califano, 590 F. 2d 1070 (D.C. Cir. 1978), and Herron v. Heckler, 576 F. Supp. 218 (N.D. Cal. 1983). We are very grateful to Nicholas Parrillo for the citations in this and the previous footnote. In *Rodway*, Judge Skelly Wright tells the Department of Agriculture that if it issues a regulation (here labeled a "policy statement"), it becomes "law" and must be enforced. Reading between the lines, the Department seems rather surprised by the court interpretation.

212 APA §706. Some rules must be based on "substantial evidence," and there is controversy over whether these standards actually are different in practice. In Ass'n of Data Processing Serv. Org. v. Fed. Res., 745 F. 2d 677, 683–4 (1985), Judge (now Justice) Scalia argues that the difference between the substantial evidence and the arbitrary and capricious standard is "largely semantic." He goes on to say that the substantial evidence test simply signals to judges in formal proceedings that they can look only to the closed record of the proceedings.

213 Review is only de novo when the agency's statute provided that "the facts are subject to trial de novo by the reviewing court," APA §706 (2) (F). Suits must seek relief "other than money damages," APA §702. Money damages are available in a limited class of cases involving torts committed by the government under the Federal Tort Claims Act, 60 Stat. 842 (1946) codified at 28 U.S. C. §1346(a) and by public officials, most notably so-called Bivens Actions under the Civil Rights Act of 1871, 42 U.S.C. §1983. *See* Breyer et al., Administrative Law and Regulatory Policy 799–811 (7th ed., 2011).

However, many developments in the courts since its passage cannot be so easily tied to legislative incentives.

Certain violations of the APA rulemaking process seldom occur because violations are transparent and compliance is straightforward. Posting a notice in the Federal Register and holding a hearing are routine. The key issue is whether notice and comment rulemaking is required when a policy is being made; if it is, public notice and hearings follow of necessity. However, standards of judicial review of the comment process and of the agency's reasoning remain contested. Furthermore, the APA framework is in the midst of adapting to the Internet age with its multitude of routes for public input.[214]

The agencies' own interest in surviving court review of their rules has led them to assemble extensive documentation of submitted comments and their responses.[215] Review of process has pushed agencies toward holding more extensive public hearings and facilitated the posting of comments. When it issues a rule under the APA, the agency must include a "concise statement of basis and purpose,"[216] but under judicial scrutiny, concision is not enforced, and these statements have become hefty volumes of justification for the path chosen.[217] The lower federal courts, especially the D.C. Circuit, which hears many rulemaking challenges, have filled in gaps in the vague language of the APA, especially after environmental and social regulation began to dominate their caseload. However, the Supreme

[214] For an overview consult the E-rulemaking website of the Penn Program on Regulation, directed by Cary Coglianese: https://www.law.upenn.edu/academics/institutes/regulation/erulemaking/papersandreports.html

[215] White House review of major rules under Executive Order (EO) 12866 requires departments and agencies in the cabinet structure of government to justify their rules using a cost/benefit test. This is not a judicially enforceable mandate, but it surely influences the nature of the record before a court if the rule is challenged. Unless statutory language prohibits such a balancing test, the executive's balancing efforts will be part of the reason-giving documentation. For a discussion of the strengths and weakness of the EO and references to the relevant literature, *see* Susan Rose-Ackerman, *Putting Cost-Benefit Analysis in Its Place: Rethinking Regulatory Review*, **65** University of Miami Law Rev. 335 (2011).

[216] APA §553(c).

[217] Occasionally, however, the courts express their frustration at the length and complexity of the record, including the statement of reasons. For example, the D.C. Circuit remarked in a case with a record that spanned more than 10,000 pages: "[T]he record presented to us ... is a sump in which the parties have deposited a sundry mass of materials that have neither passed through the filter of rules of evidence nor undergone the refining fire of adversarial presentation.... The lack of discipline in such a record, coupled with its sheer mass ... makes the record of informal rulemaking a less than fertile ground for judicial review [Natural Resources Defense Council, Inc. v. SEC, 606 F. 2d 1031, 1052 (D.C. Cir. 1979)]. We are grateful to Wendy Wagner for providing this citation.

Court constrained the lower courts' efforts to interpret APA procedural requirements in the *Vermont Yankee* opinion.[218]

Judge David Bazelon's D.C. Circuit opinion in the *Vermont Yankee* litigation held that a rulemaking of the Nuclear Regulatory Commission was procedurally insufficient under the National Environmental Policy Act, an act that requires an assessment of environmental impacts. However, he left it to the agency to decide exactly how to respond. He did not require court-like procedures, although "limited cross-examination" was one of the options that he mentioned. He argued that in technical areas the courts should review procedure and not substance, and he went on to explain that a good procedure should create "genuine dialogue," listing a range of options including:

> informal conferences between intervenors and staff, document discovery, interrogatories, technical advisory committees comprised of outside experts with differing perspectives, limited cross-examination, funding independent research by intervenors, detailed annotation of technical reports, surveys of existing literature, memoranda explaining methodology. We do not presume to intrude on the agency's province by dictating to it which, if any, of these devices it must adopt to flesh out the record. It may be that no combination of the procedures mentioned above will prove adequate, and the agency will be required to develop new procedures to accomplish the innovative task of implementing NEPA [National Environmental Policy Act] through rulemaking. On the other hand, the procedures the agency adopted in this case, if administered in a more sensitive, deliberate manner, might suffice. Whatever techniques the Commission adopts, before it promulgates a rule limiting further consideration of waste disposal and reprocessing issues, it must in one way or another generate a record in which the factual issues are fully developed [footnote omitted].[219]

This open-ended list does not seem very intrusive on its face. However, the Supreme Court read its very permissiveness as opening the way for detailed court review of procedures over and above those mandated by the APA. Justice Rehnquist, writing for the Court, worried that agencies would respond to Judge Bazelon's opinion by using increasingly time-consuming and legalistic procedures. According to him, agencies "would undoubtedly adopt full adjudicatory procedures in every instance.... [A]ll the inherent advantages of informal rulemaking would be totally lost." He claims that

[218] Vermont Yankee Nuclear Power Corp. v. Natural Resources Defense Council, 435 U.S. 519 (1978).

[219] Natural Res. Def. Council, Inc. v. U.S. Nuclear Regulatory Comm'n, 547 F. 2d 633, 653–4 (D.C. Cir. 1976) *cert. granted, judgment vacated sub nom.* Baltimore Gas & Elec. Co. v. Natural Res. Def. Council, Inc., 435 U.S. 964 (1978) and *rev'd sub nom.* Vermont Yankee.

the D.C. Circuit is attempting to influence policy "under the guise of judicial review." Rather, the courts should set aside agency choices "only for substantial procedural or substantive reasons."[220] At that level of generality Judge Bazelon would agree with Justice Rehnquist. To Bazelon, the review of process in technical areas is exactly how the courts should approach review if they have little or no expertise; the acceptable processes should not be slavishly adopted from the courtroom.

The difference between Judge Bazelon and Justice Rehnquist turns on the level of deference to agency procedures. Bazelon would give agencies considerable scope, but they would have to defend their practices in court if challenged. Rehnquist would defer to both Congress and the agencies in the design of rulemaking procedures; the courts should only check to be sure that the agency applied the APA correctly. The use of additional procedures should be discretionary for agencies. In his view, it is up to Congress to pass laws with strong procedural protections if it sees the need.

Justice Rehnquist's opinion in *Vermont Yankee*, with its deep deference to the other branches, is in striking contrast to his failed effort to revive the non-delegation doctrine a few years later in the *Benzene* case, discussed earlier.[221] There he adopted a positive political economy view of Congress under which members have incentives to draft vague statutes as a way to forge compromises and pass statutes. He had no difficulty arguing that the courts should step in to limit the operation of these political imperatives. A strong non-delegation doctrine would surely chill the legislature and reduce the number of statutes passed. Even those who share his description of Congress may well disagree with his proposed cure, but our point here is that he was willing to give the federal courts a strong oversight role in that case. In the rulemaking context, in contrast, Rehnquist expresses a rather idealized view of both legislative drafting and agency rulemaking and a rather crabbed description of judges' notion of process. Neither side of this claim seems obviously correct as an empirical matter. Some agencies have been captured by the industries they are supposed to regulate. If that occurs, they will not set up broadly participatory procedures unless required to do so by an enforceable statutory provision. Narrow interests may capture agenda setters in Congress as well. Of course, capture is not inevitable, but it does not seem overly intrusive to allow the courts to nudge agencies in a more democratic direction. If courts did tilt the administrative process in the direction of court-like procedures, the political branches

[220] Vermont Yankee, 435 U.S. at 558.

[221] Industrial Union v. American Petroleum Inst., 448 U.S. at 685.

might react by amending the relevant statutes to limit that tilt, unless partisan concerns intervene.

A key aspect of administrative law is the overlap between substance and process in reason-giving. We have already discussed the procedural implications of a reason-giving requirement in judicial review of the constitutionality of statutes. Similar issues arise in administrative law. The APA states that agencies must issue a statement of reasons when they issue rules. This is a procedural requirement; yet it also has substantive content. Courts use the statement of reasons to check if a rule is substantively lawful in light of the underlying statute delegating authority to the agency. *Chevron v. Natural Resources Defense Council* illustrates the overlap.[222] There, the Supreme Court deferred to an agency's interpretation of the substantive law. The Court permitted a new presidential administration to reinterpret a statutory term in the Clean Air Act and to issue a new rule. The Court wrote that it would defer to an agency's statutory interpretation so long as Congress had not spoken directly to the question at issue and the agency's interpretation was reasonable. A new administration with policy priorities that differed from its predecessor was thus given some policy space to reverse a prior policy so long as the new policy was consistent with the underlying statute.[223] Recall our description of the U.S. legislative process and our claim that Congress commonly does not speak clearly. Thus, in practice, there will be considerable space for agency interpretations.

The *Chevron* case did not deal directly with the administrative process, but its review of the agency's statutory interpretation inevitably required the Court to confront the agency's use of expert information and its adequacy and completeness. Both in *Chevron* and elsewhere this has led federal judges to debate their own role in resolving highly technical cases. The tension was famously stated, before the *Chevron* decision, in two concurrences in *Ethyl Corp. v. EPA*.[224] Judge Bazelon asserts that federal judges should only review process, not substance, in cases "of great technological complexity." Consistent with his later (overturned) opinion in *Vermont Yankee*, he argues that judges are not competent to review the technical merits of agency decisions and should instead "establish a decision-making process

[222] Chevron, U.S.A., Inc. v. Natural Resources Defense Council, 467 U.S. 837 (1980).

[223] Kevin Stack observes that the opinion does not mention the judicial review portions of the APA and argues that the two are inconsistent because the APA instructs the courts to decide all questions of law. Kevin M. Stack, *The Statutory Fiction of Judicial Review of Administrative Action in the United States*, in Effective Judicial Review: A Cornerstone of Good Government 317, 319–20 (Christopher Forsyth, Mark Elliott, Swati Jhaveri, & Anne Scully-Hill, eds., 2010). He makes a similar point about the *Ethyl* case.

[224] Ethyl Corp. v. EPA, 541 F. 2d 1.

that assures a reasoned decision that can be held up to the scrutiny of the scientific community and the public."[225] In that regard, he criticized the EPA for failing to keep a record of its procedures that would have permitted judicial review.[226] Judge Harold Leventhal responds that this may not be possible given the interlocking nature of substance and process. Judges must act with restraint but not abdicate responsibility for substantive review. Unlike the legislative context, the courts should ask if the agency's rule is an adequate response to the statutory mandate. Judges recognize that there is seldom one best response, but they should ask if the agency can defend its approach. Leventhal's so-called hard look review seeks to determine if the agency took a hard look at the available options – a procedural requirement but one that may require the courts to review the substantive information justifying the policy. The limited substantive review he advocates can only occur if courts get "sufficient background information" on the issues. Otherwise, the courts will not be carrying out their responsibilities to police the delegation of legislative policy choices to the executive.[227]

Thus, under "hard look" review the federal courts sometimes interpret the substantive bases of review quite aggressively and in ways that necessarily blur the substance/procedure line. For example, in *Motor Vehicle Manufacturers' Ass'n. v. State Farm*, the Supreme Court held that the repeal of a regulation must follow the same procedures as its promulgation; hence, revocation of a prior rule requires more justification than failure to act in the first instance.[228] That sounds like a purely procedural ruling, but it was supported by claims that the agency had made a glaring error in evaluating the substance. The error occurred in part because the agency was rushing to fulfill President Reagan's mandate to aid the auto industry, and it did not adequately follow APA notice and comment procedures.

More recently, in *FCC v. Fox* (*Fox I*) a divided court ruled that an FCC order on "fleeting expletives" was not arbitrary and capricious under the judicial review provisions of the APA.[229] (It remanded the case to the Court of Appeals to consider the constitutional issues.)[230] Justice Scalia's majority

[225] *Id.* at 66.

[226] *Id.* at 67.

[227] *Id.* at 68.

[228] Motor Vehicle Manufacturers' Ass'n. v. State Farm Mutual Automobile Insurance Co., U.S. 29 (1983).

[229] FCC v. Fox Television Stations, Inc., 556 U.S. 502 (2009) (Fox I). The statutory provision is APA §706 (2) (A).

[230] The Second Circuit found the policy vague and invalidated it on First Amendment grounds; Fox v. FCC, 613 F. 3d 317 (2nd Cir. 2010). The Supreme Court agreed the policy was impermissibly vague, but it overturned the enforcement actions, not on First

opinion stresses substance and finds the FCC's actions legally acceptable. Even though the FCC's action was not a rulemaking under the APA, Justice Breyer's dissent frames the case in terms of policymaking procedures. To him, the "arbitrary and capricious" standard is "not so much a particular set of substantive commands but rather a *process*, a process of learning through reasoned argument, that is the antithesis of the 'arbitrary.' This means that agencies must follow a 'logical and rational' decisionmaking 'process.'"[231] Also, in making policy the agency must act consistently and must explain the basis for any changes. In other words, he argues that certain procedural values tied to reasoned argument ought to be read into the "arbitrary and capricious" standard whenever "the policy is important, the significance of the issues clear, the failures near complete."[232] He claims that this would be an easy case for a remand if the FCC had been operating under APA rulemaking procedures. Thus, he articulates a broad role for the Court in the review of policymaking processes, but, of course, he was in a minority of four in that case. Notice, however, that he stresses rational justification, not public input and participation. It is Justice Scalia who links the FCC's action to hearings and legislative activity in Congress that might reflect evolving popular viewpoints.

In spite of Justice Scalia's lack of interest in the administrative process in *Fox I*, the courts generally give more deference to a rule promulgated through notice and comment procedures compared to one that avoids those safeguards.[233] If notice was inadequate, the comment period truncated, or the statement of reasons cursory, a decision may be remanded to the agency for further proceedings.[234]

These decisions are all made in light of the *Chenery I* doctrine, which holds that an agency cannot substitute or add reasons during the litigation

Amendment grounds, but as a violation of due process because the stations did not have "fair notice"; FCC v. Fox Television Stations, Inc., 132 S. Ct. 2307, 2320 (2012) (Fox II). However, because the Court did not address the constitutionality of the current indecency policy, the Commission is "free to modify its current indecency policy in light of its determination of the public interest and applicable legal requirements. And it leaves the courts free to review the current policy or any modified policy in light of its content and application." [*id.*]

231 *Fox I*, 556 U.S., at 548.

232 *Id.* at 562.

233 U.S. v. Mead, 533 U.S. 218 (2001).

234 Compare the statutory requirements of the APA with the United Kingdom, where the courts in reviewing policymaking processes are "cautiously" experimenting with a "duty to consult" and even something that looks like "hard-look" review. *See* Richard Rawlings, *Changed Conditions, Old Truths: Judicial Review in a Regulatory Laboratory*, in The Regulatory State: Constitutional Implications, 283, 291–2 (Dawn Olivier, Tony Prosser, & Richard Rawlings, eds., 2010).

period that were not articulated at the time the decision was made.[235] The *Chenery* litigation involved an individual administrative order, not a rule, and it was decided before the passage of the APA. Nevertheless, the basic principle still holds, although it has a different justification in the rulemaking context. In rulemaking the doctrine fits well with the claim that the administrative procedures should further public participation, transparency, and justification to the citizenry; they are not simply designed to persuade the courts. The process responds to the concern that broad delegations to the executive may undermine democratic accountability. Agency policymaking processes substitute for more directly accountable legislative processes.[236]

However, the courts sometimes rule that procedural lapses are "harmless errors" that did not affect the final result. Because it is difficult for the courts to judge if a violation was "harmless," this doctrine is applied sparingly in rulemaking cases.[237] See, for example, *Sugar Cane Growers v. Veneman* where the Court of Appeals held that a Department of Agriculture (DoA) program notice in the Federal Register, combined with a press release, was a "rule"

[235] The opinion states that "an administrative order cannot be upheld unless the grounds upon which the agency acted in exercising its powers were those upon which its action can be sustained," SEC v. Chenery, 318 U.S. 80, 95 (1943) (Chenery I).

[236] The view of *Chenery I* expressed in the text is made forcefully in Kevin M. Stack, *The Constitutional Foundations of* Chenery, 116 Yale Law J., 952, 992–4 (2007). Stack also argues that reason-giving promotes predictability in enforcement because it commits the agency to a particular interpretation of its own rules; Kevin Stack, *Interpreting Regulation*, **111** Michigan Law Rev. 355 (2012).

[237] The principle generally applies to adjudications. Cases arise as exceptions to the *Chenery* doctrine, *Chenery I*, 318 U.S. at 95. The federal courts will not remand or reverse an individual decision if the alleged error "clearly had no bearing on the procedure used or the substance of the decision reached," Massachusetts Trustees of Eastern Gas & Fuel Associates v. United States, 377 U.S. 235, 248 (1964). *See* Sahara Coal Co. v. Office of Workers' Comp. Programs, 946 F. 2d 554, 558 (7th Cir. 1991) ("harmless-error doctrine is available in judicial review of administrative action; it is an exception to the *Chenery* principle"). The principle is related to the clause in the APA §706 stating that "due account shall be taken [by the court] of the rule of prejudicial error." *See* Nate Hausman, *Monsanto Co. v. Geertson Seed Farm; Breathing a Sigh of Equitable Relief* **25** Tulane Environmental Law J. 155, 195–206 (2011). For a discussion *see* Richard Murphy, Chenery *Unmasked: Reasonable Limits on the Duty to Give Reasons*, **80** University of Cincinnati Law Rev. 817, 863–6 (2012). Murphy discusses NLRB v. Wyman Gordon Co., 394 U.S. 759 (1969) that upheld an order of the NLRB in the face of procedural inadequacies because the agency's action would not have changed on remand. However, a majority of the justices chastises the agency for engaging in rulemaking in a prior adjudication. The implication of the plurality opinion plus the dissents is that the Court will not generally permit agencies to make binding rules outside of the notice and comment process.

that required notice and comment procedures. It rejected the Department's harmless error claim, stating that following its lead would "virtually repeal section 553's requirements."[238] However, a few years later the D.C. Circuit upheld a Federal Communications Commission (FCC) order on harmless error grounds. Its reasoning illustrates the federal courts' focus on process. *United States Telecom Ass'n v. FCC* held that an FCC order was permissible so long as the agency complied with the notice and comment provisions of the APA.[239] The court upheld the order because the FCC followed the requirements of §553 with respect to notice, opportunity for comment, and reason-giving, even though the agency claimed that it was not required to comply with the APA in this case. Failure to label their actions correctly was harmless error.[240]

In both the DoA and the FCC cases, the Appeals Court enforced the APA's requirements without engaging in an elaborate effort to test if the procedural requirements made a difference in the outcome. This reflects the federal courts' general stance. There are two reasons for this approach. First, courts are often poorly equipped to judge if a procedural lapse was "harmless" in the sense of affecting substance, and, second, democratic legitimacy is one goal of notice and comment rulemaking, independent of its specific effects on a challenged rule. Minor procedural lapses that do not limit public input and transparency may be excused, however, to discourage trivial lawsuits.[241] In that sense the case law is similar to the enrolled bill rule discussed earlier. As the Ninth Circuit stated: "To avoid gutting the APA's procedural requirements, harmless error analysis in administrative rulemaking must therefore focus on the process as well as the result."[242]

Furthermore, if an agency makes policy under one of the exceptions to notice and comment rulemaking, it may face court challenges to its

[238] Sugar Cane Growers Coop. of Florida v. Veneman, 289 F. 3d 89, 95–7 (D.C. Cir. 2002). An interesting feature of this case is that it is an example of the courts holding the Department of Agriculture to its voluntary acceptance of notice and comment rulemaking even if its programs fall under the APA's exemptions. *See* TAN 209–10.

[239] United States Telecom Ass'n v. FCC, 400 F. 3d 29, 39 (D.C. Cir. 2005).

[240] *Id.* at 30, 40–2. Interestingly, the FCC lawyers had not themselves had the wit to make this argument (*id.* at 40, n. 20). They avoided making this argument because under the APA the FCC would have had to prepare a Regulatory Flexibility Analysis (RFA) documenting the costs imposed on small business. The court upheld the order for large entities and suspended the order and remanded it to the FCC so it could perform an RFA (*id.* at 42).

[241] For example, *see* Long Island Care at Home, Ltd. v. Coke, 551 U.S. 158, 174–6 (2007) (dismissing a claim that notice was inadequate and holding the government's explanation to be adequate. In other words, it had not erred.).

[242] Riverbed Farms, Inc. v. Madigan, 958 F. 2d 1479, 1487 (9th Cir. 1992) (discussed in Hausman, *supra* note 237, at 199).

authority to "legislate" without a consultation process. A policy announced without notice and comment can be subject to challenge when the agency applies it in individual cases.[243] In contrast, if a rule promulgated through APA procedures has survived judicial review, it cannot be relitigated in subsequent applications.[244] Thus, unlike review of legislation, courts have checked to see if there has been public input into the agency's deliberations over rules with legal force.

Judge Richard Posner, in *Hoctor v. U.S. Department of Agriculture*, provides a particularly clear statement of the reasons for requiring consultation before an agency issues a rule.[245] Hoctor challenged an interpretive rule promulgated without notice and comment; the rule set eight feet as the minimum height for the containment fences for dangerous wild animals, such as lions and tigers. Here, a "structurally sound" fence is clearly called for, but any *precise* height is difficult to defend, based either on the statutory language or on purely technical grounds. As a result, Posner demands more process as a way to ensure democratic legitimacy. A clear rule is "reasonable" because the regulated entities benefit from a precise height rule that can shield them from enforcement actions, but any particular height cannot be defended on principled grounds against other nearby options. He writes:

> [This case concerns] … the making of reasonable but arbitrary (not in the "arbitrary or capricious" sense) rules that are consistent with the statute … under which the rules are promulgated but not derived from it, because they represent an arbitrary choice among methods of implementation. A rule that turns on a number is likely to be arbitrary in this sense. There is no way to reason to an eight-foot perimeter-fence rule as opposed to a seven-and-a-half foot fence or a nine-foot fence or a ten-foot fence. None of these candidates for a rule is uniquely appropriate to, and in that sense derivable from, the duty of secure containment. This point becomes even clearer if we note that the eight-foot rule actually has another component – the fence must be at least three feet from any animal's pen. Why three feet? Why not four? Or two?
>
> … Legislators have the democratic legitimacy to make choices among value judgments, choices based on hunch or guesswork or even the toss of a coin, and other arbitrary choices. When agencies base rules on arbitrary choices

243 McLouth Steel Products Co. v. Thomas, 838 F. 2d 1317 (D.C. Cir. 1988); American Mining Congress v. Marshall, 671 F. 2d 1251 (10th Cir. 1982).

244 Some rules are reviewed before they are enforced. This possibility may preclude review at the enforcement stage even if no one challenged the rule prior to enforcement, e.g., under the Clean Water and Clean Air Acts. In other cases, review at either stage is permitted. *See* NLRB Union v. FLRA, 834 F. 2d 191 (D.C. Cir. 1987) for an overview.

245 Hoctor v. Dept. of Agriculture, 82 F. 3d at 165.

> they are legislating, and so these rules are legislative or substantive and require notice and comment rulemaking, a procedure that is analogous to the procedure employed by legislatures in making statutes. *The notice of proposed rulemaking corresponds to the bill and the reception of written comments to the hearing on the bill.*
>
> The common sense of requiring notice and comment rulemaking for legislative rules is well illustrated by the facts of this case. There is no process of cloistered, appellate-court type reasoning by which the Department of Agriculture could have excogitated the eight-foot rule from the ... [underlying legal text]. The rule is arbitrary in the sense that it could well be different without significant impairment of any regulatory purpose. But this does not make the rule a matter of indifference to the people subject to it. There are thousands of animal dealers, and some unknown fraction of these face the prospect of having to tear down their existing fences and build new, higher ones at great cost. The concerns of these dealers are legitimate and since, as we are stressing, the rule could well be otherwise, the agency was obliged to listen to them before settling on a final rule and to provide some justification for that rule, though not so tight or logical a justification as a court would be expected to offer for a new judge-made rule. *Notice and comment is the procedure by which the persons affected by legislative rules are enabled to communicate their concerns in a comprehensive and systematic fashion to the legislating agency. The Department's lawyer speculated that if the notice and comment route had been followed in this case the Department would have received thousands of comments. The greater the public interest in a rule, the greater reason to allow the public to participate in its formation* [emphasis added].[246]

Notice Judge Posner's use of the term "arbitrary" to characterize the agency's choice and the way he links the substantive choice to process. *Hoctor* analogizes the notice and comment process to the process of enacting statutes in the legislature. Not all of the case law is so explicit, and sometimes judicial opinions view the record of the notice and comment process as primarily designed to aid judicial review, not to enhance democratic legitimacy. Some critics view it that way as well.[247]

It is an empirical question whether notice and comment actually serves the legitimating function that we see as its primary normative justification. Does it combine openness to the contesting views of the public and the affected interests with the competent application of scientific and social scientific data and analysis? In the case of dangerous animals, the aim is not to

[246] Hoctor v. Dept. of Agriculture, 82 F. 3d at 171. One complication of the case is that the interpretive rule that required an eight-foot-high fence was actually an interpretation of a rule that had been promulgated by notice and comment. However, that rule was very open-ended and did little to narrow the USDA's discretion under the statute.

[247] E. Donald Elliott. *Re-inventing Rulemaking*, **41** Duke Law J. 1490, 1492–6 (1992).

have the affected dealers determine the policy, but rather to assure that their views and interests are heard as the USDA weighs the options. Because the courts cannot judge the merit of any particular standard within some broad range, they are only competent to judge the process. In Posner's view the APA sets out the required procedures; he does not attempt to add on other processes or to evaluate the effectiveness of the APA.[248]

IV. CONCLUSIONS

The U.S. Constitution says nothing about executive rulemaking, but the APA mandates rulemaking procedures subject to judicial review. The Constitution gives the legislature the power to make its own rules and imposes only structural constraints that do not cover internal lawmaking processes. Even statutes designed to tie the hands of Congress lack judicial review provisions, and the federal courts seldom reach out to apply the Constitution to the legislative process. We have argued that this state of affairs is consistent with congressional incentives. In addition, the U.S. case raises two normative issues central to our other cases.

The first concerns review of statutes for conformity with constitutional norms. We have argued that the review of substance may have indirect procedural effects – effects that can be deeply inconsistent with the reality of lawmaking in a presidential system. In particular, we critique recent closely divided cases that deal with federalism. Intrusive review of this type would be less problematic in a parliamentary system simply because the government can respond more easily to demands for justification and reason-giving. We illustrate that claim when we discuss South Africa and Germany. Second, we argue that notice and comment rulemaking, followed by limited judicial review that focuses on the administrative process and the rule's conformity with statute is a strength of the American legal system. Although derived from statutory law and judicial interpretations, not the text of the Constitution, these U.S. practices have lessons for executive rulemaking in parliamentary systems and in the European Union, where the political imperative to enact such statutes is weak. We discuss each of these issues in turn.

[248] In particular substantive areas one can go beyond the APA to study the way agencies actually carry out their mandates. This is the approach of ESKRIDGE & FEREJOHN, *supra* note 18, in their case studies. Particularly relevant here is their study of the Equal Employment Opportunity Commission and its deliberative processes (*id.* at 30–3).

is whether these canons are a way for the Court to try to figure out what congressional drafters intended or whether they are independent interpretive rules that Congress, in turn, ought to follow because they have been articulated by the Court. However one comes out on the normative issue, in fact, only a few canons appear to be clear and visible enough to affect the legislative drafting process, according to the extensive interviews carried out by Abbe Gluck and Lisa Bressman.[253]

The federal courts "in theory at least" assume that the legislature is politically accountable, but political reality means that many statutes are neither logical nor clear. This has not led the courts either to insist on clarity or to focus on the democratic aspects of process. The U.S. courts sometimes assert jurisdiction over purely procedural challenges to legislative actions, but they are not willing to intervene unless procedural infirmities either harm an individual's rights – especially if the person is accused of a crime – or violate the chamber's voting rules.

This hands-off approach is consistent with the U.S. constitutional structure. However, the Supreme Court could exercise limited judicial review of the legislative process in ways that would enhance democratic legitimacy. Unfortunately, that has not been the trend. If the Supreme Court follows its current direction and provides aggressive review of reason-giving in more areas of law, it will chill the legislative process, not improve it. The Court majority, often only five members, is beginning to impose heavy strictures on Congress that it is structurally unable to meet given its lack of a unitary hierarchical structure. Requirements of something close to "findings" in the judicial sense could impose higher burdens on the legislature than on the administration when it makes rules. The organization of Congress is complex and multifaceted, and members must make compromises that frequently result in unclear drafting. It would be deeply undemocratic for a small majority of the Supreme Court to interfere aggressively with legislative procedures in ways that do not enhance democracy but only entrench one interpretation of the Constitution that cannot claim broad public support. Review of substance has procedural implications if it is predicated on congressional reason-giving.

Canons, **113** Columbia Law Rev. 531 (2013). John Manning provides a more nuanced defense of new and more moderate forms of textualism. For his more recent contributions, *see* John F. Manning, *What Divides Textualists from Purposivists?* **106** Columbia Law Rev. 70 (2006) and John F. Manning, *Second Generation Textualism* **98** California Law Rev. 1287 (2010). He stresses that statutes are the product of compromises and are inevitably messy.

[253] Gluck & Bressman, *supra* note 174.

Some have proposed introducing legislative provisions, now contained in many state constitutions, such as single-subject rules, and rules that require the titles of bills to express their content.[254] These proposals would keep any challenged statute in effect for a time in order to give Congress an opportunity to correct the problem. A positive political economy view of legislative incentives, however, suggests that legislatures are unlikely to introduce these proposals. As an outside possibility, Congress might suffer from such a degree of deadlock and illegitimacy in the eyes of the public that it decides to reform itself. Congress does frequently change its rules, and sometimes in directions that further accountability and legitimacy. The successful effort in 2013 to end the filibuster for executive appointments and lower court judges is one example.[255] The flurry of state constitutional amendments dealing with legislative drafting in the second half of the nineteenth century is another.[256]

Courts need not take a completely hands-off position, however. Modest judicial efforts to review the democratic character of the legislative process could be both effective and constitutional. The Court could enhance the deliberative and democratic character of the legislative process so long as it recognizes the reality of lawmaking in the American presidential system. However, what can be feasibly expected of courts?

Hans Linde lays out a vision of a legislative process that meets his minimum conditions for democratic acceptability:

> A member who never attends the committee meetings should at least examine the record of evidence before casting a vote, or be told about it, and should certainly never vote by proxy. The committee must explain its factual and value premises to the full body. Surely, there is no place for a vote on final passage by members who have never read even a summary of a bill, let alone a committee report, or a resume, or a resume of the factual documentation.[257]

Linde's list of the minimum responsibilities of a legislator, however, would be difficult for the courts to enforce. One alternative is for the courts to monitor outputs as a way of improving inputs. Rose-Ackerman, for example, has argued that the U.S. Supreme Court should encourage deliberation and limit interest group deals by requiring consistency between statutory

[254] *See, e.g.*, Denning & Smith, *Truth-in-Lending*, *supra* note 92 (proposing a single subject and clear title rule as a constitutional amendment), and John Martinnez, *Rational Legislating*, **34** Stetson Law Rev. 547 (2005) (proposing a rational legislating statute).

[255] Peters, *supra* note 59.

[256] *See* Williams, *supra* note 75, although, as Williams points out, these provisions have seldom been vigorously enforced.

[257] Linde, *supra* note 98, at 224.

preambles and the body of the statute and between stated goals and funding. In the face of an inconsistency, it would send the statute back to Congress to revise the language within a set time period or else the statute would be struck down.[258] The goal is to improve the democratic legitimacy and perhaps also the competence of Congress. This proposal for internal consistency seems potentially enforceable and is consistent with the basic thrust of Linde's remarks. Of course, there would be hard cases under any standard of review, but there will surely be some relatively clear violations of such a rule.[259]

B. Review of Rules

To us, the American rulemaking process furthers basic democratic values for policymaking in the executive and the independent agencies. Although aspects of the process could surely use reform, we are critical of the widespread use of the term "ossification" to describe its operation.[260] Almost by definition, notice and comment rulemaking will be time-consuming for major rules that attract public attention. Many rulemaking dockets attract few comments, but as Judge Posner states: "The greater the public interest in a rule, the greater reason to allow the public to participate in its formation."[261]

Those who examine the way policy is made in federal independent agencies and cabinet departments point to a range of avoidance behaviors that coexist with agencies' voluntary efforts to achieve the ideals of notice and comment rulemaking over and above statutory requirements. Wendy Wagner canvasses the options that range from using other regulatory forms, such as guidance documents, to informal negotiations with important stakeholders, to delay or outright abandonment of a policy.[262] Jerry Mashaw and David Harfst study the experience of the National Highway

[258] Susan Rose-Ackerman, Rethinking the Progressive Agenda: The Reform of the American Regulatory State, 43–79 (1992). *See also* Jerry Mashaw, *Constitutional Deregulation: Notes toward a Public, Public Law* **54** Tulane Law Rev. 849 (arguing that citizens have a right to demand the laws be public).

[259] Rose-Ackerman, *supra* note 258, at 43–79. One case involved a statute that claimed to be aimed at helping consumers as well as dairies and dairy farmers [Block v. Community Nutrition, 467 U.S. 340 (1984)]. In fact, it harmed some groups of consumers. The Court did not take the preamble seriously. A case involving financing is Pennhurst State School v. Halderman, 451 U.S. 1 (1981), which upheld a statute where there was a large gap between the stated aims and funding.

[260] McGarity, *supra* note 21, at 1403.

[261] Hoctor v. Department of Agriculture, 82 F. 3d 165.

[262] Wagner, *supra* note 199, canvasses the options.

Traffic Safety Administration, which shifted from rulemaking to product recalls, at least in part, as a way to limit judicial review.[263] However, even though some agencies seek to avoid rulemaking to save time and hassle, the threat of judicial disapproval does not seem particularly troublesome. First, the remedy is usually only a remand to the agency to fix the offending procedural lapse.[264] Second, as William Eskridge has documented, agencies win most cases where rules are challenged in court on both substantive and procedural grounds.[265] Third, even if some agencies would prefer not to engage in notice and comment rulemaking, most continue to do so,[266] and some use the process even when not required because it increases the legitimacy of their policies. Judicial review adds extra time, but does not imply that rulemaking itself is under threat.

Proposals for reform should, we argue, concentrate both on making the process smoother and less time-consuming and on facilitating the involvement of underrepresented groups affected by the rules. As a recent essay on the Securities and Exchange Commission stated, individual prosecutions for wrongdoing grab the headlines and get public attention; the rulemaking process seems technical and boring in contrast.[267] Yet regulation cannot proceed effectively in most areas without rules to inform regulated entities and to guide enforcement. Thus, rulemaking is here to stay, and hence, reforms ought to seek to help diffuse groups overcome collective action problems, aid the participation of poorly funded interests, and inform the public about the implications of policy choices. Some criticize government funding for participation because it seems to put public officials in the position of judging who is both worthy and resource constrained. Other (more well-funded) participants argue that giving agencies discretion to fund

263 Jerry L. Mashaw & David L. Harfst, The Struggle for Auto Safety (1990).

264 Wagner, *supra* note 199.

265 Matthew R. Christiansen & William N. Eskridge Jr., *Congressional Overrides of Supreme Court Statutory Interpretation Decisions, 1967–2011*, Draft, Faculty Workshop, Yale Law School, January 27, 2014.

266 There are generally 2,500 to 4,500 final rules promulgated by federal agencies each year. Maeve P. Carey, Congressional Research Service, Counting Regulations: An Overview of Rulemaking, Types of Federal Regulations, and Pages in the Federal Register 5 (May 1, 2013).

267 Nicholas Lemann, *Street Cop*, New Yorker, Nov. 11, 2013, at 52 ("[I]t has been more than three years since President Obama signed Dodd-Frank into law, and much of it – including the Volcker Rule – has not been implemented, because the S.E.C. and other agencies have not finalized the rules. The financial industry is intensely engaged in trying to shape these rules, while the rest of the country has lost interest. The economy is in better shape. Prosecution is retrospective, and narratively riveting. Regulation is prospective, and boring and technical.")

participants could skew the process. This is, of course, a rather ironic claim given the existing tilt toward prosperous economic interests, at least in the volume of comments, but the critics do make a serious point. Although some evidence suggests that agency officials compensate for the biased nature of comments in making policy,[268] it would surely be beneficial for them to hear a wide range of voices. There are ways to overcome this objection given modern methods of communicating through the Internet. First, agencies could follow the lead of the EPA and others in beginning open and transparent consultation processes before the legally mandated APA procedures begin.[269] Second, agencies could make more concerted efforts at broad outreach.[270] Third, they could build on submitted comments to reach out through social media to those who might either oppose the rule or further develop issues raised in comments. Such actions would be less subject to accusations of bias because one point of view or information source is already in the docket. Fourth, funding the expense of participation – both travel funds and easy access to information – can help level the playing field. However, decisions about whom to fund and how much should not be made by the agency itself. Here legislation would be needed to set standards and assure legality. Perhaps either a cadre of administrative law judges or the GAO could take on this role.[271]

268 *See, e.g.*, David C. Nixon et al., *With Friends like These: Rule-Making Comment Submissions to the Securities and Exchange Commission*, **12** J. of Public Administration Research & Theory 59, 72–3 (2002) ("[C]ommenters one would expect to be more advantaged before the commission were more often rebuffed than the generic category of commenters.").

269 Wagner, *supra* note 199.

270 Some agencies are already making an outreach effort. For example, the Small Business Administration maintains a blog, The Small Business Watchdog, to post announcements of proposed rulemakings of interest to its readership, including those of other agencies. *See, e.g.*, *Small Business Regulatory Alert: Deadline Extended for Comments on Passenger Vessel Accessibility Guidelines*, The Small Business Watchdog (Aug. 14, 2013), http://weblog.sba.gov/blog-advo/?p=2397 (blog post); *Regulatory Alerts: FDA Issues Two Draft Rules on Safety of Imported Food*, The Small Business Watchdog (Aug. 8, 2013), http://weblog.sba.gov/blog-advo/?p=2390 (blog post). *See also*, Cary Coglianese, Federal Agency Use of Electronic Media in the Rulemaking Process: Final Report to the Administrative Conference of the United States 8–11 (Dec. 5, 2011) (evaluating the development of agency online outreach efforts and noting that the EPA and the Commodities Futures Trading Commission have developed easily accessible and comprehensive online portals to their respective rulemaking processes).

271 This last proposal differs from existing review by the Office of Information and Regulatory Affairs in the White House. That review focuses on substance under a cost/benefit test, not participation, and it is housed in a highly political location, even if its heads assert their commitment to expert competence. *See* Rose-Ackerman, *supra* note 215 (recommending that OIRA be made independent of the White House).

These reforms focus on agency actions to enhance the democratic legitimacy and competence of rulemaking, some of which require legislative action. The courts could enter the picture consistent with their ongoing role in overseeing the administrative process. They already understand that one goal of the rulemaking process is to further democratic legitimacy. It does not seem a particularly large step to add to that mandate a concern for the representative character of these procedures. They could nudge agencies in that direction by reviewing the range of opinions and participants that came before the agency, not only to see if their comments were taken into account, but also to ask if there are important gaps in coverage.

However, there are inherent limits to judicial activism in this area. Even if judges wanted to take on this type of review, no one might bring cases. After all, if a group is unable to participate for financial reasons or does not even know that a rulemaking is occurring or understand its implications, it is unlikely to bring a suit and may be denied standing if it does.[272] The particular problems with the American administrative law of rulemaking seem unlikely to be solved by lawsuits. Reform will require pressure on agencies and Congress by those concerned with weaknesses in the rulemaking process; it will not occur in the courts.

C. The United States as a Case Study

As we noted in our introduction, the United States is a special case compared with South Africa, Germany, and the European Union. The key point to remember is the sharp distinction in the United States between judicial review of legislative and administrative rulemaking processes. Broad policy is made in both fora, but the courts only provide intensive review of administrative agency procedures. Congress is largely left to make and enforce its own rules. As an empirical matter, we argue that this asymmetry arose from the presidential structure of government that is missing from

[272] In some areas of law, one-sided fee-shifting rules permit civil society groups that win a suit (or substantially prevail) to have their legal fees paid by the government, but these provisions only come into play ex post. Congress has passed more than 150 fee-shifting provisions [Ruckelshaus v. Sierra Club, 463 U.S. 680, 684 (1983)]. Fee shifting is especially prominent in environmental law, where such provisions are found in all major U.S. environmental statutes except for the National Environmental Policy Act, the Federal Insecticide, Fungicide and Rodenticide Act, the Coastal Zone Management Act, the Oil Pollution Act of 1990, and the Pollution Prevention Act of 1990. Lucia A. Silecchia, *The Catalyst Calamity: Post-Buckhannon Fee-Shifting in Environmental Litigation and a Proposal for Congressional Action*, **29** Columbia J. of Environmental. Law 1, 10–11 (2004).

our other cases. The legislature has an incentive to ask the courts to review administrative procedures because it is unable adequately to do so itself. However, we show that the asymmetry, although valid, misses some recent developments. Absent statutory texts, the Supreme Court has sometimes intruded on legislative procedures to resolve constitutional challenges. We argue, however, that rather than furthering democratic values, its interventions seem inconsistent with those values. We will consider interventionist decisions by the courts in our other cases and ask if they raise similar worries or if they further democratic legitimacy.

Furthermore, we see much of value in judicial oversight of rulemaking in the executive, a practice that one seldom observes in the other cases. In parliamentary systems, the legislature has little incentive to enact a law like the U.S. APA absent intense outside pressure. Yet such procedural constraints may be just as valuable in such systems because widespread policymaking delegation occurs there, as well, in spite of, or even because of, the unitary structure of government. Thus, we will examine judicial review of executive and agency rulemaking in our other cases, and we critique their experiences in light of the values of democracy, competence, and rights protection.

3

South Africa

We begin our exploration of parliamentary states with South Africa, an intriguing case of an emerging democracy with a constitutional court that is developing a distinctive jurisprudence. The German Constitution with its focus on rights was one of the more important sources drawn on during the constitution-drafting process. Legitimacy through the protection of rights is very important in a society where rights were long denied to many and where the judiciary was accused of excessive deference during the apartheid era. However, South African constitutionalism also displays a distinctive concern for democratic legitimacy and, especially, for openness and public participation.

The apartheid history exerts pressure on the courts to act firmly in support of rights and values, but judges also seek to uphold the benefits of technical competence and efficiency in their engagement with the new constitution. Their departure point in responding to the constitutional changes was the often restrictive pre-1994 understanding of the judicial role inherited from the British Westminster system. Prior to 1994, South African law distinguished sharply between judicial review of legislative and administrative activity. Much as in the United States, judicial scrutiny of legislative processes was confined to a few cases of blatant noncompliance with explicit formal requirements for the passage of legislation.[1] Judicial scrutiny of administrative acts was much more extensive. There was no review of the procedural fairness of rulemaking activity, although pre-

[1] Harris v Minister of the Interior 1952 (2) SA 428 (A); Minister of Interior v Harris 1952 (4) SA 769 (A). Even these clear violations proved very controversial, and the two *Harris* judgments led to the packing of the Appellate Division, then South Africa's highest court. On the saga and its outcome, *see* DENNIS DAVIS & MICHELLE LE ROUX, PRECEDENT AND POSSIBILITY: THE USE AND (AB)USE OF LAW IN SOUTH AFRICA (2009), chapter 1.

1994 reformers drew on the U.S. example to argue for such review.[2] Courts generally required procedural fairness in administrative decisions affecting individuals, but they were cautious about overburdening the government by extending these requirements to activities such as rulemaking that affected large groups of people.[3] The substance of the rules and their impact on individuals could, however, be subject to fairly extensive review.

The transition to full democracy and the passage of the 1993 and 1996 Constitutions as well as the Promotion of Administrative Justice Act (PAJA) in 2000 ushered in major changes whose full implications are still being worked out. Because all legislative and executive powers are now subject to an expansive, value-driven constitution, the traditional distinctions between the judicial review of legislative and administrative power, and of different kinds of administrative decision, have eroded somewhat.[4] The Constitutional Court has articulated a "due delegation" doctrine, reviewed the legislative process to determine whether reasonable steps have been taken to facilitate public participation, and analyzed statutory substance under several legal rubrics. It has yet to decide whether PAJA applies to administrative rulemaking. However, it may reach that question soon because the Supreme Court of Appeal has stated that PAJA does apply to rulemaking.[5] The presence of broader constitutional values binding all exercises of public power, however, means that rulemaking is, in any event, subject to quite extensive judicial review. Because of the presence of these overarching norms, judicial review across policymaking arenas appears to

[2] See, e.g., Lawrence G. Baxter, *Rule-making and Policy Formulation in South African Administrative-law Reform*, in ADMINISTRATIVE LAW REFORM 176–8, 183 (T. W. Bennett et al., eds., 1993); and Catherine O'Regan, *Rules for Rule making: Administrative Law and Subordinate Legislation* in *id.* at 162–74.

[3] CORA HOEXTER, ADMINISTRATIVE LAW IN SOUTH AFRICA (2ND ED.), 407–8 (2012). *See also* Minister of Health v New Clicks South Africa (Pty) Ltd 2006 (2) SA 311 (CC), para. 617: "In the pre-democratic South African administrative law tradition, little attention was given to the process by which administrative rules or standards were formulated by public authorities" (judgment of Sachs J).

[4] For a review of both the rejection of old categories and the introduction of new technicalities under some of the definitions in the Promotion of Administrative Justice Act 3 of 2000 [hereinafter, PAJA], *see* Geo Quinot, *Substantive Reasons in Administrative-law Adjudication* 3 CONSTITUTIONAL COURT REV. 111, 114–18 (2010) [hereinafter, *Substantive Reasons*].

[5] City of Tshwane Metropolitan Municipality v Cable City (Pty) Ltd 2010 (3) SA 589 (SCA), para. 10; *see* further Geo Quinot, *Administrative Law* ANNUAL SURVEY OF SOUTH AFRICAN LAW 41, 53 (2010) [hereinafter, *Administrative Law*]. For the Constitutional Court's non-definitive statements to date, *see* Jonathan Klaaren & Glenn Penfold, *Just Administrative Action*, in CONSTITUTIONAL LAW OF SOUTH AFRICA (2ND ED.), 63–38 – 63–44 (Stu Woolman & Michael Bishop, eds., 2005).

be converging, but it remains an open question how far this convergence will extend. In many areas the law remains unsettled, and our conclusions are tentative.

We discuss how the South African courts have reviewed both substance and public participation in legislative and administrative decision-making processes. South Africa is essentially a parliamentary system. The constitutional structure includes a president, but he is elected by the National Assembly at its first sitting after parliamentary elections or whenever there is a vacancy.[6] He is both head of state and chief executive and can be removed by a vote of no confidence.[7] Thus, he is effectively a prime minister.

The standard incentives in parliamentary systems accordingly apply. Even though the general thrust of the trend is overwhelmingly toward more constitutional control – reflecting the revolutionary postapartheid shift from parliamentary to constitutional supremacy – the standard incentives are clearly visible in the pattern administrative law reforms have taken. The constitution drafters introduced a bold new fundamental right to just administrative action in s 24 of the 1993 interim text, but they added some limitations in subsequent drafts because "such rights were seen as having a potentially inhibitory effect" on the new government's ability to act.[8] When the 1996 Constitution was being drafted, the African National Congress (ANC) already had experience in government, and some members pushed to remove the administrative justice right altogether. The subsequent compromise retained the right in the 1996 text, but suspended its operation pending the enactment of legislation to give it effect.[9]

The resulting legislation, PAJA, reflects the desire to temper the new administrative justice regime, producing the oddity that the constitutionally mandated statute giving effect to the right to just administrative action appears to be of narrower application than the right itself. PAJA contains a quite restrictive definition of administrative action. One judge has commented that the definition "serves not so much to attribute meaning

6 Constitution of the Republic of South Africa, 1996 [hereinafter, 1996 Constitution], s 86(1).

7 *Id.*, ss 83(a), 84–5, 102(2).

8 Hugh Corder, *Administrative Justice in the Final Constitution* **13** South African J. on Human Rights 28, 30 (1997).

9 *Id.*, at 30–4; Jonathan Klaaren, *Constitutional Authority to Enforce the Rights of Administrative Justice and Access to Information* **13** South African J. on Human Rights 549 (1997). As they note, the decision also reflected U.S. law professor Michael Asimov's recommendation that legislation be enacted in order to ensure that the broad rights in the text stayed manageable: *see* Michael Asimov, *Administrative Law under South Africa's Final Constitution: The Need for an Administrative Justice Act* **113** South African Law J. 613 (1997).

to the term as to limit its meaning by surrounding it with a palisade of qualification."[10] This attempt at definitional limitation has also produced the long uncertainty over PAJA's application to rulemaking.

The legislature also chose to omit some of the more expansive elements of the draft PAJA prepared by the South African Law Reform Commission. The Act's most radical innovation in the South African context is its application to large-scale administrative decision making in s 4.[11] However, the final Act gives officials considerable discretion in implementing s 4, and decisions about whether to conduct public participation are not themselves reviewable.[12] The final Act also delayed the coming into effect of s 4 in order to give officials more time to prepare,[13] and the statute of limitations for claims under PAJA is 180 days, which is much shorter than usual.[14]

This pattern reflects a key aspect of the play of forces in South Africa. The constitution drafters, with visionary aims, instituted bold new ideas in administrative law as they did in other contexts, but the standard incentives of ordinary parliamentary government tempered their implementation, in line with our expectations. Indeed, these incentives are particularly clear-cut in South Africa. The ANC has held a clear majority in Parliament since 1994 and has never needed to govern in coalition. It has also exercised strong party discipline, particularly during the Mbeki administration (1999–2008), which concentrated power in the presidency. As a result,

[10] Grey's Marine Hout Bay (Pty) Ltd v Minister of Public Works 2005 (6) SA 313 (SCA), para. 21, per Nugent JA.

[11] *See, e.g.*, Cora Hoexter, *The Future of Judicial Review in South African Administrative Law* **117** SOUTH AFRICAN LAW J. 484, 496–7, 514–19 (2000). She also comments, in line with our analysis, that "[i]t seems unlikely that the government will ever again have the necessary incentive to impose further tedious administrative procedures on itself"; *Id.* at 499.

[12] PAJA, s 1(i)(b)(*ii*). The section does not prevent courts from reviewing, in terms of PAJA, the adequacy of the public participation processes that officials choose to conduct – *see* the cases discussed later in this chapter. Furthermore, decisions about whether to conduct public participation are subject to general constitutional norms even if the PAJA does not apply. This seems to be the only way to invalidate a decision for failure to conduct a public participation process, where the relevant regulation gave the official discretion to conduct a public participation "if necessary … in the circumstances," in Shear v Eye of Africa Development (Pty) Ltd 2010 (5) SA 129 (GSJ). The decision does not consider s 4 or s 1(i)(b)(*ii*) of PAJA. The appeal court upheld the decision, but the point is not clear from its judgment either: *see* Eye of Africa Developments (Pty) Ltd v Shear 2012 (2) SA 186 (SCA).

[13] *See* Margaret Beukes, *The Constitutional Foundation of the Implementation and Interpretation of the Promotion of Administrative Justice Act 3 of 2000*, in THE RIGHT TO KNOW: SOUTH AFRICA'S PROMOTION OF ADMINISTRATIVE JUSTICE AND ACCESS TO INFORMATION ACTS, 11 (Claudia Lange & Jakkie Wessels, eds., 2004).

[14] Compare PAJA, s 7(1) with the Prescription Act 68 of 1969, providing for periods from three to thirty years.

Parliament has been even less likely to act to constrain "its" executive than standard incentives imply.[15]

Despite these concessions to political pressures, however, bold ideals do remain in the Constitution and amount to a potentially expansive grant of jurisdiction to the judiciary. Judicial review of lawmaking procedures and of legal substance is active and expanding. Of particular importance is the 1996 Constitution's unusually strong concern for public accountability and participation that responds to South Africa's history of political exclusion. The case law also reflects the Constitutional Court's strong commitment to furthering democratic values and rights, which has driven some expansive readings of the text. This broad backdrop means that less turns on the details of particular statutory provisions or rights. In Germany, administrative rulemaking is not subject to specific legislation, and this legal lacuna limits judicial review. By contrast, the fate of the judicial review of rulemaking in South Africa does not only depend on judicial interpretations of the scope of PAJA but also rests on the broad underlying constitutional norms that can provide a substantial basis for judicial review.

This might seem to imply an acrimonious pattern in which Parliament and the ANC seek to limit constitutional restrictions while the judiciary works to impose them. This, however, has not generally been the case. One explanation is that the constitutional order is relatively new: As in the EU, institutional boundaries and roles are still being settled, and so decisive battles have yet to be joined. Another reason is that the judiciary has often been cautious in cashing out new provisions, which further avoids or defers conflict.[16] As we will see, judges have also generally been alive to the need to respect democratic authority and the separation of powers, and to avoid imposing onerous requirements that would hobble administrative efficiency, as our model envisages. Finally, the attitude of the ANC government is important. It has generally respected judicial authority.[17] In addition, the

[15] *See, e.g.*, Richard Calland, Anatomy of South Africa: Who Holds the Power? 58–9, 85–114 (2006); William Gumede, Thabo Mbeki and the Battle for the Soul of the ANC, 76, 156–61, 169–76 (updated ed., 2007); Heinz Klug, The Constitution of South Africa: A Contextual Analysis 168–81 (2010); Sujit Choudhry, *"He Had a Mandate": The South African Constitutional Court and the African National Congress in a Dominant Party Democracy* **2** Constitutional Court Rev. 1, 10–12 (2009), and further sources there cited.

[16] *See* Theunis Roux, The Politics of Principle: The First South African Constitutional Court, 1995–2005, e.g., 288–92 (2013).

[17] Klug, *supra* note 15, at 7, 248–9, 295; Roux, *supra* note 16, chapter 4; and generally James Fowkes, Building the Constitution: The Practice of Constitutional Interpretation in Post-Apartheid South Africa (Yale JSD thesis, 2014).

values in the Constitution often align with the party's substantive commitments – unsurprisingly, considering the ANC's leading role in creating the document. Of course, the party does not always live up to those commitments, but judicial enforcement of values has often not meant imposing ideas sharply out of step with the ideals of those in government.[18]

South African constitutionalism is highly expansive. Rather than a limited set of checks on power, the 1996 Constitution aspires to be a blueprint for the whole system. Instead of rights being a constitutional variable limiting and limited by the other two variables of democracy and efficiency, all three variables find a place *within* constitutional doctrine to a degree greater than in the other systems we examine. Witness the fact that administrative justice is a fundamental right, and one that itself makes explicit reference to efficiency.[19] Or consider the way that the Constitution treats democracy as a pervasive value, to be built into rights analysis and to be actively promoted by the judiciary as a good in itself – something that has had a profound, distinctive effect on South African constitutional review.[20]

The emerging result is a general – and, partly because of its generality, often quite vague – set of value-based doctrines applying to all public power. Judicial review asks all institutions the same constitutional question: What does giving effect to constitutional values require of this actor in this context? Institutional differences still matter, of course. The balance between rights, democracy, and efficiency will be struck differently if a court is dealing with an elected institution compared with an unelected one. The various roles that institutions play can lead to differences in what is required of them in particular situations. But nevertheless, constitutional supremacy implies that the courts should ask the question of all institutions equally. Judicial review in South Africa increasingly reflects this simple, paradigm-shifting fact. Its effect will by no means be to obliterate the

[18] *See, e.g.*, Klug, *supra* note 15, at 241: "Despite … at times, blatant disrespect for rights by some government officials, government consistently and publicly asserts the notion that South Africa is building a culture of rights based on the new Constitution." The best example in the present context is *Doctors for Life*; see *infra* note 35. One of us has argued that this pattern has been a more general feature of South Africa's constitutionalism since the demise of apartheid and that the ANC's stance has underwritten the Constitutional Court's celebrated decisions to a much greater degree than it usually acknowledged – see Fowkes, *supra* note 17.

[19] 1996 Constitution, s 33(3) states that the legislation that must be enacted to give effect to the right must "(c) promote an efficient administration." Efficiency is also one of the values governing public administration – s 195(1)(b).

[20] For the leading articulation of this idea, see Theunis Roux, *Democracy*, in Constitutional Law of South Africa (2nd ed.) (Stu Woolman & Michael Bishop, eds., 2005).

distinction between legislative and administrative review, but in area after area, the two standards are converging.

I. "DUE DELEGATION"

Prior to the enactment of the 1993 interim Constitution, parliamentary supremacy prevailed, closely following the Westminster model of parliamentary democracy. The legislature could delegate power as it saw fit, and it sometimes gave the president the authority to amend or repeal statutes.[21] Although neither the 1993 text nor its 1996 successor contains an express limit on delegation, the Constitutional Court has read these texts as imposing much greater constraints on the delegation of power to the executive than was acceptable under the prior constitutional order.[22]

Limits on delegated power in the 1996 Constitution are drawn from the doctrine of separation of powers and from particular constitutional provisions. As a general matter, the legislature has the responsibility to pass laws. This means that plenary legal power should not be delegated, save in exceptional circumstances; it must be "due delegation." Furthermore, specific constitutional constraints on delegation relate to particular powers. If the Constitution specifically states that a matter is to be determined by legislation, the Court will treat that as a strong indication that the power cannot be delegated and that the matter must be regulated by statute.[23]

The Court has also placed rights-based limitations on delegation. Where rights are at stake, the Court has required Parliament to guard against abuses and, where necessary, to provide statutory guidance for the exercise of delegated power.[24] For example, the Court invalidated a statute that delegated wide-ranging decision-making powers on the grounds that it did not contain the internal constraints necessary to ensure that fair procedures were observed in their exercise, as the fundamental right to just administrative

[21] Hoexter, *supra* note 3, at 263.

[22] Beginning with Executive Council, Western Cape Legislature v President of the Republic of South Africa 1995 (4) SA 877 (CC), decided under the 1993 interim constitution. The principles in that decision are applicable under the 1996 Constitution: see Executive Council, Western Cape v Minister for Provincial Affairs and Constitutional Development 2000 (1) SA 661 (CC), para. 124.

[23] See Michael Bishop & Ngwako Raboshakga, *National Legislative Authority* in Constitutional Law of South Africa (2nd ed.), 17–47–17–48 (Stu Woolman & Michael Bishop, eds., 2005) and Justice Alliance of South Africa v President of the Republic of South Africa 2011 (5) SA 388 (CC).

[24] Dawood v Minister of Home Affairs; Shalabi v Minister of Home Affairs; Thomas v Minister of Home Affairs 2000 (3) SA 936 (CC), esp. paras 42–8.

action required.[25] Like its German counterpart, the Court has recognized that it might not always be feasible for the legislature to give statutory guidance, for example in the case of very complex decisions involving the consideration of a large number of factors.[26] The legislative duty to promote, protect, and fulfill rights does not, therefore, result in a duty to give specific statutory guidance every time it delegates power. But this qualification notwithstanding, "the reasoning employed in these cases yields up a fairly rigorous anti-delegation principle."[27]

Some limited moves to oversee delegation have come from the provincial legislatures. In 2008, the Gauteng Provincial Legislature enacted a statute that provided for the legislative review of delegated legislation, as contemplated (though not required) in the Constitution.[28] The original statute required the executive to submit all delegated legislation to the legislature after enactment. In 2011, the legislature strengthened the mechanism to provide for pre-enactment review: All delegated legislation must be submitted in draft form to the legislature for scrutiny and approval or disapproval. The legislature is also obliged to ensure that all such legislation is recorded in a central, publicly accessible index.[29] In 2012, the KwaZulu-Natal provincial legislature enacted a much blunter statute that simply withdraws all previous delegations, but suspends the withdrawal for a year to permit the legislature to review and extend the delegation if it wishes. It does not, however, create a permanent mechanism of the sort established in Gauteng.[30]

These statutes represent the high water mark of legislative efforts. Earlier proposals to establish a general review mechanism for delegated legislation in the national parliament appear to have stalled.[31] This is not, however, due to a constitutional obstacle of the sort that arose in the United States in *INS v. Chadha*. The Constitution certainly permits the National Assembly to establish a review mechanism, and may in fact oblige it to do so, and

[25] Janse van Rensburg v Minister of Trade and Industry 2001 (1) SA 29 (CC), paras 24–5.

[26] *Dawood*, para. 53.

[27] Hoexter, *supra* note 3, at 265; *see also* Bishop & Raboshakga, *supra* note 23, at 17–48 - 17–51.

[28] Gauteng Scrutiny of Subordinate Legislation Act 5 of 2008; for the constitutional mandate, *see* 1996 Constitution, ss 140(3) and (4); Jonathan Klaaren & Sanele Sibanda, *Introducing the Gauteng Scrutiny of Subordinate Legislation Act* **25** South African J. on Human Rights 161, 161 (2009).

[29] Scrutiny Act, *supra* note 28, ss 2–6 (as amended in the Gauteng Scrutiny of Subordinate Legislation Amendment Act 2 of 2011); we have benefited from correspondence with Jonathan Klaaren on this point.

[30] KwaZulu-Natal Delegation of Powers Repeal Act 3 of 2012.

[31] Klaaren & Sibanda, *supra* note 28, at 169–70.

Parliament has included legislative veto mechanisms in statutes in the past without judicial objection.[32]

II. STANDING

The 1993 and 1996 Constitutions contain expansive provisions for standing to enforce fundamental rights, and the Court has taken a generous approach to the issue. A party may raise rights violations in the public interest or on behalf of others even if they have not themselves suffered harm, and these broad standing rules have been extended to constitutional issues other than rights violations.[33]

However, standing is not completely unlimited.[34] For one thing, the Constitutional Court has indicated that it will adopt a more restrictive approach to standing in the context of challenges to legislative procedures, on the ground that it is important to avoid undue interference with the legislature's functioning. In the *Doctors for Life* case, discussed in detail later in this chapter, it held that standing will not usually be granted where a person has not approached the legislature first.[35] This is in line with the Court's decision in *New National Party*, where it ruled that a political party lacked standing to challenge whether a government department was sufficiently respecting the Electoral Commission's independence in its dealings with it. The Court found that the Commission was maintaining its own independence successfully. The decision illustrates the balance the Court is seeking to strike: Important institutions should generally be

32 1996 Constitution, s 55(2) reads: "The National Assembly must provide for mechanisms (a) to ensure that all executive organs of state in the national sphere of government are accountable to it; and (b) to maintain oversight of (i) the exercise of national executive authority, including the implementation of legislation; and (ii) any organ of state." *See also* Klaaren & Sibanda, *supra* note 28, at 171–3, and the discussion later in this chapter of another part of s 55 on public participation. For a legislative veto mechanism, *see, e.g.*, the Local Government Transition Act 209 of 1993, s 50(4)(b); the Constitutional Court reviewed the statute in *Executive Council* (1995), *supra* note 22, but the inclusion of the legislative veto mechanism was not challenged or questioned in that case.

33 1996 Constitution, s 38 (broad standing in rights cases), which has in turn been generously construed by the Constitutional Court: Ferreira v Levin NO; Vryenhoek v Powell NO 1996 (1) SA 984 (CC), paras 165, 227–30. On standing in non-rights constitutional cases, *see* Kruger v President of the Republic of South Africa 2009 (1) SA 417 (CC), para. 23; Freedom Under Law v Acting Chairperson: Judicial Services Commission 2011 (3) SA 549 (SCA), para. 19; and the cases discussed in the following paragraphs.

34 Contrary to the comment to this effect in Van Rooyen v S 2001 (4) SA 396 (T), 423G-H.

35 Doctors for Life International v Speaker of the National Assembly 2006 (6) SA 416 (CC), paras 216–21.

permitted to operate free from interference, and hence individuals will be granted standing only when this is necessary to ensure that the institutions operate constitutionally.[36] That said, the Court has yet to refuse a challenge to parliamentary procedures on standing grounds (although it has done so on grounds of jurisdiction, as we discuss under the next heading).

The Court has also recently clarified that standing to challenge procedures is somewhat more restricted if the applicant cannot demonstrate a general public interest.[37] Standing in such cases is still often available because the fundamental right to administrative action in s 33 is at stake, and the generous constitutional provisions on standing to enforce fundamental rights therefore apply.[38] (A similar approach applies to cases dealing with the general constitutional principle of legality; hence, nothing turns on whether the procedure in question is adjudged "administrative" for the purposes of the s 33 right.)[39] However, a litigant who does not demonstrate a public interest will need to show some direct personal interest in the decision in order to challenge the procedure.[40] This is in keeping with the principle of protecting institutions from challenges not necessary to protect rights, while preserving generous space for judicial review for those whose interests are genuinely affected.[41]

[36] New National Party v Government of the Republic of South Africa 1999 (3) SA 191 (CC), para. 107; *Doctors for Life*, *supra* note 35, at para. 221.

[37] Giant Concerts CC v Rinaldo Investments (Pty) Ltd 2013 (3) BCLR 251 (CC).

[38] *Id.*, paras 28–9. The Court there endorses Cora Hoexter's criticism of an earlier High Court judgment that had implausibly held that because PAJA was only a statute, the broader constitutional rules of standing did not apply and its s 6(1) conferring standing on "any person" to institute review proceedings should be more narrowly interpreted. *See* Democratic Alliance v Acting National Director of Public Prosecutions (North Gauteng High Court), unreported judgment handed down February 22, 2011, paras 19–37; HOEXTER, *supra* note 3, at 491–500. The Supreme Court of Appeal decision, also criticizing the High Court, is discussed in the next footnote.

[39] Democratic Alliance v Acting National Director of Public Prosecutions 2012 (3) SA 486 (SCA), paras 38–45. The case was heard as an appeal to a restrictive High Court approach to standing under PAJA – *see* the preceding footnote – but the SCA decided the case on the basis of the general legality principle rather than PAJA.

[40] *Giant Concerts*, *supra* note 37, at paras 41, 55.

[41] *See esp.* in this context Minister of Home Affairs v Eisenberg & Associates In re: Eisenberg & Associates v Minister of Home Affairs 2003 (5) SA 281 (CC), recognizing the own-interest standing of an attorney to challenge the validity of regulations on the basis that they were made without a required public consultation procedure. In that case the attorney's practice was deeply concerned with the immigration-law substance of the regulations. *See also* the discussion of *Eisenberg* and other related cases in *Giant Concerts*, *supra* note 37, at paras 36–42, 50–1.

III. JURISDICTION

The 1996 Constitution is expansive, and so, as a result, is the jurisdiction of the courts.[42] This is readily apparent in the administrative context, where conduct may be reviewed under PAJA, or failing that under the s 33 right to just administrative action, or failing *that* based on general constitutional principles, such as legality. The principle of legality is understood to impose several traditional administrative law standards, and there are additional possibilities of review under other rights and values.[43] The all-pervading presence of rights and values in the Constitution means that the courts will never lack a potential basis for jurisdiction whenever they think that review is desirable.

This broad view of jurisdiction holds for the review of a legislature's internal procedural decisions.[44] Apartheid-era legislation permitting Parliament to order the termination of any judicial proceedings on grounds of parliamentary privilege was repealed in 2004.[45] The courts have repeatedly confirmed their jurisdiction to review such matters (and have made a number of findings of unconstitutionality, discussed under the next heading). However, the Constitutional Court has also recognized significant restrictions on the exercise of this jurisdiction. It has held that it has jurisdiction to review legislative activity prior to the completion of the legislative process, but only in the most extraordinary circumstances where serious constitutional harm cannot otherwise be prevented.[46] It has also held that it has jurisdiction to engage in abstract review of statutes prior to their being signed by the president, but only in accordance with special constitutional

[42] 1996 Constitution, ss 165(1), 167(3)-(5), 172(1).

[43] For a recent illustration, *see* the firm rejection by the Supreme Court of Appeal of the half-hearted contention that because a prosecutorial decision fell outside PAJA, it was not subject to constitutional review except perhaps on very narrow grounds: *Democratic Alliance v Acting NDPP*, *supra* note 39, at paras 23–32. *See also New Clicks*, *supra* note 3, in which the judges disagreed on which legal norm was applicable but, nevertheless, considered many of the same doctrines and questions.

[44] Speaker of the National Assembly v De Lille 1999 (4) SA 863 (SCA), para. 14; *see* further under the next heading.

[45] Privileges of Parliament Act 91 of 1963, s 5, repealed by the Powers, Privileges and Immunities of Parliament and Provincial Legislatures Act 4 of 2004. (The whole of the 1963 Act has now been repealed, following the 2004 Act and the Financial Management of Parliament Act 10 of 2009.) S 5 had in fact earlier been ruled unconstitutional in De Lille v Speaker of the National Assembly 1998 (3) SA 430 (C), para. 41, but for some reason the order was not referred to the Constitutional Court for confirmation as required by s 172(2)(a) of the Constitution and so the invalidation was without effect.

[46] *Doctors for Life*, *supra* note 35, at paras 67–72; Glenister v President of the Republic of South Africa 2009 (1) SA 287 (CC), paras 28–51 and cases there discussed.

provisions for this review on the application of the president or members of Parliament.[47] In addition, the separation of powers naturally tempers any exercise of jurisdiction over decisions by the legislature, including its internal rules of procedure.[48]

IV. REVIEW OF THE LEGISLATIVE PROCESS

The expansive or novel elements of the Court's emerging approach to review of the legislative process can all be traced to its idea of democracy. The Court views legislative procedures as serving certain democratic ideas, including effective representation and public participation. The Court will invalidate procedures that fail to live up to these ideals, as well as any legislation arising from them.

A. Review of Public Participation in National and Provincial Legislative Processes

Most notably, the Constitutional Court has taken several cases that sought review of the legislative process to determine the adequacy of public participation. In two cases, it has invalidated statutes on this basis. The cases are all quite recent, and some later cases indicate that the Court will limit its reach. Nevertheless, in the context of our review of the U.S. and German cases, these decisions represent quite striking developments.

Unlike the U.S. and German constitutions, the 1996 South African Constitution explicitly provides that the National Assembly must "facilitate public involvement in the legislative and other processes of the Assembly and its committees."[49] Equivalent provisions apply to the National Council of Provinces, which is the second house of Parliament similar to the German Bundesrat, and to the provincial legislatures.[50] The text offers no further guidance.

In *Doctors for Life International v Speaker of the National Assembly*, the most famous case, the Court treated this language as the basis for a judicially

[47] *Doctors for Life*, *supra* note 35, paras 42–56. 1996 Constitution, ss 79–80 provide for abstract constitutional review in the national legislative process; ss 121–2 make analogous provision in the context of provincial legislation.

[48] *See* the comments in Lekota v Speaker, National Assembly (Western Cape High Court), unreported judgment handed down December 11, 2012, esp. paras 19–22, 39–40, 44, and further cases discussed under the next heading.

[49] 1996 Constitution, s 59(1)(a).

[50] 1996 Constitution, s 72(1)(a) (National Council of Provinces), s 118(1)(a) (provincial legislatures).

enforceable obligation of legislative bodies to take reasonable steps to facilitate public participation in the drafting of legislation.[51] The case concerned a challenge to several pieces of legislation, including statutes, on the sensitive issues of abortion and traditional healers, but also including an unremarkable bill on dental laboratory technicians. The National Council of Provinces (NCOP) had determined that provinces should hold public hearings or receive submissions from the public on the bills. Most provinces, however, did not do so. Some provincial legislatures indicated that they wanted to engage the public but were unable to do so within the time constraints imposed by the NCOP.

The majority judgment held that citizens have an implied fundamental right to political participation, and that the Court will apply the relatively demanding reasonableness standard in assessing legislative efforts to give effect to that right, although there is no mention of reasonableness in the relevant text.[52] It held that public participation is one of the requirements for the passage of legislation, so a failure to take reasonable steps to facilitate participation in the legislative process makes the legislation constitutionally invalid. With respect to the controversial bills on abortion and traditional healers, where there had been a good deal of public interest, it held that the paltry efforts made by several provincial legislatures were not reasonable. It placed considerable reliance on the fact that several legislatures had stated that hearings would be appropriate but then had not held them. By contrast, it held that it was not unreasonable to have held no hearings dealing with the legislation on dental technicians, which had attracted no public comments and little interest.[53] Thus, the scope of the duty to facilitate public participation varies with context. The *Doctors for Life* Court also suspended its order of invalidity to allow the legislatures concerned time to remedy the defect.

These judicial findings represent a bold, purposive reading of the text. The Constitution does not explain what it means to "facilitate public involvement," beyond affording people the opportunity to vote and participate in the activities of political parties. Section 59(1)(a) and its equivalents are not part of the process for the passage of legislation set out in the text. One might read the text as simply requiring the legislature to have a general policy for facilitating public participation, just as it must have in place measures providing for openness to the public and the media, the topic of the

[51] *Doctors for Life*, *supra* note 35.

[52] The reasonableness standard is discussed later in this chapter.

[53] *Doctors for Life*, *supra* note 35, at paras 167–92.

rest of the relevant sections. Read that way, judicial review would go no further than inquiring whether the legislature had such a policy in place.[54] The majority's approach, by contrast, goes much further. It reads these sections as implying significant judicial scrutiny of public participation processes. It is based on a robust conception of the inclusive, participatory democracy that the 1996 Constitution is said to envisage, and the opinion supports its arguments by reference to international and foreign sources that emphasize citizen participation as an important basis of established democracies.

These findings potentially considerably expand judicial oversight of parliamentary procedures, but it is not clear how far the Court will go. To date, it has invalidated four pieces of legislation on this basis – one of them a constitutional amendment. *Doctors for Life* invalidated two, and *Matatiele v President of the Republic of South Africa (2)*, handed down the same day, invalidated the other two statutes.[55] The Court has yet to invalidate any other legislation on this ground. The explanation may lie in the fact patterns of the cases. Each instance of invalidation involved failures at the provincial level. At least some of the provincial legislatures failed to hold public hearings on the draft legislation or held them in a grossly defective manner. For example, in one case traditional healers were given less than a day's notice of an opportunity to comment on draft legislation affecting their activities.[56] As the dissenting judgment of Justice Van der Westhuizen in *Doctors for Life* noted, it is not difficult to find a violation on those sorts of facts.[57] The subsequent cases concerned processes that were much less obviously flawed.

The later cases also illustrate some of the difficulties courts face in reviewing legislative procedures. In *Merafong Demarcation Forum v President of the Republic of South Africa*, the litigants claimed that a legislature that had heard from the public was obliged to return and re-consult when new facts made the legislature reverse its position. The Gauteng provincial legislature had held public hearings on the local implications of a proposed

[54] *See esp.* the dissenting judgment of Justice Yacoob in *Id.*

[55] Matatiele Municipality v President of the Republic of South Africa (No. 2) 2007 (2) SA 477 (CC).

[56] *Doctors for Life*, *supra* note 35, at para. 170 (day's notice given to traditional healers of hearing in Gauteng Provincial Legislature on Traditional Health Practitioners Act; on procedures in relation to that act *see generally* paras 167–81; on procedures in relation to the Choice of Termination of Pregnancy Amendment Act *see* paras 182–9. Challenges to two other pieces of legislation were rejected. In *Matatiele (2)*, *supra* note 55, compare the findings on the Eastern Cape Provincial Legislature, which was found to have complied with its duties (paras 70–3) with those on the KwaZulu-Natal Provincial Legislature, which did not (paras 74–84).

[57] *Doctors for Life*, *supra* note 35, dissenting judgment of Justice Van der Westhuizen, para. 244(6). *See also* Bishop & Raboshakga, *supra* note 23, at 17–72–17–73.

constitutional amendment that would shift provincial boundaries. The case arose because a particular municipality, Merafong, was to be located in the North West province. At the hearings, the majority of those who spoke favored inclusion in Gauteng instead. As a result, the legislature decided to support the constitutional amendment on the condition that Merafong be relocated to Gauteng. The National Council of Provinces, however, claimed that the legislature was obliged to vote yes or no on the whole amendment and could not propose specific changes. With local elections looming, the legislature acquiesced and supported the amendment unchanged. In the subsequent legal challenge, a divided Constitutional Court held that the legislature was well aware of the community's views but had decided it could not give effect to them, and that this was acceptable in a representative democracy. The decision not to hold further hearings was thus not unreasonable and so was not unconstitutional. It might have been courteous to do so, but in a democratic system it was for voters to decide whether their representatives had been disrespectful and vote accordingly.[58]

Poverty Alleviation Network v President of the Republic of South Africa was the sequel to *Matatiele (2)*. The legislature had sought to fix the public participation process that had earlier been found defective. The applicants contended that the legislature was just going through the motions and that the process was a mere charade designed to meet the legal requirements for a predetermined result. The Court, however, decided unanimously that the legislative officials had held hearings, had engaged with the people, and had listened. The Constitution did not require anything more.[59] The case shows the difficulties of testing this sort of procedural obligation. Extreme cases aside, deciding whether officials are just going through the motions requires the court to make judgments about the mental state and intentions of individual legislators, something the justices understandably resist doing. Nor can the mere fact that legislators stick to the same position after consultation mean that participation was inadequate; legislators can be obliged to listen, but they cannot be constitutionally obliged to do what the majority says in every case.[60] In two more recent cases, the Court unanimously rejected similar challenges.[61]

58 Merafong Demarcation Forum v President of the Republic of South Africa 2008 (5) SA 171 (CC).

59 Poverty Alleviation Network v President of the Republic of South Africa 2010 (6) BCLR 520 (CC).

60 *Merafong*, *supra* note 58, at para. 50; *Poverty Alleviation Network*, *supra* note 59, at para. 62; *see also* Michael Bishop, *Vampire or Prince? The Listening Constitution and Merafong Demarcation & Others v President of the Republic of South Africa* **2** CONSTITUTIONAL COURT REV. 313 (2009), esp. 338–40 [hereinafter, *Listening Constitution*].

61 *Glenister*, *supra* note 46; Moutse Demarcation Forum v President of the Republic of South Africa 2011 (11) BCLR 1158 (CC).

As these cases illustrate, the full implications of *Doctors for Life* remain somewhat uncertain. The *Doctors for Life* inquiry remains potentially rich soil for litigants who are given inadequate notice of hearings, are maliciously or carelessly excluded from processes, or are not provided with the materials to engage in an informed manner. Groups may have a plausible case if they are excluded because of particular vulnerabilities such as poverty, illiteracy, or geographic remoteness, if the legislature does not do enough to overcome these handicaps.[62] The failure of later challenges may simply reflect that the later cases concerned processes that were much less defective in these terms, and so one should not perhaps make too much of their failure.[63]

There is also a revealing backstory to this line of cases. Their most revolutionary premise, in a parliamentary system, is the idea that a court can get involved in judging how legislatures choose to conduct their business. But this premise has provoked little resistance from the legislatures in any of the cases. Opposing arguments have been confined to contending that whatever the justiciable threshold is, the legislature had met it, not that judicial review is inappropriate in this context in the first place. Indeed, in *Doctors for Life*, none of the respondents raised the jurisdictional questions or questioned the Court's competence to invalidate legislation in these circumstances. The Court itself had to ask for argument on these points.[64]

This attitude suggests that government actors have come to accept judicial authority even with respect to their own procedures.[65] But it also reflects the extent to which the dominant ANC government agrees with the idea behind the Court's findings. The ANC has long stressed the importance of involving the public in government, an idea emphasized during the drafting of the 1996 Constitution.[66] In 2005 – prior to the decision in *Doctors for*

[62] *Matatiele (2)*, *supra* note 55, at para. 68 held: "The more discrete and identifiable the potentially affected section of the population, and the more intense the possible effect on their interests, the more reasonable it would be to expect the Legislature to be astute to ensure that the potentially affected section of the population is given a reasonable opportunity to have a say." *See also Moutse*, *supra* note 61, at paras 57–60.

[63] Michael Bishop has also remarked on the fact that *Merafong* was "far trickier" a case than either *Doctors for Life* or *Matatiele (2)*: *see* Bishop, *Listening Constitution*, *supra* note 60, at 328. Athanosios Psygkas agrees that the later decisions represent "much less clear-cut cases of failure": Athanosios Efstratios Psygkas, *Revitalizing the "Liberty of Ancients" through Citizen Participation in the Legislative Process* 5 Annuaire International des Droit de l'Homme 720, 741 (2010).

[64] *Doctors for Life*, *supra* note 35, at paras 8–10; Directions issued by the Chief Justice dated September 22, 2005, available at www.constitutionalcourt.gov.za

[65] *See* text accompanying note 17, *supra*.

[66] *See, e.g.*, Hassen Ebrahim, The Soul of a Nation: Constitution-making in South Africa, 13–14, 240–2 (1998); Klug, *supra* note 15, at 114, 282; Vusi Gumede, *Public Policy-*

Life – a report to the Second World Conference of Speakers of Parliaments in New York took note of the "whole range of activities" initiated by the South African parliament to involve the public.[67] Efforts in this direction have also been made by provincial legislatures, although there have been some capacity problems.[68] One of the ANC's major policy initiatives since coming to power in 1994 has been to extend local government structures throughout South Africa, an initiative motivated in part by a wish to bring government closer to the people.[69] So the Court is being less radical than it may appear at first glance: it is codifying what legislatures already do or feel should be done, rather than imposing novel obligations in the face of political resistance. Furthermore, the ANC has responded to citizens' complaints

making in South Africa, in GOVERNMENT AND POLITICS IN THE NEW SOUTH AFRICA (3RD ED.) 164 (Albert Venter & Chris Landsberg, eds., 2006); MPHO PUTU, THE ROLE OF WARD COMMITTEES IN ENHANCING PUBLIC PARTICIPATION IN RUSTENBERG MUNICIPALITY: A CRITICAL EVALUATION (2006), available at http://www.ewisa.co.za/eWISAWaterworks/misc/MunicipalDocuments/NWDDisBonjala_Platinum/LMRustenberg/ward_committee_promoting_citizen_participation.pdf, 4.

67 INTER-PARLIAMENTARY UNION, PARLIAMENTARY INVOLVEMENT IN INTERNATIONAL AFFAIRS (Report to Second World Conference of Speakers of Parliaments, September 2005) available at www.ipu.org/splz-e/sp-conf05/involvement-rpt.pdf, 21. The report was noted by the Court in *Doctors for Life*, *supra* note 35, at paras 132–3.

68 *See, e.g.*, SUSAN DE VILLIERS WITH RICHARD CALLAND & EBRAHIM FAKIR, A PEOPLE'S GOVERNMENT: THE PEOPLE'S VOICE – A REVIEW OF PUBLIC PARTICIPATION IN THE LAW AND POLICY-MAKING PROCESS IN SOUTH AFRICA, (June 2001), available at http://idasa.org.za/media/uploads/outputs/files/Public%20Participation%20in%20South%20Africa.pdf, esp. 37, 48–55; Dirk Besdziek *Provincial Government*, in GOVERNMENT AND POLITICS IN THE NEW SOUTH AFRICA (3RD ED.) 11 (Albert Venter & Chris Landsberg, eds., 2006); Yolanda Sadie, *Political Parties, Interest Groups and Social Movements*, in GOVERNMENT AND POLITICS IN THE NEW SOUTH AFRICA (3RD ED.) 221–2 (Albert Venter & Chris Landsberg, eds., 2006).

69 *See esp.* White Paper on Transforming Public Service Delivery (October 1, 1997) (local government obliged to engage community), referenced by Emile Raubenheimer, *Section 4 of PAJA: The Constitutional Standard for Participative Provisions in Land Use Management* **22** SOUTH AFRICAN PUBLIC LAW/SUID-AFRIKAANSE PUBLIEKREG 491 (2007); the White Paper on Local Government (March 9, 1998), available at http://www.info.gov.za/view/DownloadFileAction?id=108131; and the provisions of the Municipal Systems Act discussed under the next heading. *See also* Raenette Taljaard & Albert Venter, *Parliament*, in GOVERNMENT AND POLITICS IN THE NEW SOUTH AFRICA (3RD ED.) 29–30 (Albert Venter & Chris Landsberg, eds., 2006), (local government participation in national legislative process via South African Local Government Association); Werner Zybrands, *Local Government*, in GOVERNMENT AND POLITICS IN THE NEW SOUTH AFRICA (3RD ED.) 144–7 (Albert Venter & Chris Landsberg, eds., 2006) (public participation in Integrated Development Plans at the local level); STU WOOLMAN & BRAHM FLEISCH, THE CONSTITUTION IN THE CLASSROOM: LAW AND EDUCATION IN SOUTH AFRICA 1994–2008, 15–16 (2009) (ANC commitment to the idea of local democratic participation in the context of school governing bodies). Note that these efforts may have suffered somewhat during the centralizing efforts of the Mbeki administration – *see, e.g.*, Gumede, *supra* note 66, at 180–1 and sources cited in note 15, *supra*.

and demands for further engagement even in cases where the Court's ruling upheld its original process. Although *Merafong* held that no further consultation was constitutionally required, the ANC, under electoral pressure, chose to reengage with the community anyway and ultimately passed another amendment placing the community in the province it desired.[70] In the most recent case, arising out of the same reorganization of provincial boundaries but in a different municipality, the Court postponed judgment in order to allow the government to resolve the situation politically. During this time, the government of its own accord gave the applicants' legal representatives confidential cabinet minutes setting out the steps it was taking.[71]

The decision to make public participation justiciable illustrates how court involvement in such areas can bring highly politicized issues into the court's jurisdiction, requiring it to tread carefully to retain its legitimacy as it moves between its roles of adjudicator and mediator. The process of striking this balance is only beginning, as new decisions in related contexts reveal.

B. Review of Public Participation in Local Government

At the local government level, municipal councils have mixed legislative and executive competence. Public participation in their activities is not the subject of a specific constitutional provision, as in the context of national and provincial legislatures.[72] But there is a statutory analog, and it has recently received judicial attention.[73]

[70] See, e.g., *ANC Meets Forum over Merafong Demarcation* Mail & Guardian June 25, 2008; *Merafong to Be Returned to Gauteng* Mail & Guardian April 9, 2009. For a more detailed account of the turnaround, *see* Bishop, *Listening Constitution*, *supra* note 60, at 366–9.

[71] *Moutse*, *supra* note 61; *see* the court orders dated November 18, 2008 (postponement to seek political solution) and May 21, 2009 (disclosure of cabinet reports). Judgment was ultimately handed down on August 23, 2011 after a further hearing on March 11, 2011.

[72] 1996 Constitution, s 160(6) empowers municipal councils to prescribe rules for their own internal arrangements and proceedings, but the wording makes no reference to democracy or public involvement in the way that the equivalent provisions for national and provincial legislatures do. *See* Roux, *supra* note 20, at 10–38 n4. Note, however, that among the "Objects of local government" is the duty "to provide democratic and accountable government for local communities" – s 152(1)(a) – and the s 160(6) powers are to be read in light of these objects and other constitutional provisions: *see Executive Council, Western Cape* (2000), *supra* note 22, at para. 98.

[73] Local Government: Municipal Systems Act 32 of 2000, ss 16–22, 50–1. The provisions were implicated at the margins of one other unsuccessful challenge, South African Municipal Workers Union v City of Cape Town 2004 (1) SA 548 (SCA), paras 10–11, but the recent decisions are the first to apply it squarely.

Two recent Supreme Court of Appeal judgments invalidated decisions by municipal councils, holding that public participation processes did not meet the statutory threshold. *Democratic Alliance v eThekwini Municipality* holds that even though there is no equivalent constitutional provision that applies to local governments, the same reasonableness standard used by the Constitutional Court to assess provincial and national legislatures applies here.[74] The decision echoes key features of the Constitutional Court's judgments: the most important basis for the finding is that the municipal council had not lived up to its own views about what procedures are required. It also holds, in line with *Merafong*, that the electorate rather than the courts must ultimately be the judge of substantive decisions made on political grounds, and it is troubled about the inadequately short notice given to the public, just as in *Doctors for Life*.[75] The latter finding illustrates the considerable room that remains in the *Doctors for Life* standard to attack defective processes.

The second decision, *South African Property Owners Association v Johannesburg Metropolitan Municipality*, is more problematic. It adopts a position in some tension with *Merafong*, but makes no reference to that decision or any of the Constitutional Court's other public participation cases, or to the earlier decision in *eThekwini Municipality*. The municipality involved in the case had conducted the statutory public participation procedures in relation to a particular increase in taxes for nonresidential property. It had done so using a set timetable that did not provide for the possibility of amendments to the budget or further public participation in relation to any amendments. It then changed its mind and adopted a significantly larger tax increase and pushed it through using a much-truncated process. The court held that this was inadequate and ordered the municipality to reengage the public after the change.[76]

The judgment once again relies on the fact that the council had not complied with its own officials' views of what public processes would be appropriate, and that it had not given the parties adequate notice. However, it appears to treat the duty to reengage as a justiciable legal requirement, and not merely a matter of non-justiciable political courtesy as *Merafong* did.[77]

[74] Democratic Alliance v eThekwini Municipality 2012 (2) SA 151 (SCA), paras 24–5.

[75] *Id.* at paras 26, 29 (council's own standards); paras 31, 38 (electoral accountability); paras 27–8 (inadequately short time periods for public response).

[76] South African Property Owners Association v Johannesburg Metropolitan Municipality 2013 (1) SA 420 (SCA). Note that review of public participation in national and provincial legislatures falls within the exclusive jurisdiction of the Constitutional Court – 1996 Constitution, s 167(4)(e) – so the SCA has no case law of its own on that topic.

[77] *South African Property Owners Association*, *supra* note 76, at paras 22–4, 33–4, 38, 40.

The judgment does not consider this discrepancy. It is doubtful that one can explain it simply by the different institutional context. The municipality was exercising legislative competence in this case, and it has independent democratic and constitutional status; hence, it is not clear why judicial review should be stricter than for provincial or national legislatures.[78]

A more plausible basis for distinguishing the decisions is that further public participation in *Merafong* would not have produced new information or opinions. No new arguments were implicated by a decision to accept one side of a binary debate rather than the other, and so more engagement would have been of little substantive value to either state or participants. By contrast, a decision to adopt a significantly greater tax increase in response to unforeseen budgetary constraints may well have raised new issues or significantly more serious versions of old ones, so there was potentially something new for everyone to learn from further public engagement in the situation that arose in *South African Property Owners Association*. This interpretation would comport with the idea that the courts are not a substitute for the electoral process. Under this view, judges would require officials to engage with the public in order to promote good decision making; the government, therefore, must redo defective processes to further that aim. But courts will not require reengagement when, as in *Merafong*, the public has had a real opportunity to be heard and additional hearings would not contribute anything further to the decision-making exercise.[79]

This is speculative: it remains to be seen what the Constitutional Court will make of the issue. The Supreme Court of Appeal's decisions illustrate the wider implications of *Doctors for Life*, but also show that important details of the public participation doctrine remain to be worked out.

C. Review of Other Internal Legislative Decisions

Judicial review of legislative procedures based on general constitutional ideas of democracy has implications that extend beyond the public participation context. In the 1999 decision in *De Lille*, the Supreme Court of Appeal issued a narrowly tailored judgment in response to an application by an MP who had been suspended from the National Assembly for fifteen

[78] On the powers of local government, see, e.g., Fedsure Life Assurance v Greater Johannesburg Metropolitan Council 1999 (1) SA 374 (CC), para. 26; Mazibuko v City of Johannesburg 2010 (4) SA 1 (CC), para. 129; Nico Steytler & Jaap de Visser, *Local Government*, in Constitutional Law of South Africa (2nd ed.), 22–1, 22–35, 22–37 (Stu Woolman & Michael Bishop, eds., 2005).

[79] *See esp. Merafong*, *supra* note 58, at paras 58–9.

days. The suspension was a punishment for making an accusation during a parliamentary debate that certain people, including other MPs, had been apartheid spies. The relevant constitutional provision simply provides that MPs "have freedom of speech in the Assembly and its committees, subject to its rules and orders."[80] As with the constitutional text in *Doctors for Life*, it is far from obvious that this text empowers the court to act, and it is certainly possible to read it as leaving the matter to the legislature to regulate. However, the Supreme Court of Appeal held that the provision did not empower the Assembly to suspend a member in this way. Permitting the suspension would not promote the constitutionally enshrined importance of free speech in the Assembly, which was crucial to "representative government in a democratic society."[81]

A recent High Court decision has, however, upheld a lesser sanction in such a case. An MP stated that the president had violated his oath of office, but he simply made a free-standing accusation without seeking to bring a substantive motion of improper conduct. The court upheld the Speaker's decision to ask the MP to withdraw the remarks not made in terms of a substantive motion, and then to ask him to leave the chamber for the day when he declined to do so. The decision follows *De Lille* in exercising jurisdiction but also illustrates its respectful limits.[82]

Other decisions have confirmed that parliamentary rules are subject to review for compliance with democratic values.[83] In *Oriani-Ambrosini v Sisulu*, a minority MP successfully challenged National Assembly rules under which an MP could only introduce a bill in the Assembly with the permission of the Speaker and approval by a vote following a committee process.[84] Once again, the bare constitutional text can be read both ways.[85]

80 1996 Constitution, s 58(1). Similar provisions apply in respect of the National Council of Provinces – s 71(1) – and provincial legislatures – s 117(1).

81 *De Lille* (SCA), *supra* note 44, at para. 29.

82 *Lekota*, *supra* note 48, at paras 19–22, 39–40, 44.

83 Earlier challenges of this variety failed on the merits: *see* United Democratic Movement v President of the Republic of South Africa (No. 2) 2003 (1) SA 495 (CC); Democratic Alliance v African National Congress 2003 (1) BCLR 25 (C) (both challenges to floor-crossing legislation); Democratic Alliance v Masondo NO 2003 (2) SA 413 (CC) (challenge concerning the allocation of seats on a mayoral council to members of the opposition). However, the allocation of seats on the executive committee of a local council was successfully challenged in Democratic Party v Brakpan Transitional Local Council 1999 (4) SA 339 (W). For differing assessments of these cases, *see* the (pre-*Doctors for Life*) discussion in Roux, *supra* note 20, at 10–37–10–45, and Fowkes, *supra* note 17, chapters 3 and 7.

84 Oriani-Ambrosini v Sisulu, Speaker of the National Assembly 2012 (6) SA 588 (CC); *see* at paras 5–7 for rules.

85 As the Court explicitly recognized: *id.*, para. 33. The Constitution vests the power to "initiate or prepare legislation" in the National Assembly as a whole – s 55(1)(b) – while also

The Court held that recognizing the right of every MP to initiate bills accorded with "the principles of multi-party democracy, representative and participatory democracy, responsiveness, accountability and openness."[86] It held that this was consistent with the Assembly's right to control its own affairs because the Assembly retained discretion about procedural specifics, and any bill remained subject to majority approval.[87]

These decisions show that the legislative public participation decisions are simply the most high-profile and innovative manifestations of a general, value-based doctrine of review of legislative conduct. The Constitution is understood to give effect to certain values; constitutional supremacy means that legislatures are subject to them; and legislative procedures and procedural decisions are therefore subject to judicial review to the extent that they do not vindicate these values.[88]

This argument is borne out by the Court's understanding of its review powers in the most traditional of cases: requiring that a statute be passed using the proper formal procedures. For example, the Court quite strictly enforces compliance with the special procedures that the constitution requires when provincial interests are implicated, including overturning legislatures' rulings about when these interests are and are not implicated.[89] This sort of review is familiar; what is important is that the Court understands it in the same way as its more creative decisions, with an emphasis on the aim of the rules – here, the proper balance of federal interests.[90] This

providing that "Any bill may be introduced in the National Assembly" – s 73(1) – and that "Only a Cabinet member or a Deputy Minister, or a member or committee of the National Assembly, may introduce a Bill in the Assembly" – s 73(2). It was conceded by the Speaker that s 73(2) empowers an MP to introduce a bill, but in his view this was only as a part of a collective act of the Assembly as a whole because that was where s 55(1)(b) vested the power.

86 *Oriani-Ambrosini*, *supra* note 84, at para. 46 [footnotes omitted]. *See generally* paras 43–9. For reliance on the public participation cases, *see id.* para. 46 n43 and n45; para. 47 n48.

87 *Id.*, paras 50, 63.

88 *See further* Bishop & Raboshakga, *supra* note 23, at 17–91 – 17–96; and *see also* the recent exercise of jurisdiction by the majority in Mazibuko v Sisulu 2013 (6) SA 249 (CC).

89 Tongoane v National Minister for Agriculture and Land Affairs 2010 (6) SA 214 (CC), paras 90–109, and earlier cases there discussed. *See also* recently in a related context Premier, Limpopo Province v Speaker of the Limpopo Provincial Government 2011 (6) SA 396 (CC); Premier, Limpopo Province v Speaker of the Limpopo Provincial Government 2012 (4) SA 58 (CC).

90 *Tongoane*, *supra* note 89, at paras 60–72. Thus, in an earlier case, the Court held that it would be "formalistic in the extreme" to invalidate legislation enacted according to an incorrect procedure where the only effect was that a more onerous procedure than required was followed: *see* Ex parte President of the Republic of South Africa: In re Constitutionality of the Liquor Bill 2000 (1) SA 732 (CC), para. 26; *Tongoane*, *supra* note 89, at paras 98–103.

reverses the more formal pre-1994 approach; it also shows how the Court's review of legislative procedures, in familiar cases and strikingly novel ones, is cut from the same purposive cloth.[91]

D. Conclusions

A set of recent cases incorporates into legislative review features previously confined to the administrative context. How far might this convergence proceed?

Basic institutional differences still matter. For example, legislators' motivations are hard to assess, and they may in any event act for purely political reasons. This practical constraint affects the review of legislators as opposed to administrators, especially in the context of reason-giving.[92] The fact that legislators are elected is also significant because it means that the courts are not the only check on their behavior. The effects of this are apparent in *Merafong*'s distinction between constitutional requirements and mere political courtesy. That said, the way that the distinction is drawn implies that the Court will defer to the voters only when the alleged misstep is not of great constitutional significance, that is, when it is no more than a matter of courtesy. In a case on local government, the Court indicated that it will take into account the need for efficiency in government business when determining requirements for minority party involvement.[93]

The precise extent to which the Court will defer to the legislatures' internal decisions on democratic grounds remains unsettled (although no doubt the boundary will be perennially contested). In the provincial and national context, the status of legislatures is already expressed in the constitutional finding that only the Constitutional Court has jurisdiction to review these decisions, whereas all courts may review the constitutionality of statutes, subject to confirmation by the Constitutional Court. The Court has held that this reflects the specially politicized nature of these decisions.[94] That distinction, however, may be largely symbolic. Parliament's internal decisions continue to enjoy considerable respect, certainly, but this respect does

[91] For the earlier approach, which was wary of requiring too much substance over form, compare the two *Harris* decisions, *supra* note 1, with Collins v Minister of the Interior 1957 (1) SA 552 (A).

[92] *Merafong*, *supra* note 58, at para. 73; *Poverty Alleviation Network*, *supra* note 59, at paras 73–4; *Democratic Alliance*, *supra* note 39, at para. 20; *see also UDM (2)*, *supra* note 83, at para. 56.

[93] *Masondo NO*, *supra* note 83, at para. 22.

[94] *Doctors for Life*, *supra* note 35, at para. 26. *See also*, e.g., *Democratic Alliance v ANC*, *supra* note 83, at 41; Roux, *supra* note 20, at 10–40.

not seem to be greater than that afforded its other decisions and policy choices, such as those expressed in statutes. So long as the Constitution imposes procedural and other requirements on legislatures that can be subject to court enforcement, it appears that the Constitutional Court will restrict the legislatures' traditional internal autonomy.

This general principle has potentially important implications for the future development of this area of the law. A comparison with Germany shows how the review of legislative procedure might develop. It might encompass a legislative obligation to monitor and update legislation, or to defend the methodology used in legislative decision making, as in the calculation of social benefits in the German *Hartz IV* decision to be discussed later. These possibilities are not textually outlandish in the South African context, and both these examples already constitute grounds for review in the context of policy-laden decisions made in the exercise of *executive* power.[95] The erosion of the distinction between administrative and legislative review potentially opens the way for continuing court review of South African legislative processes.

V. REVIEW OF ADMINISTRATIVE PROCEDURES

Just administrative processes are a fundamental right under the South African Constitution. The right requires legislation to give it concrete effect, and PAJA was duly enacted in 2000.

A. Public Participation Requirements

The law of public participation in administrative decision making is still quite uncertain. This is particularly true of rulemaking, given the long uncertainty about whether it falls under PAJA.[96]

Section 4 of PAJA sets out the steps administrators should take to comply with the constitutional right to procedurally fair administrative action in cases that affect "the rights of the public." It provides for public hearings and notice and comment procedures. Officials have discretion to adopt

[95] An ongoing legislative obligation is a natural way to understand the s 7 duty of the legislature to give effect to the Bill of Rights in light of evolving circumstances, and we discuss similar ideas in the context of reasonableness review. *See also* the support for the *Hartz IV* model expressed in passing by Dennis Davis in a book review, *Socio-Economic Rights: Adjudication under a Transformative Constitution* **127** South African Law J. 557, 561 (2010).

[96] Hoexter, *supra* note 3, at 181–2, 200–2.

either or both of these procedures, and they have the discretion to depart from these procedures where this is deemed reasonable and justifiable in the circumstances.

Other statutes also impose public participation requirements. Of particular importance is the National Environmental Management Act (NEMA), a framework statute that includes public participation as a general objective and requires notice and comment procedures for all environmental regulations and in the designation of particular activities and areas as environmentally sensitive.[97] Another example is the Mineral and Petroleum Resources Development Act, which incorporates NEMA's general principles and requires notice and comment procedures before the granting or renewal of prospecting and mining licenses.[98]

The Constitutional Court has held that in case of an overlap, there must ordinarily be compliance with both the requirements of PAJA and those of the other statute.[99] However, PAJA is very flexible. It generally permits officials to follow fair but different procedures set out in another statute, and, as noted, s 4 also gives officials general discretion to depart from its provisions.[100] Compliance with a reasonable procedure in another statute will therefore usually satisfy PAJA. Furthermore, although it is constitutionally mandated, PAJA is still only a statute, so the legislature has the power to vary its requirements in subsequently enacted statutes. The truly binding norms are only those of the s 33 constitutional right to just administrative action.[101]

[97] National Environmental Management Act 107 of 1998 [hereinafter, NEMA]. *See* s 2 (general principles, including several with implications in this context); s 23(2)(d) (public participation a general objective of activity in terms of the statute); s 24A (notice and comment procedures for environmental designations); s 47(1) (same requirements for regulations). *See also* the current regulations for Environmental Impact Assessments, GN R543 in GOVERNMENT GAZETTE 33306, June 18, 2010, and the brief discussion of them by Michael Kidd, *Environmental Law*, 401, 401–9, ANNUAL SURVEY OF SOUTH AFRICAN LAW (2010).

[98] Mineral and Petroleum Resources Development Act 28 of 2002. *See* s 6 (providing for a general obligation of procedural fairness in terms of the Act, subject to PAJA); s 10(1) (notice and comment procedures for grants of licenses); s 37(1) (incorporating the general principles in s 2 of NEMA).

[99] *See Eisenberg, supra* note 41, at paras 50, 59 n32; Zondi v Member of the Executive Council for Traditional and Local Government Affairs 2005 (3) SA 598 (CC), para. 101; Islamic Unity Convention v Minister of Telecommunications 2008 (3) SA 383 (CC), paras 59–60; Walele v City of Cape Town 2008 (6) SA 129 (CC), para. 51.

[100] PAJA, ss 3(5), 4(4).

[101] Caroline Mass, *Section 4 of PAJA and Procedural Fairness in Administrative Action Affecting the Public: A Comparative Perspective*, in THE RIGHT TO KNOW: SOUTH AFRICA'S PROMOTION OF ADMINISTRATIVE JUSTICE AND ACCESS TO INFORMATION ACTS 63 (Claudia Lange & Jakkie Wessels, eds., 2004).; Klaaren & Penfold, *supra* note 5, at 63–13 – 63–14.

Procedures in other statutes are only really subject to the broad terms of that right.[102]

Hence, if another statute requires a notice and comment procedure or some other specific process, it, and not the very open-ended s 4, will tend to be the focus of inquiry.[103] This is one reason for the limited judicial engagement with s 4 to date. However, PAJA still remains important as a source of standards expressing what s 33 of the Constitution requires. This is obviously true in situations where the statute regulating a particular activity contains no provision for public participation. But so far a subtler influence has been more important, and it does not arise from s 4. The general standards of procedural fairness, associated with s 3 of PAJA, are affecting the procedures used in cases affecting the public.

It is quite common for statutes to distinguish between actions that are only provisional or investigative and actions that make final, enduring decisions about rights and interests – and to attach much weaker procedural requirements to the former than the latter. This statutory practice is at odds with a recent trend in South African administrative law under which judges focus on the impact of an action and place less emphasis on whether it represents a final step. A merely provisional decision, or one made on the way to a final decision, may still have a serious impact on affected parties, and in these cases the courts have often been quite demanding in requiring procedural fairness at these early stages.[104] The trend is not unlimited, and it ultimately depends on the facts.[105] However, it does mean that judges

[102] *See Zondi*, *supra* note 99, at paras 99, 106–16, where the Court held that "PAJA cannot be used to evaluate a constitutional challenge" and tested the constitutionality of challenged provisions against s 33 of the Constitution and not PAJA. One must therefore be cautious of statements that all statutory public participation provisions are subject to the requirements of s 4 of PAJA: see, e.g., Raubenheimer, *supra* note 69, 498.

[103] See, e.g., Earthlife Africa (Cape Town) v Director General, Department of Environmental Affairs and Tourism 2005 (3) SA 156 (C), paras 48–9; Muckleneuk/Lukasrand Property Owners and Residents Association v Member of the Executive Council, Department of Agriculture, Conservation and Environment, Gauteng Provincial Government [2007] 1 All SA 1265 (T), both focused on procedures required by the Environmental Conservation Act 73 of 1989, NEMA's predecessor.

[104] Director: Mineral Development, Gauteng Region v Save the Vaal Environment 1999 (2) SA 709 (SCA), paras 16–20. *See also*, e.g., Oosthuizen's Transport (Pty) Ltd v Member of the Executive Council, Road Traffic Matters, Mpumalanga 2008 (2) SA 570 (T); South African Heritage Resources Agency v Arniston Hotel Property (Pty) Ltd 2007 (2) SA 461 (C); Stock v Minister of Housing 2007 (2) SA 9 (C); *Earthlife*, *supra* note 103, at paras 35–6.

[105] *See esp.* the recent decision in Viking Pony Africa Pumps (Pty) Ltd t/a Tricom Africa v Hidro-Tech Systems (Pty) Ltd 2011 (1) SA 327 (CC), paras 38–9 and the discussion by Hoexter, *supra* note 3, at 229–32, 436–43.

may end up requiring more from the earlier or provisional stages of an administrative process than statutes expressly require.

The full implications of this trend for public participation depend on its conjunction with a second general administrative law trend. A line of cases suggests that an opportunity to make representations implies, at least, that parties should be able to engage with the materials and facts available to the final decision maker and to have the decision maker engage with their submissions. Again, there are limits to this: a hearing is not mandatory, and the decision maker may engage via a summary prepared by subordinates.[106] But together, the two trends imply that repeated engagement will often be necessary. The first trend appears to require that officials should hear from interested and affected parties early in the process. But any conclusions formed at that early stage are likely to be reconsidered in light of new facts and the general input they receive. So it is likely that what reaches the final decision maker will not be what the parties engaged with initially. The second trend then seems to imply that the parties should have a further opportunity to engage with the final materials.

This result is not unappealing – continuous engagement or dialogue with stakeholders can be valuable – but it can set a rather unwieldy precedent for mass participation exercises. It is probably significant that existing cases have tended to focus on a particular applicant's opportunity to make submissions. Even if a decision is one of public importance, so that s 4 applies, the cases have focused on a particular individual's experience. Judges tend to note the applicability of s 4, but quickly move on to the more specific procedural fairness standards for general administrative conduct involving individuals under s 3 of PAJA.

This is a second reason for the limited judicial engagement with s 4 to date; and it also makes it deceptively easy to set standards for procedural fairness that look more plausible in the case of an individual than if they were generalized across a public process. Decisions in this area invariably acknowledge the need to avoid overburdening officials with procedural requirements.[107] It is not, however, always clear that judges ask whether

[106] *Earthlife*, *supra* note 103, at paras 67–8; *Muckleneuk/Lukasrand*, *supra* note 103, at para. 48; Robinson v Minister of Justice and Constitutional Development 2006 (6) SA 214 (C), 224E-227E; and *see also* the Constitutional Court's findings on these points in *New Clicks*, *supra* note 3, at paras 153–8, 185 (judgment of Chaskalson P), supported by a majority: *see* the judgments of Yacoob J, para. 792 n502 (four other judges concurred in his judgment); O'Regan J, para. 846; and Langa DCJ, paras 842–5.

[107] *Earthlife*, *supra* note 103, at paras 74–6; *Muckleneuk/Lukasrand*, *supra* note 103, at para. 48; both following the Constitutional Court's remarks on this in the administrative context

a standard that is acceptable for individual claims would be sustainable if generalized to regulatory policymaking processes.[108]

That said, current decisions show signs of a healthy pragmatism. In *Earthlife Africa v Director General, Department of Environmental Affairs and Tourism*, the Western Cape High Court reviewed a decision to build a new nuclear power plant. The Department of Environmental Affairs gave the public an opportunity to comment on an initial draft of a report on the decision, but not on the substantially different final draft. The High Court held that this did not meet the requirements of procedural fairness.[109] A later decision of the North Gauteng High Court, dealing with public consultation on the routing of a new high-speed rail link, criticized *Earthlife* because it was unduly burdensome to require such involvement in the final decision-making stage. But in that case, the applicants had made submissions to the decision maker on some six occasions and, as the court held, "it is difficult to see how anything of great importance, hitherto unmentioned, will make its appearance in a seventh submission."[110] The contrast with *Earthlife* is sharp, and it illustrates that the central point is whether the parties who are seriously affected by the process have had a meaningful opportunity to engage and to make submissions. This reading of the *Earthlife* precedent is consistent with its later treatment in the courts in other contexts.[111] Its fact-driven emphasis on the meaningfulness of a particular engagement in a particular context also recalls the fact-driven reading we offered of public participation cases in the legislative context. At this early stage, it suggests that although South Africa has begun the process of incorporating U.S.-style notice and comment procedures and other standards of review for large-scale administrative decisions, the final standards are likely to be more flexible and contextually sensitive than in the United

more generally in Premier, Province of Mpumalanga v Executive Committee of the Association of Governing Bodies of State Aided Schools 1999 (2) SA 91 (CC), para. 41.

[108] *See, e.g.*, the decision in another administrative law context in *Walele*, *supra* note 99, where only the dissent, written by O'Regan J, shows due concern for the practical consequences of a procedural ruling.

[109] *Earthlife*, *supra* note 103.

[110] *Muckleneuk/Lukasrand*, *supra* note 103, at paras 45–51.

[111] Minister of Economic Development and Others v Competition Tribunal; South African Commercial, Catering and Allied Workers Union (SACCAWU) v Wal-Mart Stores Inc (110/CAC/Jul11, 111/CAC/Jun11), unreported judgment (March 9, 2012), paras 83–90; South African Predator Breeders v Minister of Environmental Affairs and Tourism [2009] ZAFSHC 68, unreported judgment June 11, 2009, paras 51–5. [The judgment was overturned on appeal, but on other grounds, and this aspect of it was not considered: *see* South African Predator Breeders Association v Minister of Environmental Affairs and Tourism [2011] 2 All SA 520 (SCA)]; *Robinson*, *supra* note 106, at 224E-226C.

States, but potentially more demanding in certain cases. This reflects both the generally more open-ended statutory requirements, and the strong emphasis on the substantive value of participation rather than on mere compliance with formal requirements. This conclusion must be somewhat speculative, and its practicability remains to be seen. As yet, the administrative context has not seen the general challenges to the entire process that have arisen in the legislative arena because the focus has been on particular applicants' entitlements. However, the pragmatic approach suggested by the *Earthlife* line of authority should provide a salutary basis for review of mass administrative processes if such challenges do arise.

B. Giving Reasons

Reason-giving is a crucial element of administrative review. However, South Africa is still adjusting to the possibility that reason-giving might be required in large-scale contexts, such as rulemaking, which in South African law remains quite a novel idea.

Historically, South African administrative law required that reasons be given only in individual administrative decisions.[112] Section 33(2) of the 1996 Constitution provides that everyone "whose rights have been adversely affected by administrative action has the right to be given written reasons." The implications of this right for rulemaking, however, remain uncertain under PAJA (and also under general constitutional principles for the exercise of public power).

In *New Clicks*, Justice Sachs's judgment reflected the traditional view in stating that "reason-giving is just not the stuff of delegated legislation."[113] To an American student of reason-giving in APA rulemakings, this sounds distinctly odd. Admittedly, the policymaking processes that generate rules may be as difficult to reduce to a set of coherent "reasons" as the legislative processes that produce statutes, but Justice Sachs's statement ignores the fact that this kind of reason-giving is commonplace in the United States. There may be broad analytic reasons that justify a general rule even if it is the product of a group effort that mixes technical knowledge and pragmatic compromise.

So should PAJA be read to dislodge the traditional view? Justice Sachs, in fact, thought that PAJA *did* impose a general reason-giving requirement,

[112] Hoexter, *supra* note 3, at 460, 466–7; Baxter, *supra* note 2, esp. 176–84.

[113] *New Clicks*, *supra* note 3, at para. 603. Justice Sachs did not speak for a majority on this point.

but given his views on reason-giving in the rulemaking context, he saw this as a reason to think that PAJA did not apply to rulemaking.[114] Because the emerging consensus is that PAJA *does* apply to rulemaking, does this mean there is now a general, U.S.-style obligation to give a statement of reasons justifying an administrative rule?

The answer is not clear. PAJA does provide for a general right of any person affected by administrative action to request reasons for a decision. It also provides that if reasons are not provided, there is a rebuttable presumption that the action was taken without good reason. (This is a formal version of German judges' greater willingness to invalidate a decision when reasons are not given.) But in keeping with the general flexibility of PAJA, an administrator is permitted to inform the requester that she declines to provide reasons: she is empowered to depart from the requirement if she deems it reasonable and justifiable in the circumstances. She is also permitted to follow a fair but different procedure set out in another empowering provision.[115] Thus, *if* one believes that reason-giving is "just not the stuff of rule-making," and if other statutes follow tradition in not requiring reasons, there is room within PAJA to argue that this approach is reasonable and therefore lawful.

This is a particularly significant argument because the most common procedure employed in rulemaking and other large-scale decisions is the notice and comment procedure – and under s 4 of PAJA, a "notice and comment procedure" is distinguished from a "public inquiry" in part because only in the latter case is there an obligation under PAJA to "compile a written report of the inquiry and give reasons for any administrative action taken or recommended."[116] The public inquiry rule recalls the traditional practice for commissions of inquiry. In contrast, the responsible minister has the delegated power to determine the details of the notice and comment procedure, and the resulting regulations do not provide for a general duty of reason-giving.[117]

In other words, the general obligation to provide reasons created by s 5 of PAJA can be freely departed from when another reasonable procedure is in place, and the most common other procedure is a notice and comment

[114] *New Clicks*, *supra* note 3, at paras 596–7, 603; for his full argument, *see generally id.* at paras 586–610.

[115] PAJA, s 5.

[116] PAJA, s 4(2)(b)(iii).

[117] Regulations on Fair Administrative Procedures, GN R1022, *GG* 23674, July 31, 2002. Mirroring s 4 of PAJA, Reg. 5 provides for a written report in connection with a public inquiry but there is no such requirement otherwise.

procedure that does not currently carry a general duty to give reasons. Contrary to the view of Justice Sachs, then, a finding that rulemaking does fall under PAJA does not settle the question of whether rulemaking must be accompanied by reasons.

This result is consistent with our hypothesis that a parliamentary government lacks incentives to impose restrictions on itself. This is another instance in which the specifics of PAJA and other legislation tone down the implications of the post-1994 sea change in constitutional law. Justice Sachs suggested that it would be preferable for the legislature to enact separate procedures for rulemaking, rather than for judges to extend PAJA.[118] However, under our hypothesis, it seems unlikely that a parliamentary government will impose a U.S.-style regime on its "own" executive.

This is, however, not the end of the matter. This reading of PAJA is a plausible one, but can a general refusal to give reasons for rules really be considered "reasonable and justifiable" under South African law? The balance of constitutional rulings in related contexts and the government's own principles tend to suggest that it cannot, though Justice Sachs's judgment is symptomatic of a general hesitancy to make this change at a stroke.

For one thing, it seems now to be settled that principles, such as the accountability of the public administration and the legality principle, generally require the giving of reasons for decisions and acts.[119] (See also the discussion of reason-giving in rationality review, an aspect of the legality principle, later in this chapter.) These principles bind rulemaking, as an exercise of public power, irrespective of PAJA's application. Admittedly, what constitutes "adequate reasons" or a "fair procedure" is treated as flexible and context-specific.[120] Most likely, the details of the obligations imposed by these principles will vary depending on the institution under review. The Court demands relatively little, for example, of the president in firing the head of the national intelligence agency, reflecting a judicial sensitivity to the needs of the office.[121] But the Constitutional Court has held that reason-giving will "often be important in providing fairness, accountability, and

[118] *New Clicks*, *supra* note 3, at para. 598.

[119] Judicial Services Commission v Cape Bar Council 2013 (1) SA 170 (SCA), paras 43–5; Koyabe v Minister of Home Affairs 2010 (4) SA 327 (CC), para. 62; Wessels v Minister for Justice and Constitutional Development 2010 (1) SA 128 (GNP), 141J; Kiva v Minister of Correctional Services (2007) 28 ILJ 597 (E), para. 22; *see further* Hoexter, *supra* note 3, at 359 and Michael Bishop, *Rationality is dead! Long live rationality! Saving rational basis review* 25 South African Public Law / Suid-Afrikaanse Publiekreg 312, 316 (2010) [hereinafter, *Rationality*].

[120] See, e.g., *Koyabe*, *supra* note 119, at paras 36, 63, and further cases there cited.

[121] Masetlha v President of the Republic of South Africa 2008 (1) SA 566 (CC), paras 74–86.

transparency." It has also linked this to *Batho Pele* (People First), the ANC government's guiding principle in public administration, and so the judicial enforcement of procedures embodying this public idea should draw force from it, just as *Doctors for Life* did from public ideas of democracy.[122] All in all, given the prevalence of rulemaking and its impact on people's lives, these general principles support the claim that reason-giving should be required for rulemaking.

Furthermore, judges are already acting under PAJA to ensure that affected parties are given an adequate opportunity to respond to what is before the decision maker. Conceptually, it is hard for affected parties to engage with a proposal unless something is said about the reasons behind it, and a decent description of these will naturally blur into an explanation of *why* it is a desirable policy. A good notice and comment procedure, then, may entail a quite robust reason-giving requirement. The constitutional right of access to information supports this trend, as do a number of specific statutory provisions that require automatic publication of certain sorts of plans.[123]

Of course, providing information is not the same as giving reasons, and explaining reasoning incidentally during a process is not the same as giving reasons for a final decision.[124] But disclosure during a process may well end up being linked to reason-giving at its conclusion. We discuss later in this chapter the increasing tendency to build flexible reason-giving requirements into the general rationality threshold that applies to all public power. We also discuss the Constitutional Court's moves to encourage reason-giving by the government in the context of judicial review of the reasonableness of government plans, and how the Court understands this as an exercise in transparency, accountability, and participatory and deliberative democracy. If this sort of reason-giving is now required for judicial review, it may encourage officials to offer such reasons preemptively before facing court review, as has happened in the United States and in Germany.

[122] See, e.g., Van der Merwe v Taylor NO 2008 (1) SA 1 (CC), para. 71 n81; Joseph v City of Johannesburg 2010 (4) SA 55 (CC), para. 45 n39; *Koyabe*, *supra* note 119, at para. 65 n57 and the sources on Batho Pele there cited.

[123] 1996 Constitution, s 32; Promotion of Access to Information Act 2 of 2000. *See, e.g.*, NEMA, s 15(5), on the publication of environmental implementation and management plans. For other examples of statutes with such requirements, *see* Willemien du Plessis, *Access to Information*, in ENVIRONMENTAL COMPLIANCE AND ENFORCEMENT IN SOUTH AFRICA: LEGAL PERSPECTIVES, 199–205 (Alexander Paterson & Louis J. Kotzé, eds., 2009).

[124] HOEXTER, *supra* note 3, at 461–2. Reason-giving earlier in a process is also, of course, not a *substitute* for giving reasons for the final decision where that is a requirement: see, e.g., *Wessels*, *supra* note 119, at 132A, 139 C/D.

The emerging judicial view that reason-giving is required for the exercise of the s 34 right of access to courts also encourages preemptive disclosure. Parties need to be given reasons for decisions in order to know whether they can legally challenge them.[125]

Finally, the emphasis on respectful dialogue and engagement with the public blurs any sharp distinction between pre- and post-decision phases. As noted earlier, the trend in South African administrative law seems to be away from emphasizing the stage of decision making, and toward extended or repeated engagements with the public. We will also discuss the Court's emerging engagement remedy in eviction cases, reflecting a similar trend. Given these understandings of governance, pressures to be open and informative during a process are likely to affect what is expected of the process as a whole, including its conclusion.

Thus, despite the absence of clear statutory rules from the legislature on reason-giving in rulemaking, the general rights and values of the post-1994 constitutional dispensation may well lead to the judicial creation of such requirements. We should expect that any standards will have considerable built-in flexibility to allow for institutional and contextual factors and to avoid overburdening officials, but most of this development has yet to take place.

C. Consequences of Invalidation

A defective process does not necessarily lead to invalidation of the ultimate decision. Both PAJA and the Constitution grant judges broad powers to design remedies that are just and equitable.[126]

In *Mazibuko v City of Johannesburg*, for example, the Constitutional Court held that a possible procedural violation in relation to an individual would not invalidate the implementation of a general, township-wide scheme where public engagement appeared to have been generally satisfactory.[127] In *Residents of Joe Slovo Community v Thubelisha Homes*, it displayed a similarly pragmatic approach in its review of a somewhat more defective process that was part of a housing relocation scheme. Five judgments were written,

[125] *Kiva*, *supra* note 119, at paras 31–2; *see also* HOEXTER, *supra* note 3, at 471–2.

[126] PAJA, s 8; 1996 Constitution, s 172(1)(b).

[127] *Mazibuko*, *supra* note 78, at para. 134. *See also* Chairpersons' Association v Minister of Arts and Culture 2006 (2) SA 32 (T), para. 37 (reversed on appeal, but this issue not considered by the appeal court: Chairpersons' Association v Minister of Arts and Culture 2007 (5) SA 236 (SCA)); and HOEXTER, *supra* note 3, at 417–18.

but all the justices held that the various defects of public participation did not vitiate the whole process.[128]

Because procedural fairness is a contextual matter, urgency may also justify procedural defects. For example, in *Minister of Public Works v Kyalami Ridge Residents Association*, where the government was acting urgently to resettle people at risk due to flooding, the Constitutional Court accepted a rather abridged consultation with the local community.[129]

In this regard, the South African approach appears similar to the German one. However, where German law understands fair procedures chiefly in terms of their ability to produce a better quality of decision, South African law adds to this consideration a greater emphasis on public engagement and fair procedures as goods in themselves. As a result, procedural defects provide a more powerful reason for invalidation even if the quality of the decision appears unaffected. The precise line remains to be drawn. Decisions like *Mazibuko* and *Kyalami Ridge*, and especially *Joe Slovo*, show that the courts will act pragmatically, but South African law is nevertheless likely to be less forgiving of procedural defects than is German law.

PAJA grants judges a number of remedial powers when invalidating decisions, including the power to substitute their own decision, but this remains a truly exceptional remedy.[130] As in the United States, the normal remedy is to invalidate the decision, requiring the official to begin a new process.

D. Conclusions

The traditional distinction between individual and mass administrative decision making is eroding in the face of the new constitutional values. In some respects, such as the judicial willingness to engage in review at all, the traditional distinction is already a thing of the past; in others, such as the giving of reasons, its presence remains strongly felt. The erosion would have proceeded faster if there had been clearer or more rigorous statutory requirements for rulemaking and other large-scale administrative decisions. However, in line with our argument, the ANC legislature's actions to give effect to the new constitutionalism have reflected its reluctance to

[128] Residents of Joe Slovo Community, Western Cape v Thubelisha Homes 2010 (3) SA 454 (CC), paras 112, 116 (Yacoob J); 166, 174 (Moseneke DCJ); 244–6, 260 (Ngcobo J); 301–4 (O'Regan J); 378–84, 389–95, 400–9 (Sachs J). *See further* the discussion of engagement later in this chapter and sources cited in notes 185–7, *infra*.

[129] Minister of Public Works v Kyalami Ridge Residents Environmental Association 2001 (3) SA 1151 (CC), paras 103–11; *see further* the discussion under the next heading.

[130] PAJA, s 8(1)(c)(ii)(aa); Klaaren & Penfold, *supra* note 5, at 63–121 – 63–123.

impose too many restrictions on the operations of its own government. There is reason to think that the courts will act where the legislature has not. Such developments are in their early stages, and judges appear to be restrained both by tradition and concern for overburdening the executive – evident in their long avoidance of the issue of whether rulemaking falls under PAJA. However, judicial moves to require reason-giving and participation in rulemaking are arguably implied by the powerful emerging ideas of public accountability.

The same ideas underpin the similar convergence between review of procedural decisions in the administrative and legislative contexts. *Earthlife*, in light of its subsequent treatment in the courts, looks rather like *Doctors for Life* and *Matatiele (2)*: a judicial protest against an abrupt, plainly inadequate engagement of government actors with sincerely interested members of the public. By the same token, sincere and at least reasonably adequate attempts at engagement have passed muster. In both contexts, courts have emphasized the importance of affected parties having a reasonable opportunity to participate in a process and engage meaningfully with the decision maker.

There are a number of other signs of this convergence. Cases dealing with administrative and legislative matters deploy strikingly similar language.[131] Judicial review in both cases is ordinarily open only to persons who have first tried to be heard within the relevant institution.[132] In both cases a default rule requires that an application for review must be brought promptly, usually within 180 days in the administrative context and "timeously" in the legislative one.[133] There is a similar recognition that government actors have broad discretion in deciding how to involve the public.[134] In each case, there are signs of the pragmatic view that limited defects in a process will not

[131] *Merafong's* "use of the language employed in the judicial review of administrative action" is indeed striking in a legislative context: Hugh Corder, *Principled Calm Amidst a Shameless Storm: Testing the Limits of Judicial Regulation of Legislative and Executive Power* 2 Constitutional Court Rev. 239, 248 (2009). *See also* the connection drawn between the administrative law *audi alteram partem* rule and the public participation decisions in the legislative context by Bishop, *Listening Constitution*, *supra* note 60, at 337, and the discussion of substantive legislative review, which is generally understood to resemble traditional administrative law review doctrines closely, *infra*.

[132] *See Doctors for Life*, *supra* note 35, at paras 216–21; PAJA s 7(2), (generally requiring exhaustion of internal remedies).

[133] *See Doctors for Life*, *supra* note 35, at para. 216; PAJA, s 7(1) (time limit on review proceedings) read with s 9 (permitting extension of that time limit by agreement or by order of court "where the interests of justice so require)."

[134] *See, e.g.*, *Doctors for Life*, *supra* note 35, at paras 106–7, 123–9, 145; *Eisenberg*, *supra* note 41, esp. paras 51–9; PAJA, s 4(4).

vitiate the whole.[135] There is also a distinct similarity between the pragmatic way courts in the administrative context understand the duty of the final decision maker to consider materials submitted, and the legislative duty to consider the public's submissions.[136] Reasonableness and meaningfulness are common standards.

Decisions on administrative procedures, however, have yet to confront squarely the erosion of these distinctions.[137] Decisions about large-scale processes under PAJA blur into discussions of individual procedural fairness. The Constitutional Court has avoided considering the application of PAJA to engagement in more than one area of municipal activity that would appear to be closely related to both the administrative and legislative bodies of case law.[138] However, it seems clear that both the nature and extent of duties to consult more than once as a proposal evolves and the duty to give reasons will be crucial to setting the new boundaries with respect to both traditional distinctions. Both represent themes across all contexts in the review of procedure. We return to both topics in the conclusion to this chapter, but we must first discuss several important issues that arise in substantive review.

VI. REVIEW OF SUBSTANCE – PROCEDURE BY ANOTHER NAME

Judicial review of the substance of decisions existed in South Africa prior to the 1993 and 1996 constitutions as an inheritance from English law.

[135] *Compare, e.g.*, *Poverty Alleviation Network*, *supra* note 59, at paras 43–5 (serious disruptions at one meeting held by legislators counterbalanced by it being ultimately brought under control and because another, bigger meeting was held later) with the discussion of *Joe Slovo*, *supra* note 128.

[136] *Compare, e.g.*, the discussion in the administrative context in *Robinson*, *supra* note 106, at 224E-226C, citing *Earthlife*, *supra* note 103, with the discussion in the Constitutional Court's legislative public participation decision in *Moutse*, *supra* note 61, at paras 68–80.

[137] In contrast to substantive decisions, where judges regularly address the erosion of the distinction between appeal and review – *see* the discussion of reasonableness later in this chapter.

[138] The Court has avoided the question of how PAJA relates to its engagement remedy used in the eviction context, which we discuss later in this chapter – *see* Geo Quinot, *Case Review: An Administrative Law Perspective on "Bad Building" Evictions in the Johannesburg Inner City* **8**(1) ESR Rev.: Economic & Social Rights in South Africa 25 (2007). In *Mazibuko*, *supra* note at 78, it recognized that municipal executive action is excluded from the ambit of PAJA by s 1(i)(b)*(cc)* and seemed to define that power expansively, but it did not consider whether other constitutional norms impose procedural requirements on its exercise: *see esp.* paras 126–34, and also the criticism of the decision by Quinot, *Administrative Law*, *supra* note 5, at 43–4. Arguably, the latter omission reflects only the Court's view that the procedures in *Mazibuko* were generally satisfactory.

Following that system, the kind of power at issue heavily influenced the scope of review. Under the previously prevailing Westminster system of parliamentary supremacy, the substance of Parliament's decision was not subject to judicial review. Also exempt from review were certain executive powers, known as prerogatives, which included, for example, presidential pardons. Administrative decisions and delegated legislation were subject to judicial review for lawfulness and for (different) levels of reasonableness.[139]

Under the 1993 interim Constitution, the Constitutional Court began to erode these traditional distinctions between different kinds of powers. It held that the replacement of parliamentary supremacy with constitutional supremacy meant that there was now a single source of power, the Constitution. Hence, all exercises of public power were now subject to the Constitution, including legislative decisions and executive prerogatives.[140]

This approach did not make the type of power completely irrelevant for two reasons. First, the principle of separation of powers remains under the 1993 and 1996 texts, and so respect for institutional roles still matters.[141] Respect for democratic decision making still implies deference to Parliament's decisions.[142] Second, as we have seen, PAJA's cumbersome definition of "administrative action" ensured that distinctions between kinds of powers would persist. However, as with procedural review, the shift to constitutional supremacy did throw traditional distinctions in doubt. The doctrine of separation of powers is surely important, but what exactly does it mean in a system that imposes many substantive constraints on the exercise of public power without discriminating between types of power or different institutions? Courts continue to grapple with this question; we aim only to identify some important emerging trends.

We discuss three aspects of substantive review: means/end rationality, reasonableness analysis, and the constitutional limitations clause with its link to proportionality. These concepts are not always distinguished in administrative law – the line between reasonableness and proportionality, especially, can be blurry, but it is useful to distinguish them in South

[139] Jacques de Ville, Judicial Review of Administrative Action in South Africa 28–9 (2005); Hoexter, *supra* note 3, at 328–35.

[140] Key early decisions included President of the Republic of South Africa v Hugo 1997 (4) SA 1 (CC) and *Fedsure*, *supra* note 78.

[141] Ex Parte Chairperson of the Constitutional Assembly: In re Certification of the Constitution of the Republic of South Africa 1996 1996 (4) SA 744 (CC), para. 122; South African Association of Personal Injury Lawyers v Heath 2001 (1) SA 883 (CC), para. 22; Van Rooyen v The State 2002 (5) SA 246 (CC), para. 17.

[142] See, e.g., S v Lawrence 1997 (4) SA 1176 (CC), paras 42–5; Pharmaceutical Manufacturers Association of South Africa: In re Ex parte President of the Republic of South Africa 2000 (2) 674 (CC), para. 90.

African law today. We show how each of these doctrines, although nominally substantive, has implications for the constitutionality of legislative and administrative procedures, especially if rights are at stake.

A. Means/End Rationality

All government conduct is subject to rationality review. The rule of law, a founding value set out in s 1(c) of the Constitution, implies the principle of legality, which prohibits arbitrariness in any exercise of public power.[143] PAJA further makes rationality a ground of review for any exercise of public power that counts as "administrative action."[144] Rationality is also part of the test the Constitutional Court applies to the constitutional right to equality.[145] The test is deferential. The Court has enjoined courts from using rationality review to "substitute their opinions as to what is appropriate, for the opinions of those in whom the power has been vested."[146]

The Court applies the test somewhat differently in the legislative and administrative contexts. One relevant difference is the question of the mental state of the actors involved. In both contexts, rationality is treated as an objective inquiry, meaning that it does not matter whether the decision maker believed in good faith that the decision was rational, but only whether the decision was, in fact, rational.[147] However, in the legislative context this comes with a refusal to review legislative decisions for bad faith or to assess the mental states of the decision makers. For example, in a decision reviewing the constitutionality of floor-crossing legislation, the Constitutional Court refused to consider the claim that the ruling party passed the measure only to secure political advantage for itself.[148] The Court recognizes the practical impossibility of inquiring into the mental state of a multitude

[143] *Fedsure, supra* note 78, at paras 53–60 (rule of law a constitutional principle implying principle of legality); *New National Party, supra* note 36, at paras 19, 24, 25 (principle of legality discussed in *Fedsure* implies rationality). Although reported earlier, *New National Party* was decided six months after *Fedsure*.

[144] PAJA, s 6(2)(f)(ii).

[145] This is the settled interpretation of section 9(1) of the 1996 Constitution, which provides that "Everyone is equal before the law and has the right to equal protection and benefit of the law," based on judgments made in terms of the interim Constitution in Prinsloo v Van der Linde 1997 (3) SA 1012 (CC), paras 23–6; Harksen v Lane NO 1998 (1) SA 300 (CC), paras 43, 50. This approach has persisted under the 1996 Constitution.

[146] *Pharmaceutical Manufacturers, supra* note 142, at para. 90.

[147] *See id.*, which is cited for the same proposition in the context of PAJA in Trinity Broadcasting (Ciskei) v Independent Communications Authority of South Africa 2004 (3) SA 346 (SCA), para. 21.

[148] *UDM (2), supra* note 83, at para. 56. Floor-crossing legislation deals with members who "cross the floor" of Parliament to vote with another party.

of legislators, and it acknowledges that their motives may permissibly be purely political.[149] In the administrative context, however, bad faith is a separate ground of review under PAJA.[150] It was a basis for review even during the late apartheid era.[151] So while the rationality test is understood as objective in both cases, that understanding rules out review of subjective reasons in the legislative context but not in the administrative one.

A second difference concerns the link to the rationale that the government actually offers. As a matter of general practice, South African courts usually confine themselves to considering "the purposes that either appear from the face of the statute or that the government advocates in litigation ... they have not conducted the sort of speculation often evident in the U.S. courts."[152] However, there are distinctions between the courts' approach to different kinds of decisions.

In administrative review of decisions affecting individuals, the rationality test requires the courts to consider the information that officials used to make a decision. The courts ask whether there "is a rational objective basis justifying the connection made by the administrative decision maker between the material made available and the conclusion arrived at."[153] As this indicates, PAJA requires consideration of the information before the administrator as well as the reasons the administrator gives.[154] It also means that the court assesses the rationality of the decision in relation to the reasons actually given. It is not open to the administrator to offer new reasons on review, nor can the court simply ask whether there are, objectively, reasons for the decision.[155]

In the context of larger-scale administrative decisions, including rule-making, matters are evolving. The standard test under the general legality principle is whether the decision is "rationally related to the purpose for which the power was given."[156] This test usually does not include any

[149] However, when the Court reviewed a presidential decision, it made reference to his individual mental state to claim that he was acting in good faith, notwithstanding that it treated his action as an exercise in legislative power. *Pharmaceutical Manufacturers*, *supra* note 142, at paras 79, 82, 89.

[150] PAJA, s 6(2)(e)(v); on other potentially relevant PAJA provisions, *see* HOEXTER, *supra* note 3, at 311–12.

[151] *E.g.*, decisions where the courts questioned whether the real motivations of officials were racist, after repeal of racially based statutes: *see* HOEXTER, *supra* note 3, at 311.

[152] Bishop, *Rationality*, *supra* note 119, 316.

[153] *Trinity Broadcasting*, *supra* note 147, para. 21.

[154] PAJA, s 6(2)(f)(ii)(cc) and (dd).

[155] *See* National Lotteries Board v South African Education and Environment Project 2012 (4) SA 504 (SCA), paras 24–8, relying on English authority to this effect.

[156] *Pharmaceutical Manufacturers*, *supra* note 142, at para. 85.

mention of the material considered or the reasons given, and the courts have not traditionally considered these factors in the review of administrative rulemaking. There are signs, however, that this is changing. In a recent case invalidating a rulemaking, the Supreme Court of Appeal stated that the rationality test serves, in part, "to ensure the action of the functionary bears a rational connection to the facts and information available to him and on which he purports to base such action."[157] The decision holds that the test generally applied to individual administrative decision making applies to rulemaking as well. This result is also inherent in the same court's recent holding that PAJA applies to rulemaking because rationality under PAJA is assessed in terms of the reasons actually given by the decision maker.[158] These remain isolated decisions, but their potential impact is large. They strengthen the trends toward reason-giving in the emerging procedural standards.

The Constitutional Court's decision in *Albutt v Centre for the Study of Violence and Reconciliation* is a further indication of the judiciary's willingness to hold the executive to both substantive limits and participatory procedures. The decision reviewed the use of presidential pardons for individuals convicted of crimes that they alleged were political acts committed during the struggle against apartheid but that had not been dealt with by the Truth and Reconciliation Commission. It, therefore, dealt with an executive power that the courts had traditionally not reviewed. The decision tends to contradict the idea that the Court will apply rationality analysis more deferentially to these more sensitive powers. The judgment holds the president tightly to his announced purposes (reconciliation and nation building) in the use of the pardon power in that particular case, rather than asking whether his exercise of it was rationally linked to the general purposes of the pardon power. On this basis, it holds that it was irrational for the president to exclude victims from a process intended to be reconciliatory. Furthermore, rationality is held to imply participatory *procedures* where they are implied by the purpose of the action.[159]

[157] *SA Predators Breeders* (SCA), *supra* note 111, at paras 21, 40–5, applying the logic of *Trinity Broadcasting*, *supra* note 147, which concerned an individual administrative decision, in the context of delegated legislation.

[158] *City of Tshwane*, *supra* note 5.

[159] Albutt v Centre for the Study of Violence and Reconciliation 2010 (3) SA 293 (CC), paras 53–69. *See further* The Citizen 1978 (Pty) Ltd v McBride 2011 (4) SA 191 (CC), paras 77–8; Alistair Price, *Rationality Review of Legislative and Executive Decisions: Poverty Alleviation Network and Albutt* **127** South African Law J. 580, 585–7 (2010) and the discussion of "procedural irrationality" in Bishop, *Listening Constitution*, *supra* note 60, at 336, 349–51.

The decision limits itself to the special context of postapartheid reconciliation, but the links to broader ideas of democracy, such as those animating *Doctors for Life*, are clear.[160] (The Court has subsequently explicitly linked the two decisions.)[161] In *Masetlha* a majority of the Court had earlier refused to hold that fair procedure is required by rationality or by the legality principle more generally.[162] *Albutt* places at least some qualification on this holding. It suggests that *Masetlha* is now challengeable at least to the extent that participation follows from the purpose for which a power is exercised: a potentially broad exception indeed, given the importance generally assigned to public inclusion.[163]

A subsequent decision of the Court strengthens this suggestion. In a challenge to an appointment made by the president to the position of head of the National Prosecuting Authority, the Court confirmed that rationality implicates the process as well as the merits of a decision. It held that the president's decision "can be successfully challenged only if a step in the process bears no rational relation to the purpose for which the power is conferred *and* the absence of the connection colors the process as a whole and hence the ultimate decision with irrationality."[164] This reflects pragmatism and the Court's effort to strike the proper institutional balance.

[160] *Albutt, supra* note 159, at para. 75. *See also* the separate concurring judgment of Froneman J, in which two other judges concurred, which also states that the decision was limited to the particular context, but links the finding to general ideas of participatory democracy and cites *Doctors for Life, supra* note 35, and *Matatiele (2), supra* note 55, strongly implying that the ruling has application beyond cases of postapartheid reconciliation (*Id.* at paras 90–2); and Melanie Murcott, *Procedural Fairness as a Component of Legality: Is a Reconciliation between Albutt and Masetlha Possible?* 130 South African Law J. 260 (2013).

[161] Schubart Park Residents' Association v City of Tshwane Metropolitan Municipality 2013 (1) SA 323 (CC), para. 43; *see also* the comments of Cameron JA on *Albutt* and participatory democracy in *The Citizen, supra* note 159, at para. 77.

[162] *See Masetlha, supra* note 121, at paras 77, 83–4; compared to paras 177, 182–90, 195–7 (per Ngcobo J, dissenting on this point and linking rationality to procedural standards) and 233–7 (per Sachs J, disagreeing with Ngcobo J's conclusion on the facts but agreeing with the broad construction of the legality principle to include duties of fairness); *see further* Bishop, *Listening Constitution, supra* note 60, at 335–7, 349–52; Klaaren & Penfold, *supra* note 5, at 63–17 – 63–18.

[163] In favor of a broad reading of *Albutt* is that, although *Masetlha* frames its finding in general terms, it emphasizes the importance of not unduly constraining the president in the context of firing the head of the National Intelligence Agency. That is quite a specialized context suggesting an unusual degree of deference.

[164] Democratic Alliance v President of the Republic of South Africa 2013 (1) SA 248 (CC), paras 33–7, 39, 41–5. The finding of irrationality in the case could be explained on the facts simply as a failure to take relevant considerations into account – *see id.* at paras 62, 69–70, 74, 76–7, 81, 84, 88–9 – but the judgment states clearly that rationality analysis implicates the means adopted to a particular end, including the process used.

This reading is also supported by the similarly broad post-*Masetlha* reading of the legality principle that the Court offered in *Koyabe* in the context of reason-giving. That decision leaves room for the possibility that reason-giving might not be required in certain institutional contexts, but suggests that those will be exceptions, with reason-giving the default.[165] The Supreme Court of Appeal, too, has interpreted *Albutt* to mean that courts can review a decision in terms of the legality principle "on essentially the same grounds as those set out in s 6(2) of PAJA" – meaning that the standards applied to individual administrative decision making are generally applicable to all exercises of public power.[166] It has, however, continued to show sensitivity to institutional context when applying this expansive principle, just as the Constitutional Court has.[167]

Despite being a nominally deferential standard, then, rationality analysis is expanding. Courts are working out the procedural implications of its traditional prohibition on arbitrariness, and they are linking democratic ideas to its traditional requirement that there must be reasons for government action by assessing government conduct increasingly in terms of the reasons actually given. These developments appear, however, to be accompanied by a pragmatic awareness that the rationality standard applies across a range of contexts with different institutional realities.

B. Reasonableness

Reasonableness is a more demanding standard than rationality, but like rationality, its assessment varies somewhat from context to context. It is used in administrative law as an explicit element of the s 33 right to just administrative action and as a ground of review listed in PAJA. It is also used by the courts to measure the state's fulfillment of certain positive obligations in terms of rights and other constitutional provisions. We discuss this more general usage first. Once again, there are signs that the two standards are evolving toward each other.

The Constitutional Court has used reasonableness in connection with a variety of constitutional obligations, including but not limited to rights. Its most famous application is in socioeconomic rights cases.[168] It has also

[165] *See* text accompanying notes 119–22, *supra*.

[166] JDJ Properties CC v Unmgeni Local Municipality 2013 (2) SA 395 (SCA), para. 23, citing, inter alia, *Albutt*.

[167] *See, e.g., Judicial Services Commission*, *supra* note 119, at paras 43–51.

[168] The seminal case was Government of the Republic of South Africa v Grootboom 2001 (1) SA 46 (CC). In its first socioeconomic rights case, the Court referred to both reasonableness

been used in other contexts, including a challenge to measures to provide security on public rail transport,[169] challenges to election planning brought under the right to vote,[170] and challenges to the adequacy of public participation in legislative decision making, as we saw earlier. The reasonableness standard is drawn, in some instances, from the text of individual provisions. The text dealing with socioeconomic rights, for example, refers to the state's obligation to take "reasonable ... measures" to realize the rights.[171] But reasonableness is also employed without a textual hook, as in the other examples mentioned. The Court has not explained when the standard applies and when it does not.[172]

At present, the standard is hard to define because the courts have left it as a flexible, case-by-case test (and also because courts have only applied it in a relatively small number of cases). But that said, the test appears to be evolving into a crucial mechanism for the courts to keep government transparent and accountable.[173] The reasonableness test increasingly involves scrutiny of the state's reasons. The Court stresses the contextual nature of its inquiry and considers detailed evidence in applying it. As with rationality review, reasonableness review is subject to the caveat that courts should not use it to assume a policymaking role.

Two recent decisions that involve socioeconomic rights are of special interest. In *Mazibuko*, the Constitutional Court's first decision on water rights, the government submitted a great deal of information about its water policies in the residential areas that were the subject of the litigation.

and rationality without choosing between them: see Soobramoney v Minister of Health (KwaZulu-Natal) 1998 (1) SA 765 (CC), para. 25 ("unreasonable" and "rationally"), para. 29 ("rational").

169 Rail Commuters Action Group v Transnet Ltd. t/a Metrorail 2005 (2) SA 359 (CC), paras 84, 86.

170 *See*, most recently, Richter v Minister of Home Affairs 2009 (3) SA 615 (CC) and AParty v Minister of Home Affairs 2009 (3) SA 649 (CC). These broader applications of reasonableness are not always acknowledged by analysis that focuses on socioeconomic rights cases: *see further* Fowkes, *supra* note 17, chapter 8.

171 1996 Constitution, ss 26(2), 27(2), 29(1)(b), 29(2).

172 There is also some variation in the way reasonableness is used *within* public law. For example, the Court's formulation in the voting rights context – "Parliament is obliged to provide for the machinery ... that is reasonably capable of achieving the goal of ensuring that all person who want to vote ... are able to do so" per *New National Party*, *supra* note 36, at para. 23 – is not identical to the one used in the railway security decision – the plan or conduct must "fall within the range" of what "a reasonable decision-maker in the circumstances could have adopted," per *Rail Commuters*, *supra* note 169, at para. 86. These discrepancies do not affect the more general points made here.

173 *See, e.g.*, Minister of Health v Treatment Action Campaign (No. 2) 2002 (5) SA 721 (CC), para. 123 (reasonableness implies policy transparency).

The Court was impressed by the serious engagement of the government with the issue and declined to find a violation. It understood the process as an exercise in accountability. "A reasonableness challenge requires government to explain the choices it has made," which requires it to "provide information it has considered and the process it has followed to determine its policy."[174] The judgment understands the application of reasonableness analysis to positive rights obligations as a way to "foster a form of participative democracy that holds government accountable and requires it to account between elections over specific aspects of government policy" [*sic*].[175] Notably, in contrast to the other countries we consider, the democracy-promoting motivation is explicit: it is not just about requiring evidence to facilitate judicial review.

This aspect of the judgment's logic potentially applies to legislatures as well because democratic accountability "between elections" is important for legislatures too. As it happens, in South Africa it is more likely to be the executive that generates the detailed plans that a court is reviewing, but if the legislature were to do this (as was the case in Germany in *Hartz IV*), then the same rights- and democracy-based logic would seem to apply. The *Mazibuko* Court's requirement that an agency disclose "the process that it has followed" and "what it has done to formulate the policy: its investigation and research, the alternatives considered, and the reasons why the option underlying the policy was selected" looks a lot like the *Hartz IV* inquiry discussed in the German case study.[176] Of course, a court might be more deferential in applying that test to an elected legislature. The Court has been cautious of judging legislative decisions based solely on the written documents produced during the process, and it has been sensitive to the ways legislatures inform themselves by deliberation and committee activity.[177] But considerable deference is already built into the reasonableness approach that the Court uses in these decisions,[178] and ultimately the legislature is obliged to respect rights just as much as the executive.[179] As discussed earlier, this is an area where there is room for legislative review standards to evolve closer to administrative ones.

[174] *Mazibuko*, *supra* note 78, at para. 71.

[175] *Id.* at para. 160.

[176] *Id.* at para. 161; *see also* para. 164. 125 BVerfGE 175 [Hartz IV decision] available in English at http://www.bverfg.de/entscheidungen/ls20100209_1bvl000109en.html

[177] *See* the discussion in *Moutse*, *supra* note 61, at paras 68–80.

[178] *Mazibuko*, *supra* note 78, at paras 46–68, 161 discusses the earlier relevant cases; *see* also *Moutse*, *supra* note 61, at para. 81.

[179] 1996 Constitution, s 7.

A second decision signals further erosion of traditional restraints on the judicial review of legislative reasons. *Blue Moonlight Properties* was an eviction case, raising a city's obligations under the right to housing to provide temporary accommodation to persons it evicted at the behest of private owners. The judgment concerned a municipality, understood in South African constitutional law to have mixed executive and legislative competence. The municipality objected that it could not afford to provide accommodation. Breaking with a tradition in which budgetary decisions are the government's purview, the Court ruled that its "determination of the reasonableness of measures within available resources cannot be restricted by budgetary and other decisions," because the budgetary decisions may not have been informed by a proper understanding of the rights at stake.[180] Because the municipality provided no evidence that it could not afford to provide temporary housing, the Court ordered it to do so.[181]

The significance of the decision is twofold. The Court did not decide whether the local government decisions it was reviewing were executive or legislative in nature. That supports the suggestion, made earlier, that what is critical to the application of the reasonableness test is not the type of power being exercised but how it affects rights. The Court also refused to accept the traditionally inviolate nature of budgetary decisions. This, too, suggests that the enforcement of rights-based obligations is eroding traditional constraints on judicial review of legislative decisions. Just as the budgetary nature of a decision is not a bar to reasonableness review (though it may be grounds for restraint), the fact that the budgetary decision is made by a national or provincial legislature should not bar it either, especially given the Court's willingness to subject legislative decisions about public participation to reasonableness analysis.

From a comparative perspective, it is striking that the Constitutional Court has been willing to examine public participation procedures in some detail, but has been slower to do this in relation to other aspects of the processes used by legislators and officials – such as the examination of the evidentiary basis for a statutory provision that German courts examine or the detailed examination of process that forms part of U.S. "hard-look" review in the administrative context. Admittedly, there is arguably a clearer textual basis in South Africa for review for public participation than some of these other types of review. The constitutional text speaks of involving the public in legislative deliberations, as does s 4 of PAJA. However, the existing cases

[180] City of Johannesburg Metropolitan Municipality v Blue Moonlight Properties 39 (Pty) Ltd 2012 (2) BCLR 150 (CC), paras 68–74.

[181] *Blue Moonlight*, *supra*, at paras 73, 75, 95, 96.

dealing with reasonableness provide an ample foundation for the sort of review conducted in these other countries. As noted, the reasonableness test contemplates inquiries into the process followed and the evidence considered, and it refers to ideas such as coherence that bear a close resemblance to the sort of review that the Constitutional Court conducted in Germany.[182] (Aspects of this type of inquiry, in both Germany and South Africa, can also fall under proportionality analysis, discussed later.)

The potential for development in directions that follow the U.S. and German examples is therefore clear, and both *Mazibuko* and *Blue Moonlight* appear to be moves in that direction. *Mazibuko* requires the government to respond to socioeconomic rights challenges by disclosing its ongoing efforts to give effect to the right. As in Germany, this sort of review inevitably implicates substance, but the *Mazibuko* judges focus on responsiveness, inclusiveness, and the coherence of the state's process, rather than reconsidering the merits of the water policy. In *Blue Moonlight*, similarly, the Court does not tell the government how to spend its money. It only says that when the government decides how to allocate funds, it has to consider the rights implications of its policies and budget accordingly. If it wishes to conduct a housing renewal, it has to budget for those evicted, and it cannot later use its own failure to do this as a reason for not meeting its rights obligations in relation to those people.

These cases show that reasonableness, like rationality, is developing a significantly procedural component. The most detailed development of this sort has occurred in the context of socioeconomic rights, and some further aspects of it are instructive for our argument here.

South African socioeconomic rights review has been described, in admiration and in criticism, as following a significantly administrative law model. Initially, this was a description of *Grootboom*, under which socioeconomic rights triggered review of a government's housing plan (as opposed to grounding more concrete entitlements).[183] However, the

[182] See, e.g., *Grootboom*, *supra* note 168, at para. 41 (reasonableness requires "a *coherent* public housing program"); para. 54 (relevant to reasonableness that the "allocation of responsibilities and functions has been *coherently* and *comprehensively* addressed" and that the plan represents "a *systematic* response to a pressing social need"); para. 95 ("section 26 [the right to housing] does oblige the state to devise and implement a *coherent* and *co-ordinated* program"), italics added. For a summary of the reasonableness standard's features, *see* Sandra Liebenberg, Socio-Economic Rights: Adjudication under a Transformative Constitution 152–3 (2010).

[183] *See* Liebenberg, *supra* note 182, at 173–5; Marius Pieterse, *Procedural Relief, Constitutional Citizenship and Socio-Economic Rights as Legitimate Expectations* **28** South African J. on Human Rights 359, 359–63 (2012), and the earlier sources there cited.

basis for the description has since expanded, and its accuracy may have increased. In *Joseph*, for example, the Court created a fundamental right to service delivery and linked it explicitly to PAJA, requiring procedural checks before services could be discontinued.[184] The most prominent new example is the engagement remedy, developed in the context of eviction and now expanding to other cases where rights of occupation are seriously disrupted.[185] The Court orders state and property owners to engage meaningfully with evictees to determine the details of an eviction, including the provision of alternative accommodation where evictees would otherwise be left homeless. In effect, the parties negotiate about what is reasonable in the circumstances, operating under (to date, loose) court supervision, with the court then granting an order for eviction or some other step in light of agreements reached. The result is that the Court has created a general procedural remedy applicable to every attempt at eviction, coupled with substantive orders, including specific orders to provide accommodation or refit buildings, that are case specific and do not create precedents. It thus affords some relief to the parties, while limiting its own policymaking role (which, as with the *Grootboom* model, is an achievement variably valued by scholars).[186] This is most obviously understood as a response to the challenges of making substantive judicial rulings in complex, policy-laden contexts, but the Court has also linked it explicitly to the inherent value of fair procedures and respectful dealings by the state with the public, citing *Doctors for Life*.[187]

[184] *Joseph*, *supra* note 122.

[185] *See esp.* Port Elizabeth Municipality v Various Occupiers 2005 (1) SA 217 (CC); Occupiers of 51 Olivia Road, Berea, and 197 Main Street, Johannesburg v City of Johannesburg 2008 (3) SA 208 (CC); *Joe Slovo, supra* note 128. Engagement has also now been applied in an action for restoration of possession – *Schubart Park, supra* note 161 – and it has been held that the constitutional prohibition on eviction without a court order, in terms of which engagement is ordered, applies to other instances in which occupation is disrupted – *see* Motswagae v Rustenberg Local Municipality 2013 (2) SA 613 (CC), paras 12–13.

[186] See, e.g., Kirsty McLean, *Meaningful Engagement: One Step Forward or Two Back? Some Thoughts on Joe Slovo* **3** Constitutional Court Rev. 223 (2010); Brian Ray, *Proceduralisation's Triumph and Engagement's Promise in Socio-economic Rights Litigation* **27** South African J. on Human Rights 107 (2011); Sandra Liebenberg, *Engaging the Paradoxes of the Universal and Particular in Human Rights Adjudication: The Possibilities and Pitfalls of "Meaningful Engagement"* **12** African Human Rights Law J. 1 (2012); Brian Ray, *Evictions, Avoidance and the Aspirational Impulse* **5** Constitutional Court Rev. (2014).

[187] See, e.g., *Schubart Park, supra* note 161, at para. 43, linking engagement in the eviction context to its general importance in a range of other contexts, including the legislative public participation cases.

Others generally discuss this resort to procedure as a response to the challenges of socioeconomic rights review, but that is not our present concern. Here, we stress a significant feature of this development that is less often remarked on. The cases stand for the large-scale importation of administrative law standards into a rights-based standard that applies to all public power and draws on the reasonableness test as used in that context. However, they also go further – because, as we have seen, reasonableness in rights review incorporates ideas of engagement and other procedural duties that are not part of reasonableness in administrative law.

This development has the potential to be confusing, especially because, as noted, the Court has not always confronted the question of how the two reasonableness standards in the two spheres relate to one another. *Joseph*, a rights case, establishes a link to PAJA, but the rights-based engagement cases in the eviction context do not. The rights-based holding in *Mazibuko* recognizes that PAJA does not apply to municipal executive power without investigating whether other standards, such as the legality principle, might apply.[188] The standards are also evolving and many details remain to be worked out. However, one can nevertheless see emerging the same sort of convergence in the review of administrative and non-administrative power that we have seen in other contexts.

Once again, the Court is applying broad ideas of democratic participation and accountability, drawn from rights, and blurring traditional institutional boundaries as a result. Once again, however, decisions like *Mazibuko*, *Joe Slovo*, and *Nokotyana v Ekurhuleni Metropolitan Municipality* show that, the expansions of reasonableness and engagement notwithstanding, the courts will continue to show considerable deference to officials in other institutions.[189]

It is not yet clear, however, whether the standards of reasonableness review will vary depending on whether or not actors are elected. The signs are that this will not be the most crucial factor. Admittedly, the most far-reaching developments discussed here – including *Mazibuko*, *Blue Moonlight*, and the engagement remedy – have all arisen in relation to municipal power, rather than national or provincial legislatures. But as noted, it is not clear that less respect is due in the municipal context, where governments wield both original legislative and executive power and direct election occurs. In

[188] *Id.* at para. 43. *See* Liebenberg, *supra* note 182, at 296–7; McLean, *supra* note 186, at 239–40 and further sources cited in n 186, *supra*.

[189] Nokotyana v Ekurhuleni Metropolitan Municipality 2010 (4) BCLR 312 (CC) was another case in which, as in *Mazibuko* and *Joe Slovo*, the Court sought to avoid unduly disrupting an ongoing government program.

addition, this reasonableness review is a rights-based test, and rights bind all public officials. The likeliest speculation, then, is that institutional differences will continue to make themselves felt, but at the level of detail. The expansion of rationality analysis has produced, for example, quite a close review of presidential conduct in *Albutt* and quite a deferential one in *Masetlha*, and the best reading is that this difference arises from the details of the context and purpose of the power being exercised. Similarly, the extent of institutional deference in reasonableness review can be expected to depend above all on the substantive details of the power and its impact in a particular context, rather than the formal institution involved.

If we turn to consider the question from the perspective of the reasonableness standard in administrative law, there are signs of the same trend. In the administrative context, the s 33 right explicitly provides that everyone has the right to "reasonable" administrative action. Although PAJA includes reasonableness as a ground of review, according to its formulation, judges may review conduct only if it is "so unreasonable that no reasonable person could have" acted as the official did. This suggests the comparatively weak *Wednesbury* concept of unreasonableness derived from English law (and, as such, appears to be another example of the legislature seeking to use PAJA to tone down the restraints on government action imposed by s 33 of the Constitution). However, the Court has not followed this restrictive implication, and it has defined a reasonable administrative decision simply as one a reasonable decision maker could reach.[190]

Stated at this level of generality, it is similar to the other reasonableness test used in rights review. Admittedly, in articulating the administrative law version of the test, the Court stressed distinctively administrative law features. For example, it stated that it would assess reasonableness in relation to the information before the decision maker and the reasons given.[191] But as the preceding discussion shows, these features may no longer serve to sharply distinguish the reasonableness test used in administrative law from the one used in rights review. In the wake of *Mazibuko*, the trend now seems to be to require the government to inform the court about its evidence and reasons under both tests.

Other differences also appear less than sharp. Courts have traditionally deployed the administrative law reasonableness test only in relation to

[190] PAJA, s 6(2)(h). For the *Wednesbury* test, *see* Associated Provincial Picture Houses Ltd v Wednesbury Corporation [1947] 2 All ER 680 (CA). For the Constitutional Court's approach, *see* Bato Star v Minister of Environmental Affairs 2004 (4) SA 490 (CC), paras 42–4.

[191] *Bato Star*, *supra* note 190, at para. 45.

narrow administrative decisions affecting individuals (and the PAJA test is framed accordingly), whereas reasonableness in the general rights context is most commonly deployed against larger-scale policy decisions like government housing plans. However, scale cannot distinguish the two tests. One can challenge any kind of action on rights grounds, and nothing prevents a litigant from challenging large-scale conduct on administrative law grounds provided it constitutes administrative action. The seminal administrative law case on reasonableness, for example, concerned the allocation of fishing quotas across an entire industry.[192] The courts express similar concerns for the role and place of other branches in both small- and large-scale cases.[193] Applications of reasonableness in the two contexts generally look similar.[194] Indeed, some commentators raise this similarity as evidence that the Court has given socioeconomic rights little substantive content of their own.[195]

There are also some signs of convergence toward the reasonableness standard used in rights review in other administrative law doctrines. (As noted, the rights review reasonableness standard has come to encompass more than the administrative law reasonableness standard.) The decision in *Pepcor Retirement Fund* is noteworthy. Traditionally, following English law, South African administrative law has only treated mistakes of fact by a decision maker as reviewable if they are "jurisdictional" facts – that is, the official thought he had legal authority to act whereas, in fact, he did

[192] *Id.* Several earlier challenges, under the pre-reasonableness administrative action right in the interim Constitution, implicated province-wide allocations of funds to public schools: see, e.g., *Premier, Mpumalanga*, *supra* note 107; Permanent Secretary, Department of Education and Welfare, Eastern Cape v Ed-U-College (PE) 2001 (2) SA 1 (CC); Bel Porto School Governing Body v Premier of the Western Cape Province 2002 (3) SA 265 (CC).

[193] For example, the resistance shown by the Court to a more intrusive "minimum core" interpretation of socioeconomic rights in *Grootboom*, *supra* note 168, and *Treatment Action Campaign (2)*, *supra* note 173, is grounded on the same sorts of separation of powers concerns as the Court's resistance to introducing too strong a substantive fairness test in the administrative procedure context in *Bel Porto*, *supra* note 192, or the concern with the distinction between appeal and review (discussed later in this chapter) shown by it in *Bato Star*, *supra* note at 190, and by the Supreme Court of Appeal in its earlier judgment in the same matter, Minister of Environmental Affairs and Tourism v Phambili Fisheries (Pty) Ltd [2003] 2 All SA 616 (SCA), paras 52–4.

[194] Geo Quinot & Sandra Liebenberg, *Narrowing the Band: Reasonableness Review in Administrative Justice and Socio-economic Rights Jurisprudence in South Africa* **22** Stellenbosch Law Rev. 639 (2011) also note this similarity between public law reasonableness (they consider only socioeconomic rights cases) and administrative review, which, as they note, is understudied. *See id.* at 639.

[195] The most important contributions to this debate are cited in *Id.*, 639 n1–2. For this criticism in the context of the *Mazibuko* decision, *supra* note 78, see Quinot, *Substantive Reasons*, *supra* note 4, esp. 127–8.

not.[196] Recently, however, the Supreme Court of Appeal has relied on the legality principle and the constitutional right to just administrative action to hold that any mistakes of fact can be a basis for reviewing a decision. Its reason appears to be that constitutional principles require decisions to serve the public interest.[197] Where a material error of fact results in a mistaken decision in an area of public importance – the facts of *Pepcor* related to pension fund administration – the public interest is not served, and a court should review the decision. Whether such a review will succeed "will depend on a consideration of the public interest in having the decision corrected and other factors, and in particular, the interests of the person in whose favor a decision has been taken."[198]

Pepcor resembles reasonableness review in the rights context in its restrained but, nevertheless, substantive review of a rather obviously flawed policy decision. Furthermore, the *Pepcor* court was openly concerned that its decision should not eliminate the common law distinction between appeal and review.[199] That distinction, inherited from English law, is intended to draw a line between a judge asking whether a decision was right on the merits (appeal), and merely asking whether it was legally authorized and taken in accordance with the required procedures (review), with a judge in the administrative law context ordinarily being confined to the latter.[200] *Pepcor*'s concern is, therefore, essentially the same as the concern expressed in rights cases that reasonableness review not turn into judicial second guessing of policy decisions. The decision, which has since become settled law, is evidence that the convergence of the usages is a product of the movement of *both* reasonableness standards toward the other.[201] The Supreme

[196] An exception is a mistake that triggers one of the other grounds of review; for example, if the mistake were malicious such that the decision maker could be said to be acting in bad faith.

[197] Pepcor Retirement Fund v Financial Services Board 2003 (6) SA 38 (SCA), para 47, *see also* paras 41–5; Hoexter, *supra* note 3, at 260–74.

[198] *Pepcor, supra* note 197, para 48.

[199] *Id.* at para 48.

[200] See, e.g., De Ville, *supra* note 139, at 27–31. On the tendency of the reasonableness standard to narrow the distinction between review and appeal, see, e.g., Klaaren & Penfold *supra* note 5, at 63–104 – 63–106, Hoexter, *supra* note 3, at 316–17; Elmene Bray, *Administrative Justice*, Environmental Compliance and Enforcement in South Africa: Legal Perspectives, 178–83 (Alexander Paterson & Louis J. Kotzé, eds., 2009); and the comments in *Bato Star, supra* note 190, at para 45, on how reasonableness incorporates a substantive element into administrative review but that the appeal/review distinction is of continued significance.

[201] The *Pepcor* ruling on this point has become settled law: *see esp.* Bullock NO v Provincial Government, North West Province 2004 (5) SA 262 (SCA), para 16; Oudekraal Estates (Pty) Ltd v City of Cape Town 2004 (6) SA 222 (SCA), para 25; *Chairpersons' Association,*

Court of Appeal's subsequent statements that *Pepcor* applies to the review of *all* exercises of public power, not just those that count as "administrative action" also supports this conclusion.[202]

Another sign of this convergence concerns review for vagueness. This has historically been an aspect of reasonableness review in administrative law under South African common law. It applies to both delegated legislation and individual administrative decisions.[203] This type of review continues to be important under the 1996 Constitution, but courts now review legislation for vagueness as well. The basis for legislative review is the principle of legality (not the rights-based reasonableness test): like *Pepcor*'s mistake of non-jurisdictional fact, vagueness is a ground of review of any exercise of public power.[204]

The technical lines are far from neat. A general reasonableness standard used in rights review, abetted by the legality principle, applies to all public power, while a narrower reasonableness standard used in administrative law, abetted by other traditional administrative law doctrines like mistake of fact, applies only to administrative action. Some things that fall under one reasonableness standard fall under different headings in the other context. But while the courts' usage of reasonableness and legality seems less than systematic, we can nevertheless see the broader trend toward convergence through the tangle. Institutional differences may still drive variations in the assessment, but increasingly they do not drive sharp differences in the standards being applied, and similar imperatives seem to be at work across the different contexts.

C. Proportionality and the Limitations Clause

Reasonableness and rationality do not exhaust the review standards available in either the administrative or legislative review context. As noted,

(2007) supra note 127, para. 48; and Chairman, State Tender Board v Digital Voice Processing (Pty) Ltd; Chairman, State Tender Board v Sneller Digital (Pty) Ltd 2012 (2) SA 16 (SCA), paras 35–6.

202 See esp. Democratic Alliance v President of the Republic of South Africa 2012 (1) SA 417 (SCA), para. 112 n18; *Bullock NO, supra* note 201, at para. 16. The relationship between this sort of review and PAJA therefore remains problematic: *see further* Clive Plasket, *Administrative Law* 25, 37–8 Annual Survey of South African Law (2007).

203 Hoexter, *supra* note 3, at 332–3.

204 Affordable Medicines Trust v Minister of Health 2006 (3) SA 247 (CC), paras 108–9; *Kruger, supra* note 33, at paras 65, 67; *see also* De Lange v Smuts NO 1998 (3) SA 785 (CC), paras 46–7; Hoexter, *supra* note 3, at 356–7, and further cases there discussed. Note that Chaskalson CJ states that vagueness falls under s 6(2)(i) even though it is not specifically mentioned in PAJA – *New Clicks, supra* note 3, at para. 246, Wandisile Warwa-Mandlana & Clive Plasket, *Administrative Law* Annual Survey of South African Law, 104, 117 (2005).

reasonableness is used in a variety of rights contexts, but there are also other, rights-specific tests of various kinds. Similarly, administrative law offers a range of other grounds for review. However, we confine ourselves here to a final example that is of particular relevance to the comparison between the two areas: proportionality analysis. Proportionality is embodied in the Constitution's limitations clause in section 36, and according to some, it was part of the pre-1994 administrative law conception of reasonableness.[205] Commentators today argue that it is, at least, implicit in both the public law and administrative law reasonableness tests that the courts currently use.[206]

Section 36 is another key provision that can oblige the government to provide reasons in the legislative context. In South African law the complainant must first establish a violation, after which the inquiry shifts to whether that violation can be justified under the limitations clause. At that stage, the government bears what the Court has called "an onus of a special type."[207] Deciding whether a limitation is justified often means considering evidence – for example, the impact of the impugned measures on society.[208] The government has a duty to provide this evidence to the court. If it seeks to defend the limitation, failure to submit the necessary supporting material can lead to a finding of invalidity.[209] Functionally, the court is requiring the government to submit reasons for a decision. Because the limitations clause applies to any "law of general application," its reason-giving requirements apply in the context of legislation, as well as to administrative rulemaking.

[205] See, e.g., YVONNE BURNS, ADMINISTRATIVE LAW UNDER THE 1996 CONSTITUTION (REV. ED., 1999) 193–4; LAWRENCE BAXTER, ADMINISTRATIVE LAW 528–9 (1984).

[206] HOEXTER, *supra* note 3, at 343–6; Cora Hoexter *Unreasonableness in the Administrative Justice Act* in THE RIGHT TO KNOW: SOUTH AFRICA'S PROMOTION OF ADMINISTRATIVE JUSTICE AND ACCESS TO INFORMATION ACTS, 154–6 (Claudia Lange & Jakkie Wessels, eds., 2004); Sandra Liebenberg *Interpretation of Socio-Economic Rights* in CONSTITUTIONAL LAW OF SOUTH AFRICA (2ND ED.), 33–39 – 33–40 (Stu Woolman & Michael Bishop, eds., 2005); LIEBENBERG, *supra* note 182, at 161; Quinot & Liebenberg, *supra* note 194, at 646–7, 650–1, 654–5, 659–61; Bray, *supra* note 200, at 181–2; Alistair Price, *The Content and Justification of Rationality Review* **25** SOUTH AFRICAN PUBLIC LAW/SUID-AFRIKAANSE PUBLIEKREG 345, 356–9, 361 n71 (2010); Danie Brand, "Introduction to Socio-economic Rights in the South African Constitution," in SOCIO-ECONOMIC RIGHTS IN SOUTH AFRICA 51 (Danie Brand & Christof Heyns, eds., 2005).

[207] Minister of Home Affairs v National Institute for Crime Prevention and the Re-integration of Offenders (NICRO) 2005 (3) SA 280 (CC), para. 34.

[208] IAIN CURRIE & JOHAN DE WAAL, THE BILL OF RIGHTS HANDBOOK (5TH ED.), 167 (2005).

[209] Moise v Greater Germiston Transitional Local Council 2001 (4) SA 491 (CC); *NICRO*, *supra* note 207.

As currently understood, the s 36 limitations inquiry is objective in the sense that it simply asks whether there are reasons to think the limitation is justified. It does not focus on particular reasons that the relevant state actors offer to justify the offending action. In fact, in principle, the s 36 inquiry does not even depend on the reasons that the government offers in court. A failure by the government to offer justifications for review does not necessarily lead the court to find that the limitation is unjustified – although this tends to be the result in practice. The judges must still satisfy themselves that the limitation is, in fact, unjustified. (The onus on the government is said to be of "a special type" because failure to discharge it does not inevitably mean that the legal point is decided against the government.)[210]

Proportionality may not be confined to s 36.[211] It is arguably also an element of the reasonableness standard both in administrative law and in the context of rights review. Proportionality is not mentioned as a ground of review in PAJA and has so far received the explicit support in this context of only one Constitutional Court judge (Justice Sachs). Hoexter, however, argues that it is substantially incorporated into the understanding of administrative law reasonableness set out in *Bato Star*.[212] Only one Constitutional Court judge (Justice O'Regan, in dissent) has conducted a proportionality inquiry as part of a reasonableness analysis in the context of rights review – that is, in determining whether a right has been limited, rather than in deciding whether that limitation of the right is justified (under s 36). Nevertheless, some commentators argue that the inquiry is latent in the existing case law, although judges have yet to go so far as to apply it.[213]

[210] *NICRO*, *supra* note 207, at paras 35–6; *see further* Stu Woolman & Danie Brand, *Limitations*, in CONSTITUTIONAL LAW OF SOUTH AFRICA (2ND ED.), 33-44 – 33-45 (Stu Woolman & Michael Bishop, eds., 2005); CURRIE & DE WAAL, *supra* note 208, at 166–7.

[211] We leave to one side the technical problem of how to relate proportionality analysis at the interpretive stage to proportionality analysis under section 36 that tests whether a limitation is justified, although it may have played a role in restraining the development of proportionality analysis. *See* Woolman & Brand, *supra* note 210, at 34-31 – 34-42; Kevin Iles, *Limiting Socio-economic Rights: Beyond the Internal Limitations Clauses* **20** SOUTH AFRICAN J. ON HUMAN RIGHTS 448, 450–3 (2004) and sources there cited.

[212] HOEXTER, *supra* note 3, at 349–50; *see* Sachs J in *New Clicks*, *supra* note 3, at paras 637, 661.

[213] The one example (not usually recognized as such) is the lone dissent of O'Regan J in *New National Party*, *supra* note 36. For further analysis of her dissent in this regard, *see* FOWKES, *supra* note 17, chapter 3. On proportionality as part of the Court's public law reasonableness test and its absence in the application of that test, *see* Theunis Roux, *Legitimating Transformation: Political Resource Allocation in the South African Constitutional Court* **10** DEMOCRATIZATION 92, 96–7 (2003) and sources cited in *supra* note 206.

(It is worth noting, in passing, that the similarly minimal development of the standard in both contexts reflects the general judicial concern for the separation of powers. It also supports the claim that similar considerations are in play in both contexts. As elsewhere, it produces convergence: here, a convergence of caution.)

In principle, the inquiry under both sorts of reasonableness analysis is objective, like the s 36 inquiry: the test is whether the decision or conduct is reasonable, not whether the relevant actor offered reasons at the time showing that it was reasonable. In principle, the duty of the state to offer evidence and reasons for a decision affecting socioeconomic rights, under *Mazibuko*, looks a lot like the "onus of a special type" of the s 36 inquiry. As with the s 36 duty, a failure by the state to comply with the *Mazibuko* obligation is not, in principle, fatal to its case, but, in practice, one expects that it will have that effect. The explanation may simply be an inference that an official who does not offer a justification in court is an official who cannot provide one. But the more judicial review seeks to further openness and participatory democracy as goods in themselves, as we saw earlier in various contexts including *Mazibuko*, the more courts might come to focus on the reasons that the officials actually offer. Whether this will occur remains to be seen, but this speculation raises the possibility that current trends may affect the s 36 inquiry. The distinctively democratic focus of South African review in general may in time produce a distinctive proportionality inquiry.

VII. CONCLUSIONS ON SOUTH AFRICA

South Africa is a hybrid case. It is essentially a parliamentary system. Hence, the legislative majority does not have an incentive to impose constraints on rulemaking into the executive. However, the drafting of the new constitutions was a special moment. The drafters sought to entrench the postapartheid values of responsiveness, openness, and accountability, and to prevent future executives from denying fair procedures to any South African, as had so often been the case in the past. This history accounts for the unusual extent to which the Constitution expresses these values and for the attitude of the ANC government. Rights-based legitimacy plays an important role, as in the German and U.S. cases, but in South Africa considerations of rights are bound up with ideas of participatory democracy and inclusion.

The courts have further developed the constitutional supports for public participation. Participatory values influence decision-making processes both in the legislatures and in the administration. In contrast, the decision to include various restrictions on the scope of PAJA, passed in 2000 some years after the transition, looks consistent with our claim that parliamentary systems lack special incentives to constrain rulemaking. However, although the text of PAJA is not always clear, its sometimes restrictive wording has not stopped the courts from giving effect to constitutional values of participation and democratic accountability.

South African judges and legislators are responding to a new constitutionalism in which all public power is subject to judicial review. Rights and values such as accountability, transparency, and participatory democracy now apply to all exercises of public power. The courts no longer treat certain institutions and powers as off limits to judicial review. Even where democratic values are most dominant, as in review of legislative power, the Constitutional Court has been willing to intervene in the name of these values, albeit with some caution. Furthermore and as a consequence, the standards of review across different contexts are converging.

In the wake of these changes, the judiciary is seeking to be sensitive to the greater democratic legitimacy of other branches and the need not to disrupt their efficient functioning, consistent with the need to give effect to the new constitutional values and to protect individual rights. Their jurisprudence recognizes both that rights certainly still matter and that the courts need to respect the elected legislature and the expertise of the executive. In spite of the convergence of legislative and administrative review, South African jurisprudence recognizes that differences remain between the institutional roles of the two branches. For example, a major difference between the treatment of administrative and legislative conduct is the application of the doctrine of bad faith; courts do not apply it to political decisions made by multi-member legislatures. This may seem like a practical consideration, but, at bottom, it recognizes that courts should not always demand of elected legislators – who are accountable to the electorate – the sorts of reason-giving that courts would require of unelected officials. To do so would inject the courts too far into the substance of lawmaking.

In general, the judiciary has focused on procedure. The courts review the way public bodies reach decisions and the reasons they offer. These procedural requirements are driven by substantive concerns related to the protection of rights. Rather than deciding substantive questions outright, the courts prefer to ask if the process was based on law, was open and accountable, and took account of relevant considerations. This represents a compromise between the preservation of these new rights, on the one hand, and established reasons for judicial restraint, such as democratic legitimacy and the separation of powers, on the other.

Because these considerations play out differently when applied to legislative and administrative conduct, one would expect continuing differences in the judicial review of these powers, even if the tests are word-for-word identical. However, many of those distinctions remain to be drawn. The new South African doctrine of separation of powers remains a work in progress. Two particularly important sites of activity concern duties of repeated engagement as a process unfolds, and the duty to give reasons. In a number of contexts, judges grapple with whether public participation is a one-off procedural step to be ticked off or a more substantive exercise that may require repeated steps until a body can claim to have engaged in meaningful consultation. Much will depend on the interpretation of *Merafong* and on the Constitutional Court's reaction to the Supreme Court of Appeal's decisions on public participation in the municipal context. Similarly, reason-giving is expanding into new areas, but it remains to be seen if it will become a general requirement in areas such as administrative rulemaking or even legislative activity. These developments, in turn, have implications for judicial review, especially because courts will have to decide how to react if the government gives the court reasons that differ from those it offered to affected members of the public at the time. The more judicial review is understood as an exercise in supporting accountable and participatory democracy, the less satisfying it will be to focus on an objective inquiry into whether there are adequate reasons for a decision, as distinct from the state actor's engagement with the public in articulating reasons for it.

Much remains uncertain, but the evidence of convergence across a variety of institutional contexts shows that rights and principles remain the dominant force behind the expansion of review, producing standards that are consistent across the types of power that the courts review. Because of the richer conception of democracy in its constitutionalism, South Africa has a head start compared with German public law in fostering public participation in rulemaking processes.

In the United States, administrative rules that make policy are subject to procedural constraints that improve their democratic legitimacy. The deliberative process in the legislature is not subject to judicial control and is constrained only by electoral and other political pressures. In contrast, South African constitutionalism directly expresses the value of participatory democracy, openness, and inclusion in the making of policy, wherever it occurs. Although expressed in open-ended terms, this explicit approach gives the courts a clear role in assuring democratic legitimacy, alongside and as part of its role in upholding rights. It is an important case to watch as its courts struggle to balance this constitutional mandate with their desire not to step too intrusively into political disputes.

4

Germany

In Germany judicial review of both statutes and executive rules emphasizes legal substance, especially the protection of rights. Constitutional norms contain very few procedural obligations, but they set out strong substantive requirements, derived especially from the key principles of proportionality and equality. Even the Federal Constitutional Court's (*Bundesverfassungsgericht*) weakest level of proportionality review is stricter than the U.S. rational basis test.[1] Statutes do not impose detailed and coherent procedural standards either on the legislative process or on executive rulemaking – consistent with our claim that parliamentary systems are unlikely to impose general procedural constraints on the executive. However, we document situations where statutes do impose certain procedures on executive rulemaking or permit legislative checks. Nevertheless, these constraints have only limited impact on rulemaking procedures. Procedural provisions in German law are often more hortatory recommendations than legal mandates. The situation is in flux, however; both the rights-based nature of review and the process of European integration are pushing policymaking in the direction of more transparency and more reliance on outside expertise. The latter move, however, need not imply greater openness to the general public.

1 *See* Daniel Halberstam, *The Promise of Comparative Administrative Law: A Constitutional Perspective on Independent Agencies*, in COMPARATIVE ADMINISTRATIVE LAW 185 at 196 (Susan Rose-Ackerman & Peter L. Lindseth, eds., 2010) on the scope of Art. 12 GRUNDGESETZ FÜR DIE BUNDESREPUBLIK DEUTSCHLAND [GRUNDGESETZ] [GG] [Basic Law], May 23, 1949, BUNDESGESETZBLATT [BGBl.] [hereinafter, GG] at 1, available in English at http://www.gesetze-im-internet.de/englisch_gg/index.html (translated by Christian Tomuschat and David P. Currie; the subsequent citations from the Basic Law are taken from this translated version). Halberstam compares 7 ENTSCHEIDUNGEN DES BUNDESVERFASSUNGSGERICHTS [BVERFGE] [Federal Constitutional Court] 377 (1958) with Williamson v. Lee Optical Co., 348 U.S. 483 (1955).

Nevertheless, even if a shift toward greater openness occurs, the judiciary seems unlikely to seek to enhance the democratic accountability of executive rulemaking. So far, at least, their efforts parallel those of the U.S. Supreme Court majority in its recent reviews of statutes that implicate federalism values. In both countries, the burden of proof that the courts impose on legislators or government officials is designed to help the courts evaluate constitutional challenges; any impact on the state's democratic accountability to citizens is a secondary by-product.

There are no sharp distinctions and some overlaps between administrative rules and statutes. The government exercises a strong influence on executive rulemaking in order to assure that the rules accord with its policy agenda. The courts check to be sure that the resulting rules are consistent with the statutes that granted rulemaking authority. However, access to the courts is not generally available for individual actions that challenge the democratic legitimacy and competence of the state without affecting rights. The Constitutional Court does not emphasize public input as a source of democratic legitimacy either for statutes or for secondary legislation promulgated by the executive and the agencies. Compared to South Africa, German law, thus, takes a significantly different approach to the establishment of procedural rules. The Constitutional Court has, however, examined the quality of the technical information available to the legislature and has found rights violations when the legislature could not justify the factual assumptions behind certain laws. Such "strict scrutiny" occurs in the United States as well, but with fewer substantive constitutional rights, a detailed examination of the factual underpinnings of legislation rarely occurs. The exceptions, noted earlier, are the cases dealing with federal legislative power vis-à-vis the states.

The German Constitution or Basic Law (*Grundgesetz*) includes structural provisions for the passage of legislation and explicitly permits the delegation of rulemaking authority to the executive. The Constitutional Court enforces these requirements, but it does not otherwise consider the democratic legitimacy of policymaking processes in the legislature or in the government. The German conception of democracy has moved beyond a strict separation of powers between the executive and legislature and recognizes their interdependence and the value of supplementary democratic "routes."[2] Nevertheless, the Court views elections as the primary route for

[2] *See* Niels Petersen, *Demokratie und Grundgesetz – Veränderungen des Demokratieprinzips in Art. 20 Abs. 2 GG angesichts der Herausforderungen moderner Staatlichkeit*, **58** Jahrbuch des Öffentlichen Rechts der Gegenwart, 137, 168–70 (2010) (arguing for a deliberative model of democracy that is based on plurality and expertise).

public accountability and distrusts calls for more public participation in policymaking.[3] More direct participation could undermine the influence of both elected representatives and technical experts. Consequently, the Court generally abstains from demanding democratic legitimation of policymaking through procedural routes, such as requirements for public participation.[4] Hence, the German case stands in contrast to South Africa where the Constitution and its interpretation by the Constitutional Court emphasize the values of public participation and openness for legislative and administrative lawmaking based on a strong commitment to the democratic value of inclusiveness.

The German courts do intervene when rights are at stake. Both the administrative courts and the Constitutional Court focus on their preservation. The Basic Law begins with a long list of rights and gives individuals access to the courts to defend these rights.[5] As the final arbiter, the Constitutional Court analyzes the constitutionality of the challenged state action, often concluding with a review of proportionality. The principle of proportionality derives from the rule-of-law principle and forms a crucial ingredient of fundamental rights review.[6] It requires legislative provisions and other state actions to fulfill three conditions. First, the measure must be suitable to promote a legitimate aim; second, it must use the least restrictive means available; and third, it must be proportionate to the predicted costs and benefits of the legislative solution using a balancing test. Individuals can only bring cases to the Constitutional Court if their rights are at stake – whether the case concerns a legislative or an executive matter.[7] This focus on rights covers all types of rulemaking because, unlike American law, the jurisprudence of the Constitutional Court does not distinguish sharply

[3] *Id.* at 14–16 (explaining that despite new approaches, the recent adjudication of the Constitutional Court still follows a formal concept of democracy based on representation).

[4] *But see* 107 BVerfGE 59, 91 f. (stating in the context of self-government: "Within the framework of popular government based on representation, the Basic Law also allows for special forms of participation of the affected parties when executing public tasks").

[5] Basic Law articles 1–20. Other rights are scattered throughout the Basic Law, for example at article 20(4), article 33, article 38, article 101, article 103, and article 104. Article 19(4) guarantees judicial review.

[6] David P. Currie, *Lochner Abroad: Substantive Due Process and Equal Protection in the Federal Republic of Germany*, 1989 The Supreme Court Rev. 333, at 353 f. (comparing the elements of proportionality to "the American tests both for substantive due process and for the necessity and propriety of federal legislation").

[7] Individuals have standing to bring constitutional complaints only if they can claim a subjective rights violation, Basic Law article 93(1) no. 4a. Disputes between state organs can reach the court without any rights-based claims, Basic Law article 93(1) no. 1.

between the judicial review of statutes and secondary legislation. The third type of legitimacy, competence and expertise, is not an independent basis of review. However, challenges to the evidentiary basis of a rule sometimes are at the core of rights-based cases. In order for a limitation of rights to be judged proportional, the courts often demand that the rule have a rational factual basis. Of course, even if the protection of rights motivated a lawsuit, a decision that requires transparent and well-justified statutes and regulations may indirectly affect the democratic accountability of public policymaking.

Hence, the three types of legitimacy overlap. The Constitutional Court's focus on rights leads it to require competent, well-reasoned justifications for policies that affect rights, and that requirement, in turn, can enhance the public accountability of procedures in both the legislature and the executive. However, the Court's focus on rights leaves gaps – closing some routes to Constitutional Court review. For example, legislative and executive decisions concerning the allocation of monetary resources or economic policy, which could affect a large number of people in the long run, largely escape review because the rules rarely have direct, immediate consequences for individuals.

To some extent, the courts have filled these gaps by invoking fundamental rights to push decision makers to explain the underlying factual bases of policies. There is, however, no clear judicial recognition of the benefit for democracy of more open and participatory rulemaking in the executive and of well-justified statutory drafting procedures in the legislature. Rather, procedural safeguards are still seen as essentially a way to protect fundamental rights (*Grundrechtsschutz durch Verfahren*).[8] Fundamental rights impose substantive limitations on state action, and the Constitutional Court demands the use of procedures that help individuals enforce their rights. The Constitutional Court generally views transparency and reason-giving as ways to make it easier for the courts to judge if there has been a violation of substantive rights. It seldom characterizes such processes as preconditions for accountable, democratic government.

[8] 53 BVerfGE 30, 59 f., 65; 49 BVerfGE 89, 139 f.; Eberhard Schmidt-Assmann, Das allgemeine Verwaltungsrecht als Ordnungsidee [hereinafter, Schmidt-Assmann, Verwaltungsrecht] 305, 309 f. (2nd ed., 2006) (criticizing the confinement to the "serving function" of procedural law); Udo Di Fabio, Risikoentscheidungen im Rechtsstaat [hereinafter, Di Fabio, Risikoentscheidungen] 21–6 (1994) (stating that the development of complex new regulatory tasks challenges the focus of German administrative law on individuals and their subjective rights).

Recall our general expectation that in a parliamentary system the legislative majority would have little incentive to constrain the policymaking process inside government ministries. Furthermore, an active constitutional court charged with protecting rights would not, in principle, distinguish between statutes and secondary legislation, but might, in practice, review the legislative process more carefully simply because it is more transparent than executive rulemaking procedures. These expectations seem broadly consistent with the German case. The Administrative Procedures Act[9] does not govern rulemaking. Instead, if detailed statutory mandates are either impractical or politically difficult, the legislature itself sometimes retains the power to exercise substantive control through the review of executive regulations. These controls comport with German views of the central role of the parliament in lawmaking, but one might suppose that the cabinet would not be enthusiastic. However, the government may accept these provisions not only because ministers recognize the dominance of parliament in lawmaking but also because the risks of deadlock and controversy are relatively small. Review would be carried out by the body whose majority formed the government, and the procedures themselves are usually time limited and do not allow the opposition to impose long delays. The main exception here would be a minority party coalition partner wishing to highlight its power to challenge the government.

Beyond legislative-executive relations, the open-ended nature of constitutional rights gives the Constitutional Court the option of reviewing the actions of both the administration and the legislature. Its recent forays in that direction, although grounded in the jurisprudence of rights, suggest that German public law may be open to reconsidering established legal doctrine in light of increased demands for public accountability.

We begin with a discussion of the separation of powers as it applies to the non-delegation doctrine. Then, we discuss judicial review of the legislative process and of the substance of statutes. Finally, we contrast review of legislation with review of the administrative process.

I. SEPARATION OF POWERS: THE NON-DELEGATION DOCTRINE

In the German Basic Law the "separation of powers" principle divides state authority into the three conventional branches: the legislature, the executive,

[9] Verwaltungsverfahrensgesetz [VwVfG] [Administrative Procedures Act], Jan. 23, 2003, BUNDESGESETZBLATT TEIL 1 [BGBL I] 102 [hereinafter VwVfG], most recently amended by article 3 of the act of July 25, 2013, BGBL I 2749.

and the judiciary (horizontal separation of powers).[10] The Basic Law takes account of the interdependence of the branches, but actual political practice also has had a strong influence on the understanding of the separation of powers.[11] Interactions between the legislative and executive branches have shaped the modern German political system.[12] The coalition parties in parliament elect the government, whose members head the respective ministries and thus are at the top of the hierarchical executive structure. The center of legitimacy, nevertheless, lies in the directly elected parliament, whose structure and procedures aim to ensure debate, minority participation, control, and transparency. Accordingly, the Basic Law requires that debates in parliament must be open to the public. Conversely, a principle of confidentiality has long governed executive action[13] – a principle that is increasingly in tension with recent developments emphasizing freedom of access to information. The parliament confers democratic legitimation on the government and in chains of legitimacy (*Legitimationsketten*) down the hierarchical ladder in the executive.[14] Additionally, the parliament creates a basis for legitimacy by enacting statutes. To guard this power, the non-delegation doctrine governs the distribution of lawmaking authority between the legislature and the executive.

[10] Helmuth Schulze-Fielitz, *Artikel 20 Grundgesetz (Rechtsstaat)*, in GRUNDGESETZ-KOMMENTAR, BAND 2 ¶ 69 [hereinafter, Schulze-Fielitz, *Artikel 20 Grundgesetz*] (Horst Dreier, ed., 2nd ed., 2006). The vertical separation of powers refers to the division between the federal level and the states. Peter Häberle, *Das Verständnis des Rechts als Problem des Verfassungsstaates*, in DIE SPRACHE DES RECHTS, BAND 1: RECHT VERSTEHEN, VERSTÄNDLICHKEIT, MISSVERSTÄNDLICHKEIT UND UNVERSTÄNDLICHKEIT VON RECHT 155, at 158 f. (Kent D. Lerch, ed., 2004) (on the notion of horizontal and vertical separation of powers).

[11] Udo Di Fabio, *§ 27 Gewaltenteilung*, in HANDBUCH DES STAATSRECHTS DER BUNDESREPUBLIK DEUTSCHLAND, BAND II VERFASSUNGSSTAAT ¶ 31, 35 (Josef Isensee & Paul Kirchhof, eds., 3d. ed., 2004).

[12] Eberhard Schütt-Wetschky, *Gewaltenteilung zwischen Legislative und Exekutive?*, **50** AUS POLITIK UND ZEITGESCHICHTE B 28/2000, 5, at 9 f. (2000) (describing the development from the classic separation of powers concept envisioned by the Parliamentary Council to the "new" understanding as a separation of powers between the government and the opposition originating in the 1960s).

[13] BERNHARD W. WEGENER, DER GEHEIME STAAT, ARKANTRADITION UND INFORMATIONSFREIHEIT 3, 7, 223–57 (2006) (providing a detailed overview of the tradition of secrecy in the executive as opposed to the openness of parliamentary debates). Article 42(1) Basic Law requires that parliamentary debates must be open.

[14] Ernst-Wolfgang Böckenförde, *Demokratie als Verfassungsprinzip*, in STAAT, VERFASSUNG, DEMOKRATIE, STUDIEN ZUR VERFASSUNGSTHEORIE UND ZUM VERFASSUNGSRECHT 289, at 299 (Ernst-Wolfgang Böckenförde, ed., 2nd ed., 1991); HERMANN PÜNDER, EXEKUTIVE NORMSETZUNG IN DEN VEREINIGTEN STAATEN VON AMERIKA UND DER BUNDESREPUBLIK DEUTSCHLAND 102 f. (1995).

The Basic Law's principles of democracy and the rule of law require that certain state actions must be grounded in a parliamentary statute (*Vorbehalt des Gesetzes*).[15] In particular, fundamental rights can only be limited through a statute. The Constitutional Court developed this principle further and stated that the legislature itself has to make all "essential" decisions in such situations (*Wesentlichkeitstheorie*).[16] Additionally, the Basic Law explicitly allows and limits the delegation of rulemaking to the executive, thus acknowledging both the demand for regulation and the limited capacity of the legislature.[17] Executive rulemaking has to be linked to a parliamentary statute that delegates power to a particular executive organ that is responsible to the parliament. The text of the Basic Law is much more explicit about the delegation of rulemaking authority to the executive than the U.S. Constitution. Article 80(1) Basic Law states:

> The Federal Government, a Federal Minister or the Land governments may be authorised by a law to issue statutory instruments [regulations]. The content, purpose and scope of the authority conferred shall be specified in the law. Each statutory instrument [regulation] shall contain a statement of its legal basis. If the law provides that such authority may be further delegated, such subdelegation shall be effected by statutory instrument [regulation].

In the early years of the Basic Law, shortly after World War II, the Constitutional Court gave a rather rigid interpretation to the content, purpose, and scope of the delegation in empowering statutes in recognition of the misuse of executive regulation under the Nazi regime.[18] By the 1960s, however, the Court began to apply these constraints more loosely in response to the changing imperatives of modern government.[19] Contrary

[15] 33 BVerfGE 125, 158; Schulze-Fielitz, *Artikel 20 Grundgesetz*, *supra* note 10, at 105–27.

[16] 33 BVerfGE 125, 158; 40 BVerfGE 237, 248 ff.; 49 BVerfGE 89, 126 f. and many subsequent decisions (settled case law).

[17] 8 BVerfGE 274, 311, 321 f.; 101 BVerfGE 1, 35; Hartmut Bauer, *Artikel 80 Grundgesetz*, in Grundgesetz-Kommentar, Band 2 ¶ 11, 14 (Horst Dreier, ed., 2nd ed., 2006) (stating that, statistically, the number of regulations is around three times higher than the number of enacted statutes on a federal level, with 30–40 percent of regulations needing approval of the Bundesrat, ¶14); Statistisches Bundesamt (ed.), Statistisches Jahrbuch 2011 für die Bundesrepublik Deutschland 111 provides statistical data on the number of regulations and statutes for the 14th to 16th legislative periods of the German parliament, available under https://www.destatis.de/DE/Publikationen/StatistischesJahrbuch/StatistischesJahrbuch2011.pdf?__blob=publicationFile).

[18] 1 BVerfGE 14, 59 f. (explicitly referring to the experiences in the Weimar Republic).

[19] Roland Geitmann, Bundesverfassungsgericht und "offene" Normen, 167 ff. (1971) (providing an extensive overview of adjudication showing that, since the 1960s, hardly any regulation has been struck down on the basis of article 80 Basic Law); Pünder, *supra* note 14, at 68 (stating that the Constitutional Court has not voided any

to current American legal doctrine, which has essentially abandoned the non-delegation doctrine, the Constitutional Court limits legislative delegation by requiring that the use and content of the regulation should be "foreseeable" from the statutory language.[20] The Court deems an empowering provision sufficiently specific if the content, purpose, and scope can be derived from a systematic, teleological, or historic interpretation of the statute as a whole.[21] The level of specificity required depends on the issue in question, the intensity of the regulation, the complexity of the issue, and the likelihood that conditions will change over time.[22] The statute's empowering provision can thus be set out in a quite general standard.[23] Delegation of regulatory authority has increased because of the growing importance of risk regulation, which depends on scientific-technical data (e.g., energy and environmental law), the need to steer economic processes (e.g., telecommunication law), and the flexibility required in areas such as financial, economic, transport, and social law.[24] In those areas, the legislature often enacts abstract general provisions and leaves the concrete, detailed implementation to the administration.[25] The courts have generally accepted the validity of such wide delegations, especially in technically complex areas.

empowering statute for a violation of specificity principle since 23 BVerfGE 208, 223); Johannes Saurer, Die Funktionen der Rechtsverordnung 289 ff. (2005); Armin von Bogdandy, Gubernative Rechtsetzung 338 (2000); Thomas von Danwitz, Die Gestaltungsfreiheit des Verordnungsgebers 102 f. (1989); Fritz Ossenbühl, *§ 103 Rechtsverordnung*, in Handbuch des Staatsrechts der Bundesrepublik Deutschland, Band 5 [hereinafter, Ossenbühl, *§ 103 Rechtsverordnung*] ¶ 4, 15 (Josef Isensee & Paul Kirchhof, eds., 3rd ed., 2007).

20 1 BVerfGE 14, 60; 2 BVerfGE 307, 334; 78 BVerfGE 249, 272 (settled case law).

21 8 BVerfGE 274, 307 (settled case law); *see also* the case law of the Federal Administrative Court 30 Entscheidungen des Bundesverwaltungsgerichts [BVerwGE] [Federal Administrative Court] 287, 292; 65 BVerwGE 323, 326; 68 BVerwGE 277, 280 f.

22 58 BVerfGE 257, 277 f. (citing more examples); *see* more recently 103 BVerfGE 332, 384 f.

23 48 BVerfGE 210, 222 f. (regarding the area of tax law); 101 BVerfGE 1, 32 f. (settled case law) (regarding indeterminate legal language in § 2 Animal Protection Act).

24 Ossenbühl, § 103 Rechtsverordnung, *supra* note 19, at 4, 15; Hans Schneider, Gesetzgebung – Ein Lehrbuch 231, footnote 4 (3rd ed., 2002). For example, provisions of the Federal Emissions Control Act delegate many different responsibilities to the executive and mandate the purpose, scope, and content of the regulation (and thus comply with article 80 Basic Law) but nevertheless leave a wide margin of discretion.

25 The legislature uses general terms such as the *Stand von Wissenschaft und Technik* (state of the scientific and technical knowledge), *see* Gesetz über die friedliche Verwendung der Kernenergie und den Schutz gegen ihre Gefahren [Atomgesetz] [Nuclear Energy Law], July 15, 1985, BGBl I 1565, most recently amended by article 5 of the act of Aug. 28, 2013, BGBl I 3313, § 7(2) Nr. 3 and Gesetz über die Haftung für fehlerhafte Produkte [Produkthaftungsgesetz – ProdHaftG] [Product Liability Law], Dec. 15, 1989, BGBl I 2198, most recently amended by article 9 sect. 3 of the act of July 19, 2002, BGBl I

Sometimes parliament limits delegation not through detailed substantive language but, instead, by giving the parliament certain rights to participate in the production of secondary norms.[26] Then, the parliament's role in executive rulemaking processes compensates for the general language in wide delegations.[27] The Constitutional Court has accepted the legality of these options as consistent with parliamentary dominance. Parliamentary participation as a way to increase the democratic legitimacy of rulemaking stands in sharp contrast to the United States, where rulemaking legitimacy depends on extensive administrative procedures involving the public, and where legislative vetoes are unconstitutional. This again shows the fundamentally different approaches. In Germany, the main form of legitimacy, even for executive rulemaking, derives from elections, whereas in the United States, public participation plays a strong, legitimizing function, over and above the president's legitimacy as an independently elected chief executive.

Yet the grounding of legitimacy in the parliament seems at odds with the reality of political power. Under the German system, the party or party coalition that controls the majority in the Bundestag organizes the cabinet, and statutes are usually drafted in the cabinet ministries. Hence, one might expect broad delegation because open-ended mandates give the governing

2674, § 1(2) no. 5; Ossenbühl, *§ 103 Rechtsverordnung*, *supra* note 19, at 4, 15; Helmuth Schulze-Fielitz, *Technik und Umweltrecht*, in HANDBUCH DES TECHNIKRECHTS [hereinafter, Schulze-Fielitz, *Technik*] 455, at 465, 470 ff. (Martin Schulte & Rainer Schröder, eds., 2nd ed. 2011); HORST DREIER, HIERARCHISCHE VERWALTUNG 164 ff. (1991) (critically comparing the speed of passing new statutes and updating them); SAURER, *supra* note 19, at 87 ff. with further references.

26 For example, Gesetz zum Schutz vor schädlichen Umwelteinwirkungen durch Luftverunreinigungen, Geräusche, Erschütterungen und ähnliche Vorgänge [Bundes-Immissionsschutzgesetz – BImSchG] [Federal Emission Control Act], May 17, 2013, BGBl I 1274), most recently amended by article 1 of the act of July 2, 2013, BGBl I 1943 (an English version (last updated 2009) is available at http://www.bmub.bund.de/fileadmin/bmu-import/files/english/pdf/application/pdf/bimschg_en_bf.pdf), § 48b lists some of the delegating provisions and makes executive regulations enacted according to them subject to approval by the Bundestag.

27 The Basic Law by constraining delegation rules out statutes that give a minister the power to repeal or amend a statutory provision, even if such actions are approved by the legislature. The United Kingdom calls such provisions Henry VIII clauses after the monarch who exercised such powers, and they now must be clearly authorized by Parliament and are subject to more procedural constraints than ordinary exercises of delegated power. Thus, ministers must consult widely, put their proposal before Parliament, and obtain an affirmative vote. Any rules that are classified as statutes must be voted on favorably by Parliament. Dawn Oliver, *Regulation, Democracy, and Democratic Oversight in the UK*, in THE REGULATORY STATE: CONSTITUTIONAL IMPLICATIONS 243, 251 (Dawn Oliver, Tony Prosser, and Richard Rawlings, eds., 2010).

party or coalition the maximum freedom of action while in power. In addition, because laws are relatively easy to amend or repeal, detailed statutory language cannot lock in future governments. The government's political interest in broad delegation is in tension with the prominence of the legislature in the German constitutional framework. In addition, as a factual matter, the legislative branch is not inevitably a rubber stamp that accepts a passive role. The cabinet does not dominate every legislative policy debate. In situations where the legislature fears bureaucratic overreaching or where the cabinet and the party leaders are in conflict, perhaps in a coalition government, the Bundestag can seek to ensure compliance with its policies.

II. REVIEW OF THE LEGISLATIVE PROCESS

The Basic Law only includes rules for the "external" legislative procedures that govern the various formal steps of enacting federal legislation.[28] It does not govern the internal decision-making processes and methods inside either house. Judicial review of legislation is the sole competence of the Constitutional Court, which examines adherence to the formal and substantive requirements of the constitutional text but with some interesting twists. The Basic Law lists the claims that can be brought before the Constitutional Court and opens up two main paths to review of the legislative process.[29] First, the Court has jurisdiction over disputes between certain state organs and over cases brought by state or federal governments, or by one-fourth of the members of the Bundestag, concerning abstract review of the procedural and substantive constitutionality of statutes. Second, the Court also hears complaints brought by individuals against state actions alleged to violate their constitutional rights. Such cases can lead the Court to review the constitutionality of the statute that is the basis of the concrete implementing act. If a lawsuit challenges a statute directly or as applied, the Court can examine its compliance with both the procedural and the substantive requirements of the Basic Law.[30] According to the Court, everyone's

[28] On the distinction between the internal and external legislative procedure, *see* HERMANN HILL, EINFÜHRUNG IN DIE GESETZGEBUNGSLEHRE 61 (1982); on the legislative duties regarding the internal procedure, see Gunther Schwerdtfeger, *Optimale Methodik der Gesetzgebung als Verfassungspflicht*, in HAMBURG, DEUTSCHLAND EUROPA, BEITRÄGE ZUM DEUTSCHEN UND EUROPÄISCHEN VERFASSUNGS-, VERWALTUNGS- UND WIRTSCHFTSRECHT, FESTSCHRIFT FÜR HANS PETER IPSEN ZUM 70. GEBURTSTAG 173, at 173 f. (Rolf Stödter & Werner Thieme, eds., 1977).

[29] Articles 93(1) no. 1 and 93(1) no. 2 Basic Law provide for review of claims brought by state organs; article 93(1) no. 4a Basic Law provides for review of claims brought by individuals.

[30] 6 BVERFGE 32, 37 f. (establishing the complete review in the so-called *Elfes* decision); Horst Dreier, *Artikel 2(1) Grundgesetz*, in GRUNDGESETZ-KOMMENTAR, BAND 1 [hereinafter, Dreier, *Artikel 2(1) Grundgesetz*] ¶ 38 ff., 46 (Horst Dreier ed., 3rd ed., 2004); Currie,

fundamental right to the "free development of her personality" in article 2(1) Basic Law protects all human behavior. Hence, an individual rights violation is possible any time the state restricts human action.[31] This inclusive interpretation of fundamental rights lowers the bar for individuals to access the Constitutional Court.[32] To prevent an excessive caseload, however, the Court only decides cases of fundamental constitutional importance, as defined by the Court itself.[33]

A. Procedural Duties in the Basic Law

The Basic Law guides the legislative process beginning with submission of a draft and ending with the passage of a statute.[34] The legislature has two houses – the directly elected Bundestag or parliament, and the Bundesrat, representing the Länder (states).[35] A statutory draft can be initiated by the federal government, the Bundesrat, or from inside the parliament (article 76(1) Basic Law). If the federal government submits the draft, it goes first to the Bundesrat for comments before the Bundestag considers it. This assures the early influence of the Länder.[36] After the Bundestag passes a bill, the Bundesrat either has to positively approve the statute or not veto it, depending on the nature of the statute.[37] Once passed, the statute must be certified

supra note 6, at 360 f., 363 (concluding that "Article 2(1), in conjunction with the proportionality principle, is thus the heart of substantive due process in Germany").

31 6 BVerfGE 32, 36 (settled case law); Dreier, *Artikel 2(1) Grundgesetz, supra* note 30, ¶ 20.

32 Fundamental rights also provide a way to review the parliament's participation in and delegation to supranational organizations. Under article 38(1) Basic Law the entire citizenry is called upon to elect representatives and thereby to legitimize the exercise of state power. The parliament itself cannot undermine this right by widely shifting its competences to supranational actors. If it does, German citizens can bring a constitutional complaint before the Constitutional Court based on their right to elect political representatives.

33 Gesetz über das Bundesverfassungsgericht [Bundesverfassungsgerichtsgesetz – BVerfGG] [Federal Constitutional Court Act], Aug. 11, 1993, BGBl I 1473, most recently amended by article 1 of the act of Aug. 29, 2013, BGBl I 3463, §§ 93a, 93b, 93d.

34 Helmuth Schulze-Fielitz, *Gesetzgebung als materiales Verfassungsverfahren*, **2** Neue Zeitschrift für Verwaltungsrecht [NVwZ] 709, at 712 (1983) (pointing out its fragmentary nature); Christoph Gusy, *Das Grundgesetz als normative Gesetzgebungslehre?*, **18** Zeitschrift für Rechtspolitik [ZRP] 292 (1985) [hereinafter, Gusy, *Grundgesetz*].

35 37 BVerfGE 363, 380 (pointing out that the Bundesrat represents the states and is not an equal second chamber); Brun-Otto Bryde, *Artikel 77 Grundgesetz*, in Grundgesetz-Kommentar, Band 2 ¶ 3 (Ingo von Münch & Philip Kunig, eds., 6th ed., 2012).

36 Basic Law article 76(2) reads: "Federal Government bills shall first be submitted to the Bundesrat. The Bundesrat shall be entitled to comment on such bills within six weeks." The time for review can be reduced to three weeks for urgent matters.

37 *See* Basic Law article 77(2a), (3). Unless the Basic Law explicitly makes a statute's enactment dependent on positive approval, the Bundesrat only has veto power, which, in turn, can be overturned by a vote of the Bundestag.

by the federal president, who needs a prior countersignature by the chancellor or the competent federal secretary (article 58 Basic Law). The statute is then promulgated in the Federal Law Gazette (*Bundesgesetzblatt*, article 82(1) sentence 1 Basic Law).

The Basic Law does not govern the drafting process, which often takes place inside the executive prior to the bill's submission to the legislature. Nevertheless, the internal order of the federal ministries gives some guidance on the drafting procedure. Among other things, the order requires an impact assessment, participation of the affected federal ministries, the Ministry of Justice, and "the Länder, national associations of local authorities and representatives of the Länder to the Federation," as well as of "central and umbrella associations and of the expert community at the federal level."[38] These are internal guidelines enacted for organizational purposes, not legally enforceable requirements.[39] They do not create rights for those outside of the state organs that are subject to them. Hence, a violation of an internal order, such as a failure to carry out an impact assessment or to consult with an association, does not make the enacted statute invalid, unless there is a violation of constitutionally guaranteed principles.[40]

Likewise, the Basic Law does not contain explicit rules covering the internal decision-making processes inside the Bundestag and Bundesrat after they receive a draft. However, the Constitutional Court has derived certain formal rules of debate, voting procedures, and committee work from the principle of democracy, but it has left the actual decision-making procedures to the discretion of the legislature. Additionally, the Bundestag and Bundesrat have enacted internal orders governing their procedures.[41]

[38] Gemeinsame Geschäftsordnung der Bundesministerien [GGO] [Joint Rules of Procedure of the Federal Ministries], July 26, 2000, GEMEINSAMES MINISTERIALBLATT [GMBL] 526, most recently amended through resolution of Sept. 1, 2011, GMBL 576, §§ 44–7, available in English at http://www.bmi.bund.de/cae/servlet/contentblob/150474/publicationFile/13399/Moderner_Staat_-_Moderne_Id_23340_de.pdf

[39] KLAUS STERN, DAS STAATSRECHT DER BUNDESREPUBLIK DEUTSCHLAND, BAND II 307 (1980); Fritz Ossenbühl, *§ 102 Verfahren der Gesetzgebung*, in HANDBUCH DES STAATSRECHTS DER BUNDESREPUBLIK DEUTSCHLAND, BAND 5 [hereinafter, Ossenbühl, *§ 102 Verfahren*] ¶ 4 (Josef Isensee & Paul Kirchhof, eds., 3rd ed., 2007).

[40] Michael Kloepfer, *Was kann die Gesetzgebung vom Planungs- und Verwaltungsrecht lernen?*, **3** ZEITSCHRIFT FÜR GESETZGEBUNG [ZG] 289, at 290 (1988) (expressly referring to the GGO); Gerhard Hoffmann, *Das verfassungsrechtliche Gebot der Rationalität im Gesetzgebungsverfahren*, **5** ZG 97, at 101 (1990).

[41] Article 40(1) sentence 2 Basic Law creates the so-called *parlamentarische Geschäftsordnungsautonomie* upon which the Bundestag enacted the Geschäftsordnung des Bundestages [GOBT] [Internal Order of the Bundestag], July 2, 1980, BGBL I 1237, most recently amended according to the announcement of April 23, 2014, BGBL I 534. The Bundesrat enacted the Geschäftsordnung des Bundesrates [GOBR] [Internal Order of

According to the internal order of the Bundestag, a bill is given three readings before the final vote, with committee work taking place after the first reading.[42] The parliament is free to hear associations and experts, but constitutional law does not obligate it to do so.[43] The internal rules require a statement of reasons for legislative drafts – although there is no equivalent duty for enacted statutes.[44] However, these internal orders lack external effect, and thus outsiders cannot enforce them.[45] Moreover, the parliament can abandon its internal order as a whole by a simple majority vote or can vote to deviate from individual provisions by a two-thirds majority of the members present, as long as the abandoned rules are not mandatory requirements derived from the Basic Law.[46]

To the extent that the Basic Law mandates procedural rules, explicitly or implicitly, the Constitutional Court can review the legislative process for compliance with these rules. Its interpretation takes into consideration all state actors with the right to participate in the legislative process, such as opposition parties and the Bundesrat. The Court has, for example, ruled that the allocation of seats in parliamentary committees must be in proportion (a "mirror image") of the party distribution in the parliament as a whole.[47] The Court has also overseen the procedural aspects of calling a conference committee (*Vermittlungsausschuss*) in case the Bundestag and Bundesrat cannot agree on a legislative text.[48] Another ruling concerned

the Bundesrat], Nov. 26, 1993, BGBl I 2007, most recently amended by the decision of the Bundesrat of June 8, 2007, BGBl I 1057.

42 GOBT §§ 78, 80, 86.

43 36 BVerfGE 321, 321 holding 1, 330; Rupert Stettner, *Artikel 77 Grundgesetz*, in Grundgesetz-Kommentar, Band 2 ¶ 8 (Horst Dreier, ed., 2nd ed., 2006).

44 Drafts are regulated in GOBT § 76(2), GOBR §§ 24, 26(2), sentence 2, GGO §§ 42–4. There is no constitutional duty to provide a formal statement of reasons for statutes; *see* only recently Kyrill-A. Schwarz & Christoph Bravidor, *Kunst der Gesetzgebung und Begründungspflichten des Gesetzgebers*, **66** Juristenzeitung [JZ] 656 (2011); Timo Hebeler, *Ist der Gesetzgeber verfassungsrechtlich verpflichtet, Gesetze zu begründen? – Grundsätzliche Überlegungen anlässlich des Bundesverfassungsgerichtsurteils zur Leistungsgestaltung im SGB II*, **63** Die Öffentliche Verwaltung [DÖV] 754, at 756 (2010).

45 *See* 29 BVerfGE 221, 234; Ossenbühl, § *102 Verfahren*, *supra* note 39, at 3; Michael Kloepfer, *Abwägungsregeln bei Satzungsgebung und Gesetzgebung*, **110** Deutsches Verwaltungsblatt [DVBl.] 441 f. (1995) [hereinafter, *Abwägungsregeln*]; Martin Morlok, *Artikel 40 Grundgesetz*, in Grundgesetz-Kommentar, Band 2, ¶ 21 (Horst Dreier, ed., 2nd ed., 2006).

46 GOBT § 126; Ludger-Anselm Versteyl, *Artikel 40 Grundgesetz*, in Grundgesetz-Kommentar, Band 2, ¶ 21 (Ingo von Münch & Philip Kunig, eds., 6th ed., 2012).

47 70 BVerfGE 324, 362–4, 80 BVerfGE 188, 222, and 84 BVerfGE 304, 323 (establishing this "mirror image rule").

48 112 BVerfGE 118 (ruling on the basis of article 77 Basic Law that the "mirror image rule" applies to the conference committee but has to be balanced with the necessity of allowing the formation of a solid majority within the committee); 72 BVerfGE 175, 190,

the voting process in the Bundesrat. The Basic Law demands that each state delegation vote as a bloc.[49] The Court overturned a statute because the Bundesrat used a voting procedure where one state's delegation cast a split vote.[50] Furthermore, under article 38(1) Basic Law, each member of parliament is an elected representative of the German people. The Court interpreted that clause to require rules of debate in the plenum that ensure each representative's right to speak, question, and ask for information.[51] All these decisions focus on "disputes concerning the extent of the rights and duties of a supreme federal body or of other parties vested with rights of their own by this Basic Law or by the rules of procedure of a supreme federal body" (article 93(1) no. 1 Basic Law). Such cases, which concern the internal affairs of the national parliament, can only be brought to the Court by the Bundesrat, party factions, or members of parliament.

B. The Legislative Process in the Jurisprudence of the Federal Constitutional Court

The Constitutional Court has been reluctant to impose further procedural duties linked to democratic accountability, citing its respect for the democratic legitimacy of the legislature.[52] Nevertheless, the Court has articulated procedural duties derived from the fundamental rights of individuals.[53] Initially, the Court sought to strike a balance between acknowledging parliamentary autonomy and the effective protection of rights.[54] It focused on

101 BVerfGE 297, 306–8, and 120 BVerfGE 56, 74–80 (all three decisions ruling on the limits of changes or amendments to the statutory draft originating in the committee); 106 BVerfGE 253 (dealing with the mathematical method employed for distributing the seats in the conference committee to obtain a "mirror image"; the dissent by Justice Broß argues for the unconstitutionality of the method challenged).

49 Basic Law article 51(3) sentence 2.

50 106 BVerfGE 310.

51 10 BVerfGE 4, 12 (right to speak); 13 BVerfGE 123, 125 (right to question); 67 BVerfGE 100, 129; 70 BVerfGE 324, 355 (right to inform and debate); 80 BVerfGE 188, 218 (providing a coherent summary).

52 *See* Uwe Kischel, Die Begründung: Zur Erläuterung staatlicher Entscheidungen gegenüber dem Bürger 304 f. (2003) (pointing to the difference between the legislature and the executive).

53 Jakob Nolte, *Rationale Rechtsfindung im Sozialrecht*, **52** Der Staat 245, 248 (2013) (pointing out that the Constitutional Court has created requirements for the internal drafting of statutes since the middle of the 1970s); Philipp Dann, *Verfassungsgerichtliche Kontrolle gesetzgeberischer Rationalität*, **49** Der Staat 630, 633 (2010) (explaining that the Constitutional Court has increasingly used consistency arguments since the late 1980s).

54 Niels Petersen, *Gesetzgeberische Inkonsistenz als Beweiszeichen, Eine rechtsvergleichende Analyse der Funktion von Konsistenzargumenten in der Rechtsprechung*, **138** Archiv des öffentlichen Rechts [AöR] 108, 114 (2013) [hereinafter, Petersen, *Inkonsistenz*].

the fundamental principles of proportionality and equality in reviewing the rationality of parliamentary statutes. This line of cases imposed indirect constraints on legislative procedures, and recent decisions have increasingly emphasized what can be seen as procedural duties. Relying on the principles of consistency and transparency, the Court has carried out detailed reviews of legislative decision making. These decisions have shaped procedures and could have an impact on the connection between the legislature and the citizenry.

1. Individual Rights as a Basis for Procedural Duties

In conducting fundamental rights review, the Constitutional Court acknowledges that the legislature has a "margin of discretion." Within that margin, the legislature can realize its goals through a variety of options. The Court does not try to enforce a standard of "optimal legislation." Because legislators often face high levels of uncertainty, abstract and general norms are legitimate in statutory language.[55] The Constitutional Court reviews compliance with the fundamental rights in the Basic Law by applying the proportionality standard; the Court's intensity of review varies depending on a statute's impact on fundamental rights.[56] In areas where the legislature has wide discretion, the Constitutional Court has increasingly abstained from reviewing the legislative output, but it compensates for this deference by checking the factual bases of statutes and reviewing the decision-making process.[57] There is thus a connection between substantive standards and procedural duties; but the exact nature of this connection remains uncertain.[58] The case law lacks clear guidelines on when and how the Court will review legislative processes.[59] Nevertheless, in complex areas the justices acknowledge the need to allow greater legislative discretion as to substance, and, as a consequence, they focus instead on technical competence and process.[60]

55 49 BVerfGE 168, 181 ff. *See generally* Indra Spiecker genannt Döhmann, Staatliche Entscheidungen unter Unsicherheit (2012); Gusy, *Grundgesetz*, *supra* note 34, at 297.

56 Nolte, *supra* note 53, at 249.

57 Nolte, *supra* note 53, at 249; Dann, *supra* note 53, at 630 (arguing that the Constitutional Court hereby exceeds its competences).

58 Klaus Meßerschmidt, *The Race to Rationality Review and the Score of the German Federal Constitutional Court*, **6** Legisprudence 347, 350 (2012) (describing this relationship as "the triangle of judicial review" consisting of "substantive review, procedural review, and impact review").

59 Nolte, *supra* note 53, at 248 f.

60 *See* 103 BVerfGE 293, 307 (emphasizing the legislature's margin of discretion regarding the labor market, the social system, and the economic system).

According to the Court, the substantive standard of proportionality implicitly compels the legislature to calculate the present and future costs and benefits of legislation that will affect fundamental rights.[61] Such information can then lay the groundwork for a balancing test and can justify unequal treatment.[62] In some cases, the Court explicitly demands that statutes be grounded in factual reality.[63] Because steps two (least restrictive means) and three (balancing) of any proportionality review are not tied to absolute values, the Court tries to protect legislative discretion while ensuring effective rights protection. Its case law thus requires legislators to investigate causation in complex areas and to apply state-of-the-art empirical social research instead of merely pointing to official statistics.[64] The legislature has to draw on existing knowledge by using the available material, consulting experts, and conducting hearings in the preparatory as well as the enactment stage.[65] Moreover, even if a statute is constitutional at the time of enactment, the legislature has to monitor the statute's development, especially the validity of initial prognoses, and it should, if necessary, take corrective steps to ensure continuous compliance with the Constitution and its proportionality principle.[66] Notice, however, that even though the Court speaks of the legislature's obligations, these responsibilities are often, in fact, the work of the government ministries. Committees chaired by opposition politicians as well as individual members with dissenting views may be a source of alternative views and data. The Bundestag, however, has limited staff, and given the parliamentary structure, the government performs much of the basic work.

As in South Africa, a lack of information justifying a statute can sometimes prompt the Court to strike down a law. In the United States, courts may also review the factual underpinnings of a statute if constitutional

[61] 39 BVerfGE 210, 225 f.; 50 BVerfGE 290, 333 f.; 65 BVerfGE 1, 55 (settled case law); *see also* Gusy, *Grundgesetz, supra* note 34, at 293; *see also* Meßerschmidt, *supra* note 58, at 363 (calling the proportionality principle "the Trojan horse of due deliberation and impact review").

[62] This duty follows indirectly from the intensive substantial control exercised by the Constitutional Court in areas related to fundamental rights, where it reviews the factual background for statutory decisions in great detail, *see* especially 7 BVerfGE 377, 415 (on the limitation of pharmacies); 11 BVerfGE 30, 45 (on a *numerus clausus* for doctors); *see* Hebeler, *supra* note 44, at 756.

[63] *See* 50 BVerfGE 290, 331 f.; 65 BVerfGE 1, 55; Nolte, *supra* note 53, at 248.

[64] 65 BVerfGE 1, 55; Gusy, *Grundgesetz, supra* note 34, at 292 f.

[65] 50 BVerfGE 290, 334; 65 BVerfGE 1, 55; Gusy, *Grundgesetz, supra* note 34, at 293.

[66] 25 BVerfGE 1, 13; 49 BVerfGE 89, 130; 50 BVerfGE 290, 335; 65 BVerfGE 1, 55 f.; Gusy, *Grundgesetz, supra* note 34, at 294 (stating that it is unclear how to institutionalize this duty as selective judicial review cannot be sufficient).

rights and principles are at issue, but the United States has a narrower set of protected rights than our other cases. Although the U.S. courts do sometimes review factual justifications, the range of issues where rights are at stake is narrower than in either Germany or South Africa. However, as we discussed earlier, review based on other constitutional provisions, especially those dealing with federalism, has led the present Supreme Court to provide quite aggressive review of the stated justifications for a wider range of statutes.

One prominent German example in which the Constitutional Court derived procedural duties from fundamental rights is its interpretation of the principle of equality as applied to tax law.[67] According to the Court, the principle of equality has to be fleshed out in an area-specific way.[68] Tax law, with its underlying goal of revenue generation for the state, offers no guidance for the concrete implementation of the principle.[69] Hence, the Court itself developed a principle of consistency as a way of defining the principle of equality.[70] The principle (sometimes also described as the principle of a just system or *Prinzip der Systemgerechtigkeit*[71]) obliges the legislature to act

[67] Petersen, *Inkonsistenz*, *supra* note 54, at 128 (also examining the Constitutional Court's adjudication on election law); Dann, *supra* note 53, at 632–4 (reviewing the Constitutional Court's decision 122 BVerfGE 210 on commuter tax relief); Mehrdad Payandeh, *Das Gebot der Folgerichtigkeit: Rationalitätsgewinn oder Irrweg der Grundsrechtsdogmatik*, **136** Archiv des öffentlichen Rechts 578, 589–602 (2011) (examining the principle of consistency in the context of the general principle of equality, as well as the areas of tax and election law).

[68] 75 BVerfGE 108, 157; Werner Heun, *Artikel 3 Grundgesetz*, in Grundgesetz-Kommentar, Band 1 [hereinafter Heun, *Artikel 3 Grundgesetz*] ¶ 73 (Horst Dreier, ed., 3rd ed., 2004); Kyrill-A. Schwarz, *"Folgerichtigkeit" im Steuerrecht*, in Festschrift für Josef Isensee zum 70. Geburtstag 949 [hereinafter, Schwarz, *"Folgerichtigkeit"*], 949 f. (Depenheuer et al., eds., 2007); Joachim Englisch, *Folgerichtiges Steuerrecht als Verfassungsgebot*, in Gestaltung der Steuerrechtsordnung – Festschrift für Joachim Lang zum 70. Geburtstag 167, 167 ff. (Tipke, Seer, Hey, & Englisch, eds., 2010).

[69] Schwarz, *"Folgerichtigkeit,"* *supra* note 68, at 955.

[70] *See only* 84 BVerfGE 239, 274, 283; 126 BVerfGE 400, 417; Heun, *Artikel 3 Grundgesetz*, *supra* note 68, at 75. For more extensive treatment, *see* Schwarz, *"Folgerichtigkeit,"* *supra* note 68, at 956; Paul Kirchhof, *§ 118 Steuern*, in Handbuch des Staatsrechts der Bundesrepublik Deutschland, Band 5 ¶ 172, 178 ff. (Josef Isensee & Paul Kirchhof, eds., 3rd ed., 2007).

[71] Payandeh, *supra* note 67, at 581 f. (emphasizing the conceptual similarities of the principle of a just system with the principle of consistency and explaining that the Constitutional Court has long argued with the former, but replaced it with the latter); *but see* Lerke Osterloh, *Folgerichtigkeit – Verfassungsgerichtliche Rationalitätsanforderungen in der Demokratie*, in Demokratie-Perspektiven, Festschrift für Brun-Otto Bryde zum 70. Geburtstag 429, 434 (Michael Bäuerle, Philipp Dann, & Astrid Wallrabenstein, eds., 2013) (pointing out the more demanding nature of the principle of a just system in comparison to the principle of consistency).

consistently and to achieve equality in the resulting statutory order.[72] This is a substantive requirement linked to the preservation of individual rights, but the legislature can defend itself against a constitutional challenge by presenting evidence of consistency or by giving reasons why the rights violation is justified in a particular instance.[73] Thus, as with all reason-giving requirements, the principle mixes substance and process. However, the collection of information and the statement of reasons are for the benefit of the Court and of the affected individuals, but not of voters in general. The aim is to aid the Court, not to improve the democratic legitimacy of the parliamentary process.

Because the Constitutional Court may scrutinize the factual basis of a statute, the legislature has an incentive to make its analysis visible and reviewable, which implies transparency and documentation.[74] The Court has not struck down statutes merely because of a legislative failure to collect solid evidence of a law's effects. Nevertheless, judicial review of rights violations could have implications for the legislative process, especially with respect to the factual justifications for new laws. In particular, two recent decisions, the so-called *Hartz IV* judgment and the subsequent decision on the Asylum Seekers Benefits Act, discussed later, might open the door for more stringent Constitutional Court review of the information basis of statutes.

2. Legislative Duties in the *Hartz IV* Decision and Beyond

In February 2010, the Constitutional Court's *Hartz IV* decision imposed a new level of procedural obligations on the legislature although, as usual, the constitutional basis was substantive rights, not democratic legitimacy.[75] The Court reviewed the validity of the legislature's information-gathering processes when it enacted a law on social benefits that amended the German

[72] Schwarz, "*Folgerichtigkeit*," *supra* note 68, at 957 (stating that an inconsistency only indicates but does not prove a violation of equality); Heun, *Artikel 3 Grundgesetz*, *supra* note 68, at 76 (emphasizing that a strict adherence to equality in tax law is practically impossible).

[73] *See* Meßerschmidt, *supra* note 58, at 356 (stating that "in all proportionality issues the burden of proof rests with the legislator").

[74] Gusy, *Grundgesetz*, *supra* note 34, at 294.

[75] 125 BVerfGE 175 [hereinafter, 125 BVerfGE 175, *Hartz IV* decision] available in English at http://www.bverfg.de/entscheidungen/ls20100209_1bvl000109en.html. Subsequent quotes are taken from this English version of the judgment. This section relies heavily on Stefanie Egidy, *Casenote – The Fundamental Right to the Guarantee of a Subsistence Minimum in the Hartz IV Decision of the German Federal Constitutional Court*, 12 German L.J. 1961 (2011).

Code of Social Law.[76] In July 2012, the Court ruled on the adequacy of the basic cash benefits included in the Asylum Seekers Benefits Act and essentially affirmed the *Hartz IV* judgment.[77] Both decisions were based on the "fundamental right to the guarantee of a subsistence minimum" derived from human dignity in article 1(1) of the German Basic Law in conjunction with the principle of the social welfare state in article 20(1) Basic Law – a human right that is independent of citizenship. It gives every individual an enforceable, subjective right (*subjektives Recht*) to the "material prerequisites which are indispensable for his or her physical existence and for a minimum of participation in social, cultural and political life."[78] This obligates the legislature to pass statutes that ensure a subsistence minimum to all individuals.[79] In doing so, the legislature has latitude to specify the levels of standard benefits because they depend on the state of society and the prevailing conditions of life.[80]

In the *Hartz IV* case, the Court declared that the social law's standard benefits for adults and children were unconstitutional, primarily because the provisions were not entirely based on an underlying statistical investigation by the legislature. The Court found that instead of conducting separate empirical research, the legislature based parts of the calculation of standard benefits on "'random' estimates."[81] The Court ruled that even though the legislature has discretion to choose which statistical models to use to calculate benefits, it must exercise this discretion consistently and transparently. Instead of declaring the level of social benefits unconstitutional, the Court concentrated on the procedure used to determine the subsistence minimum and found that it violated the Constitution.

The Court analyzed the legislature's calculations under the view that a constitutionally acceptable procedure would result in a constitutionally acceptable outcome.[82]

[76] Sozialgesetzbuch Zweites Buch – Grundsicherung für Arbeitssuchende [SGB II] [Social Code Book II], May 13, 2011, BGBl I 850, 2094, most recently amended by article 1 of the act of July 28, 2014, BGBl I 1306.

[77] 132 BVerfGE 134 [hereinafter, 132 BVerfGE 134, *Asylum Seekers Benefits Act* decision] available in English at http://www.bverfg.de/en/decisions/ls20120718_1bvl001010en.html.

[78] 125 BVerfGE 175, *Hartz IV* decision at 175, headnote 1.

[79] 125 BVerfGE 175, *Hartz IV* decision at 223 f.

[80] 125 BVerfGE 175, *Hartz IV* decision at 224 f.

[81] 125 BVerfGE 175, *Hartz IV* decision at 237–9. The court issued a declaration of incompatibility rather than immediately striking the legislation down, which would have eliminated the statutory basis for all social benefits (at 255 f.). The legislature was given until December 31, 2010 to make the necessary corrections by following the procedural instructions the court developed (at 257 f.).

[82] 125 BVerfGE 175, *Hartz IV* decision at 225 f.

> The Federal Constitutional Court hence examines … whether within its [i.e., the Bundestag's] margin of appreciation it has selected a calculation procedure that is fundamentally suited to an assessment of the subsistence minimum, whether, in essence, it has completely and correctly ascertained the necessary facts and, finally, whether it kept within the bounds of what is justifiable in all calculation steps with a comprehensible set of figures within this selected procedure and its structural principles.[83]

Using this standard of review, the Court intensely examines the statistical analysis underlying the legislature's determination of the standard benefits. It concludes that even though the legislature relied on suitable empirical methods, it failed to apply these tools consistently throughout the calculations. For instance, the legislature selected households from the lowest income quintile as a reference group. Using their monthly expense as a baseline in determining the subsistence minimum, the legislature chose to deduct certain types of expenses it deemed inessential. The Court went into considerable detail to criticize these exclusions because they were undertaken without factual justification.[84] In the subcategory of furniture, for example, the formula disallowed expenses for camping furniture and works of art without evidence that the lowest quintile of households actually spent money on these items.[85] The Court similarly held that the legislature failed to use sufficient data to calculate the needs of children, as it merely applied a certain percentage to the standard benefits for adults based on the child's age.[86]

In determining the levels of social benefits, the Court acknowledges that the legislature has substantive latitude, while emphasizing the duties of consistency and transparency. These two duties are related but conceptually distinct. They can be read either as logical substantive requirements or as background procedural requirements. In this case, they are a little of both. The aim is to reach an acceptable result through the application of clear and consistent rules.[87] The Court does not dictate any concrete procedural steps; however, the legislature must use consistent methods that justify the statutory provisions. Hence, in contrast to prior case law, this decision emphasizes the necessity of using certain procedures that compensate for

[83] 125 BVerfGE 175, *Hartz IV* decision at 226.

[84] 125 BVerfGE 175, *Hartz IV* decision, para. 173.

[85] 125 BVerfGE 175, *Hartz IV* decision, para. 175.

[86] 125 BVerfGE 175, *Hartz IV* decision, paras. 190–8 (pointing out that "[C]hildren are not small adults," at 246).

[87] Ralf Rothkegel, *Ein Danaergeschenk für den Gesetzgeber, Zum Urteil des Bundesverfassungsgerichts vom 9. Februar 2010* – 1 BVL 1, 3, 4/09, **49** Zeitschrift für die Sozialrechtliche Praxis [ZFSH/SGB] 135, at 140 f. (2010).

the substantive latitude the Court gives to the legislature in this area of law.[88] With this reasoning, the Court imposes procedural duties on the legislature en route to an acceptable substantive result.[89]

The 2012 decision regarding the benefits provided under the Asylum Seekers Benefits Act takes the *Hartz IV* reasoning and applies it to the group of asylum seekers. The Court again used the fundamental right to a subsistence minimum to declare the challenged provisions unconstitutional. First, the benefits, which had not been updated since 1993, were currently more than 30 percent lower than the subsistence minimum provided by the *Hartz IV* legislation.[90] This sum was held to be patently insufficient to meet the subsistence minimum that human dignity required, and it, therefore, violated that human right.[91] Second, in addition to the unconstitutional legislative outcome, the amounts had not been determined comprehensively in a transparent and appropriate procedure based on real needs.[92] The legislature appeared not to have used reliable data, instead merely estimating the program's overall budgetary costs.[93] Despite granting the legislature a margin of discretion, the Court demanded that the benefits be justifiable on the basis of reliable figures and coherent means of calculation that take into account the relevant facts completely and accurately. Accordingly, all steps of the calculation have to stay within the chosen procedure and its structural principles. However, the Court stated that these requirements impose no specific procedural duties on the legislature and leave room for political compromise.[94] This last concession responds to criticism of *Hartz IV* without changing the obligations imposed on the legislature. It might, however,

[88] Michael Brenner, *Das innere Gesetzgebungsverfahren im Lichte der Hartz IV-Entscheidung des Bundesverfassungsgerichts*, **26** Zeitschrift für Gesetzgebung [ZG] 394, at 394 (2011); Nolte, *supra* note 53, at 247; Petersen, *Inkonsistenz*, *supra* note 54, at 110, 113, 114 (emphasizing compensation); Dann, *supra* note 53, at 637 f. (criticizing this decision as an intrusion into parliamentary competences); *see also* Bernd Grzeszick, *Rationalitätsanforderungen an die parlamentarische Rechtsetzung im demokratischen Rechtsstaat*, **71** Veröffentlichungen der Vereinigung der Deutschen Staatsrechtslehrer 49, 70–4 (2012) (critically analyzing the possibility of a compensation for deficits in legitimacy).

[89] Brenner, *supra* note 88, at 394; Nolte, *supra* note 53, at 247, 250; Dann, *supra* note 53, at 636 f.; Petersen, *Inkonsistenz*, *supra* note 54, at 114.

[90] According to 132 BVerfGE 134, *Asylum Seekers Benefits Act* decision, at 148, in 2009, 121,918 foreigners of different immigration status received benefits according to the Asylum Seekers Benefits Act, Asylbewerberleistungsgesetz [AsylbLG] [Asylum Seekers Benefits Act], Aug. 5, 1997, BGBl I 2022, most recently amended by article 3 of the act of Nov. 22, 2011, BGBl I 2258.

[91] 132 BVerfGE 134, *Asylum Seekers Benefits Act* decision, 166–70.

[92] *Id.* at 170–3.

[93] *Id.* at 170.

[94] *Id.* at 162 f.

be read as limiting the impact of that decision.[95] The Court implicitly confirms that these requirements straddle the division between substance and procedure – they help to achieve a constitutional result and give a basis for review, but the legislature can fulfill them only if it uses consistent methods. So, ultimately, the legislature will have to follow certain procedures, if only to consistently apply the method that it has chosen. The exact requirements, however, remain unclear.

The legislature's duty of consistency could ultimately give individuals the possibility of challenging the legislative process as long as the statute touches on a fundamental right.[96] The principle of consistency obliges the legislature to adhere to a chosen standard, which is a stricter requirement than the prohibition against arbitrary decisions.[97] The principle of consistency has a forty-year tradition in tax law, although there it is not tied so closely to process as it was in *Hartz IV*.[98] The Court had also previously applied the principle of consistency in conducting proportionality review of statutes, examining whether the legislature had consistently pursued the aim chosen.[99] In the *Sports-betting* decision the Court struck down the state's monopoly on conducting sports bets because the statute in question was not well designed to achieve the legislative goal of fighting gambling addiction and other negative consequences of a private betting system, making it disproportionate.[100] Similarly, in its *Nonsmoker* decision the Court struck down a statute that banned smoking in public restaurants because it did

95 Nolte, *supra* note 53, at 262.

96 *See*, e.g., Stephan Rixen, *Verfassungsrecht ersetzt Sozialpolitik? „Hartz IV" auf dem Prüfstand des Bundesverfassungsgerichts*, **14** SOZIALRECHT AKTUELL 81 [hereinafter, Rixen, *Verfassungsrecht*], at 81 f. (2010); Rothkegel, *supra* note 87, at 141.

97 Lothar Michael, *Folgerichtigkeit als Wettbewerbsgleichheit, Zur Verwerfung von Rauchverboten in Gaststätten durch das BVerfG*, **63** JURISTENZEITUNG [JZ] 875, at 879 (2008).

98 23 BVERFGE 242, 256; 120 BVERFGE 125, at 155; 122 BVERFGE 210, at 231 (settled case law); recently 127 BVERFGE 224; Michael, *supra* note 97, at 880; *see also* Oliver Lepsius, *Anmerkung*, **64** JURISTENZEITUNG [JZ] 260 (2009) (criticizing the Constitutional Court's use of the principle of consistency in its decision on commuter tax relief in 122 BVERFGE 210).

99 Osterloh, *supra* note 71, at 431–3 (analyzing the use of the notion of consistency (*Folgerichtigkeit*) in the adjudication of the Constitutional Court, starting as early as 1 BVERFGE 14 in 1951); Christian Bumke, *Die Pflicht zur konsistenten Gesetzgebung – Am Beispiel der privaten Vermittlung staatlicher Lotterien und ihrer bundesverfassungsgerichtlichen Kontrolle*, **49** DER STAAT 77 (1010) at 80, 87–91 (describing the development since the late 1990s of expanding the constitutional principle of consistency as a paradigm shift).

100 115 BVERFGE 276 (sports-betting decision); *see* Josef Franz Lindner, *Konsequente Zweckverfolgung als Verfassungspflicht des Gesetzgebers*, **22** ZEITSCHRIFT FÜR GESETZGEBUNG [ZG] 188 (2007); Petersen, *Inkonsistenz*, *supra* note 54, at 129 f.

not consistently implement the concept of protecting against smoke and was thus disproportionate.[101] Both cases were based on a violation of the right to occupational freedom (article 12 Basic Law) and focused on the substantive outcome, not the legislative procedure. The Court redirected its focus in the *Hartz IV* decision, and in the *Asylum Seekers Benefits Act* case it showed that the same reasoning is applicable throughout all areas of social benefits law. The Court even made its own interim regulations on the benefits for asylum seekers applicable retroactively, beginning January 2011. It argued that after *Hartz IV*, the legislature had to prepare itself for the possible unconstitutionality of the respective provisions of the Asylum Seekers Benefit Act.[102] The justices have not indicated whether they will extend the reasoning of *Hartz IV* beyond the social welfare field to other constitutional rights; however, the focus on process and especially the emphasis on consistency could extend far beyond social benefits law.[103]

Transparency was a key aspect of *Hartz IV*, which stated: "In order to facilitate this constitutional review, there is an obligation for the legislature to disclose the methods and calculations used to determine the subsistence minimum in the legislative procedure."[104] Transparency was only marginally mentioned in the *Asylum Seekers Benefits Act* case, and neither decision explicitly imposed a duty of publicity on the legislature. However, in order to make the legislation transparent to the relevant audience, the records of the decision-making process effectively have to be published.[105] Prior to *Hartz IV*, this was seen as good constitutional practice; the *Hartz IV* decision appears to transform this practice into an enforceable constitutional duty.[106] Beneficiaries can implicitly expect the state to justify a certain subsistence

[101] 121 BVerfGE 317, 362 f. (*nonsmoker* decision); *see* Rixen, *Verfassungsrecht*, *supra* note 96, at 84 f.; *see also* Petersen, *Inkonsistenz*, *supra* note 54, at 111 f. (critical toward the court's use of consistency in this case); and Dann, *supra* note 53, at 634 f. (criticizing the court's application of the principle of consistency).

[102] 132 BVerfGE 134, *Asylum Seekers Benefits Act* decision, at 178.

[103] Michael, *supra* note 97, at 876 (examining the nonsmoker decision, argues that the decision may have implications beyond the protection of nonsmokers in restaurants and refers to a similar line of argument in the dissenting opinions of Justices Brun-Otto Bryde and Johannes Masing in 121 BVerfGE 317, 380, 383). Payandeh, *supra* note 67, at 584 states that while it is possible to use consistency as a general principle, the Constitutional Court has not gone that far. He also refers to the contrary position of Bumke, *supra*, note 99, at 91, 93 (arguing that a general duty of consistency derived from the rule of law principle is the inevitable consequence of the recent development). *But see* Hebeler, *supra* note 44, at 762.

[104] 125 BVerfGE 175, *Hartz IV* decision, at 226.

[105] *See* Rothkegel, *supra* note 87, at 146.

[106] *Id.* (criticizing untransparent changes made in the conference committee).

minimum.[107] The scope of this transparency requirement seems broad, and some German commentators have criticized its reach. First, the executive often prepares statutes and conducts the background analysis; hence, full transparency might go beyond legislative decision-making processes and impose duties on the executive.[108] Second, one can read the transparency requirement as requiring the legislature to give a statement of reasons as the last step of the legislative process, a requirement that some see as encroaching on legislative prerogatives.[109] However, the Constitutional Court merely demands that the legislature disclose its underlying methods, which does not imply a duty to provide a statement of reasons for the entire statute. Nevertheless, through the gateway of subjective rights, the decision may, in fact, make the legislative process more open to all observers, not just those whose subjective rights are affected. Here, transparency is a by-product of a decision that facilitated the review of fundamental rights. South African constitutional developments, in contrast, go one step further, with the Court holding that the promotion of transparency is an explicit aim of legislative rulemaking and of constitutional checks on legislative behavior. Under that view of judicial review, the purported drawbacks of *Hartz IV* become advantages tied to the democratic accountability of the legislative process.

In July 2014 the Constitutional Court upheld *Hartz IV* in reviewing an April 2012 decision of the Social Court of Berlin.[110] The lower court held that the revised version of the standard benefits violated the fundamental right to a subsistence minimum and referred the case to the Constitutional Court.[111] The Berlin court examined whether the legislature calculated the standard benefits in a consistent and transparent way and criticized, for example, the legislative change of the reference group from the lower 20% of households to the lower 15% as arbitrary, erroneous, and

[107] Anne Lenze, *Hartz IV Regelsätze und gesellschaftliche Teilhabe, Das Urteil des BVerfG vom 9.2.2010 und seine Folgen*, WISO Diskurs 4, 8 f. (May 2010).

[108] Nolte, *supra* note 53, at 252.

[109] *Id.*

[110] Federal Constitutional Court, decision of July, 23, 2014, 1 BvL 10/12.

[111] Social Court of Berlin, decision of April 25, 2012, file number S 55 AS 9238/12. *See* Nolte, *supra*, note 53, at 262–265 (pointing to this court decision and conducting an in-depth analysis); Stephan Rixen, *Sind die neuen "Hartz-IV"-Regelleistungen verfassungsgemäß?*, Soziale Sicherheit [SozSich] 73 (2013); Peter Schmitz, Anwalt/Anwältin im Sozialrecht [ASR] 120 (2012) (agreeing with the decision although pointing out the probably limited impact of a decision by the Constitutional Court); Ricarda Langer, Rechtsdienst der Lebenshilfe [RdLH] 58 (2012) (also expressing agreement); Ulrich Wenner, Soziale Sicherheit [SozSich] 238 (2012).

inconsistent.[112] It also criticized the legislature's exclusion of certain goods and services from the standard benefits, and it held that the legislature failed to give statistical evidence or other reasons for its normative assumptions. For example, the court questioned the reduction of benefits allocated for the purchase of high-proof alcoholic beverages, pointing out that the legislature failed to consider the social relevance of (moderate) alcohol consumption and its use as a gift.[113] This judgment shows the extent to which judges can use the principle of consistency as a check on the legislature, blurring the line between technical and political analysis.[114] If the Constitutional Court had followed the reasoning of that judgment, the potential impact on the legislative margin of discretion would have been large, because all lower courts can – and might even be under the obligation to – refer cases to the Constitutional Court if they deem a statute to be unconstitutional.[115] The courts could have questioned political choices if the legislature fails to give sufficient reasons and to engage in proper statistical analysis. Alive to these implications, the Constitutional Court upheld the legislature's response to *Hartz IV* and stressed the limitations expressed in the original decision. In its July decision, it is beginning to delineate the precise scope of the doctrine of consistency and transparency.[116] The Court is wary of becoming widely involved in the kind of second-guessing that the lower-court decision illustrates. In our view, this caution is warranted; going forward, it should apply the doctrine expressed in *Hartz IV* as a procedural, not a substantive, requirement. A reason-giving requirement inevitably mixes process and substance, but the Constitutional Court could articulate how it will strike the balance in future cases.

It is noteworthy that the procedural violations before the Constitutional Court involved harm to an individual rights holder, not the problems facing the general public as it seeks to evaluate the policy impact of a law and to hold politicians to account. The procedural requirements are linked to the violation of individual rights, not the promotion of broad democratic

[112] Social Court of Berlin, decision of April 25, 2012; Nolte, *supra* note 53, at 254.

[113] Social Court of Berlin, decision of April 25, 2012; Nolte, *supra* note 53, at 257.

[114] Nolte, *supra* note 53, at 257; Petersen, *Inkonsistenz, supra* note 54, at 132 f. (stating that the legislature only seemingly keeps its full political autonomy, since comparisons, even in statistical analysis, are per se evaluative, which is, however, an essential part of judicial review); Dann, *supra* note 53, at 630 (stating that the abstract nature only pretends to be neutral and thus subtly shifts the power balance between the parliament and the Constitutional Court).

[115] Nolte, *supra* note 53, at 254.

[116] *Id.* at 262–265 (listing ways the Court could make its reasoning more precise and limit it to keep it to its actual application); Petersen, *Inkonsistenz, supra* note 54, at 134.

values.[117] The Court demands transparency primarily to facilitate judicial review, not to improve the democratic accountability of the legislature. One might think that basing a decision on improper procedures would be less confrontational than subjecting social welfare legislation to full substantive control and ordering an increase in benefits. However, process control is not always less intrusive than substantive review.

In the United States, legislative procedures are the preserve of Congress with substantive judicial review for violations of constitutional rights. As we have seen in Chapter 2, the Supreme Court generally does not review the validity of the data and statistical analyses behind statutory provisions, even though the courts frequently do examine this material in administrative law. In the U.S. context, review of statutory substance is usually seen as less, not more, confrontational than interfering with the internal procedures of Congress.[118] We have criticized recent U.S. legal developments where narrow majorities of the Supreme Court struck down statutes on federalism grounds and demanded something like formal "findings" from the legislature – a reason-giving requirement that seems inconsistent with U.S. political realities. As we have argued, such a requirement would be less intrusive in a parliamentary system such as Germany's, but even here, it could go too far if it enmeshes the courts in the details of policy.

C. The Practical Limits of Procedural Duties

Even after the *Hartz IV* decision, the Constitutional Court does not require that statutes reflect the best expert knowledge; in its view, to do so would be overly intrusive.[119] The democratically elected Bundestag consists of representatives who need have no special qualifications or expert knowledge.[120] The parliament is a forum for political decision making and is not structurally conducive to the systematic accumulation of expert knowledge or the production of "optimal" statutes.[121] The executive consists of a professional

[117] *See* 125 BVerfGE 175, *Hartz IV* decision; *see also* Meßerschmidt, *supra* note 58, at 352, 357 (calling the review of procedural aspects on the basis of alleged rights violations "procedural review writ large," following and citing the categorization of Ittai Bar-Siman-Tov, *The Puzzling Resistance to Judicial Review of the Legislative Process*, **91** Boston University Law Rev. 1915, 1924 (2011), who describes this review as "semi-procedural judicial review").

[118] *See* Bar-Siman-Tov, *supra* note 117.

[119] 132 BVerfGE 134, *Asylum Seekers Benefits Act* decision, 162 f.

[120] The Basic Law only sets a minimum age requirement, Basic Law article 38(2); Gusy, *Grundgesetz*, *supra* note 34, at 297 f.; Hebeler, *supra* note 44, at 762.

[121] Gusy, *Grundgesetz*, *supra* note 34, at 297 f.; Georg Lienbacher, *Rationalitätsanforderungen an die parlamentarische Rechtsetzung im demokratischen Rechtsstaat*, **71** Veröffentlichungen

civil service overseen by the cabinet and is organized by subject area so that expert knowledge can be more easily brought to bear on policy choices.[122] According to Christoph Gusy, although statutory drafters often draw on the expertise and staff of the executive, the Basic Law envisages the legislative process not as a process of cognition (*Erkenntnisverfahren*) but as a process of decision making (*Entscheidungsverfahren*) that requires political compromise.[123]

In spite of the potential impact of the *Hartz IV* decision on legislative drafting, the Court is unlikely to move beyond its focus on individual rights to take on broad questions of the democratic accountability of legislative procedures not linked to violations of rights. Even if it did wish to do so, the principle of consistency would not be a good place to start. Although the Court does not demand the "purity of a legislative system" (*Systemreinheit*), consistency is hard to apply to the lawmaking process overall where the drafting process is shaped by the necessity of compromise.[124] Even if the same party coalition controls the majority of the Bundestag and the Bundesrat, the party factions and the parties themselves have to come to an agreement. Consensus, dissent, and compromise are basic necessities of democratic decision making (*Grundbedingungen der Demokratie*), facts of political reality, and inherent in the work of parliament. As a result of compromise, the legislature might not always be able to explain the origin of and motive behind every legislative act in principled, consistent terms.[125] In addition, the lack of clear rules for applying the principle of consistency creates the danger of arbitrary, case-by-case enforcement by the Court, which provides no guidance to legislative bodies.[126] In his dissenting opinion in

der Vereinigung der Deutschen Staatsrechtslehrer 7 (2012) at 13–15; Hebeler, *supra* note 44, at 762; Nolte, *supra* note 53, at 251 f.; Petersen, *Inkonsistenz*, *supra* note 54, at 130 f.

122 Gusy, *Grundgesetz*, *supra* note 34, at 297.

123 *Id.* at 298; *see also*, Lienbacher, *supra* note 121, at 16 f.

124 Michael, *supra* note 97, at 879; Rixen, *Verfassungsrecht*, *supra* note 96, at 85; Claudia Bittner, *Casenote – Human Dignity as a Matter of Legislative Consistency in an Ideal World: The Fundamental Right to Guarantee a Subsistence Minimum in the German Federal Constitutional Court's Judgment of 9 February 2010*, **12** German L.J. 1941, 1954 (2011); Hebeler, *supra* note 44, at 762; Dann, *supra* note 53, at 640.

125 Christoph Engel, *Inconsistency in the Law: In Search of a Balanced Norm*, in Is there Value in Inconsistency? 221, 225 (Christoph Engel & Lorraine Daston, eds., 2006) (examining the conflict between rationality of law and the political process).

126 Payandeh, *supra* note 67, at 590–3, 595–9, 600–2 (using the examples of tort law, the commuter tax relief, and election law to illustrate that the principle of consistency lacks content and its use is, at least to a certain extent, arbitrary); Grzeszick, *supra* note 88, at 58–60 (highlighting the arbitrary nature of the principle of consistency's implicit orientation at any legislative goal using the example of the nonsmoker decision to); *see also* Rixen, *Verfassungsrecht*, *supra* note 96, at 85.

the Court's *Nonsmoker* decision, Justice Bryde argues that a certain amount of generalization and simplification is necessary, criticizing the majority for demanding a level of consistency and purity in legislative drafting that cannot be met – requirements that endanger the ability of the political system to adapt to change.[127] Accepting that concern, the Constitutional Court, in the *Asylum Seekers Benefits Act* case, now explicitly states that the Basic Law "allows for negotiations and for political compromise."[128]

The future relationship between the Court and the legislature will depend on whether the Court itself applies the principles of consistency and transparency to the legislature in a consistent and transparent way.[129] We have shown that the Constitutional Court has recently tilted in the direction of monitoring the parliament's use of expert knowledge. Despite the lack of constitutional provisions mandating competent research or the inclusion of expert, statistical, and scientific data,[130] the Constitutional Court has imposed these obligations on the legislature through its fundamental rights jurisprudence. Its aim is not to strengthen democratic functioning but to preserve rights in spite of democratic choices that may limit rights.[131]

Such an effort would be virtually impossible in the United States, where the greater number of veto gates assures that all legislation will be a political compromise. The U.S. Supreme Court may find that a statute violates rights, but its response is to hold the act unconstitutional, not require some change in legislative procedures. We have already critiqued its decisions in the federalism area that seem to misunderstand the nature of the legislative process, but outside that area, a decision is usually democratically legitimate if it follows the proper constitutionally mandated procedures, independently of whether it represents a compromise.

In Germany some statutes pass virtually unchanged from the government's draft. In addition, statistical analyses, expert hearings, and participation of private and state actors are already part of the normal legislative practice.[132] A strong party in control of the government with a coherent policy agenda can enact its preferred policies into law, whatever the legislature's internal

[127] Dissent of Justice Brun-Otto Bryde in 121 BVerfGE 317, 380 f.

[128] 132 BVerfGE 134, *Asylum Seekers Benefits Act* decision, at 162.

[129] This is pointed out by Michael, *supra* note 97, at 881 f.; *see* Bumke, *supra* note 98, at 80 (criticizing the Constitutional Court's inconsistent application of the principle of consistency).

[130] Gusy, *Grundgesetz*, *supra* note 34, at 298.

[131] Hebeler, *supra* note 44, at 762.

[132] *See* Helmuth Schulze-Fielitz, Theorie und Praxis parlamentarischer Gesetzgebung – besonders des 9. Deutschen Bundestages (1980–1983) 490–507 (1988) (using the legislative period from 1980–3 to analyze the regard for rationality in legislative practice).

procedures. However, a coalition government or a weak and divided ruling party may face difficult drafting choices. Furthermore, if a different political coalition controls the upper house, the government will need to anticipate its position when it drafts the text. Although court rulings that affect the legislative process will be less troublesome in the German parliamentary system compared to the United States, they still can be overly intrusive if they are predicated on a level of rationality and consistency not suitable to the political process of passing statutes. The substantive law may be inconsistent or vague so long as it complies with fundamental rights.[133] The outcome is clearly the result of *Entscheidungsverfahren*, not *Erkenntnisverfahren*.

III. REVIEW OF ADMINISTRATIVE REGULATIONS AND GUIDELINES

Regulations outnumber formal statutes in Germany and shape whole areas of law.[134] Their legal and practical consequences often affect individuals more strongly than statutes standing alone.[135] Thus, regulations are not only quantitatively but also qualitatively the dominant form of legal constraint.[136] As the core form of secondary legislation, they are at the center of our study of the administration.

Judicial review of secondary legislation in Germany is not fundamentally different from review of the legislative process and of the substance of statutes. Here too, the violation of rights plays a prominent role. As a result, the system produces some of the same lacunae as for statutes. The ministries and agencies that make rules and the bodies that produce ordinances, however, have less claim to democratic legitimacy than does the directly elected legislature. For that reason, judicial review of administrative rulemaking could help strengthen the democratic legitimacy and

[133] WERNER HEUN, DAS MEHRHEITSPRINZIP IN DER DEMOKRATIE 79 ff. (1983); Christoph Gusy, *Das Mehrheitsprinzip im demokratischen Staat*, **106** ARCHIV DES ÖFFENTLICHEN RECHTS [AöR] 329, at 337 ff. (1981); Klaus Schlaich, *Die Verfassungsgerichtsbarkeit im Gefüge der Staatsfunktionen – Besteuerung und Eigentum*, **39** VERÖFFENTLICHUNGEN DER VEREINIGUNG DER DEUTSCHEN STAATSRECHTSLEHRER [VVDStRL], 99, at 109 (1981).

[134] For the latest figures, *see* STATISTISCHES BUNDESAMT (ed.), *supra* note 17; *see* Ossenbühl, *§ 103 Rechtsverordnung*, *supra* note 19, at 15 (calling regulations the "most common public source of law"); von Danwitz, *supra* note 19, at 21 (making a similar claim).

[135] Ossenbühl, *§ 103 Rechtsverordnung*, *supra* note 19, at 15.

[136] SAURER, *supra* note 19, at 188; LIV JAECKEL, GEFAHRENABWEHRRECHT UND RISIKODOGMATIK 196, 199 (2010) (emphasizing the "high practical relevance"); RAINER SCHRÖDER, VERWALTUNGSRECHTSDOGMATIK IM WANDEL 268 (2007) (pointing out their major role in technical and environmental law); DI FABIO, RISIKOENTSCHEIDUNGEN, *supra* note 8, at 338; SCHMIDT-ASSMANN, VERWALTUNGSRECHT, *supra* note 8, at 122, 325 f.

transparency of policymaking by reviewing compliance with the statutory frame. Indeed, that is one of the motivations for judicial review of administrative rulemaking in the United States. It plays a less important role in Germany. In addition to rights-based judicial review, the delegation of lawmaking authority to the executive is constrained and checked by formal and informal inter-branch and internal executive control mechanisms. Under the law, broad public participation is not a separate route to democratic legitimacy. German law often requires inter-branch or intergovernmental consultation but not broad public participation.

Recently, the similarities between executive and legislative rulemaking procedures were the subject of several decisions by the State Social Court of Berlin-Brandenburg.[137] Building on the *Hartz IV* decision, the court applied the principles of consistency and transparency to executive rulemaking. It examined health policy guidelines enacted under the Fifth Book of the German Social Code, § 92, by the Federal Joint Committee, which consists "of the joint self-government of physicians, dentists, hospitals and health insurance funds."[138] However, as Jakob Nolte points out, this application blurs an important distinction between judicial review of legislative and executive rules.[139] The legislative margin of discretion in shaping fundamental rights protection does not extend to the area of executive rulemaking. The courts often subject executive rules to detailed substantive review because the empowering statute limits subsequent rulemaking. In cases of wide delegations in complex subject areas, the executive has some discretion to create certain policies. Nevertheless, the empowering statute has to determine the content, purpose, and scope of the regulations. As a result, the courts cannot concentrate on process as a way of avoiding substantive review.[140]

137 Nolte, *supra* note 53, at 258 f. (citing and analyzing the decisions of the State Social Court of Berlin-Brandenburg, decision of Dec. 6, 2011, file number L 1 KR 184/11 ER at section II.2.1.4, published in Pharma Recht [PharmR] 100 (2012); State Social Court of Berlin-Brandenburg, decision of June 22, 2012, file number L 1 KR 296/09 KL at section 2.1, published in PharmR 398 (2012); State Social Court of Berlin-Brandenburg, decision of August 17, 2011, file number L 7 KA 77/08 KL at section D.1, published in Zeitschrift für das gesamte Medizin- und Gesundheitsrecht [ZMGR] 386 (2011); State Social Court of Berlin-Brandenburg, decision of December 21, 2011, file number L 7 KA 77/10 KL section D.1, published in Krankenhaus-Rechtsprechung [KRS] 11.106).

138 Cited from the English Web site of the Federal Joint Committee (available at http://www.english.g-ba.de), which is established by Sozialgesetzbuch Fünftes Buch – Gesetzliche Krankenversicherung [SGB V] [Social Code Book V], Dec. 20, 1988, BGBl I 2477, 2482, most recently amended by article 1 of the act of August 11, 2014, BGBl I 1346, § 91.

139 Nolte, *supra* note 53, at 260 f.

140 *Id.*

A. The Production of Secondary Legislation

Secondary legislation consists of three types of rules: regulations, ordinances, and administrative guidelines. Only regulations and ordinances are secondary legislation with external effect. The executive enacts regulations under delegations of lawmaking authority in formal statutes that dictate the scope and procedural requirements of the respective regulations. According to article 80(1) sentence 1 Basic Law, regulatory authority can be delegated to the federal government, a federal secretary, or any of the state governments. Federal regulations require a collegial decision by the coalition parties, and regulations enacted by one minister must be presented to the cabinet. Hence, any conflicts between coalition parties will most likely be solved within the government and not be brought to public attention.[141]

Ordinances, the second type of secondary lawmaking, are enacted by self-governing institutions. These institutions only have autonomy to regulate within particular areas; therefore, ordinances have limited scope and influence.[142] Administrative guidelines are intra-administrative rules that guide executive behavior. Theoretically they only have internal effects and are not subject to externally imposed procedures.[143] Despite their internal character, guidelines can have strong practical effects, so that government bodies sometimes use guidelines and regulations as functional equivalents. In certain areas, most prominently in environmental law, guidelines are subject to some formal procedural requirements.[144] Their use is limited when

141 Markus Möstl, *§ 2. Teil: Normative Handlungsformen*, in ALLGEMEINES VERWALTUNGSRECHT § 20 para. 5 (Hans-Uwe Erichsen & Dirk Ehlers, eds., 14th ed., 2010).

142 These institutions include but are not limited to municipalities, municipal organizations, universities, chambers, public broadcasters, and social insurance bodies; HARMUT MAURER, ALLGEMEINES VERWALTUNGSRECHT [hereinafter, MAURER, VERWALTUNGSRECHT] § 4 para. 24 (18th ed., 2011); Fritz Ossenbühl, *§ 105 Satzung*, in HANDBUCH DES STAATSRECHTS DER BUNDESREPUBLIK DEUTSCHLAND, BAND II VERFASSUNGSSTAAT ¶ 4 ff. (Josef Isensee & Paul Kirchhof, eds., 3rd ed., 2007).

143 78 BVERFGE 214, 227; MAURER, VERWALTUNGSRECHT, *supra* note 142, § 24 paras. 20–31 (stating that various concepts argue for external effects of guidelines, e.g., through an application of the principle of equality); Möstl, *supra*, note 141, § 20 paras. 16–19; 72 BVERWGE 300 (320 f.); 107 BVERWGE 338 (340 ff.); 129 BVERWGE 209 (212) (emphasizing their function to define general terms in statutes in the area of environmental law, so called *normkonkretisierende Funktion*); SAURER, *supra* note 19, at 219 ff. (providing an extensive analysis of their legal character).

144 SAURER, *supra* note 19, at 79 ff.; *see* the empowerment to enact regulations, Gesetz zur Förderung der Kreislaufwirtschaft und Sicherung der umweltverträglichen Bewirtschaftung von Abfällen [Kreislaufwirtschaftsgesetz – KrWG] [Life-Cycle Resource Management Act], Feb. 24, 2012, BGBL I 212, most recently amended by § 44 sect. 4 of the act of May 22, 2013, BGBL I 1324, § 16(1); Schulze-Fielitz, *Technik*, *supra* note 25, at 487.

implementing European law requirements, however, because their merely internal validity means that they do not create the subjective rights for third parties mandated by EU law.[145]

Although the Basic Law mentions all three legal instruments,[146] there is no single coherent normative system that governs their enactment. The Basic Law includes very limited formal requirements that outline the authority of the government to issue these instruments, leaving aside the internal process leading up to the final version.[147] In addition to the participation of the Bundestag and Bundesrat, which will be discussed in more detail later in this chapter, regulations and ordinances have to be signed and published, and the regulatory text must cite its legal basis.[148] The Constitution does not require a formal statement of reasons.[149] The Federal Administrative Procedures Act and similar state-level acts complement the Basic Law by comprehensively outlining the procedures for issuing administrative acts – that is, adjudications or other individual decisions – and forming administrative contracts. They do not, however, cover the process of producing either regulations with the force of law or legal guidelines.[150] In the absence of an Administrative Procedures Act for rules and norms, the procedural constraints for executive rulemaking are fragmented, with requirements

[145] Since 1991 the ECJ prohibits the implementation of binding EU law through the use of guidelines because their lack of external effects prevents judicial review; *see* most prominently the decisions regarding the TA Luft, Case C-361/88 Commission v Germany [1991] ECR I-2567, at paras. 15 ff., and regarding the implementation of procurement law, Case C-433/93 Commission v Germany [1995] ECR I-2303, at paras. 17 ff.; Saurer, *supra* note 19, at 81 f., 155 ff., 329 ff.; Anke Frankenberger, Umweltschutz durch Rechtsverordnung 65 (1998).

[146] Basic Law articles 80, 119, 132 (mentioning regulations); Basic Law article 28 (regulating ordinances); Basic Law articles 84(2), 85(2), 86, 87b(2), 108(7), 129 (mentioning guidelines).

[147] Kischel, *supra* note 52, at 315; Maurer, Verwaltungsrecht § 13 para. 10; Hartmut Maurer, Staatsrecht, Band 1 [hereinafter, Maurer, Staatsrecht] § 17 paras. 150–2 (6th ed., 2010).

[148] Basic Law article 82, GGO §§ 66–8, GOBReg § 30 (demanding publication in the *Bundesanzeiger* or *Bundesgesetzblatt Teil I*); *see also* Basic Law article 80(1) sentence 3.

[149] Saurer, *supra* note 19, at 85; Kischel, *supra* note 52, at 307 ff.; Ossenbühl, *§ 103 Rechtsverordnung*, *supra* note 19, at 72 ff. (pointing to the value and necessity of a formal statement of reasons as an internal or external means of control); Panagiotis Skouris, Die Begründung von Rechtsnormen 96–101 (2002).

[150] *See* VwVfG § 9; Eberhard Schmidt-Aßmann, *§ 109 Verwaltungsverfahren*, in Handbuch des Staatsrechts der Bundesrepublik Deutschland, Band II Verfassungsstaat ¶ 18 (Josef Isensee & Paul Kirchhof, eds., 3rd ed., 2007); Susan Rose-Ackerman, Controlling Environmental Policy: The Limits of Public Law in Germany and the United States 82–93 (1995) [available in German as: Umweltrecht und politik in den Vereinigten Staaten und der Bundesrepublik Deutschland, 1995].

spread throughout the legal system at the European level and at the federal and state levels in Germany.[151]

On the federal level, the empowering statutes often include area-specific procedural rules for the enactment of a regulation. For ordinances, the statutes enacted by the German Länder contain detailed procedural requirements applicable to every ordinance enacted by a municipality, complemented by even stricter federal rules especially in the area of planning/zoning law. There is no equivalent system for regulations, however.[152] Thus, again, the enactment of regulations only must conform to specific, selective procedural constraints – there is no overall set of rules.[153]

In spite of the dearth of coherent constitutional or statutory procedural rules, the government has issued internal orders to guide the preparation, issuance, and promulgation of regulations by federal organs. The most important guideline is the Joint Rules of Procedure of the Federal Ministries (GGO), which, among other things, governs the issuance and promulgation of regulations.[154] Its provisions are comparable to the rules that apply to statutory drafts. They include the duty to issue an explanatory memorandum and an impact assessment and to consult with federal ministries, the Länder, and relevant federal associations and experts.[155] The

[151] Ossenbühl, *§ 103 Rechtsverordnung*, *supra* note 19, at 68; Michael Gerhardt & Wolfgang Bier, *§ 47*, in VERWALTUNGSGERICHTSORDNUNG: VwGO 88 ff. (Friedrich Schoch, Eberhard Schmidt-Aßmann, & Rainer Pietzner, eds., 22nd ed., loose leaf, Sept. 2011).

[152] Some state statutes govern the enactment of regulations at the state level and contain procedural requirements (e.g., Bayerisches Gesetz über das Landesstrafrecht und das Verordnungsrecht auf dem Gebiet der öffentlichen Sicherheit und Ordnung [Landesstraf- und Verordnungsgesetz – BayLStVG] [Bavarian Act on State Administrative Offenses and Regulatory Law in the Area of Public Safety and Order], Jan. 1, 1957, BAYERISCHE RECHTSSAMMLUNG [BAYRS] II, 241, most recently amended by § 1 no. 29 of the regulation of July 22, 2014, BAYERISCHES GESETZ- UND VERORDNUNGSBLATT [GVBL] 286 and Allgemeines Verwaltungsgesetz für das Land Schleswig-Holstein [Landesverwaltungsgesetz – LVwG] [State Administrative Act of Schleswig-Holstein], June 2, 1992, GESETZ- UND VERORDNUNGSBLATT SCHLESWIG-HOLSTEIN [GVOBL] 243, 534, most recently amended by the act of June 21, 2013, GVOBL 254). However, these requirements mainly concern the formal requirements authorizing rulemaking, not requirements for notice, participation, and reason-giving.

[153] SCHMIDT-ASSMANN, VERWALTUNGSRECHT, *supra* note 8, at 327 f. (stating that procedural rules for regulations need to be further developed ensuring equal and transparent participation as well as plurality); PÜNDER, *supra* note 14, at 149.

[154] GGO §§ 62–8.

[155] The GGO requires usage of the Manual on Legal Drafting issued by the Federal Ministry of Justice (GGO § 42(4)); the duty to issue an explanatory memorandum (GGO §§ 42, 43); assessing and providing information on the regulatory impacts (GGO § 44), involvement of the affected federal ministries (GGO § 45) and the Federal Ministry of Justice (GGO § 46); and prompt and early information and involvement of "the Länder, national

government can void a rule that does not comply.[156] However, these guidelines do not have external effect, and hence their violation alone will not affect the validity of a regulation or give anyone a right to bring a challenge to the courts.[157]

Within this general framework, the Constitutional Court has sometimes required the executive to make a rational balancing decision between competing fundamental rights. This is a way to uphold rights in sensitive areas where the executive has significant discretion and review of the result seems insufficient.[158] For example, administrative regulations governing the distribution of university resources affect the scope of occupational freedom, a constitutional right.[159] Hence, according to the Constitutional Court, the executive rule maker must research the state of experience and knowledge properly, consider the underlying facts, and use a rational, comprehensible method of balancing competing interests.[160] Here again, the Court is concerned with the substantive balancing decision and does not impose any specific procedural duties. Even though there is no obligation to give a formal statement of reasons, the rulemaking body may well want to guard against invalidation by being sure that the courts can reconstruct the process used and the motivation for the rule.[161] Overall, however, there is no constitutional duty to grant hearing or participation rights to experts, the public, or affected groups.[162]

associations of local authorities and representatives of the Länder to the Federation," as well as of "central and umbrella associations and of the expert community at federal level" (GGO § 47).

156 Ulrich Battis, *§ 165 Der Verfassungsverstoß und seine Rechtsfolgen*, in HANDBUCH DES STAATSRECHTS DER BUNDESREPUBLIK DEUTSCHLAND, BAND VII ¶ 62 (Josef Isensee & Paul Kirchhof, eds., 1st ed., 1992); FERDINAND KOPP & WOLF-RÜDIGER SCHENKE, VERWALTUNGSGERICHTSORDNUNG: VwGO § 47 para. 120 (debating this issue in regard of EU law in paras. 99, 125).

157 Ossenbühl, *§ 103 Rechtsverordnung, supra* note 19, at 70; Ossenbühl, *§ 104 Autonome Rechtsetzung der Verwaltung*, in HANDBUCH DES STAATSRECHTS DER BUNDESREPUBLIK DEUTSCHLAND, BAND II VERFASSUNGSSTAAT ¶ 21 (Josef Isensee & Paul Kirchhof, eds., 3rd ed., 2007); KOPP & SCHENKE, *supra* note 156, at § 47 para. 120; Kloepfer, *Abwägungsregeln, supra* note 45, at 441 f.

158 KISCHEL, *supra* note 52 at 309 ff., 326.

159 Basic Law article 12(1).

160 85 BVERFGE 36, 56 f.; 54 BVERFGE 173, 197; 66 BVERFGE 155, 179 f.; *see* KISCHEL, *supra* note 52, at 310 ff. (analyzing these decisions). According to Heun, *Artikel 3 Grundgesetz, supra* note 68, at 87, the principle of equality is applied in a particular strict way in the area of article 12 Basic Law.

161 KISCHEL, *supra* note 52, at 309 ff. (criticizing the Constitutional Court's limited emphasis on the value of transparency for judicial review, arguing for greater duties of transparency).

162 42 BVerfGE 191, 205; PÜNDER, *supra* note 14, at 142; ARMIN VON BOGDANDY, GUBERNATIVE RECHTSETZUNG 398 (2000); Möstl, *supra* note 141, § 19 para. 18.

The more direct route to democratic accountability through hearings, public participation, and reason-giving is thus largely absent for regulations, although some scholars argue for a constitutional duty to balance the democratic deficit by providing a statement of reasons when the government promulgates secondary legislation.[163] However, as in the case of statutes, the Constitutional Court imposes procedural constraints only when individual rights are at stake or in the case of abstract challenges by certain state organs.[164] The courts value transparency mainly because it can ensure better legal protection for citizens.[165] They do not justify it as a route to more effective citizen participation in rulemaking.

Hence, contrary to the U.S. APA, German administrative law does not impose a duty on the executive to give reasons when it makes rules. In this, the law is similar to the South African case where the legislature has not yet passed a clear statutory rule that mandates reason-giving or public participation for secondary legislation. Nevertheless, the prospects for judicially created rules of this type are much greater in South Africa than in Germany, again highlighting the South African courts' drive to further a participatory and inclusive democracy.

B. Area-Specific Procedural Rules

Thus, in general, the law imposes weak procedural constraints on secondary lawmaking, supplemented by rather strong substantive requirements. Nevertheless, in certain limited areas, substantive statutes mandate procedures for enacting rules, for example regarding the regulation of risk, especially in environmental law and planning law. The regulatory demands in these areas differ from ordinary secondary rulemaking.[166] With modern

[163] Ossenbühl, *§ 103 Rechtsverordnung*, *supra* note 19, at 72 ff.; Kischel, *supra* note 52, at 304 ff. (deriving a duty to give a statement of reasons by drawing a connection to judicial review, which implicitly presupposes the existence of subjective rights); Jörg Lücke, Begründungszwang und Verfassung, Zur Begründungspflicht der Gerichte, Behörden und Parlamente 13 (1987) (arguing for a general constitutional duty to give a statement of reasons); Ulrich Ramsauer, *Artikel 80 Grundgesetz*, in Alternativkommentar, Kommentar zum Grundgesetz für die Bundesrepublik Deutschland 74b (2002) (assuming such a duty only for certain areas); Gerhardt & Bier, *supra* note 151, at 95 & n. 516 (arguing for a duty only in cases of a statutory basis).

[164] Kischel, *supra* note 52, at 309 f.; Maurer, Staatsrecht, *supra* note 147, § 17 para. 150 (discussing the argument that merely publishing the final regulation does not provide for publicity of the procedure).

[165] Kischel, *supra* note 52, at 309 f., 311 f.

[166] Jaeckel, *supra* note 136, at 17, 48 (emphasizing the uncertainties of risk regulation in the areas of nuclear technology, genetic engineering, and nanotechnology).

technologies advancing at an unprecedented speed and with increasingly complex environmental interdependencies, substantive steering by the legislature has reached the limits of its capacity.[167] Therefore, the legislature has compensated for its anemic substantive influence by imposing procedural duties on the executive that are geared toward exploring and including the various affected interests.[168] This creates tensions between German law's traditionally skeptical attitude toward procedural constraints and the procedural emphasis of modern risk regulation. In such cases, the empowering statute specifies the duties of the regulatory authority and includes obligations such as a statement of reasons or periodic reports on the rule's impact.[169] It may also specify certain groups or types of people who should be heard. Commentators justify such consultation with outsiders as a way to improve the regulatory result by hearing from those with expertise and experience.[170] The Constitutional Court has enforced these positive duties.[171]

The need for expert knowledge is one reason that the legislature both delegates legislative authority and also requires certain types of consultation.[172] The legislature can guide the process and create time-intensive procedural requirements, as long as the executive preserves a certain amount

[167] *Id.* at 178 f., 182 f., 197 f., 263; SCHRÖDER, *supra* note 136, at 195 f.

[168] JAECKEL, *supra* note 136, at 324.

[169] SAURER, *supra* note 19, at 79 (stating that the executive is permitted to exceed its obligations and provide additional hearings and information); *see also* JAECKEL, *supra* note 136, at 224 (referring to VwVfG §§ 26(1) and 65 allowing the executive to make use of external expertise).

[170] Ossenbühl, *§ 103 Rechtsverordnung*, *supra* note 19, at 66; SCHNEIDER, *supra* note 24 at 263; JAECKEL, *supra* note 136, at 197 f. (emphasizing the purpose of improving the quality of the rationality and quality of decision making); PÜNDER, *supra* note 14, at 144 f., 234 (emphasizing that the participation of the public is much wider in the United States).

[171] This is the core of a recent decision of the Constitutional Court, 127 BVerfGE 293. In 2002 article 20a was added to the Basic Law to "protect the natural foundations of life and animals." In the Animal Protection Act, the legislature delegated rulemaking authority to the executive, but required consultation with the Animal Protection Commission prior to the drafting of a final regulation in order to promote the protection of animals. The Länder Government of Rhineland-Palatinate brought an abstract review procedure to the Constitutional Court challenging certain provisions of a federal regulation on the specifics of keeping laying hens as farm animals. The Constitutional Court held the regulation to be unconstitutional because the authorities failed to comply with the hearing requirement and thus violated higher law and article 20a Basic Law.

[172] *See* Schulze-Fielitz, *Technik*, *supra* note 25, at 465, 477 f., 485, 498; *see also* SCHMIDT-ASSMANN, VERWALTUNGSRECHT, *supra* note 8, at 84–6, 308 (emphasizing the value of procedures to ensure rationality in line with democracy and rule of law principles); PÜNDER, *supra* note 14, at 233 f. (arguing that U.S. law places more emphasis on the value of expertise in executive rulemaking than does the German system because of its use of independent experts and delegation to independent agencies).

of rulemaking responsibility.[173] Different regulatory tasks correspond to different procedural requirements.[174] Environmental law emphasizes precaution and requires consultation with nonstate actors from listed sectors.[175] Statutes like the Genetic Engineering Act that concern modern risk regulation stress the gathering of expert knowledge and hence require consultation with experts.[176] In these areas, the executive has to regulate under conditions of uncertainty due to unknown causal links and the indeterminate consequences of technical instruments.[177] The processes mainly aim at good substantive results, not better democratic legitimacy through participation.[178]

The mandated consultations most commonly prescribe a hearing of concerned parties or experts whom the executive individually selects.[179] The participation of private actors is often ad hoc, but can also have a more institutionalized structure. However, there are no overall participatory rights for external bodies or citizens even in the statutes that mandate some level of consultation.[180]

For example, the Federal Emissions Control Act requires a "Hearing of the Parties Concerned" and sets up an ad hoc group.[181]

> Where the issuance of ordinances and general administrative provisions requires a hearing of the parties concerned, an ad-hoc group shall be heard which is to be constituted in each individual case from representatives of the

[173] SAURER, *supra* note 19, at 234; Gertrude Lübbe-Wolff, *Verfassungsrechtliche Fragen der Normsetzung und Normkonkretisierung im Umweltrecht*, **6** ZEITSCHRIFT FÜR GESETZGEBUNG (ZG) 219, 244 (1991); *see* also more generally ERHARD DENNINGER, VERFASSUNGSRECHTLICHE ANFORDERUNGEN AN DIE NORMSETZUNG IM UMWELT- UND TECHNIKRECHT (1990).

[174] DI FABIO, RISIKOENTSCHEIDUNGEN, *supra* note 8, at 26.

[175] BImSchG § 51; KrWG § 68; SAURER, *supra* note 19, at 111.

[176] Gesetz zur Regelung der Gentechnik [Gentechnikgesetz – GenTG] [Genetic Engineering Act], Dec. 16, 1993, BGBL I 2066, most recently amended by article 4 sect. 14 of the act of Aug. 7, 2013, BGBL I 3154, §§ 4, 5; SAURER, *supra* note 19, at 111.

[177] Schulze-Fielitz, *Technik*, *supra* note 25, at 475 ff.; SAURER, *supra* note 19, at 61 f.

[178] Schulze-Fielitz, *Technik*, *supra* note 25, at 462 f., 470 f.; SCHMIDT-ASSMANN, VERWALTUNGSRECHT, *supra* note 8, at 305, 310 (stating that this "serving function" does not do justice to the independent value of procedures to steer toward good results).

[179] *See* BImSchG § 4(1), § 7(1), § 10(10), § 22(1) sentence 2, § 23(1) sentence 1; SAURER, *supra* note 19, at 78 f.

[180] CLAUS PEGATZKY, PARLAMENT UND VERORDNUNGSGEBER 60 ff. (1999); SAURER, *supra* note 19, at 366 ff.

[181] BImSchG § 51 (*see* English version, *supra* note 26). Similarly KrWG § 68 and Gesetz zum Schutz vor schädlichen Bodenveränderungen und zur Sanierung von Altlasten [Bundes-Bodenschutzgesetz – BBodSchG] [Federal Soil Protection Act], Mar. 17, 1998, BGBL I 502, most recently amended by article 5 sect. 30 of the act of Feb. 24, 2012, BGBL I 212, § 20.

> scientific community, the parties affected and, where applicable, the business community and the transport sector, as well as of the supreme Land authorities responsible for emission control.

The notion of the "parties affected" is interpreted very broadly, and covers environmental protection organizations, consumer protection organizations, and associations of citizens' initiatives.[182] The executive can chose whom to hear, however, and groups with no right to be heard cannot raise a legally enforceable objection.[183] In contrast, the Federal Nature Conservation Act gives recognized associations that aim at protecting the environment vested rights to comment and examine expert opinions when the government prepares regulations.[184] As with the Emissions Control Act, the regulatory authority can decide which groups to recognize. Participation is not open-ended.[185]

Likewise, the Genetic Engineering Act established the Central Commission for Biosafety, which is a permanent body composed of experts and qualified persons affiliated with certain organizations that must be heard before the government enacts regulations.[186] Another example is the Committee on Hazardous Substances, which consists of representatives of "the employers, the trades unions, the state authorities, the statutory accident insurance institution and other suitable persons, especially from the scientific community."[187] Such institutions have a filtering function, which

[182] Hans D. Jarass, BImSchG, § 51 para. 2 (9th ed., 2012); Hans-Joachim Koch, *§ 51*, in GK BImSchG, at para. 26 (Hans Joachim Koch, Eckhard Pache, & Dieter H. Scheuing, eds., 2011); Klaus Hansmann, *§ 51*, in Umweltrecht Kommentar, Band I, BImSchG, at paras. 9, 11 (Robert von Landmann & Gustav Rohmer, eds., 2009, loose leaf, last update April 1, 2013).

[183] Hansmann, *supra* note 182, § 51 paras. 18–20, 31–2; Jarass, *supra* note 182, § 51 para. 5; Koch, *supra* note 182, § 51 para. 43.

[184] Gesetz über Naturschutz und Landschaftspflege [Bundesnaturschutzgesetz – BNatSchG] [Federal Nature Conservation Act], July 29, 2009, BGBl I 2542, most recently amended by article 4 sect. 100 of the act of Aug. 7, 2013, BGBl I 3154, § 63.

[185] There is no systematic information on which groups are, in fact, heard, or on their impact on the final results. The regulation will only state that the parties concerned were heard. There is a list of associations (with 2,190 entries as of August 1, 2014, available under https://www.bundestag.de/dokumente/lobbyliste) that can represent their interests before the parliament and the government. However, this list does not include public associations and does not give any information on who is actually heard.

[186] The Commission is established in GenTG §§ 4, 5 and is given hearing rights in GenTG §§ 6, 7, 14, 30.

[187] Verordnung zum Schutz vor Gefahrstoffen [Gefahrstoffverordnung – GefStoffV] [Hazardous Substances Ordinance], Nov. 26, 2010, BGBl I 1643, 1644, most recently amended by article 2 of the ordinance of July 15, 2013, BGBl I 2514, § 20, an English version is available at http://www.baua.de/en/Topics-from-A-to-Z/Hazardous-Substances/Hazardous-Substances-Ordinance.html.

facilitates the incorporation of public input and expert knowledge by condensing it into a single report. However, part of the filtering occurs up front when the government draws up a list of those to consult.

Given that the same coalition controls both the Bundestag and the cabinet, one may ask why the executive accepts or even proposes such constraints on its own freedom of action. Lacking in-depth research on this issue, the answer to this question contains a speculative element. First, even governing party MPs may want some assurance from the government that it will administer a particularly controversial act fairly and competently, and procedural requirements can help to reassure the legislators. Second, the government itself may seek these provisions as a way of increasing the legitimacy of its actions in contested areas. Of course, it can always carry out such processes on its own, but placing them in the statute is a stronger guarantee. Third, one should not overstate the real bite of these requirements. They seldom give anyone the right to go to court to object to their inadequate implementation. Thus, they provide a check but not a very stringent one, especially because existing internal guidelines include similar provisions.

The issue of public participation also arises when private actors have the authority to draft rules. Rules developed by transnational or private actors are today an important source of regulatory norms. Yet their incorporation into German law raises the issue of democratic legitimacy in a particularly stark form. Although the parliament can threaten to refuse to transpose these rules into (national) law, its practical influence is limited by the complexities of (international) lawmaking and by prior commitments favoring incorporation of privately designed rules.[188] The rules that private or transnational bodies develop derive some legitimacy from these bodies' expertise, reputation, and acceptance. Their weak or nonexistent parliamentary legitimacy, however, gives the parliament the incentive to impose special procedural duties on the enactment of these rules in order to promote public accountability.[189] As recognized by the concept of

[188] *See* for example the contract between the Federal Republic of Germany and DIN Deutsches Institut für Normung (June 5, 1975, available under http://www.din.de/sixcms_upload/media/2896/Vertrag_BRD_DIN.pdf), giving DIN the status as the exclusive national standardization organization. The DIN is, in turn, required to consider the public interest, and the final lawmaking authority of course remains with the state; *see* JAECKEL, *supra* note 136, at 258.

[189] JAECKEL, *supra* note 136, at 250, 253 f. (describing the "legitimacy paradox" as the discrepancy between increased legitimacy through higher quality and a democratic deficit due to a lack of a legitimacy chain); SCHMIDT-ASSMANN, VERWALTUNGSRECHT, *supra* note 8, at 331.

"legitimacy through procedure" (*Legitimation durch Verfahren*),[190] transparency and procedural rules, such as equal representation and participation, information, and documentation, can help to increase legitimacy.[191] Examples exist in financial market regulation, environmental law, and also in the setting of industry standards.[192] However, the legislature has not created a widely accepted and coherent framework for such procedural requirements.[193]

These developments represent important efforts to reach beyond the bureaucracy and top political appointees to draw on a wider knowledge base. They hark back to an old German tradition of relying on private bodies to draft rules related to the safety of products and workplaces.[194] Seen as a whole, not limited to specific areas of environmental law, however, participation of private actors in the process of enacting regulations is the exception, not the rule.[195] Moreover, procedural requirements for regulations are less detailed and less strict than those for statutes, which require three readings, publicity, and participation by the Bundesrat and the Bundespräsident.[196] The procedural rules for regulations mostly consist of hearing and information requirements, often requiring consultation only with a body of experts and with affected groups handpicked by the ministry.

[190] 49 BVerfGE 89, 139 f.; 53 BVerfGE 30, 56 f.; Lübbe-Wolff, *supra* note 173, at 242 ff.; Niklas Luhmann, Legitimation durch Verfahren, 27 ff. (3rd ed., 1978) (from a sociological point of view); *see* generally Utz Schliesky, Souveränität und Legitimität von Herrschaftsgewalt 149 ff. (2004).

[191] Christian Calliess, *Finanzkrisen als Herausforderung der internationalen, europäischen und nationalen Rechtsetzung*, 71 Veröffentlichungen der Vereinigung der Deutschen Staatsrechtslehrer [VVDStRL] 113 (2012) (discussing ways to ensure democratic legitimacy of financial regulation by informal and private bodies); Matthias Schmidt-Preuß, *Verwaltung und Verwaltungsrecht zwischen gesellschaftlicher Selbstregulierung und staatlicher Steuerung*, **56** VVDStRL 160, 202–6 (1997) (arguing that, e.g., regulations promulgated by the DIN fulfill "minimum standards of democracy and the rule of law," at 205).

[192] For example, the norms promulgated by the German Institute for Norms (DIN). Schmidt-Preuß, *supra* note 191, at 202–6; Rose-Ackerman, *supra* note 150, at 63–5.

[193] Jaeckel, *supra* note 136, at 257 (stating that the development of such a concept is necessary); Di Fabio, Risikoentscheidungen, *supra* note 8, at 468 (criticizing the lack of due process due to the lack of transparency of expert participations and the lack of clarity regarding the legal impact of expert opinions and demanding the development of procedures and promotion of transparency when setting standards).

[194] Rose-Ackerman, *supra* note 150, at 63–5.

[195] Saurer, *supra* note 19, at 366 f.

[196] Saurer, *supra* note 19, at 86 f. (stating that there is no duty to conduct three readings, which leads to less publicity; there are fewer participatory rights of the Bundesrat, and no involvement and thus no competency of the president to examine the statute before signing).

C. Parliamentary Influence on Lawmaking in the Executive

Despite the general lack of procedural duties, German secondary rulemaking procedures do have one unique feature compared to the United States. In the United States, formal ex post involvement of the legislature in rulemaking is unconstitutional, and federal rules never require approval by the states. Of course, both members of Congress and state officials will weigh in on rules that affect them and their political supporters, but there are no legal requirements beyond a rather toothless effort to get around the Supreme Court case that held the legislative veto unconstitutional.[197] In Germany, the Basic Law allows and sometimes even requires consultation and approval of regulations by the Bundesrat and Bundestag. The legislature also can, under certain circumstances, exercise direct influence by modifying regulations itself.

Under the Basic Law, the Bundesrat must approve a regulation if it was enacted under a statute that itself needed Bundesrat approval, unless these participatory rights are waived through a statute.[198] Hence, the Bundesrat's rights are weaker here than in the legislative process.

The Bundestag's influence on rulemaking in the executive takes a variety of forms; the Basic Law only sets wide outer limits. As a general matter, the parliament obtains information either through the executive's obligations to inform the parliament and to answer questions posed by members or through informal channels, such as members of the cabinet who are also members of parliament and members of parliament who are on agencies' boards of directors.[199] Furthermore, the legislature can push back against regulatory decisions and policies by making statutory changes or withdrawing the initial delegation, although in Germany's parliamentary system that is not a common occurrence.

Over and above such generic influences, individual statutes include a variety of requirements for Bundestag participation in the promulgation of secondary norms.[200] These often go hand in hand with comparatively wide

[197] Legislative vetoes of rules were found unconstitutional in I.N.S. v. Chadha, 462 U.S. 919 (1983). The statute is Congressional Review Act, 5 U. S. C. §§ 801–8 [U.S. 417 (1998)] (requiring major rules to be submitted to Congress for a possible joint resolution of disapproval that must be signed by the president to become binding).

[198] Basic Law article 80(2).

[199] CHRISTOPH MÖLLERS, DIE DREI GEWALTEN: LEGITIMATION DER GEWALTENGLIEDERUNG IN VERFASSUNGSSTAAT, EUROPÄISCHER INTEGRATION UND INTERNATIONALISIERUNG 131 (2008).

[200] For a detailed analysis *see* Ossenbühl, *§ 103 Rechtsverordnung*, *supra* note 19, at 58 ff.; SAURER, *supra* note 19, at 371 ff.; Christian Seiler, *Parlamentarische Einflussnahmen auf*

delegations of lawmaking authority to the executive, seemingly compensating for the uncertainty of the empowering provisions.[201]

For example, when the executive drafts a rule, the delegating statute might mandate certain procedures. Most importantly, the parliament may include statutory provisions that give it the right to deny consent or demand alterations prior to a regulation's enactment, or to reject it within a certain time limit after its enactment.[202] These rights require specific empowering provisions because there is no general right of Bundestag oversight. Although the parliament regularly makes use of these possibilities, this form of influence does not dominate state practice. From 1949 to 1999 only approximately sixty-five delegating statutes required some form of consent by the parliament.[203] In its most common statutory form, the enactment of a regulation depends on prior approval by the Bundestag; this either has to be given expressly or is assumed after a certain period of time

den Erlass von Rechtsverordnungen im Lichte der Formenstrenge, 16 Zeitschrift für Gesetzgebung [ZG] 50 (2001); Schneider, *supra* note 24 at § 9 paras. 253 ff.; Maurer, Staatsrecht, *supra* note 142, § 17 para. 155. For an analysis of the influence of Länder parliaments *see* Wito Schwanengel, Einwirkungen der Landesparlamente auf die Normsetzung der Exekutive, Verordnungsgebung unter Parlamentseinfluss (2002).

201 57 BVerwG 130, 139 f. (showing openness toward the idea of compensation); Ossenbühl, *§ 103 Rechtsverordnung*, *supra* note 19, at 63 (also emphasizing compensation); von Danwitz, *supra* note 19, at 125 ff, is critical, as is Johannes Schmidt, Die Beteiligung des Bundestags beim Erlasss von Rechtsverordnungen – Zur verfassungsrechtlichen Beurteilung parlamentarischer Mitwirkungsvorbehalte (2002) 144–75 (examining whether it is constitutionally permissible for the Bundestag to compensate legitimacy deficits by retaining influence on the enactment of regulations).

202 For example, Gesetz über die Umweltverträglichkeitsprüfung [UVPG] [Environmental Impact Assessment Act], Feb. 24, 2010, BGBl I 94, most recently amended by article 10 of the act of July 25, 2013, BGBl I 2749, § 3(1) sentence 4, 5 (making the enactment of regulations dependent on the approval of the Bundestag, which is deemed as given if not denied within three weeks); BImSchG § 48b (giving the Bundestag a right to veto or alter a draft regulation within a four-week window); KrWG § 67 (giving the Bundestag a right to veto or alter a draft regulation within a three-week window); Umwelthaftungsgesetz [UmweltHG] [Environmental Liability Act], Dec. 10, 1990, BGBl I 2634, most recently amended by article 9 sect. 5 of the act of Nov. 23, 2007, BGBl I 2631, § 20(2) (giving the Bundestag a right to veto or alter a draft regulation within a three-week window); Außenwirtschaftsgesetz [AWG] [Foreign Trade Act], June 6, 2013, BGBl I 1482, § 12(4) (giving the Bundestag a right to veto a regulation within four months after its promulgation); Gesetz zur Förderung der Stabilität und des Wachstums der Wirtschaft [StabG] [Economic Stability and Growth Act], June 8, 1967, BGBl I 582, most recently amended by article 135 of the regulation of Oct. 31, 2006, BGBl I 2407, § 20(5) (giving the Bundestag a right to veto a regulation within six weeks after its promulgation).

203 Ossenbühl, *§ 103 Rechtsverordnung*, *supra* note 19, at 57 referring to the official count from 1949 to 1999 listing sixty-five statutes, *see* Datenhandbuch zur Geschichte des Deutschen Bundestages 1949 bis 1999 2593 f. (Peter Schindler, ed., 1999).

has passed.[204] Parliament sometimes conditions its consent on certain substantive changes. Generally, these provisions are an accepted part of legislative practice, especially because, as an alternative, the legislature can always withdraw the entire delegation of lawmaking power.[205]

Given the German constitutional structure, such a continuing legislative role is in line with the prevailing view of democracy under which the legislature retains some formal influence even when delegating to the executive. The Basic Law grants the executive derivative rulemaking power and only permits it to perform essentially legislative activity when the legislature deems it necessary to implement a public policy. The Constitutional Court only requires that the parliament have a legitimate reason for retaining influence over delegated rulemaking.[206] For example, sometimes wide delegation to the executive can permit flexible and speedy adaption of rules that implement very important aspects of legislative policies.[207] A legislative veto can accompany such delegation. Examples are rules that set tariffs or prices.[208] Hence, delegation is a functional necessity, but the legislature has the authority to monitor the enactment and content of the regulations, although it need not do so.

Academic commentators debate the constitutionality of the blurring of executive and legislative powers in such statutes,[209] and the Constitutional Court has not ruled on the constitutionality of all the different mechanisms included in statutes. Some legal scholars argue that Bundestag oversight ought to have limits. They claim that, under the Basic Law, the legislature cannot intervene in rulemaking as a way to circumvent the parliamentary process. Once a delegation has occurred, the substantive responsibility for making policy ought to remain with the executive.[210] Its draft rules can be subject to various types of input from the Bundestag, ranging from consultation to outright disapproval, but the authority to issue the rules ought to

[204] Arnd Uhle, Parlament und Rechtsverordnung 109, 223 (1999); Seiler, *supra* note 200, at 63 ff.

[205] 8 BVerfGE 274, 319–22 (holding that the "state practice" of demanding approval of regulations by the Bundestag is generally in conformity with the Basic Law and is based on "old role-models"); Möstl, *supra* note 141, § 20 paras. 6, 9.

[206] 8 BVerfGE 274, 321 f.

[207] *Id.*

[208] *Id.*

[209] The Constitutional Court has expressly acknowledged this problem, but held that this is not unconstitutional because in the legislative process as well, the competences of the legislature and executive are intertwined in many ways, 8 BVerfGE 274, 321–2; more on constitutionality Saurer, *supra* note 19, at 371 ff.; Maurer, Staatsrecht, *supra* note 147, § 17 paras. 157–9.

[210] Jaeckel, *supra* note 136, at 204.

remain with the executive.[211] Under this view, the parliament must make the fundamental decision to delegate when it passes a statute and ought not to revisit it during the implementation phase.

Another aspect of the complex links between statutes and regulations is pragmatic. Under certain circumstances, the legislature exercises substantive influence by enacting statutory provisions that directly modify executive regulations. The Constitutional Court points out the practical necessity and advantages of this practice.[212] Suppose, for example, the legislature wanted to reform a complicated and multifaceted area like tax or social law, which is regulated through numerous intertwined statutes and regulations. If it enacted a tax reform bill, the government would then have to modify all the relevant regulations. Leaving the task of modifying these regulations to the executive could result in inconsistent, time-consuming, and piecemeal implementation. The alternative of replacing all the relevant regulations with a formal statute would also be impractical; it would limit administrative flexibility by barring the executive from responding promptly to changed circumstances. Instead, the legislature could spell out the necessary regulatory changes in the reform statute.[213] According to a decision from the Constitutional Court, the amended or altered part of a regulation that was modified through a statute keeps its status as a regulation; the executive can revise it later following the normal regulatory process.[214] The Court, however, limits the legislature's ability directly to alter regulations to cases where these actions are part of a major overhaul of a subject area, and thus they can only occur along with substantive statutory changes.[215]

Hence, German law presently permits the legislature to influence executive rulemaking through a variety of routes. Thus, we might expect that

[211] Seiler, *supra* note 200, at 66; Möstl, *supra* note 141, § 20 para. 6.

[212] 114 BVERFGE 196.

[213] According to Seiler, *supra* note 200, at 51 f. fn. 5, this happens fairly often; all changes to the income tax implementation regulation between 1992 and 1999 were made through parliamentary statutes.

[214] 114 BVERFGE 196. The decision from 2005 was based on complaints of two state governments about the constitutionality of the enactment of statutory changes to a health care premium law, which included changes to a regulation on the basis of this statute. It settled a long-standing academic discussion and overturned the prevailing academic opinion (*see* Seiler, *supra* note 200, at 53). It contains a good summary of the current law and further references. *See* SIMON SCHNELLE, EINE FEHLERFOLGENLEHRE FÜR RECHTSVERORDNUNGEN, 2007; Frauke Brosius-Gersdorf, *Der Gesetzgeber als Verordnungsgeber: Änderungen der Bundespflegesatzverordnung durch das Beitragssicherungsgesetz zwischen Gesetzesrecht und Parlamentsverordnung*, 22 ZEITSCHRIFT FÜR GESETZGEBUNG [ZG], 305, 307 (2007) (criticizing the unconstitutional mix of statutes and regulations as well as the undermining of procedural rules).

[215] 114 BVERFGE 196, 238.

any postelection change of the governing coalition would lead to substantive changes in regulatory law. Such shifts do sometimes occur in highly disputed areas of law that rely on regulations, such as school law, which is a Länder responsibility. However, a political change in parliament, and thus a governmental switch, will more commonly lead to the enactment of new statutes. Of course, regulations will be altered as new statutes come into force, but hardly any major changes occur at the regulatory level alone. One reason for this is the constitutional requirement that essential political or policy decisions have to be made in statutes. However, this is not a very onerous constraint. Given the parliamentary structure, it is not difficult for a new government to amend and enact statutes. The drafts often originate in the executive branch, allowing for inter-branch coordination and consultation.[216] Moreover, the German bureaucracy's reliance on professional civil servants ensures continuity and depoliticizes much routine secondary rulemaking.

The decree of parliamentary involvement in rulemaking is striking to those familiar with the American system. In the U.S. presidential system, congressional involvement is either informal or tied to budgets and legislative hearings. The U.S. Supreme Court's decision in the *Chadha* case declared that legislative vetoes are unconstitutional. The opinion stresses that such vetoes violate the formal requirements for enacting statutes. German law seems less formalistic in a way that reflects the nature of parliamentary government. It permits Bundestag oversight and upholds statutes that allow the legislature to modify executive regulations even though they might leave the author of the regulation unclear.

Some members of the U.S. Congress support moves toward greater congressional oversight on the German model. However, an existing law that requires major rules to be submitted to Congress for review has little bite because rules can only be struck down by statute.[217] Requiring the U.S. Congress to approve rules obviously would have a much greater effect than in Germany because different political parties might control the executive and Congress. For example, recent efforts by the House of Representatives to rein in and oversee executive rulemaking would, if they became law, have a pronounced chilling effect on the executive and the agencies' rulemaking

[216] Seiler, *supra* note 200, at 52 f.

[217] The Congressional Review Act, 5 U.S.C. §§ 801–8, sets up an expedited process for passing a joint resolution of disapproval of a major rule, that requires the president's signature or a veto override to go into effect. Only one rule has been rescinded under this process – a workplace ergonomics rule promulgated at the end of the Clinton administrative and disapproved by the new Republican Congress and President George W. Bush.

activities. Furthermore, a 2013 bill seems to be unconstitutional because it includes what is essentially a legislative veto.[218] Ultimately, maintaining the separation of powers between the executive and legislature is a less important concern in the German parliamentary system than it is in the U.S. presidential system where congressional vetoes would have more political force.

In contrast, South Africa is similar to Germany, although legislative review of delegated legislation is still emerging. There appears to be no constitutional objection to ex ante participation and ex post control by the legislature of executive lawmaking. One province in South Africa has gone even further than Germany by requiring that all proposed delegated legislation be submitted to it for scrutiny and approval prior to enactment.

Comparing the United States to Germany (and South Africa), one can provide functional reasons for the contrasting legal doctrines. In the United States, these reasons turn on the meaning of delegation. If it is based on the need for expert input and speedy responses to fluid conditions, bringing the legislature back in to approve regulations would undermine these basic justifications for delegation, especially under divided government. In the German case, these considerations are present as well, and have led the parliament to design procedural rules that both create and limit oversight rights. Furthermore, the processes are truncated; the parliament takes a simple vote and need not go through the three readings necessary for enacting a statute. These pragmatic limits make it feasible for ex post legislative involvement to ensure political influence and control over the implementation of policies, thereby increasing democratic legitimacy. Although the chancellor and the cabinet might prefer not to have to go to the parliament for approval, the cost of doing so is relatively modest when they have secure majority support in the Bundestag.

As we have seen, German constitutional and statutory law seldom requires open-ended public input. Even though in some areas statutes constrain and manage rulemaking procedures, there is no equivalent of the judicial review of U.S. notice and comment procedures, where courts check

[218] *See* HR 367, Regulations from the Executive in Need of Scrutiny Act, which passed the House by 232 to 183 on August 2, 2013 and was referred to the Senate. It would prevent any major rule from going into effect unless ratified by a joint resolution of Congress. If no resolution is passed within seventy session days, the rule would be deemed not approved and would not take effect. It lowers the threshold for a rule to count as "major" from an impact of $100 million on the economy per year to $50 million. So far, this is purely symbolic politics as the bill will not pass the Senate and would not be signed by the president.

for conformity with that process and for consistency with the underlying substantive statute. Bundestag ex post review of executive rules is a distinctive feature of the German case, but it may not have much practical effect given the parliamentary structure of government. It could be a route for opposition party members, back-benchers, or minority party coalition members to vent their frustration, but it is unlikely to be a major check on executive action. The basic point is that in a parliamentary system there are simply less likely to be deep disagreements between the legislative majority and the administration than in the United States. If such disagreements do arise, the constitutional superiority of the German legislature clarifies the locus of power in contrast to the United States, where both the president and Congress can claim political legitimacy. That might seem to be an argument for permitting legislative vetoes in the United States, and, indeed, that argument is made by the veto's supporters.[219] Nevertheless, on the other side of the argument, requiring formal congressional approval for rules could have very negative effects on the ability of the U.S. bureaucracy to function effectively under delegated authority.

D. Judicial Review

Germany has a separate system of administrative courts, which is regulated by the Administrative Court Procedure Code.[220] Secondary rulemaking is overseen by these courts, which have a decentralized competence to review regulations and declare them invalid, either through abstract or concrete review mechanisms. Administrative courts judge whether executive actors have complied with constitutional and statutory limits. Article 19(4) Basic Law guarantees effective judicial review against executive decisions, but only if the decisions affect fundamental rights.[221] When reviewing an executive action, the administrative courts have to examine the legality of the individual decision as well as the legality of the underlying secondary norms (the Constitutional Court has a monopoly on the review of the constitutionality of parliamentary statutes). Although this administrative review includes

[219] *See* Justice White's dissent in *INS v. Chadha*, 462 U.S. at 967.

[220] Verwaltungsgerichtsordnung [VwGO] [Code of Administrative Court Procedure], Mar. 19, 1991 BGBl I 686, most recently amended by article 13 of the act of July 8, 2014, BGBl I 890.

[221] Prevailing opinion, *see* Helmuth Schulze-Fielitz, *Artikel 19 Grundgesetz*, *supra* note 10; Eberhard Schmidt-Aßmann, *Einleitung*, in Verwaltungsgerichtsordnung: VwGO 11, 18 ff. (Friedrich Schoch, Eberhard Schmidt-Aßmann, & Rainer Pietzner, eds., 22nd ed., loose leaf, Sept. 2011).

the rulemaking process, its focus is on substance – mainly the proportionality of both the regulation and its application.[222] Administrative courts do not generally consider whether rulemaking processes are consistent with accountable policymaking and democratic functioning.[223] They only review procedural requirements set out in positive law.

However, one can ask whether judicial review could help to open up administrative rulemaking processes, absent any deeper legal or statutory reforms. In the current system of administrative judicial review, the answer is basically no. Three factors determine the capacity and effectiveness of judicial review as a way to enforce procedural rules for secondary rulemaking: the availability of review to challenge procedures, standing requirements, and so-called healing provisions that require the courts to overlook procedural violations if they have no effect on substance.

First, in German administrative law, judicial review is available to challenge procedural flaws. However, administrative law does not provide a uniform review process. Individuals can challenge federal regulations in the abstract before the Higher Administrative Court, after exhausting administrative review before the Constitutional Court, or in state courts, in the case of state regulations.[224] In contrast to the United States, the plaintiff needs to show that the regulation negatively affected his or her own legal rights or interests, not just to obtain standing, but also to make the claims justiciable.[225] Furthermore, the Constitutional Court will only hear cases brought by private individuals if the plaintiff's fundamental rights are at stake. Time limits apply to legal challenges to regulations, but often, the plaintiff's legal rights or legally protected interests are only affected after those time limits have expired when the rule is implemented in individual

[222] Schmidt-Assmann, Verwaltungsrecht, *supra* note 8, at 222; also Pünder, *supra* note 14, at 221–30, 269 f. (comparing the German and U.S. systems of review and emphasizing the German focus on individual rights).

[223] Schmidt-Aßmann, *supra* note 221, at 9; Pünder, *supra* note 14, at 212.

[224] *See* 1 BVerfGE 184, 196; 111 BVerwGE 276; Ossenbühl, *§ 103 Rechtsverordnung*, *supra* note 19, at 81 ff.

[225] In the United States, grants of standing are distinct from what the plaintiff can argue once given standing. *See* FCC v. Sanders Brothers Radio Station, 309 U.S. 470 (1940). The court gave Sanders Brothers standing to appeal an FCC ruling even though it was not the addressee of the ruling. It held that the firm "had the requisite standing [under that FCC statute] to appeal and to raise, in the court below, any relevant question of law in respect of the order of the Commission." It justified this holding on the pragmatic ground that Congress "may have been of the opinion that one likely to be financially injured by the issue of a license would be the only person having a sufficient interest to bring to the attention of the appellate court errors of law in the actions of the Commission." The current law on standing is complex and unclear, but the basic distinction between legal requirements for standing and arguments on the merits remains.

cases. Hence, the individual is only entitled to concrete review of the rule as applied. If the court grants jurisdiction and standing, it will examine the contested regulation for its formal (procedural) and substantive lawfulness.[226] In the case of a violation brought in a case of abstract review, the court declares the regulation invalid *inter omnes*. In practice, this is not a productive route for challenging regulatory procedures because the courts usually find that agency procedures have no external effects, absent, of course, a specific procedural duty in the delegating statute.

Second, the administrative court can review the legality of federal and state regulations if an individual challenges an administrative act that was enacted on the basis of a regulation (concrete review). An administrative court has to refuse to enforce a regulation in the concrete case if it finds a violation of higher law. This decision only applies to the parties; hence, it is not an effective tool for challenging overall procedural requirements. Furthermore, in order to avoid burdening the courts with test cases, access to administrative (as well as constitutional) judicial review is based on subjective public rights (*subjektives öffentliches Recht*).[227] A plaintiff only has standing if he or she can claim a potential violation of such a procedural or substantive right, and not all public law provisions that are beneficial to individuals also give them subjective rights. Review is especially difficult to obtain when the plaintiff is not the addressee of an administrative act, but is, nevertheless, affected as a third party. In these cases, a subjective right exists if a norm was not only enacted to serve the public interest but also sought to advance the individual interest of a limited group of citizens. For example, § 3 Federal Emission Control Act protects "neighbors" in addition to the "general public" and thus has a subjective rights dimension in favor of those neighbors.[228] Hence, if the law grants few or no rights, regulations are very unlikely to be subject to judicial review. This filter shows, once again, that the main concern of German administrative law is the protection of individual rights, not compliance with procedural law. Furthermore, because a case may arise many years after the rules were put in place and because the executive is not required to document its rulemaking procedures, it seems

[226] *See* KOPP & SCHENKE, *supra* note 156, § 47 paras. 50, 66 (on the abstract review mechanisms provided for in VwGO § 47); FRIEDERIKE VALERIE LANGE, GRUNDRECHTSBINDUNG DES GESETZGEBERS – EINE RECHTSVERGLEICHENDE STUDIE ZU DEUTSCHLAND, FRANKREICH UND DEN USA, 172 ff. (2010).

[227] KOPP & SCHENKE, *supra* note 226, § 47 paras. 43 ff.; LANGE, *supra* note 226, at 165 f.

[228] 64 ENTSCHEIDUNGEN DES BUNDESGERICHTSHOFS IN ZIVILSACHEN [BGHZ] [Federal Supreme Court for Civil and Criminal Cases] 220, at 224; JARASS, *supra* note 182, § 3 para. 31.

unlikely that the resolution of such cases will turn on claimed procedural failures at the rulemaking stage.

Third, Germany has a number of norms and doctrines that can make procedural violations irrelevant or allow the executive to make up for omitted procedural steps while the court case is pending.[229] Some enabling statutes contain so-called healing provisions that explicitly limit the impact of procedural violations. Although these rules are not evidentiary in nature, their effect is similar to the "harmless error rule" in the United States.[230] These healing provisions are mainly applicable to administrative acts, but they sometimes also apply to rulemaking procedures. For example, the Federal Building Code lists a number of irrelevant violations of preparatory procedural norms and explicitly states that "[f]laws of procedure in the course of consideration are only significant where these have had an obvious influence on the outcome under consideration."[231] Although the executive is still nominally required to act in a lawful manner and comply with objective law, its compliance might be negatively affected by the knowledge that procedural mistakes made ex ante will not harm the validity of the norm ex post. Although some scholars regard any violation of procedural rules as crucial to the validity of regulations,[232] the prevailing opinion takes account of the weight of the violation or the character of the violated requirement.[233] According to the Federal Administrative Court, the lack of required approval from another constitutional organ makes a regulation per se invalid, but the failure to undertake other forms of participation leads only to a balancing test in which the court weighs the interests protected by the procedure against the impact of the violation on the outcome.[234] The Constitutional Court has applied this criterion in a similar

[229] Especially for administrative acts, certain procedural steps can be conducted in hindsight, even during a court proceeding challenging the administrative act (VwVfG § 45). An administrative act will not be invalid because of a violation of procedural or formal requirements when it is evident that this had no effect on the outcome of the decision (VwVfG § 46).

[230] See Chapter 2, discussing the rule's limited application to rulemaking.

[231] Baugesetzbuch [BauGB] [Federal Building Code], Sept. 23, 2004, BGBl I 2412, most recently amended by article 1 of the act of July 15, 2014, BGBl I 954, § 214, an English version is available at http://www.iuscomp.org/gla/statutes/BauGB.htm; *see also* Raumordnungsgesetz [ROG] [Regional Planning Act], Dec. 22, 2008, BGBl I 2986, most recently amended by article 9 of the act of July 31, 2009, BGBl I 2585, § 12.

[232] Ramsauer, *supra* note 163, at 74 (pointing out that this is the case even if there is no impact on the result).

[233] Saurer, *supra* note 19, at 370 f. (providing an extensive overview).

[234] 59 BVerwGE 48, 49 f. (holding that the regulation was valid despite the lack of a statutory obligation to hear the leading organizations of the competent unions when preparing the regulation); 91 BVerfGE 148, 175 (dealing with evident violations).

way.[235] Legal academics assume invalidity when officials violate an essential procedural requirement– that is, when the violation could have affected the substantive accuracy of the result.[236] A violation of nonessential procedural requirements only renders a regulation invalid if the violation is obvious.[237] In short, participation is not a value in and of itself but rather serves some other substantive purpose. Furthermore, it is the court, not the plaintiffs or the public, that decides if the procedural violation had a substantive effect – a difficult factual inquiry.

Given these restrictions, the German system is not likely on its own to open up its administrative practice to accommodate procedural values for rulemaking. Although the courts have declared regulations void insofar as they fail to comply with statutory requirements, the cases are limited and fragmented, especially when compared to the U.S. Administrative Procedure Act (APA). Moreover, healing provisions further limit the applicability of procedural rules. Also, aspects of judicial review, ranging from available procedures to the necessity of adversely affected rights, hinder an all-encompassing review of procedures.

However, judicial review of process in Germany may be shifting in response to European law. The implementation of European law relies on the maxim of *effet utile*, which requires courts to interpret domestic law to ensure the efficient enforcement of European law. Because European law is dependent on the Member States for enforcement, this principle aims to encourage the citizenry to seek judicial review to protect their rights and provides checks on the implementation of EU law through decentralized, individual court cases. European courts sometimes provide more scrutiny of Member State procedure than do the administrative courts in Germany.[238] The possibility

[235] 10 BVerfGE 221, 226 (striking down a regulation because of the failure to conduct a necessary hearing); 91 BVerfGE 148, 175 f. (stating the impermissibility of enacting regulations by the government in a circular); Rose-Ackerman, *supra* note 150, at 60. *See also* 73 BVerfGE 280, 299 (stating that a violation is irrelevant if individual rights were not violated through procedural mistakes).

[236] Gerhardt & Bier, *supra* note 151, at 13; Fritz Ossenbühl, *Eine Fehlerlehre für untergesetzliche Normen*, 49 Neue Juristische Wochenschrift [NJW] 2805 [hereinafter, Ossenbühl, *Fehlerlehre*], at 2812 (1986); Saurer, *supra* note 19, at 370 f.

[237] Ossenbühl, *Fehlerlehre*, *supra* note 236, at 2812.

[238] Schmidt-Assmann, Verwaltungsrecht, *supra* note 8, at 214 f., 358 (pointing out the EU law influence on the two most important aspects of German administrative procedures law: the focus on individual rights and the importance of substantive outcomes, not procedures); Juliane Kokott, *Europäisierung des Verwaltungsprozessrechts*, **31** Die Verwaltung 335, 336 f. (1998) (emphasizing that the Anglo-Saxon and French legal traditions view administrative procedure as a decision-making process, in which it is crucial to "play by the (procedural) rules").

of such review will likely affect national courts' use of healing provisions and might force them to take violations of procedural rules seriously. The European Court of Justice (ECJ) has applied the Aarhus Convention, dealing with participation in environmental policymaking in the executive, to Member States. It has held that national administrative courts have to relax their standing requirement and give environmental NGOs the ability to seek judicial review of rules on "the ground that that rule protects only the interests of the general public and not the interests of individuals."[239] However, so far, the EU's own internal procedural requirements emphasize harm to individuals under a "right to good administration," not procedures linked to democratic accountability. The ECJ may push Member States, such as Germany, toward more democratically accountable procedures especially in environmental rulemaking, but so far those values are not prominent inside the European Commission itself.[240]

IV. PROCEDURE AS A VALUE IN GERMANY

German constitutional jurisprudence concentrates on avoiding the violation of individual rights, and the Constitutional Court's recent procedural turn is no different. However, although couched in rights language, these decisions may have implications for the representative and democratic character of lawmaking. Democratic legitimacy may benefit from the way the Court links rights-based legitimacy to legitimacy derived from technical competence, even though this is a rather roundabout route that leaves many gaps and uncertainties.

The German concept of democracy and its interpretation by the Constitutional Court emphasize legitimacy derived from the parliament. The parliament creates public institutions, appoints the government, and regulates subject matter through statutes. The legislature faces restrictions derived from fundamental rights, with their intensive substantive standard of proportionality. Rights-based jurisprudence also increasingly imposes indirect procedural constraints. The non-delegation doctrine forces the legislature to decide all issues essential to or restrictive of fundamental rights. In contrast, the U.S. concept of democracy detaches the executive branch from interference with or substantive steering by Congress – of course, subject to the legislature's ultimate control of the budget and its ability to engage

[239] Case C-115/09 BUND, Landesverband Nordrhein Westfalen (Friends of the Earth) v. Bezirksregierung Arnsberg & Trianel Kohlekraftwerk Lünen [2011] ECR I-3673.

[240] See the discussion in Chapter 5.

in oversight. By enacting the APA, however, the U.S. Congress set up strong mechanisms of public participation that the courts enforce, compensating for weaker substantive checks. The formal and informal interdependence between the legislature and the executive in the German parliamentary system, however, leads to feedback mechanisms that ensure parliamentary steering and influence on executive rulemaking ex ante and ex post without a German APA that covers rulemaking. In most areas of German law, democratic legitimacy is maintained through the link to the Bundestag, not through open-ended public participation in rulemaking inside the executive. In the environmental and nature protection areas, the executive must often engage in some type of consultation before issuing rules, but, even there, those who are not invited to participate have no legal recourse to demand more inclusive procedures. German law also mandates procedures that further democratic values when it adopts norms produced by international and private bodies outside of the formal structure of government. Furthermore, German planning and licensing laws do require public input for individual projects.[241] Although the law recognizes the values of public consultation only in these special cases, they show an understanding of the value of policymaking procedures that enhance public legitimacy if certain conditions hold.

Our analysis has isolated two trends in judicial review of legislative and administrative processes. On the one hand, prompted by the recent *Hartz IV* decision, the Constitutional Court has emphasized the value of reason-giving in the legislature, at least if plaintiffs can link it to a violation of their rights. On the other hand, despite European pressure in favor of public participation, German administrative law seems reluctant to follow this path. In administrative law the main sources of legally mandated procedures are the Administrative Procedures Act and the municipal codes. Both have detailed procedural requirements for hearings, information gathering, and reason-giving.[242] Nevertheless, neither deals with federal or statewide regulations and guidelines, and both permit officials to remedy some procedural

[241] Rose-Ackerman, *supra* note 150, at 82–93 (1995); *see*, for instance, the plan approval procedure in VwVfG § 73.

[242] The Administrative Procedures Act governs administrative acts, that is, particular, individual applications of the law. Under this act, the executive has to conduct a hearing (VwVfG § 28), give a statement of reasons (VwVfG § 39), and be sufficiently clear (VwVfG § 37). Also the planning law (zoning law), for instance, contains detailed instructions, i.e., concerning the method of balancing. According to Federal Building Code § 1(6) the municipality has a substantive obligation to consider a wide range of concerns, and Federal Building Code § 9(8) obliges the municipal authority to provide a formal statement of reasons when enacting a zoning ordinance.

violations ex post and even to ignore them if the courts judge that they would not have had an impact on the outcome.[243]

These requirements may not seem sufficient to ordinary citizens if they view transparent, participatory processes as linked to democratic legitimacy, especially if their rights or non-justiciable interests are concerned. Big construction projects serve as exemplary cases for the lack of public acceptance of the status quo.[244] These projects are usually welcomed overall, just not in one's own backyard. Nevertheless the cases allow one to draw some conclusions about the values of public participation.

To illustrate, consider the case of *Stuttgart 21* – the collective term for the licensing and financing decisions concerning the proposal to modernize and extend the train station in Stuttgart, a German city in the state of Baden-Württemberg. The executive carried out formal procedures under zoning law and a plan-approval procedure; these included various outlets for public participation and produced the impact assessments required by zoning, planning, and environmental law.[245] However, the decision to license the project led to a public uproar that included violent demonstrations and demands for more direct participation. Finally, the citizens were asked to cast a vote on the project. In the end, the vote ratified the project, but what is important to us is that the mere existence of procedural rules and their judicial enforceability were insufficient to achieve democratic consensus and to create democratic legitimacy (*effektiver Legitimationszusammenhang*).[246] If citizens feel that public hearings are a purely formal exercise, issuing a decision after the hearing will not answer demands for democratic responsiveness. Democratic responsiveness requires public input and creates a state obligation to explain technical balancing decisions to citizens. These concerns, expressed in the outcry over Stuttgart 21, cannot be met simply by pointing to the technical quality of the data and its expert analysis.

Might the German Constitutional Court move beyond its focus on individual rights to take on broader questions of the democratic accountability of legislative and administrative procedures? At present, this development

[243] As explained earlier, the Administrative Procedures Act and the codifications of zoning law contain "healing provisions."

[244] Alexander Schink, *Öffentlichkeitsbeteiligung – Beschleunigung – Akzeptanz*, **26** Zeitschrift für Gesetzgebung [ZG], 227 footnote 6 (2011) (pointing to the relevance for other large-scale projects).

[245] Fabian Wittreck, *Demokratische Legitimation von Großvorhaben*, **26** Zeitschrift für Gesetzgebung [ZG], 209, 214, 220 (2011); Schink, *supra* note 244, at 226.

[246] Wittreck, *supra* note 245, at 209, 216, 220 (pointing out that despite 3,000 objections submitted and various judicial checks there was a discrepancy between the actual and the perceived democratic legitimacy).

seems unlikely. Nevertheless, the Court may be shifting the dividing line in favor of greater transparency and consistency, even as it maintains its focus on individual rights and the preservation of the constitutional structure. Rights-based cases may be a door that leads the Court to consider the democratic legitimacy and accountability of the government and legislative policymaking procedures.

5

The European Union

The European Union's claims to legitimacy are sharply contested. Some assert that expert administrative competence lies at the root of its authority.[1] Yet it has never been simply a technocratic body.[2] Those pointing to the European Union's "democratic deficit" argue that it ought to reform to improve its public accountability, not simply to become a better technical regulator. Furthermore, rights protection is of growing importance in the ongoing debate over the future of the European Union. The EU courts have relied on all three types of legitimacy in their review of legislation, using arguments that sometimes blend and mix democracy, rights, and expertise in novel ways. However, their jurisprudence tilts toward the protection of individual rights, a trend that is likely to continue with the accession of the European Union to the European Convention on Human Rights mandated in article 6(2) of the European Union's current Treaty on European Union (TEU).[3]

1 Compare Giandomenico Majone, *Europe's "Democratic Deficit": The Question of Standards*, **4** European Law J. 5 (1998) with the somewhat different view of Peter L. Lindseth, Power and Legitimacy: Reconciling Europe and the Nation-State (2010).

2 According to Peter Strauss: "The literature about the Commission's actions consistently imagines Commission bodies to be expert as well as consensual – their authority grounded in technocratic rather than political judgment. Popular will is in some sense feared, while judicial checking of sums is thought unnecessary, an invitation to unwonted legalism." Peter L. Strauss, *Rulemaking in the Ages of Globalization and Information: What America Can Learn from Europe, and Vice Versa*, **12** Columbia J. of European Law 645, 652 (2005–6).

3 The EU is based on multilateral treaties, which have been modified and restructured over time. When the attempt to enact a constitutional treaty failed in 2005, the Member States signed the Treaty of Lisbon in 2007. This Treaty went into force on December 1, 2009 and consists of two separate treaties, containing the primary law of the European Union: the Treaty of the European Union (Consolidated Version of the Treaty on European Union [TEU] [2012] Official Journal of the European Union [OJ] C 326/13) and the Treaty on the Functioning of the European Union (Consolidated Version of the Treaty on the Functioning of the European Union [TFEU] [2012] OJ C 326/47).

The European Union is not a conventional nation-state. Its democratic legitimacy is derived from the EU citizens' representation in the EU parliament and the involvement of the Member States. There are two routes for direct Member State involvement. The first is through the European Council composed of the heads of state or government of the Member States, together with its president and the president of the Commission; it sets general policy but is not part of the ordinary legislative process. The second is the Council of the European Union (the "Council") composed of government representatives from Member States; those who attend its meetings vary with the issues up for decision or discussion.[4] Initially, the role of the EU parliament was weak relative to the Council and the executive (the Commission).[5] The Council was traditionally the most powerful legislative body, even though it could only react to Commission proposals.[6] The Lisbon Treaty has strengthened the role of the EU parliament, making it equal to the Council as a legislative organ for most areas of EU competence. Although the European Union has a wide legislative mandate, its actions must fall within the range conferred by the treaties, and it shares power with the Member States. The EU courts actively review the legislative and regulatory activity of the EU bodies and of the Member States, including review of the legislative competence of EU bodies.

The Court of Justice of the European Union consists of two courts, the General Court (GC) and the European Court of Justice (ECJ).[7] The GC hears most initial challenges from individuals and business firms with appeal to the ECJ on points of law. References for preliminary rulings coming from Member State courts go directly to the ECJ as do requests for opinions from EU institutions. Each court has twenty-eight members, one from each

[4] TEU articles 10(1), (2), 15; TFEU articles 235–43. Armin von Bogdandy, *Grundprinzipen*, in EUROPÄISCHES VERFASSUNGSRECHT – THEORETISCHE UND DOGMATISCHE GRUNDZÜGE 13 at 64 f. (Armin von Bogdandy & Jürgen Bast, eds., 2nd ed., 2009); Philipp Dann, *Die politischen Organe*, in EUROPÄISCHES VERFASSUNGSRECHT – THEORETISCHE UND DOGMATISCHE GRUNDZÜGE 335 at 378–85 (Armin von Bogdandy & Jürgen Bast, eds., 2nd ed., 2009).

[5] *See* TEU articles 13, 14. The German Constitutional Court's decision on the Lisbon Treaty pointed out that the roles of Parliament and Council under the Treaty accord with the EU's supranational character. 123 BVERFGE 267, 367 f.

[6] The Council and the Parliament can trigger the Commission's initiative, but neither body can force it to act (TFEU articles 225, 241). The Council has had this power since the 1950s.

[7] In addition, a Civil Service Tribunal, established in 2005, is solely devoted to personnel disputes involving the European Civil Service. Appeals on points of law can be made to the General Court. Originally the General Court was called the Court of First Instance, and it handled civil service cases among other challenges to Community actions that did not originate in national courts.

Member State, who serve six-year renewable terms. Nine advocates general (AGs) prepare "opinions" that help the ECJ prepare its judgments. Both courts are divided into chambers and usually sit in panels of three[8]; as a result, the jurisprudence of the EU courts may not be internally consistent. However, because there are no dissenting opinions, it is difficult to infer internal disagreements on fundamental issues, although a published AG's opinion that conflicts with the final judgment of the ECJ would be one clue, as are cases where the ECJ overrules the GC.

As the reach of the European Union has expanded, the GC has grown in importance, with more private individuals and firms seeking access. The GC has ruled on fundamental questions concerning the EU courts' jurisdiction, standing for natural and legal persons, and the standard for review. Even though the ECJ can directly adjudicate claims between EU organs and those brought by Member States, the GC can rule on procedural challenges if they are linked to the rights of individual plaintiffs.

Peter Lindseth argues that the drafters of the original treaty envisaged the Court of Justice as a check on Community executive institutions similar to the French Conseil d'État.[9] In support of that claim, French administrative law provides the four bases for judicial control in the European Union:[10] "lack of competence, infringement of an essential procedural requirement, infringement of [the] Treaty or of any rule of law relating to its application, or misuse of powers."[11] The ECJ was "to enforce legality against administrative power in its new supranational guise."[12] Although over time the ECJ has focused more on the promotion of Union law in national courts, it continues to review Union actions, especially when individual rights are at stake.[13] As the EU executive obtained technical regulatory competence, inside the

[8] The GC sits in chambers of three or five judges, article 10 Rules of Procedure of the General Court, OJ 1991, L 136, p. 1 with corrigendum in OJ 1991, L 317, p. 34, most recently amended in OJ 2013, L 173, p. 66. In the ECJ judges sit in panels of three and, exceptionally, as a Grand Chamber of fifteen judges, articles 27, 28 Rules of Procedure of the Court of Justice, OJ 2012, L 265. In a few cases, set out in the treaties, the ECJ judges sit en banc.

[9] Lindseth, *supra* note 1, at 140–1.

[10] *Id.*, at 137–52. His focus is on the relationship between Member State courts and EU courts.

[11] Treaty establishing the European Coal and Steel Community of April 18, 1951 (Paris), article 33; Treaty establishing the European Economic Community of March 25, 1957 (Rome) article 173.

[12] Lindseth, *supra* note 1, at 141.

[13] *Id. See also* Francesca Bignami, *Creating European Rights: National Values and Supranational Interests*, 11 Columbia Journal of European Law 241 (2005); R. Daniel Kelemen, Eurolegalism (2011). Kelemen's focus is on the shift from a history of opaque, informal regulation at the Member State level to the EU's more rigid, clear, and transparent rules, enforceable by the courts. Thus, he focuses on the growing importance of lawyers in the

Commission and in the growing number of agencies,[14] the ECJ developed a countervailing jurisprudence of rights protection. Nevertheless, as we argue later in this chapter, the Court grants EU institutions a larger margin of discretion than Member States, both with respect to rights and for other aspects of Union law.

We concentrate on the EU courts' role as a check on Union institutions. This has not been a smooth development; the courts struggle with tensions between their traditional jurisprudence, treaty language, and current realities. In spite of their overall efforts to promote EU democracy, the courts have not read the EU treaties to include enforceable protections for participatory values in either legislative processes or Commission rulemaking.[15] There is a continued focus on individual rights even if the underlying issues could better be defined as ones of democratic legitimacy and accountability. However, the TEU includes a new article 11 that invokes the value of participation by citizens, "representative associations," and "civil society." The text does not precisely define these terms or mandate particular procedures.[16] In spite of the vague language, some commentators claim that this article provides a framework for rulemaking that could permit the EU courts to review administrative rulemaking processes for democratic legitimacy. Joana Mendes, for example, grounds her claim in the language of individual rights, but she sees those rights as linked to democratic legitimacy and as encompassing the right to participate in the policymaking processes of the Commission. So far, the EU courts have not adopted that position,

EU regulatory landscape; he emphasizes compliance, not the process of making norms in the first place, although the two obviously overlap.

14 *See* Giandomenico Majone, *Two Logics of Delegation: Agency and Fiduciary Relations in EU Governance*, **2** European Union Politics 103 (2001), and Johannes Saurer, *Individualrechtsschutz gegen das Handeln der Europäischen Agenturen*, **45** Europarecht 51 [hereinafter, Saurer, *Individualrechtsschutz*], 51 (2010).

15 The cases that refuse to require participation in rulemaking are: Case T-521/93, Atlanta AG v Council and Commission [1996] ECR II-1707; Case C-104/97 P, Atlanta AG and others v Commission and Council [1999] ECR I-6983. For an analysis of the cases *see* Joana Mendes, Participation in EU Rule-Making: A Rights-Based Approach (2011) [hereinafter, Mendes, Participation in EU Rule-Making], chapter 5. Some of the leading cases upholding overall democratic values are: Case 138/79 Roquette Frères v Council [1980] ECR 3333; Case 294/83 Les Verts v Parliament [1986] ECR 1339; Case C-70/88 Parliament v Council [1990] ECR I-2041; Case T-135/96 UEAPME v Council [1998] ECR II-2335.

16 TEU article 11(1) and (2). Joana Mendes, *Participation and the Role of Law after Lisbon: A Legal View of Article 11 TEU*, **48** Common Market Law Rev. 1849 (2011) [hereinafter, Mendes, *Participation*] at 1851–4, critiques the vague wording of Article 11.

but she argues that if they did so, it would be consistent with the Lisbon Treaty.[17]

In reviewing the EU's substantive law, the EU courts claim to be more deferential if the policy at issue is particularly complex and technical, but it is not obvious that they actually follow that dictum. The courts sometimes review the adequacy of procedures, not just the substantive result, but they have not set out a clear procedural framework linked to democratic accountability. If they made such an effort, they would need to confront the diverse lawmaking institutions in the European Union. The GC has sought to ensure that decisions are grounded in sound science and expertise, but it has not furthered participatory values. The EU courts sometimes examine the reasoning and evidentiary base of policy choices, but they have been unsympathetic to procedural challenges based on democratic legitimacy that seek broader participation in policymaking.[18] Their reluctance is particularly noteworthy given Commission, agency, and Council support for "Better (or Smarter) Regulation." The courts seldom give these soft law efforts legally binding and judicially enforceable effects. They have not faced the possible tensions between the Commission's push to improve the technical quality of policy documents, on the one hand, and to develop more inclusive participatory processes, on the other.[19]

U.S. law makes a sharp distinction between aggressive review of the substance and process of administrative rulemaking and hands-off review of legislation, outside of certain constitutionally problematic areas. In American public law, one argument for judicial review of rulemaking

[17] Mendes, *Participation*, *supra* note 16; *see also* Koen Lenaerts, *The Principle of Democracy in the Case Law of the European Court of Justice*, **62** Comparative Law Quarterly 271 (2013). Lenaerts is the vice president of the ECJ. Kelemen, *supra* note 13, at 28, 52–6 argues that EU citizens have demanded more transparency from the EU over and above formal treaty provisions and that the EU has responded. He claims that EU policymakers "have responded by enhancing transparency, formalizing procedures for public participation, and increasing access to justice for aggrieved parties" [at 28]. We do not disagree except to note that the first two items on the list are voluntary actions by EU institutions that have not led to rigorous court review. The third applies to individuals harmed by particular EU actions, not challenges to the democratic legitimacy of regulatory actions. If the courts are involved, the focus is, as Kelemen argues at 55–6, on the protection of rights, not democratic accountability. *See also id.* at 29–32, 43–5, critiquing the Open Method of Coordination as permitting end runs around the transparency and accountability available in the more formal procedures of the established EU institutions.

[18] *See* the *Atlanta* cases mentioned earlier.

[19] *See* Stijn Smismans, *Functional Participation in EU Delegated Regulation: Lessons from the United States at the EU's "Constitutional Moment,"* **12** Indiana J. of Global Legal Studies 599 (2005).

under the U.S. Administrative Procedure Act is to ensure that unelected bureaucrats act consistently with congressional purposes.[20] Congress gives unelected judges a limited mandate to check that the administrative process is open and that rules are publicly justified and consistent with statute.[21] It does not give the courts the same power over congressional processes. No such distinction exists in the European Union. If the litigant clears the jurisdictional and standing hurdles discussed later in this chapter, judges have not placed much emphasis on legislative and rulemaking procedures.

So far, the democratic accountability argument for judicial review of process is missing in the case law of the European Union.[22] Rather the concern is, first, with individualized harm at the hand of EU bodies and, second, with technocratic competence, tempered by the recognition that legally trained judges cannot fully evaluate the choices of other EU institutions. Rights-based legitimacy and competence are the keys to judicial review and are likely to increase in importance with the Lisbon Treaty's incorporation of the Charter of Fundamental Rights of the European Union by reference in article 6(1) TEU. However, as we discuss later in this chapter, some of the changes introduced by the Treaty of Lisbon could provide openings for the courts if they choose to take them.[23] It remains to be seen if they will shoulder this responsibility.

We provide a brief introduction to the EU institutional landscape, both legislative processes and the court system, and then turn to judicial review of EU lawmaking. We discuss standing and jurisdiction before

[20] For a general argument that the courts ought to seek to uphold congressional legislative purposes *see* STEPHEN BREYER, MAKING OUR DEMOCRACY WORK: A JUDGE'S VIEW (2010).

[21] *See* SUSAN ROSE-ACKERMAN, FROM ELECTIONS TO DEMOCRACY: BUILDING ACCOUNTABLE GOVERNMENT IN HUNGARY AND POLAND (2005); Susan Rose-Ackerman, "Introduction," in ECONOMICS OF ADMINISTRATIVE LAW xiii, xxi–xxiv (Susan Rose-Ackerman, ed., 2007).

[22] *But see* the opinion of AG Cruz Villalón in Case C-427/12, European Commission v. European Parliament and European Council (Biocides Case). He asks the ECJ to consider possible differences between articles 290 and 291 of the TFEU that establish delegated acts and implementing acts, respectively, without being clear about the distinction. Here the Commission argues that a regulation ought to have required the Commission to issue a delegated act under article 290(1) TFEU, not an implementing act under article 291(2) TFEU. We discuss these new treaty articles later.

[23] Mendes argues that they should take on this responsibility under TEU article 11, Mendes, *Participation*, *supra* note 16; and Joana Mendes, *Delegated and Implementing Rule Making: Proceduralisation and Constitutional Design*, **19** EUROPEAN LAW J. 22 (2013) [hereinafter, Mendes, *Proceduralisation*].

assessing the courts' review of process and substance. As in South Africa, the courts' jurisprudence is in some flux so our conclusions are necessarily tentative.

I. PROCEDURES FOR RULEMAKING IN THE EUROPEAN UNION

Originally, rulemaking in EU institutions did not distinguish explicitly between legislative and executive rulemaking. As in previous versions of the Lisbon Treaty, article 288 TFEU lists legal acts of the Union, but the list is not exhaustive. The legal acts include regulations, directives, and decisions. However, the Lisbon Treaty complicates matters by restructuring the rulemaking procedures and introducing a distinction between legislative acts and "non-legislative" acts.[24] According to article 289 TFEU, regulations, directives, and decisions can be adopted by the EU legislature. The Commission and other EU bodies can enact non-legislative acts, including delegated and implementing acts (articles 290, 291 TFEU). These non-legislative acts, however, can also take the form of regulations, directives, and decisions; in general, the EU institutions are free to select the type of act on a case-by-case basis.[25] The terminology is misleading, and the formal distinction between legislative and non-legislative acts seems only to lie in their author and their enactment procedures. Although the procedures are now systematically different for each form of rulemaking, the EU courts still evaluate acts of the Union in somewhat similar ways. This part will first analyze the procedural rules applicable to the various forms of rulemaking; the second part will analyze their enforcement through the judicial system.

A. Legislative Acts

In its early years the Community had an "executive-technocratic" legislative process, to use Lindseth's term – a structure that gave administrative

[24] Cosima Haselmann, Delegation und Durchführung gemäss Art. 290 und 291 AEUV 88, 54 (2012); Jürgen Schwarze, Europarecht – Strukturen, Dimensionen und Wandlungen des Rechts der Europäischen Union 701 (2012) [hereinafter, Schwarze, Europarecht] (calling non-legislative acts "quasi-legislative").

[25] TFEU articles 296, 297(2). Nigel Foster, EU Law Directions 103–4 (3rd ed., 2012). Jürgen Bast, *New Categories of Acts after the Lisbon Reform: Dynamics of Parliamentarization in EU Law*, **49** Common Market Law Rev. 885, 920 (2012) claims that, with few exceptions, "there is no convincing teleological argument to eliminate the freedom of choice on the part of the legislative institutions to opt for a particular regime of control."

law particular salience.[26] Over time, the role of the Parliament has grown, and the introduction of qualified majority voting in the Council expanded the scope for political negotiation. Under the TFEU, the ordinary legislative procedure involves a proposal from the Commission followed by a co-decision procedure under which the draft can be amended and traded back and forth between the Council and the Parliament, ending, in disputed cases, with a Conciliation Committee.[27] The Parliament votes by majority rule, and the Council usually votes by qualified majority.[28] Although the ordinary legislative process formally begins with a Commission draft, both the Parliament and the Council have long been able to shape the agenda by requesting a proposal from the Commission on a particular topic.[29] Of course, even without a formal request, Member State governments and parliamentary blocs seek to influence the Commission.

The treaties say little about internal processes in the Council, the Commission, or the Parliament, and they give the Parliament explicit authority to adopt its own rules of procedure.[30] The TFEU is mainly concerned with the interactions between the branches, voting rules, and the publicity and openness of deliberations regarding legislative acts, reflecting a concern for the necessity of public discourse in legislation.[31] The Parliament and the Council, when they deliberate and vote on draft legislative acts, shall meet publicly.[32] They "shall ensure publication of the documents relating to the legislative procedures,"[33] as well as all legislative acts

[26] LINDSETH, *supra* note 1, at 143.

[27] TFEU articles 289, 294. There are also provisions for legislative procedures limited to specific types of legislation scattered throughout the Treaty and for initiatives from groups of Member States and, via the Parliament, from the Central Bank, the Court of Justice, or the European Investment Bank (TFEU article 289). A search of the TFEU suggests that special legislative procedures, which usually require unanimity from the Council and little or no role for the Commission, are limited to areas of particular sensitivity to the Member States. Most operate like quasi-amendments to the Treaty because of the unanimity requirement.

[28] The definition of a qualified majority has changed over time and by type of legislation. As of November 1, 2014 it requires at least 55 percent of the members of the Council representing the participating Member States, comprising at least 65 percent of the population of these states, TFEU article 238(3).

[29] TFEU articles 225, 241. Strauss, *supra* note 2, at 655 claims that the original rationale for giving the Commission the sole authority to propose legislation was "to prevent the submission of legislative proposals inspired by nationalistic interests that would lead to the backsliding of Community legislation."

[30] TFEU article 232.

[31] Jürgen Bast, *Handlungsformen und Rechtsschutz*, in EUROPÄISCHES VERFASSUNGSRECHT – THEORETISCHE UND DOGMATISCHE GRUNDZÜGE 489, 553 (Armin von Bogdandy & Jürgen Bast, eds., 2nd ed., 2009).

[32] TEU article 16(8); TFEU article 15(2).

[33] TFEU article 15(3) para. 5.

and any non-legislative "[r]egulations and directives which are addressed to all Member States, as well as decisions which do not specify to whom they are addressed."[34] Moreover, article 296(2) TFEU introduces a duty to provide a statement of reasons for all legal acts (legislative and non-legislative) contained in article 288 TFEU, including administrative rules, independent of their binding character.[35] Publication and reason-giving allow citizens to understand and potentially question EU decisions. The only procedural constraint specifically directed at the Commission requires it to give reasons if it fails to submit a proposal after a request from either legislative body.[36] As in the U.S. and the German constitutions, there are no requirements for public participation in lawmaking or for consultation with experts. Despite the lack of positive procedural duties in the Treaties, the EU organs have introduced soft-law instruments to encourage "better" regulation, including greater openness to outside participation. Commission support for civil society participation arises both from some officials' interest in furthering the social policy role of the EU and as a way to counter worries about its "democratic deficit."[37] Moreover, as we will discuss later, the EU courts have created specific procedural obligations through case law, mostly by reviewing the quality of fact-finding used to justify decisions.

B. Non-Legislative Acts

Similar to national developments, the European Union increasingly engages in administrative rulemaking in response to the challenges of modern risk regulation and the limited capacity of the legislative bodies.[38] The Commission and some of the European Agencies conduct non-legislative, executive rulemakings to implement EU legislative acts. Moreover, private and semiprivate actors, such as standardization bodies, engage in

[34] TFEU article 297(2) para. 2.

[35] Schwarze, Europarecht, *supra* note 24, at 703; Alexander H. Türk, *Oversight of Administrative Rulemaking: Judicial Review*, **19** European Law J. 126, 134 (2013).

[36] TFEU articles 225, 241.

[37] Stijn Smismans, *European Civil Society; Shaped by Discourses and Institutional Interests*, **9** European Law J. 473 (2003); Smismans, *supra* note 19; Francesca Bignami, *Three Generations of Participation Rights Before the European Commission*, **68** Law & Contemporary Problems 61, 72–3 (2004–5). Recently, the former seems to dominate the latter. *See* Commission Staff Working Document, Review of the Commission Consultation Policy, SWD(2012) 422 final, Strasbourg, 12.12.2012. Additional backing for this claim is in Mendes, *Participation*, *supra* note 16, at 1854–7.

[38] Türk, *supra* note 35, at 127.

co-regulation and self-regulation.[39] The Lisbon Treaty codified the forms of delegated acts and implementing acts, although it remains unclear exactly how these different forms are defined and whether they can be clearly differentiated.

1. Delegated Acts

Unlike previous treaties, articles 290 and 291 TFEU distinguish between delegation and implementation. This new distinction creates a third (tertiary) level of EU law in addition to primary treaty law and secondary rules (legislative acts). Delegation permitted under article 290(1) TFEU allows "the Commission … to adopt non-legislative acts of general application to supplement or amend certain non-essential elements of the legislative act." Using language similar to the German Basic Law, the empowering legislative act must include the objectives, content, scope, and duration of the delegation.[40] Although the German Constitutional Court interprets the term "essential" to cover any rule essential for an individual's exercise of his or her fundamental rights, the EU courts will not necessarily interpret article 290 TFEU in a similarly rigid way.

The Commission can supplement or amend legislative acts through delegated acts, but its actions can only affect "non-essential" provisions.[41] This leaves room for the Commission not only to supply needed details and to make indeterminate legal language concrete, but also formally to alter the text and thus update provisions on a continuous basis without seeking a renewed delegation.[42] This possibility allows for flexibility, but allowing the Commission to alter the wording of the underlying legislative act makes it

[39] Herwig C. H. Hofmann, Gerard C. Rowe, & Alexander H. Türk, Administrative Law and Policy of the European Union 326–31 (2011); Deirdre Curtin, Herwig Hofmann, & Joana Mendes, *Constitutionalising EU Executive Rule-Making Procedures: A Research Agenda*, **19** European Law J. 1, 2–3 (2013).

[40] Markus Möstl, *Rechtsetzungen der europäischen und nationalen Verwaltungen*, Deutsches Verwaltungsblatt [DVBl] 1076, 1077 (2011); Haselmann, *supra* note 24, at 57 with further references.

[41] TFEU article 290(1). *See also* COM(2009)673, December 9, 2009, Communication from the Commission to the European Parliament and the Council. Implementation of Article 290 of the Treaty on the Functioning of the European Union.

[42] Martin Gellermann, *Art. 290*, in EUV/AEUV para. 6 (Rudolf Streinz, ed., 2nd ed., 2012); Thomas Christiansen & Mathias Dobbels, *Non-Legislative Rule Making after the Lisbon Treaty: Implementing the New System of Comitology and Delegated Acts*, **19** European Law J. 42, 44 (2013) stating that to amend includes "deleting, replacing or adding non-essential elements." For an example from before the Treaty of Lisbon, *see* Smismans, *supra* note 19 at 605–16, discussing the implementation of Occupational Health and Safety directives.

difficult to identify the author of the law and poses problems for democratic legitimacy and the rule of law.[43]

Just as in Germany, there are few procedural requirements for delegated executive rulemaking.[44] The treaty texts do not lay out any required procedures for such acts, and it is not yet clear how the EU courts will interpret the key terms. Article 11 TEU, a general treaty provision on process and accountability, governs all EU activity. It is not tied to the protection of rights, and one can read its text as an effort to enhance the democratic character of the European Union.[45] Nevertheless, tensions may arise if the EU courts review Commission procedures and those of other agencies and institutions. Judicial review in the name of public participation might conflict with the claims to bureaucratic competence advanced by the Commission and EU agencies. Rather, the courts may maintain their previous hands-off interpretations and only consider the objective relevance of rules in particular policy areas.[46] A 2014 case suggests that the ECJ will do just that. It rejected a challenge by the Commission, and deferred to a legislative choice of an implementing versus a delegated act – a distinction we further develop in the next section.[47] The Court may be reluctant to make decisions with procedural implications for Commission behavior and is likely to leave such actions to the legislative process.[48]

The European Parliament and the Council retain the option of repealing a delegation, and each has a veto right so that either body could stop a particular

43 Möstl *supra* note 40, at 1080–1 (stating that in German law, this provision might violate the rule of law principle).

44 *Id.* at 1083.

45 *See* Mendes, *Participation*, *supra* note 16 (also making that argument).

46 Herwig C. H. Hofmann & Alexander Türk, *Die Ausübung übertragener Normsetzungsbefugnisse durch die Europäische Kommission*, Zeitschrift für Gesetzgebung [ZG] 105, 108 (2012) (citing the previous adjudication of the ECJ on essential elements of legislation, Case C–240/90 Germany v. Commission, ECR I–5383 (1992) para. 37); Christoph Möllers & Jelena von Achenbach, *Die Mitwirkung des Europäischen Parlaments an der abgeleiteten Rechtsetzung der Europäischen Kommission nach dem Lissabonner Vertrag*, **46** Europarecht 39, 49 (2011) (noting that the EU courts have not voided any empowering acts based on a violation of this non-delegation doctrine).

47 Case C-427/12, *Biocides Case.*

48 However, for a holding dealing with the legislative process *see* Case C-355/10, European Parliament v. Council of the European Union, Judgment of the Court of Justice (Grand Chamber) of September 5, 2012. The Parliament challenged a decision of the Council by arguing that the decision involved "essential" elements of the underlying legal code and was hence beyond the authority of the Council acting alone. The ECJ agreed with the Parliament. The case involved the Council, not the Commission, and the Council's action occurred before the entry into force of the Lisbon Treaty so it does not provide a clear precedent. *See* Merijn Chamon, *How the Concept of Essential Elements of a Legislative Act Continues to Elude the Court. Parliament v. Council*, 50 Common Market Law Rev. 849

delegated act from coming into force (article 290(2)(b) TFEU). These powers ensure that the legislative bodies retain their influence and thus promote one view of democratic legitimacy.[49] These checks resemble the German construction, insofar as the Bundesrat or Bundestag has veto powers. The European Parliament and the Council do not have the right to modify the text of the delegated act.[50] Nevertheless, they can exercise substantive influence because their separate veto powers may affect the Commission's choices as it drafts delegated acts.[51] A Commission document urges the Parliament or the Council to issue a statement of reasons if one of them vetoes an act, but that is not a formal legal requirement.[52] Notice the switch compared to American law – a switch that reflects the relative power of the EU executive. Here the executive requests the legislative bodies to give reasons, whereas in the United States the legislature requires the executive to give reasons when it promulgates rules under the Administrative Procedure Act.

2. Implementing Acts

Implementing acts are a second type of non-legislative act set out in article 291 TFEU. While delegated acts allow the Commission to amend and supplement nonessential parts of legislative acts, implementing acts make the empowering provision concrete.[53] The idea seems to be that delegated acts require the Commission to make more explicit policy choices compared with implementing acts.[54] However, this terminology provides little

(2013) (critiquing the decision for not clarifying the distinction between "essential" and "non-essential" elements).

49 Möllers & von Achenbach, *supra* note 48, at 47 f., 50–2. Compare this possibility with the U.S. case of I.N.S. v. Chadha, 462 U.S. 919 (1983), declaring such legislative vetoes unconstitutional because they do not follow constitutional lawmaking procedures. Although some defend such vetoes as ways to enhance democratic legitimacy, they have a cost. The legislature may not think through the relative value of delegation ex ante because it can always overrule a rule ex post.

50 Hofmann & Türk, *supra* note 48, at 120 (emphasizing that there is "little room for substantive changes").

51 *Id.* at 117 (emphasizing that the European Parliament has full substantive control).

52 COM(2009)673 sections 5.2, 5.3.2. Delegated acts enter into force only if no objection is expressed by either a majority of the Parliament or a qualified majority of the Council, TFEU article 290(2).

53 Christiansen & Dobbels, *supra* note 42, at 44; Hofmann & Türk, *supra* note 47, at 113, 115 (pointing out the arbitrariness of the distinction between making an act concrete and supplementing the empowering provisions); *see also* Paul Craig, *Delegated Acts, Implementing Acts and the New Comitology Regulation*, **36** European Law Rev. 671 [hereinafter, Craig, *Delegated Acts*] 672–4 (2011).

54 Craig, *Delegated Acts, supra* note 53, at 672–7 (listing five sources of ambiguity).

guidance for drawing the distinction.[55] Hence, the Parliament, the Council, and the Member States each might push for the type of act most beneficial to them. According to one pair of commentators, "the Council is seen to push to limit the scope and use of delegated acts, and the Parliament often drops its insistence in return for amendments on the substance of regulations."[56]

Member States implement much EU legislation through their own legal systems. If the policy requires some uniformity across Member States, article 291 TFEU allows the Commission to set legal standards to provide guidance.[57] The EU legislature oversees the enactment of delegated acts, whereas article 291 TFEU obligates the EU to give Member States a role in order to compensate them for the intrusion into their executive autonomy.[58] That article instructs the EU legislature to set out "in advance the rules and general principles concerning mechanisms for control by Member States of the Commission's exercise of implementing powers."[59]

3. The Rebirth of Comitology?

The Lisbon Treaty formally abandoned the old comitology structure[60] under which Member State experts advised the Commission on legislative and non-legislative drafts. These committees were a form of consultation but not of public participation. The interests represented reflected both Member State concerns and technical expertise. The committees mixed technical subject matter expertise with political interests tied to the Member States.

55 Martin Gellermann, *Art. 291*, in EUV/AEUV para. 2 (Rudolf Streinz, ed., 2nd ed., 2012) [hereinafter, Gellermann, *Art. 291*]; Hofmann & Türk, *supra* note 48, at 113–15 (describing it as a "grey area" that gives the legislature discretion to select the legislative form); Mendes, *Proceduralisation*, *supra* note 23; Ulrich Stelkens, *Art. 291 AEUV, das Unionsverwaltungsrecht und die Verwaltungsautonomie der Mitgliedstaaten*, **47** EUROPARECHT 511, 542 f. (2012) (pointing out the discretion of the EU legislature insofar as articles 290 and 291 TFEU overlap).

56 Christiansen & Dobbels, *supra* note 42, at 55.

57 Compare Mendes, *Proceduralisation*, *supra* note 23, at 23 and Bast, *supra* note 25, at 920–2, on the one side, with Robert Schütze, *"Delegated" Legislation in the (new) European Union: A Constitutional Analysis*, **74** MODERN LAW REV. 661, 690–1 (2011), on the other. The latter sees article 291 TFEU as a sign of an executive federalism that limits the competence of the Union; the former two authors argue that the article has not changed the powers of the Union to adopt implementing acts.

58 SCHWARZE, EUROPARECHT, *supra* note 24, at 701.

59 TFEU article 291(3).

60 Comitology was governed by Decision 1999/468/EC. This decision was repealed by regulation (EU) no. 182/2011, February 16, 2011, article 12. *See* Christiansen & Dobbels, *supra* note 42; HOFMANN, ROWE, & TÜRK, *supra* note 39, at 279–81.

Many criticized this process for lacking democratic legitimacy because it was neither transparent nor accountable.[61]

Yet a variant of comitology seems to be reappearing, at least for implementing acts and potentially for delegated acts as well. The European Union has issued regulation 182/2011 for implementing acts that requires committees of Member States' representatives chaired by the Commission and instructs the Commission to "take into account or follow" their recommendations.[62] This appears to be a variant of the old comitology process. Member State committees now can review the Commission drafts of implementing acts. Some committees operate only in an advisory capacity, while others follow an "examination" procedure under which the Commission cannot proceed if the committee issues a negative report.[63] The process helps the Commission learn if its proposals will be feasible on the ground. This practical reason for consultation, however, does not exhaust the topics that might be of interest to the public. Implementing acts generally have broader public policy implications beyond their effects on Member State governments. However, the consultation committees are only routes for Member State input; the Commission is not required to consult organized interests or the wider public.[64]

For delegated acts under article 290, a 2011 Common Understanding between the Commission, the Council, and the Parliament elaborates the roles of these institutions. It builds on a 2009 Commission Communication that explains how to promulgate delegated acts. In that Communication the Commission states that it will "consult experts from the national authorities of all the Member States" with some role in carrying out the acts and may set

[61] Francesca E. Bignami, *The Democratic Deficit in European Community Rulemaking: A Call for Notice and Comment in Comitology*, **40** Harvard International Law J. 451 (1999); Gijs Jan Brandsma, Deirdre Curtin, & Albert Meijer, *How Transparent are EU "Comitology" Committees in Practice?* **14** European Law J. 819 (2008).

[62] Regulation 182/2011 of the European Parliament and of the Council of February 16, 2011 (laying down the rules and general principles concerning mechanisms for control by Member States of the Commission's exercise of implementing powers). *See* Schwarze, Europarecht, *supra* note 24, at 702; Gellermann, *Art. 291*, *supra* note 55, para. 18; Haselmann, *supra* note 24, at 227–9; Christiansen & Dobbels, *supra* note 42, at 43. Additionally, the Member States enacted standard rules of procedure regarding the work in the committees as well as the appeal committee. Christiansen & Dobbels, *supra* note 42, at 46; Hofmann, Rowe & Türk, *supra* note 39, at 282–3.

[63] If the committee gives no opinion, the Commission may issue the implementing act. The regulation also provides for an appeal committee, also made up of Member State representatives as voting members, Regulation (EU) 182/2011, article 6.

[64] Hofmann, Rowe, & Türk, *supra* note 39, at 284, 395. This continues the practice under the older treaty arrangements. *See* Smismans, *supra* note 19.

up committees or use existing ones.[65] The Common Understanding emphasizes the roles of the Parliament and the Council and sets time tables for cooperation between the EU organs. Nevertheless, the procedures are not binding and leave considerable gaps.[66] In order to gain more influence over delegated acts under article 290, both the Parliament and the Member States have pushed for stronger procedural rules and sought expert consultations from parliamentary bodies and Member State organizations at early points in the drafting process.[67] However, they have not advocated for broad-based civil society consultation or for judicial review. The Commission now inserts a standard recital emphasizing the importance of expert consultations into its draft proposals, a practice that involves Member State technocrats.[68]

As we noted earlier, the Commission may also favor civil society participation as a way to counter dominance by Member State experts over either delegated or implementing acts. Conflicts over the rules that should govern consultations and the selection of experts create tensions between the EU organs.[69] More fundamentally, even if some Commission officials favor broader consultation in some cases, they seek to be the ultimate judge of whether such procedures are needed, and they seldom initiate broad-based consultations not tied to EU institutional or Member State needs.[70]

[65] The Common Understanding is available at: http://register.consilium.europa.eu/doc/srv?l=EN&f=ST%208753%202011%20INIT. *See* Christiansen & Dobbels, *supra* note 42, at 49 (pointing out that this Common Understanding is based on an earlier communication by the Commission on the implementation of article 290 TFEU): European Commission, Communications from the Commission to the European Parliament and the Council, COM(2009)673 http://eur-lex.europa.eu/LexUriServ/LexUriServ.do?uri=COM:2009:0673:FIN:EN:PDF. The discussion of procedures is at pp. 6–7. *See also* Mendes, *Proceduralisation*, *supra* note 23, at 24, 25.

[66] Christiansen & Dobbels, *supra* note 42, at 49, 54.

[67] Christiansen & Dobbels, *supra* note 42, at 51 (explaining that criticism of the procedure was voiced by Denmark, the United Kingdom, and Germany who demanded a "formalisation of the preparation of delegated acts," including participation by national experts, in a submission to the Committee of Permanent Representatives dealing with the implementation of article 290 TFEU).

[68] *Id.* at 50–1 (quoting the recital: "It is of particular importance that the Commission carry out appropriate consultations during its preparatory work, including at expert level.").

[69] *Id.* at 50–1.

[70] For example, Smismans, *supra* note 19 at 614, 616, provides an example in his case study of the Chemical Agents Directive. The Commission's initial proposal in 1993 required only one procedure. The Parliament stressed that binding rules should be sent to the legislature for approval.

C. Soft Law Procedural Rules

Self-regulatory, soft-law mechanisms designed to achieve "Better Regulation"[71] (now "Smart Regulation"[72]) complement the formal text of the TFEU. The Commission's initiative to achieve Better Regulation is built on impact assessment, consultations, and expertise.[73] One of the Commission's fundamental documents is the White Paper on European Governance promoting five principles of good governance: openness, participation, accountability, effectiveness, and coherence.[74] The Commission uses these principles in drafting both legislative and so-called non-legislative acts.[75] In practice, the Commission consults both with designated stakeholders and with the broader public. Under these initiatives, technocratic analyses by the Commission and other EU agencies and commissions are an important aspect of lawmaking. The Commission uses consultation and participation procedures on a voluntary basis if it deems expert advice necessary.[76] Given that the Commission both drafts proposed statutes (regulations and directives) and issues its own norms (called "non-legislative" but similar to legally binding rules), there is no sharp distinction between the processes it uses to draft different types of legal instruments. Recently, it has extended this unified practice by applying its requirements for impact assessment to non-legislative acts. Moreover, the Commission provides extensive online

[71] Core documents are the White Paper on European Governance, COM(2001)428, the inter-institutional Agreement on Better Lawmaking, OJ 2003, C 321/1, and the Commission communication on better lawmaking, COM(2002)275. *See also* the Commission communications on consultation, COM(2002)713, and expertise, COM(2002)704.

[72] *See* the new initiatives in COM(2010)543: Smart Regulation in the European Union and COM(2012)746 EU Regulatory Fitness.

[73] An overview of key documents on "Smart Regulation" can be found under http://ec.europa.eu/smart-regulation/better_regulation/key_docs_en.htm

[74] Commission White Paper on European Governance, COM(2001)428.

[75] *See* Anne Meuwese, Ymre Schuurmans, & Wim Voermans, *Towards a European Administrative Procedure Act*, 2 Rev. of European Administrative Law 3, 10–12 (2009); *see also* the impact assessment guidelines COM(2009)92, which explain, e.g., the necessary steps and pitfalls for "gathering information and consulting stakeholders" (pp. 18–21).

[76] For a list of recent and ongoing consultations, *see* the European Commission, Your Voice in Europe, http://ec.europa.eu/yourvoice/consultations/index_en.htm. Comments submitted are available at this site after the closing of the comment period. A recent example is the spring 2014 public consultation on aspects of the EU-U.S. trade deal: European Commission, Director-General for Trade, Press Release, *Commission to consult European public on provisions in EU-US trade deal on investment and investor-state dispute settlement* http://trade.ec.europa.eu/doclib/press/index.cfm?id=1015. The press release makes

resources for the public and has set up several different "specific document registers," for example, the comitology registry and the registry for expert groups and interest representatives.[77] Procedural rules designed to enhance transparency and participation apply to EU agencies as well. As yet, few of these agencies have independent rulemaking powers, but they are deeply involved in the preparatory phases inside the Commission.[78] The procedural rules addressed to the agencies are generally self-regulatory; they cannot be enforced by outsiders. Nevertheless, the legislative acts establishing agencies increasingly include such rules.[79]

These efforts are insufficient to fill the procedural lacunae.[80] Except in the field of "social policy,"[81] they are voluntary efforts that do not create legally enforceable rights for citizens, experts, Member States, or other institutions, and thus, they cannot be enforced through litigation before EU courts.[82] For instance, the failure of the Commission to undertake an impact assessment according to its own rules does not make a legislative draft inadmissible, although the Impact Assessment Board, a formally

clear that the consultation only concerns this one aspect of the negotiations, which will continue as planned on other aspects of the deal.

[77] Curtin, Hofmann, & Mendes, *supra* note 39, at 8 f. Notice that the Commission still uses the term "comitology" to describe its processes. *See* http://ec.europa.eu/transparency/reg-comitology/index.cfm?do=FAQ.FAQ

[78] Hofmann & Türk, *supra* note 48, at 125, 132.

[79] *Id.* at 125 use several examples: The Management Board of the European Aviation Safety Agency created an elaborate set of procedural rules aimed at ensuring transparency and participation, which resembles the U.S. APA's notice and comment procedure and has become a role model for other EU agencies (pp. 126–7). The European Railway Agency is an example for procedural rules that are contained in the establishing regulation 881/2004, ABl. 2004 L 164/1 (at 128–9). The same is true for the European Medicines Agency with regulation 726/2004 (at 129–30) and the European Agency for the Cooperation of Energy Regulators with regulation 713/2009 (at 130–1). Saurer, *Individualrechtsschutz*, *supra* note 14, at 55 explains that, even though the European Aviation Safety Agency is only involved in preparatory phases of rulemaking, it has its own rulemaking department and rulemaking director.

[80] Patricia Popelier, *Governance and Better Regulation: Dealing with the Legitimacy Paradox*, **17** European Public Law 555 (2011) (arguing "that under certain conditions, BR is a useful strategy to compensate for democratic deficit problems of traditional lawmaking"); Hofmann & Türk, *supra* note 48, at 132, 137 (arguing for developing a European Administrative Procedures Law).

[81] TFEU article 154.

[82] In 2010 Smismans checked to see if the EU courts cited soft law aspects of the Lisbon Strategy, in particular the Open Method of Coordination as applied to macroeconomic and employment policy coordination. He did a word search of the courts' website and found that this material was never cited in judgments and was only mentioned three times in AGs' opinions and even these were essentially accidental. However, key Lisbon concepts of "competitiveness" and "sustainability" were frequently referenced. Stijn Smismans,

independent body headed and staffed by the Commission,[83] can ask for a resubmission of a draft impact assessment.[84] The lack of clear guidelines also raises concerns about equal access to the Commission when consultations do occur.[85] Thus, even though the TFEU clarified and expanded some procedural rules, crucial gaps remain. There is a tension between transparency as a route to greater legitimacy and worries about the efficiency of EU rulemaking. Although the Lisbon Treaty does codify the values of openness and transparency in Article 11 TEU, it does not give the EU courts much to work with if asked to review either public participation or the use of expertise. Hence, the courts will have to resolve these conflicts by themselves.[86] Little turns on the distinction between ordinary laws and delegated acts so long as the delegation itself is acceptable, and in only a few cases has process been central to legal challenges. As to general civil society participation, the only clear requirement affects environmental policymaking where the Aarhus Convention enhances administrative procedural rights both at the EU level and in the Member States. Civil society groups are using EU accession to that treaty as a route to push the European Union toward greater openness and participation. They have challenged EU procedures in court and achieved both victories and setbacks in the GC.[87] Overall, efforts to

From Harmonization to Co-ordination? EU Law in the Lisbon Governance Architecture, **18** J. of European Public Policy 504, 516–19 (2011).

[83] The European Parliament has criticized the IAB's limited independence in resolution 2010/2016(INI) of June 8, 2011, stating "that the members of the IAB are independent only in formal terms, since they are currently appointed by and subject to the instructions of the Commission President," no. 29. Available at: http://www.europarl.europa.eu/sides/getDoc.do?type=TA&language=EN&reference=P7-TA-2011–0259

[84] *See* IAB, Impact Assessment Board Report for 2013, 4 (http://ec.europa.eu/smart-regulation/impact/key_docs/docs/iab_report_2013_en.pdf) (explaining the process and giving details on resubmission rates).

[85] Popelier, *supra* note 80, at 560–1 (discussing the "legitimacy challenges" of the Better Regulation approach).

[86] Hofmann, Rowe, & Türk, *supra* note 39, at 284 (referring to the access to documents of comitology committee meetings).

[87] The formal title of the Aarhus Convention is the Convention on Access to Information, Public Participation in Decision-making and Access to Justice in Environmental Matters. It is an initiative of the United Nations Commissions for Europe and was signed on June 25, 1998 and approved on behalf of the European Community by Council Decision 2005/370/EC of February 17, 2005. One active civil society group is ClientEarth, whose EU Aarhus Center is directed by a former head of the Legal Affairs Unit of the EU Directorate for the Environment (XI), Ludwig Krämer. He cites the recent cases and critiques the Commission's lack of openness in Ludwig Krämer, *The EU, Access to Environmental Information and the Open Society*, **14** Academy of European Law Forum 463 (2013). Most cases decided by the GC have been appealed to the ECJ. One of the cases listed by Krämer was decided against the applicant: Case T-111/11, ClientEarth v. European Commission [2013].

achieve "Better Regulation" are manifold and ongoing and highlight the continuing debate over just how to implement procedural values in the highly technical areas subject to EU regulation.

D. Promoting Transparency and Participation in the EU Treaties

In contrast to the omission of concrete procedural duties for rulemaking, the Lisbon Treaty takes the remarkable and novel step of complementing representative democracy with participative elements based on openness, participation, and transparency as founding principles.[88] In making these changes, the European Union commits to a concept of democratic legitimacy that extends beyond representation. This new approach might influence the interpretation and application of the existing rulemaking procedures. The abstract and general duties to further participation and transparency could be made concrete.[89] Openness and transparency rely on public access to relevant information and decision-making procedures.[90] Participation not only can further democratic legitimacy, but also can preserve rights and promote well-founded substantive decisions.[91] In order to achieve these goals, participatory structures should ensure efficient and balanced chances to provide input.

Most prominently, article 1 para. 2 TEU announces that the "Treaty marks a new stage …, in which decisions are taken as openly as possible and as closely as possible to the citizen." In a similarly abstract manner, article 10(3) TEU asserts a fundamental democratic right guaranteeing citizens "the right to participate in the democratic life of the Union." Likewise, article 298(1) TFEU obligates all EU administrative institutions to be "open, efficient and independent." These values permeate various treaty provisions, some of which contain specific duties of EU organs and rights of citizens.

[88] Bogdandy, *supra* note 4, at 66–8; Mendes, *Participation*, *supra* note 16; Curtin, Hofmann, & Mendes, *supra* note 39, at 5–6; Schwarze, Europarecht, *supra* note 24, at 703. *See also* TEU article 10(1) emphasizing representative democracy.

[89] *See* TEU articles 10 and 11; Mendes, *Proceduralisation, supra* note 23, at 25–7; Peter Michael Huber, *Art. 11 EUV*, in EUV/AEUV para. 1, 3 (Rudolf Streinz, ed., 2nd ed., 2012) (stating that supplementing the representative concept of democracy with a participative concept increases democratic legitimacy).

[90] Christian Calliess, *Art. 1 EUV*, in EUV/AEUV para. 75–9 (Christian Calliess & Matthias Ruffert, eds., 4th ed., 2011); Mendes, *supra* note 23, at 23 footnote 3 (stating that the notions of transparency in TFEU article 15(3) and openness in TEU article 10(3), TFEU article 298(1) are used "apparently interchangeably").

[91] *See also* Mendes, *Proceduralisation*, *supra* note 23, at 39.

Attempts to increase participation and transparency can be found in article 11 TEU and article 15 TFEU. Article 11 TEU seeks to counter the often-proclaimed democratic deficit of the European Union by encouraging participation from citizens, representative associations, and the civil society.[92] It obligates EU institutions to "give citizens and representative associations the opportunity to make known and publicly exchange their views in all areas of Union action" (article 11(1) TEU) and "maintain an open, transparent and regular dialogue with representative associations and civil society" (article 11(2) TEU). When appropriate, this provision can generate a duty to conduct hearings.[93] More concretely, "[t]he European Commission shall carry out broad consultations with parties concerned in order to ensure that the Union's actions are coherent and transparent" (article 11(3) TEU). This provision is not geared toward protecting rights, but rather toward ensuring the accuracy of decision making.[94] Finally, article 11(4) TEU introduces the novel possibility of a citizens' initiative to force the European Commission "to submit any appropriate proposal ... for the purpose of implementing the Treaties."[95] One worry is that organized groups might dominate participation at the EU level at the expense of the public good.[96] Therefore, some argue that participatory processes require a strong enforcement mechanism to ensure transparency and equal access of the members of civil society. Only then can deliberation increase the democratic legitimacy of decision making.[97] It remains to be seen if the European Union will be able to organize these new procedures to fulfill democratic goals, but EU officials do seem to recognize both the promise and pitfalls of consultation.[98]

In response to these concerns, article 15 TFEU demands that "[i]n order to promote good governance and ensure the participation of civil society,

[92] Matthias Ruffert, *Art. 11 EUV*, in EUV/AEUV paras. 2–3 (Christian Calliess & Matthias Ruffert, eds., 4th ed., 2011) (mentioning the Commission's White Paper on Good Governance).

[93] Martin Nettesheim, *Art. 11 TEU*, in Das Recht der Europäischen Union, Band I EUV/AEUV para. 10 (Eberhard Grabitz, Meinhard Hilf, & Martin Nettesheim, eds., loose leaf updated to Sept. 2013) (stating that hearings would be appropriate especially in the preparatory phase of rulemaking); Mendes, *Participation*, *supra* note 16, at 1865–8.

[94] Nettesheim, *supra* note 93, para. 11. *See also* the Protocol on the Application of the Principles of Subsidiarity and Proportionality, OJ 2010, C 83/206.

[95] *See* Huber, *supra* note 89, para. 42 (emphasizing a binding effect on the Commission); likewise Nettesheim, *supra* note 93, para. 27.

[96] Huber, *supra* note 89, paras. 17, 18; Nettesheim, *supra* note 94, para. 19.

[97] Ruffert, *supra*, paras. 4, 13; Curtin, Hofmann, & Mendes, *supra*, at 11; Mendes, *Participation*, *supra* note 16, at 1862–3.

[98] COM(2009)92, at 20 (describing pitfalls in regard to information gathering and consulting stakeholders).

the Union's institutions, bodies, offices and agencies shall conduct their work as openly as possible" (article 15(1) TFEU). In addition to demanding publicity of legislative proceedings and publication of legislative materials, this provision emphasizes a general duty of each EU institution to "ensure that its proceedings are transparent" and demands that they develop general rules of procedure regarding access to documents (article 15(3) para. 3 TFEU). Most concretely, article 15(3) para. 1 TFEU gives EU citizens and residents "a right of access to documents of the Union's institutions, bodies, offices and agencies."[99]

On first glance, the EU landscape seems to be an arbitrary smorgasbord of instruments and mechanisms promoting participation and transparency that leaves gaps and often lacks clear normative content.[100] According to one study:

> The vast array of actors, forms of acts and applicable procedures make it difficult to assess to what extent constitutional values infuse executive rule-making, and more precisely how general principles are complied with across the legal system. This is all the more so since the terrain is fragmented and rather sector-specific.[101]

The treaties, nevertheless, show a clear decision to push the EU toward a strengthening of participatory values. However, the strong emphasis of the Lisbon Treaty on procedural rules that promote participation and transparency is not reflected in the provisions on legislative procedures or in the text of articles 290, 291 TFEU, including the rules governing their application.

In spite of the disjunction between the abstract and the specific, the marked procedural focus found throughout the treaties indicates a strong commitment that could influence EU institutions. The general provisions govern all EU activity, including legislative and non-legislative rulemaking.[102] They mainly reflect broad institutional goals and are not cloaked

[99] The relevant EU documents on freedom of information are Regulation 1049/2001 (regarding public access to European Parliament, Council and Commission documents) May 30, 2001; Regulation 1367/2006 (on the application of the provisions of the Aarhus Convention on Access to Information, Public Participation in Decision-making and Access to Justice in Environmental Matters to Community institutions and bodies) September 6, 2006. The Commission also proposed a new regulation in COM(2008)229 final, April 30, 2008, but it has not been adopted.

[100] Mendes, *Proceduralisation*, *supra* note 23, at 37; Oliver Mross, Bürgerbeteiligung am Rechtsetzungsprozess in der Europäischen Union 193 (2010) (using the German expression "Sammelsurium" regarding Article I-47 of the Constitutional Treaty).

[101] Curtin, Hofmann, & Mendes, *supra* note 39, at 3.

[102] Mendes, *Proceduralisation*, *supra* note 23 at 23–5, 36, 40.

in the language of rights. That is both a benefit and a cost. On the one hand, they straightforwardly seek to enhance the democratic character of the European Union. However, on the other hand, if the Commission and the legislative bodies ignore these mandates, judicial review is presently unavailable.[103] Limited implementation seems likely. Even if consultation occurs, it need not be open-ended. The notion of an "independent" administration might clash with the call for more "open" processes. In the face of any reluctance by the EU to fully embrace public participation, it is unlikely that the EU courts will read the treaty clauses to give individuals or other concerned entities the right to go to the GC to demand more transparent and participatory processes. The EU courts – as we will see later in this chapter – work under formal and substantive limitations and have generally been reluctant to impose strict procedural duties on EU institutions.

II. STANDING AND JURISDICTION TO CHALLENGE EU LEGAL ACTS

As the European Union has taken on more direct regulatory functions, private litigants are pressing the EU courts to review these decisions. However, enforcing values of participation and transparency through EU courts is not an easy task. Litigants face three limitations. First, restrictive rules on jurisdiction and standing make it difficult to challenge EU legal acts based on a lack of consultation or participation. Second, the EU courts have been rather reluctant to conduct intensive proportionality review of EU acts. There are

[103] The situation today is similar to that discussed in Strauss, *supra* note 2, at 675: "The obligation to explain proposals … is subject principally to political enforcement – by the Council or Parliament rather than the courts." He also cites a document in which both the Commission itself and an external assessment of the Commission's consultation processes rejected the option of making consultation requirements legally binding (*id.* at 665–6). The Commission claims that citizens expect that "European institutions should deliver on substance rather than concentrating on procedures" as if these were opposing goals: Communication toward a Reinforced Culture of Consultation and Dialogue – General Principles and Minimum Standards for Consultation of Interested Parties by the Commission COM(2002)704 final (Dec. 11, 2002). The external review similarly argues that "[t]he problem with a legally binding requirement to consult is that it creates an opportunity and perhaps even an incentive for those dissatisfied with a particular policy outcome to challenge proposals in court on the grounds of inadequate consultation." BETTER REGULATION TASK FORCE, GET CONNECTED: EFFECTIVE ENGAGEMENT IN THE EU 25 (Sept. 2005). The Commission has now issued a reassessment of its procedures for policymaking that does not include a recommendation for intensive judicial review. EUROPEAN COMMISSION, *supra* note 37.

only a few cases that require EU actors to use specific procedures in order to provide a sound factual basis for policy decisions.[104] If Member State legal acts infringe on fundamental freedoms, the ECJ sometimes requires a consistent pursuit of the underlying policy.[105] At the same time, the ECJ has voided very few European directives for a violation of the principle of proportionality.[106] Third, a lack of enforceable procedural rights leaves the courts with few grounds for imposing duties on EU organs. However, these limitations may bind less strongly in the future. The Lisbon Treaty weakens all three limitations by broadening the standing requirement, showing a greater concern with individual rights, and emphasizing transparency and participation as fundamental values.

The first issue is the formal threshold that private litigants have to pass in order for the EU courts to hear their claims. EU institutions and Member States have automatic access to the courts to challenge the behavior of other institutions and Member States.[107] Other litigants must establish the jurisdiction of the courts and their own standing to bring the case to the GC. A private party has standing, "against an act addressed to that person or which is of direct and individual concern to them" (article 263 para. 4 TFEU). The second part of this paragraph, added by the Lisbon Treaty, also permits challenges to "regulatory acts" if the applicant can show a direct concern (so long as the act does not entail implementing measures) (article 263 para. 4 TFEU). The notion of "regulatory acts" is not defined in the treaties and its interpretation has spurred a complex controversy that the EU courts have only recently confronted.[108]

[104] Hofmann & Türk, *supra* note 48, at 134 f.

[105] Case C-338/04, Placanica [2007] ECR I-1891 para. 53; Case C-67/98, Zenatti [1999] ECR I-7289, para. 35 f.; Case C-243/01, Gambelli [2003] ECR I-13031, paras. 62, 67.

[106] Rufolf Streinz, Europarecht, para. 759 (9th ed., 2012) (claiming that up until the enactment of the European Charter of Fundamental Rights, there was only one case in which a directive enacted by the European Parliament and Council was voided because of a violation of fundamental rights: ECJ, C-453/03 i.a. – ABNA Ltd. i.a. v Secretary of State for Health i.a., [2005] ECR I-10423, para. 85); Hofmann & Türk, *supra* note 48, at 135 (emphasizing that the ECJ has granted the EU legislature a considerable degree of discretion, citing Case C-58/08 Vodafone et al. [2010] ECR I-4999 para. 52); *see also* Verica Trstenjak & Erwin Beysen, *Das Prinzip der Verhältnismäßigkeit in der Unionsrechtsordnung*, **47** Europarecht 265, 273 f. (2012) (emphasizing the legislature's discretion).

[107] Notice the contrast with judicial review in the United States where the federal courts are very cautious in giving standing to one part of government to sue another part or even for individual members of one branch to do so. The individuals must comply with general standing requirements and show individualized harm.

[108] Wolfram Cremer, *Art. 263 AEUV*, in EUV/AEUV para. 54 f. (Christian Calliess & Matthias Ruffert, eds., 4th ed., 2011); Hofmann & Türk, *supra* note 48, at 133 f.; Alexander Thiele, *Das*

Some scholars argue that the terminology mirrors concepts in the Constitutional Treaty, and they interpret the term in light of the hierarchy between regulations and European statutes.[109] Thus, the term "regulatory act" should not apply to legislative acts under the Lisbon Treaty.[110] This interpretation excludes regulations enacted in a legislative procedure and thus is linguistically problematic.[111] Hence, other scholars read the clause as an effort to increase judicial protection, and they would define the term to include any legal act of general application, whether it is enacted in a legislative or non-legislative procedure.[112]

The ECJ adopted the former, restrictive reading of article 263 para. 4 TFEU. In *Inuit* it held that "regulatory acts" do not include legislative acts.[113] In other words, the only way for individuals to challenge a legislative act is to claim that it is of direct and individual concern to them. This will usually be difficult given the nature of most legislation.[114] Hence, if the Court continues to uphold the two prongs of the *Inuit* decision, this Lisbon Treaty provision will only slightly broaden individuals' access to the EU courts.[115]

Rechtsschutzsystem nach dem Vertrag von Lissabon – (K)ein Schritt nach vorn? – Zugleich ein Beitrag zur begrenzten Reichweite von Art. 47 Abs. 1 GRC wie auch zur Rolle der historischen Interpretation primären Unionsrechts, **45** Europarecht 30, 43 (2010); Peter Thalmann, *Zur Auslegung von Art. 263 Abs. 4 AEUV durch Rechtsprechung und Lehre*, **47** Europarecht 452 (2012) (including an overview of judicial and academic views).

109 Cremer, *supra* note 108, at 56 with further references in footnote 198; Hofmann & Türk, *supra* note 48, at 133 f.; Thiele, *supra* note 108, at 43f.

110 This was the view of the Grand Chamber of the ECJ in the appeal in Inuit, Case 583/11 P; *see also* Stephan Pötters, Christoph Werkmeister, & Johannes Traut, *Rechtsakte mit Verordnungscharakter nach Art. 263 Abs. 4 AEUV – eine passgenaue Ausweitung des Individualrechtsschutzes?*, **47** Europarecht 546 (2012) (confining regulatory acts to delegated and implementing acts).

111 Jürgen Schwarze, *Art. 263 AEUV* in EU-Kommentar para. 52 (Jürgen Schwarze, ed., 3rd ed., 2012) [hereinafter, Schwarze, *Art. 263 AEUV*].

112 *Id.*, para. 52 with further references; *see also* Bast, *supra* note 31, at 556–7; Stephan Balthasar, *Locus Standi Rules for Challenges to Regulatory Acts by Private Applicants: The New Article 263 (4) TFEU*, European Law Rev. 542, 545 f. (2010); *see* Ingolf Pernice, *Die Zukunft der Unionsgerichtsbarkeit – Zu den Bedingungen einer nachhaltigen Sicherung effektiven Rechtsschutzes im Europäischen Verfassungsverbund*, **46** Europarecht 151, 151 footnote 1, 167 f. (2011).

113 Case 583/11 P, Grand Chamber, October 3, 2013 (Inuit Tapiriit Kanatami). It holds that the term "regulatory act" is more restrictive than the term "act" and does not include legislative acts, such as the regulation at issue here that was promulgated by the Parliament and the Council (paras. 58–61); *see* Thalmann, *supra* note 108, at 456–9.

114 The ECJ follows earlier case law in searching not just for clear direct harm to the plaintiff but also for something individual or particular about that harm. In *Inuit*, case C-583/11 P, para. 73, the appeal is not admitted because even though the plaintiffs suffered harm, the act that harmed them does not single them out. It is general and applies "indiscriminately."

115 Compare with TEC article 230 para. 4. Ulrich Ehricke, *Art. 263 AEUV*, in EUV/AEUV para. 55 (Rudolf Streinz, ed., 2nd ed., 2012); Hofmann & Türk, *supra* note 48, at 134.

Here, the appellants lose both because they are not individually concerned *and* because the act they are challenging is a piece of ordinary EU legislation, not a non-legislative rule.

A. Jurisdiction

The jurisdiction of the EU courts is the first hurdle to overcome in seeking review of legislative and executive rulemaking. The EU treaties define *which* measures of *which* EU organs can be brought before the EU courts on *which* grounds. The TFEU clarified the jurisdiction of the EU courts, bringing it in line with recent court judgments.[116] TFEU article 263 para. 1 reads:

> The Court of Justice of the European Union shall review the legality of legislative acts, of acts of the Council, of the Commission and of the European Central Bank, other than recommendations and opinions, and of acts of the European Parliament and of the European Council intended to produce legal effects *vis-à-vis* third parties. It shall also review the legality of acts of bodies, offices or agencies of the Union intended to produce legal effects *vis-à-vis* third parties.

Before the TFEU, the EU courts had explicit authority to review and annul the actions of the Council and the Commission if they violated the treaty.[117] In *Les Verts* the ECJ extended its own jurisdiction to include the Parliament. It argued that the European Union is a community based on the rule of law that establishes a complete system of legal remedies and procedures. The Court explains omission of the Parliament from the text "because, in its original version, the EEC Treaty merely granted it [the Parliament] powers of consultation and political control rather than the power to adopt measures intended to have legal effects vis-à-vis third parties."[118] Now that it can adopt legally binding measures, its actions are subject to review. In asserting jurisdiction, the court focuses on harm to third parties; the ECJ will not review Parliament's own rules of proceeding.[119]

Other EU bodies make decisions under delegated authority. These delegations were not contemplated when the Treaty was originally drafted, but

[116] Saurer, *Individualrechtsschutz*, *supra* note 14, at 65.

[117] Given this authority and limits on private party standing, many early cases were brought by one institution against another, over and above the many cases brought by Member States to test the limits of Union power.

[118] Case 294/83 Parti Ecologiste "Les Verts" v European Parliament, [1986] ECR 1339, paras. 23, 24 (Les Verts).

[119] *Les Verts*, para. 44; *see* article 232 TFEU. The Green Party of France (Les Verts) was given standing to ask for the annulment of a rule governing the financing of parliamentary elections because it was directly concerned and individually harmed.

they are likely to become more important over time. Prior to the adoption of the TFEU, the Community courts applied the reasoning of *Les Verts* to assert or to deny jurisdiction over the new agencies. Once again, the TFEU formally subjects their legally binding rules to judicial review.

In 2008 the Court of First Instance (now the General Court) reviewed the procurement procedures of the European Agency for Reconstruction (EAR) that provided aid to the Balkan countries. The key point for the court was that the EAR could act on its own under the terms of its enabling statute. Thus, it distinguished this case from others where an EU agency's choice had to be, at least nominally, approved by the Commission.[120] It also distinguished cases with limited jurisdiction on various other grounds, including the advisory nature of the agency opinion, the existence of other remedies, and the special treatment of police and criminal matters.[121]

Many agencies, however, do not have final authority to make legally binding decisions – either general rules or individualized judgments. In those cases the EU courts will not review their decisions directly.[122] Rather the courts will treat those decisions as recommendations to the ultimate authority – usually the Commission – which means that the applicant must sue the Commission (or the Council), not the agency.[123] Once litigants learn which body they need to sue, however, the advisory nature of agency decisions does not pose a bar to review so long as Commission decisions have the force of law.[124] Nevertheless, agencies that issue advisory opinions or recommendations to the Member States are not subject to judicial review.

Litigation involving the European Medicines Agency (EMEA) and its Committee for Proprietary Medicinal Products (CPMP) illustrates the courts' reasoning. The EMEA and the CPMP issue expert opinions, but ultimate decision-making authority rests with the Commission although it seldom overrules the agency's recommendations. Recognizing that much

[120] Case T-411/06 Sogelma v European Agency for Reconstruction [2008] ECR II-2771, paras. 54–7. The cases cited are Case T-133/03, Schering-Plough v Commission and EMEA (December 5, 2007) and Joined Cases T-369/94 and T-85/95 DIR International Film and Others v Commission [1998] ECR II-357, both holding that the firms could only sue the Commission, not the agency.

[121] The cases are C-160/03, Spain v Eurojust [2005] ECR I-2077 (special nature of police and criminal matters), T-148/97 Keeling v OHIM [1998] ECR II-2217 (other remedies); and 1 March 2007, Joined Cases T-311/06 R I, T-311/06 R II, T-312/06 R, and T-313/06 R FMC Chemical and Others v. EFSA (nonbinding opinion of EFSA).

[122] Saurer, *Individualrechtsschutz*, *supra* note 14, at 56, 60.

[123] *Id.* at 61–3.

[124] *See* Johannes Saurer, *The Accountability of Supranational Administration: The Case of European Union Agencies*, **24** American University International Law Rev. 429 [hereinafter, Saurer, *Accountability*], 461–2 (2008–9).

of the real work goes on in the EMEA, the EU courts assert jurisdiction to review not only formal Commission decisions but also the findings of the agency.[125] As Johannes Saurer summarized the *Artegodan* case:

> the Court of First Instance not only agreed to hear a claim against a negative decision of the Commission on a pharmaceutical application, but also held that effective review requires exploration beyond the Commission's formal decision into the findings of the agency and its committee, here the EMEA and the CPMP. With that, the court acknowledged the tremendous factual importance of the agency's opinion, and stated that the Commission would necessarily have to follow the agency – unless it could come up with elaborate reasoning pointing to the contrary.[126]

The TFEU not only broadened the scope of jurisdiction regarding the Parliament, but it also gave the courts jurisdiction over other previously exempt measures. Prior to the adoption of the TFEU, EU courts had only limited jurisdiction over the second (Common Foreign and Security Policy) and third pillars (Police and Judicial Cooperation in Criminal Matters) of the EU. By abandoning this structure, the TFEU now provides jurisdiction for measures previously adopted within the third pillar,[127] while still limiting judicial review under the second pillar.[128] The older treaties contained only fragmentary provisions giving jurisdiction to the EU courts. So far, the GC and the ECJ have expressed differing views on the extent of their review authority under the TFEU, with the ECJ overturning efforts by the GC to provide review of rules with broad-ranging impacts.

For example, the ECJ dismissed a case brought by Spain and Finland that challenged language requirements in postings for job candidates at Eurojust,[129] which deals with police and judicial cooperation.[130] The Court denied jurisdiction under article 230 TEC, but it went on to say that eventually a job candidate would have access to judicial review under other treaty provisions. At that point, Member States would be able to act as formal "intervenors."[131] Thus, the ECJ held that it lacks jurisdiction to

[125] Case T-74/00, Artegodan GmbH v Commission [2003] ECR II-494. *See* Paul Craig, EU Administrative Law 159 f., 643–6 (2012) [hereinafter, Craig, EU Administrative Law]. The acronym is now EMA, not EMEA.

[126] Saurer, *Accountability*, *supra* note 124, at 461–2 (internal citations omitted).

[127] Hofmann, Rowe & Türk, *supra* note 39, at 799; Thiele, *supra* note 108, at 49 f. (welcoming this change).

[128] TEU article 24(1) para. 2 and TFEU article 275 para. 1 exclude judicial review, except in the cases of TEU article 40 and TFEU article 275 para. 2.

[129] Case C-160/03, Kingdom of Spain v Eurojust [2005] ECR I-2077.

[130] TFEU article 85.

[131] Case C-160/03, paras. 36–44. Richard L. Creech, *While the Advocate-General Finds Eurojust's Language Rules for Job Applicants Partly Contrary to Union Law, the Court*

resolve a claim brought under one treaty article by a Member State, but it asserted that it will have jurisdiction in the future to rule on the same matter if brought under another treaty article by a different plaintiff. This has detrimental consequences for consistent judicial review of EU measures because the ECJ may decide similar cases on the basis of different criteria.

In contrast, AG Miguel Poiares Maduro argued that the ECJ should decide the case, using an argument similar to ECJ's argument in *Les Verts.* His central claim was that dismissing the case "might undermine a fundamental principle of Union law."[132] In general, Eurojust "has no legislative role or decision-making power. It is a body with an essentially operational function."[133] That explains the lack of any explicit grant of review. However, when, as here, it acts in a way the AG views as legislative, it ought to be subject to review, just as the parliamentary action was in *Les Verts.*[134] Member States were in a privileged position in accessing the ECJ under title VI; they were permitted to bring cases without having to demonstrate legal harm to themselves.[135] Hence, according to AG Poiares Maduro, they were entitled to bring actions for annulment on the ground that Eurojust's actions infringe EU law.[136] In dismissing the case, the ECJ acknowledged that Member States can access the courts to pursue certain claims without a prior showing of harm. It just rejected the AG's application of the treaty provision to this case. If brought today, this case would fall within the scope of article 263 TFEU as Eurojust is no longer excluded from this jurisdiction.[137] However, article 276 TFEU imposes new jurisdictional limits in this area, which might offer an opportunity for the courts to deny jurisdiction.[138]

Dismisses Case for Lack of Standing. Decision of 15 March 2005 in Case C-160/03, Kingdom of Spain v. Eurojust **2** European Constitutional Law R. 147 (2006).

132 Opinion of the AG in Case C-160/03, Kingdom of Spain v Eurojust, delivered December 16, 2004, paras. 11–25 (at 13).

133 AG Poiares Maduro's opinion, para. 20, footnote omitted.

134 The AG would then have had the court annul parts of the call for applications and accept other parts as lawful (paras. 26–76).

135 EU (version of the Treaty of Nice) article 35(6), (7).

136 AG Poiares Maduro's opinion at paras. 23–4, citing Case 41/83 Italy v. Commission [1985] ECR 873, para. 30.

137 Johannes Saurer in a personal e-mail [May 10, 2011] argues that the case would have come out differently under the TFEU, along the lines of the AG's opinion. Eurojust is no longer in a special category in the treaty, so article 263 would apply. The TFEU, article 276 denies the ECJ jurisdiction over any matters relating to the police or other law enforcement services of a Member State and over any Member State activities "with regard to the maintenance of law and order and the safeguarding of national security."

138 *Id.*

Notice that Poiares Maduro describes Eurojust's action as "legislative," meaning that it makes policy, which it surely does. However, the Treaty now seems to say that *by definition* the Commission and the agencies do not issue legislative acts. Yet, realistically, they will continue to make policy in many areas where expertise and rapid response are needed. The ECJ accepts that reality both for the Commission and, in a recent decision, for at least some agencies. The Court appears unwilling to permit individuals and firms to seek review of executive policymaking procedures.[139] It will only provide review if the policy is applied in a particular case.

B. Standing and Legal Interest

After assuming jurisdiction, the EU courts consider whether private litigants have standing to bring the case. Member States and EU organs are not subject to this requirement. Originally, standing depended on a showing of "direct and individual concern."[140] This phrase was read very restrictively and applied to both decisions aimed at third parties and regulations (with only a few exceptions).[141] In 2002 AG Jacobs urged the ECJ to broaden standing.[142] The AG argued that a farmers' association should have standing to seek annulment of a regulation dealing with the olive oil market. Doing so would remove what Jacobs saw as an anomaly where the greater the number of persons affected, the less likely it was that there would be effective judicial review.[143] He argued that the ECJ should provide heightened review to match the growth in the European Union's powers. According to him, the weakness of the European Union's democratic and constitutional legitimacy should prompt more liberal standing rules.[144] The ECJ did not accept that reasoning; it held that the association should not get standing under article 230 para. 4 of the TEC (Consolidated Version of the Treaty establishing the European Community [TEC] [2006] OFFICIAL JOURNAL OF THE EUROPEAN UNION [OJ] C-321 E/37) (now article 263

[139] Case-270/12 United Kingdom v Parliament and Council [2014].

[140] TEC article 230 para. 4.

[141] LINDSETH, *supra* note 1, at 142. The exceptions were for antidumping, competition, and state aids.

[142] Case C-50/00 P. Unión de Pequeños Agricultores [UPA] v. Council, [2002] ECR I-6677. *See* LINDSETH, *supra* note 1, at 142–3. *See also* CRAIG, EU ADMINISTRATIVE LAW, *supra* note 125, at 305–19 (2010) (reviewing the case law).

[143] AG Jacobs opinion, para. 102. Discussed by CRAIG, EU ADMINISTRATIVE LAW, *supra* note 125, at 309–10.

[144] AG Jacobs opinion, para. 102; LINDSETH, *supra* note 1, at 142–3.

TFEU) because there was nothing peculiar about the way it was affected compared to other bodies.[145]

In addition to the standing requirements, the EU courts sometimes require that private litigants show a legally protected interest, without which a private litigant does not have the need for legal relief. This requirement is only intended to exclude cases in which the applicant cannot show any legal interest in the case. However, the Court of First Instance (now the General Court) has used the condition to avoid deciding on standing and to refuse to hear a case "because, if she [the plaintiff] has no such interest, it will be unnecessary to examine whether the contested decision is of direct and individual concern to her within the meaning of the fourth paragraph of Article 230 EC."[146] The Court of First Instance dismissed an application from a scientific expert as inadmissible.[147] The expert challenged a scientific opinion of the EMEA and its CPMP that recommended approval of a drug that her research had shown to have dangerous side effects. She challenged the procedures and the final result, but the court found that her scientific findings had been taken into account and that her reputation had not been damaged. Hence, she had no legally protected interest that permitted her to sue. Apart from limiting experts' access to judicial review on regulatory matters and avoiding the issue of standing, this case gives insight into the procedures required by the Commission.

> [T]he Community rules require the Commission to confirm that the particulars and documents provided by the applicant [pharmaceutical firm] for marketing authorisation are correct in order that it may assess the quality, safety and efficacy of that product and authorise its marketing.... [In that regard, if] the person responsible for the authenticity of the final reports relating to some of the clinical trials disputes the veracity of the information sent without her agreement by the applicant for marketing authorisation, the Commission is required, in the interest of public health, to examine that information.[148]

If the Commission does not do so, it violates the relevant regulation.[149] If the Commission "had refused to examine the information provided by her

[145] Case C-50/00, para. 37. *See also* Case C-263/02 P, Commission v Jégo-Quéré [2004] ECR I-3425, paras. 29–39 (denying standing on similar grounds). Both cases are put in context, discussed, and critiqued in Craig, EU Administrative Law, *supra* note 125, at 310–19 and in Carol Harlow, Accountability in the European Union 148–53 (2002).

[146] Case T-326/99, Nancy Fern Olivieri v. Commission and EMEA [2003] ECR II-6053 para. 66.

[147] *Id.*

[148] *Id.* paras. 78, 80.

[149] Regulation (EEC) No 2309/93 of July 22, 1993 laying down Community procedures for the authorization and supervision of medicinal products for human and veterinary use and establishing a European Agency for the Evaluation of Medicinal Products.

in the course of the procedure … or [if] there had been an implicit decision to reject that information, … [s]he would have been entitled to contest the legality of either of these decisions before the Court of First Instance."[150] The expert's interest lies in having her scientific views considered, which is sufficient for the court to examine her claims. The particular circumstances of the expert's prior involvement might make this a special case, but the court's findings are still a quite striking assertion. In American administrative law, decisions are sometimes remanded because the evidence is weak or because new information was not incorporated.[151] However, individual experts not associated with groups that are benefited or harmed by the regulation itself do not have standing to argue that their views should have been heard. In contrast, the decision is in accord with the EU courts' strong presumption in favor of the responsible use of scientific expertise. Even though the expert was unsuccessful in this case, others might be able to bring cases purely because of their professional interest in contributing to the policy choice, surely a very abstract and public-spirited notion of injury. They would, nonetheless, need to fulfill a standing requirement, which the court failed to specify in this case. The opinion relies on a mixture of individual rights and the value of expertise for competent policymaking, but because the scientist lost, its impact is unclear.[152] Access to the court depends on the scientist's claim of individualized harm, but the reasoning speaks to the importance of a technically competent decision.

At about the same time and for different reasons, the Court of First Instance reached out to give standing to the pharmaceutical company Pfizer, which sought the annulment of an EU regulation that withdrew EU authorization of an additive in animal feedstuffs.[153] The Council passed the regulation on a recommendation from the Commission. The Council noted that the "regulation is an act of general application which applies to objectively determined situations and produces legal effects on categories of persons viewed abstractly and in their entirety" and goes on to argue that the regulation is not of "individual concern" to Pfizer.[154] As with the farmers in the olive oil case, that does not mean that Pfizer is not affected, but rather

[150] Case T-326/99, Nancy Fern Olivieri v Commission, para. 81.

[151] *See, for example*, Scenic Hudson Preservation Conference v. FPC (I), 354 F. 2d 608 (2d Cir. 1965); Scenic Hudson Preservation Conference v. FPC (II), 453 F. 2d 463 (2d Cir. 1971).

[152] Mendes, Participation in EU Rulemaking, *supra* note 15, at 362–6 (analyzing this case).

[153] Case T-13/99, Pfizer Animal Health SA v Council [2002] ECR II-3305.

[154] *Id.* paras. 74, 75.

that it is just like all the other producers or potential producers and that the ban also affects farmers. In fact, Pfizer was the only producer, but according to the Commission, Pfizer's market dominance has occurred "purely by chance," and there is nothing to prevent another firm from entering the market.[155] In considering standing, the court looks for individualized harm and states that:

> [N]atural or legal persons may claim that a measure of general application is of individual concern to them only if they are affected by reason of certain attributes which are peculiar to them or by reason of circumstances in which they are differentiated from all other persons.[156]

Even if Pfizer is the only producer, that fact is not sufficient. If "the measure is applied by virtue of an objective legal or factual situation," then even if it, in practice, only affects one individual, that person will not be able to challenge it in court.[157] The Court then goes on to find that in this particular case Pfizer has standing because the Commission's procedures give it "the benefit of procedural guarantees" that distinguish it from "all other traders concerned by the regulation."[158] Pfizer's special procedural rights, not the substantive harm it suffered, give it standing. The Court's main concern in admitting Pfizer's claim is not the overall legality of the Commission's actions, but whether Pfizer has suffered a particularized harm. Pfizer received standing in court, but no right to participate in the Commission's decision.[159]

The debate over standing echoes American law to the extent that it does not allow applicants to challenge legislation applied generally and abstractly.[160] At the same time, it contrasts with U.S. law in disallowing standing to

[155] *Id.* para. 78.

[156] *Id.* para. 88. The cases cited in support of this proposition are Case 25/62 Plaumann v Commission [1963] ECR 95, para. 107; Case C-309/89, Codorniu v Council [1994] ECR I-1853, para. 20; Case T-12/93 CCE de Vittel and Others v Commission [1995] ECR II-1247, para. 36.

[157] *Pfizer*, para. 89. Citing Case C-213/91 Abertal and Others v Council [1993] ECR I-3177, para. 17; order of September 30, 1997 in Case T-122/96 Federolio v Commission [1997] ECR II-1559, para. 55.

[158] *Pfizer*, para. 104 f. *See also* para. 101 and cases cited there: Joined Cases T-481/93 and T-484/93 Exporteurs in Levende Varkens and Others v Commission [1995] ECR II-2941, para. 55; the order in Case T-585/93 Greenpeace and Others v Commission [1995] ECR II-2205, paras. 56 and 63.

[159] Mendes, Participation in EU Rule-Making, *supra* note 15, at 198–200.

[160] *See* Londoner v. Denver, 210 U.S. 373 (1908) (requiring a hearing when an individual property owner is harmed) and Bi-Metallic Investment C. v. State Board of Equalization, 239 U.S. 441 (1915) (refusing to require a hearing when the rule applies to many people).

challenge executive regulations even though the litigant is clearly harmed by the policy. In deciding standing claims, the EU courts look to the particularized nature of the harm, not the process that produced it. Except for AG Jacobs' argument that the EU institutions' weak democratic legitimacy justifies broad standing, the EU courts do not award standing as a way to enhance the political accountability of EU institutions. Rather, they have limited standing in cases that challenge acts of general applicability. Even when the claimant is challenging the quality of the expertise used to make a decision, the admissibility of the claim is tied most clearly to an individual's harm, even if the issue of public legitimacy lurks in the background.

Hence, the ECJ imposes a standing requirement that severely limits review. It polices the separation of powers and the overall legitimacy of policy choices only in cases brought by Member States or by one EU institution against another. Individuals and private bodies cannot get into court to raise these claims. However, the limits imposed by the ECJ may be about to change. In a seeming response to the debate over AG Jacobs' opinion, the TFEU dropped the requirement of "individual concern" and requires only "direct concern," but only for "regulatory acts not requiring implementing measures" (article 263 para. 4 TFEU). As discussed earlier, this shift has had limited application so far. Nevertheless, it could make it easier to obtain standing in cases challenging non-legislative acts of general application and help to gain judicial review of substance and process.[161]

One counterweight to the limits on individual appeals is the right of Member States to bring cases directly to the ECJ that challenge the behavior of EU institutions. Such suits might be supported by private interests as an indirect way to get their grievances into court. For example, in a 2014 case the United Kingdom argued that an EU legislative act violated the Treaty by giving the European Securities and Markets Authority (ESMA) the power to issue binding orders governing the financial markets in times of emergency. One assumes that this lawsuit was supported by private UK financial firms affected by the regulation. In this case, the ECJ upheld the legislation as consistent with the treaty, and the case did not deal with ESMA's processes, but only with their legal authority to issue regulations.[162] Nevertheless, in future this route to the ECJ could be used to challenge procedures if the ECJ were inclined to rule on such matters. We discuss a few cases later in this chapter that indirectly deal with process.

[161] Türk, *supra* note 35, at 127.

[162] Case C-270/12 United Kingdom v Parliament and Council [2014]. For an overview of EU securities regulation, *see* Kelemen, *supra* note 13, at 93–142. He outlines the detailed nature of the regulations that rely on disclosure and strict legal enforcement.

III. GROUNDS FOR DECISIONS: SUBSTANCE AND PROCESS

Because the EU courts dismiss many cases seeking the review of policy on standing and jurisdictional grounds, the case law setting the parameters of the policymaking process is rather thin. However, once an EU court has taken a case, it makes few distinctions between legislation that involves Parliament and the Council and tertiary legislation – that is, norms or rules promulgated by the Commission or by a combination of Council and Commission. Agencies with the power to issue legally binding rulings are treated the same as other bodies with that power.[163] This conflation of all kinds of lawmaking is a distinctive feature of EU jurisprudence. It seems to be the result of the variety of ways that the European Union can make legally binding policies combined with a parliament that still struggles to assert democratic legitimacy. Even though members of Parliament are directly elected, the Council and Commission remain key sources of political power given their links to the Member States. The new agencies, which usually include representatives from each Member State, gain their political legitimacy not from their subordination to the Parliament, but from their ability to aggregate Member State views and to claim a mantle of expertise.

A. Substance

If EU courts review the legality of acts adopted by EU organs, they decide "on grounds of lack of competence, infringement of an essential procedural requirement, infringement of the Treaties or of any rule of law relating to their application, or misuse of powers."[164] Although some provisions directly mandate certain procedures, these might also be derived from judicial review of the substance of an act. EU courts might require EU organs to show that they explored the relevant information basis of the requirements and the impact of their actions.[165] Although not tied to any specific

[163] Case T-411/06, *Sogelma*: "The general scheme of the Treaty is to make a direct action available against all measures adopted by the institutions which are intended to have legal effects (see *Les Verts* …)" (para. 36). "The general principle to be elicited from that judgment is that any act of a Community body intended to produce legal effects vis-à-vis third parties must be open to judicial review" (para. 37).

[164] TFEU article 263 para. 2.

[165] Türk, *supra* note 35, at 141 (emphasizing "the link between [the] procedural and … substantive dimension"). Citing Case C-77/09 – Gowan [2010] ECR I-13533, para. 57, which emphasizes the need to research "all the relevant facts of the individual case, facts which support the conclusions reached."

procedures, this substantive review might indirectly require EU organs to place a greater emphasis on sound procedures. We have already seen these indirect effects at the national level, for instance, in the U.S. Supreme Court's decisions dealing with rights and federalism and the German Constitutional Court's adjudication in *Hartz IV*. However, although the EU courts rigidly enforce the principle of proportionality against Member States, they seem much more reluctant to do the same regarding EU actors.[166] The inclusion of the Charter of Fundamental Rights of the European Union might be the lever with which to enforce a stronger proportionality review on the EU level. If so, the case law may develop in ways that mirror developments in the United States and Germany.

In *Spain v. Council*, the ECJ annulled a Council regulation establishing a support scheme for cotton farmers because it violated the principle of proportionality by failing to consider certain relevant costs.[167] One of the regulatory objectives was to ensure economically viable conditions for cotton production and safeguard profitability.[168] The structure of the new support scheme decreased the available support based on actual cotton production.[169] The ECJ takes a substantive approach and considers the proportionality of the challenged parts of the regulation.[170] However, the ECJ also claims to be granting the legislature a wide margin of discretion by limiting review "to verifying that the measure in question is not vitiated by any manifest error or misuse of powers and that the authority concerned has not manifestly exceeded the limits of its discretion."[171] Following this standard of review, the ECJ examines "whether the contested measures of the new cotton support scheme are manifestly inappropriate in terms of that objective."[172]

The ECJ then connects this substantive standard to the necessity of proper research, stating that "the institutions must at the very least be able to produce and set out clearly and unequivocally the basic facts which had to be taken into account as the basis of the contested measures of the act and on which the exercise of their discretion depended."[173] Thus, in this case

[166] Meuwese, Schuurmans, & Voermans, *supra* note 75.
[167] Case C-310/04, Spain v. Council [2006] ECR I-7285; *see* Meuwese, Schuurmans, & Voermans, *supra* note 75, at 14–15.
[168] Case C-310/04 at recital 5, para. 11.
[169] *Id.* para. 87.
[170] *Id.* para. 97.
[171] *Id.* para. 96.
[172] *Id.* para. 102.
[173] *Id.* para. 123.

the ECJ requires the EU decision makers to conduct proper research based on substantive review. It concludes that:

> the Council … has not shown before the Court that in adopting the new cotton support scheme established by that regulation it actually exercised its discretion, involving the taking into consideration of all the relevant factors and circumstances of the case, including all the labour costs linked to cotton growing and the viability of the ginning undertakings, which it was necessary to take into account for assessing the profitability of that crop.[174]

The EU courts have frequently expressed support for the primacy of science in the policymaking process. Thus, in the *Artegodan* case, the Court of First Instance writes:

> The procedure [in the relevant Directive] … is characterised by the vital role accorded to an objective and detailed scientific assessment by the CPMP [the scientific advisory committee] of the substances in question. Although the CPMP's opinion does not bind the Commission, it is nonetheless extremely important so that any unlawfulness of that opinion must be regarded as a breach of essential procedural requirements rendering the Commission's decision unlawful.[175]

The *Pfizer* case, discussed earlier in terms of standing, is an excellent illustration of the way the EU courts deal with expertise.[176] The challenged EU action mixes together actions involving the Council (but not the Parliament)[177] and the competence of the Commission and its scientific advisory bodies. Pfizer was complaining about a Council regulation, but, following EU practice, the regulation was drafted by the Commission based on material supplied by its scientific advisors, although it overruled those advisors' conclusions in some respects. The line between statutes and administrative regulations is not at issue in the case. The Court reviews the adequacy of the evidence in a way that parallels "hard look" review in U.S. administrative law. Just as in American law, once standing has been granted, the firm faces no limits on what it can argue. In the process of deciding the case, the Court engages with all of Pfizer's arguments even as it dismisses them all.

The Court goes into considerable detail in assessing the quality of the risk assessment process – both the factual basis and the policy choice. It

174 *Id.* para. 133.

175 Case T-74/00, para. 197.

176 Case T-13/99, Pfizer Animal Health SA v Council [2002] ECR II-3305.

177 In the terminology of the Treaty of Lisbon these actions are "non-legislative" because the Parliament is not involved. They have binding legal force and are enacted under special Treaty provisions that permit the Council to act on a proposal by the Commission, for example, in the field of agriculture.

finds that "[n]either the Treaty nor the secondary legislation … contains a definition of the precautionary principle"[178] and that the 1979 document, entitled: "Guidelines on the Application of the Precautionary Principle," is only a working document that does not impose any duties on Community institutions.[179] Because it is not bound by any legal definition of the principle, the Court itself explains what a competent scientific risk assessment under the precautionary principle entails.[180] At the same time, it asserts that the scope of judicial review is limited to "manifest error," "misuse of power," or clearly exceeding the bounds of discretion[181] because of "highly complex scientific and technical facts."[182] The Court holds that the Community institutions did not make factual errors[183] and did not err in finding a risk to human health from the contested additive.[184] Thus, the Court accepts the outcome but only after a very detailed look at the evidence and the relationship between the scientific advisory committees, on the one hand, and the Commission and the Council, on the other.[185] The Commission and the Council can ignore some of the findings of the advisory committee, as they did here, so long as they explain why in scientific terms.[186] "Scientific legitimacy is not a sufficient basis for the exercise of public authority."[187] Notice how the Court both requires the political institutions to rely on science and asserts that politics can trump the recommendations and findings of individual scientists.[188] It makes no distinction between the Council and the Commission, both of which have legal authority over third parties that the advisory bodies lack.

[178] Case T-13/99, *Pfizer*, at para. 117.

[179] *Id.* para. 121.

[180] *Id.* paras. 163–72.

[181] *Id.* para. 166.

[182] *Id.* para. 169. Notice the way this list echoes the original grounds for review under the Treaty of Rome quoted earlier: lack of competence, infringement of a procedural requirement, infringement of the Treaty or of law relating to its application, and misuse of power.

[183] *Id.* para. 311.

[184] *Id.* paras. 401–3.

[185] *Id.* paras. 197–9.

[186] *Id.* para. 199.

[187] *Id.* para. 201.

[188] In *id.* para. 202 the court distinguishes Case T-120/96 Lilly Industries v Commission [1998] ECR II-2571, para. 83. It points out that "under the provisions which applied in that case, consultation with the competent scientific committee within a period prescribed by those provisions was a pre-requisite for adoption of a Commission proposal. For that reason alone, the legal context of this case differs from that in *Lilly Industries*, which can therefore provide no support for the arguments of the interveners."

A 2012 opinion from the ECJ in an antidumping case supports a similar view under the Lisbon Treaty.[189] The opinion states that EU institutions have broad discretion in the area of commercial policy, especially trade protection, "by reason of the complexity of the economic, political and legal situations which they have to examine."[190] Notice that the justices refer not only to economic expertise but also to politics and law. Using familiar formulas, the opinion states that judicial review in complex economic situations is limited to verifying compliance with relevant procedures and to checking whether the facts have been accurately stated, and whether there was manifest error or misuse of power. Given those limitations, it holds that the GC can examine the administrative process, and it upholds the GC's finding that the Commission's process violated the firms' right of defense.[191] Thus, as in *Pfizer*, after bows in the direction of deference, the ECJ accepts the GC's quite aggressive review of facts and of the policy conclusions that follow.[192]

As there is no coherent standard of review regarding the underlying facts of a policy decision and no clear standard of proof,[193] these preliminary cases only show tendencies present in the EU courts' holdings. So far, judicial review has often been stricter when individuals were directly and individually concerned or even named in the challenged legal act.[194] The resistance of the EU courts to imposing procedural duties in rulemaking proceedings[195] might face some pressure through the inclusion of the Charter of Fundamental Rights of the European Union (CFR) in the EU

[189] Joined Cases C-191/09 P and C-200/09 P, Council and Commission v Interpipe Niko Tube and Interpipe NTRP, ECJ February 16, 2012, upholding the decision of the GC on all grounds. John Gaffney, an expert on EU law based in Ireland, directed us to the cases summarized here.

[190] *Id.* para. 63, citing Case C-351/04 Ikea Wholesale [2007] ECR I-7723, paras. 40 and 41.

[191] *Id.* paras. 68, 83, 86.

[192] However, antidumping policy may be a special case. *See* Mendes, Participation in EU Rule-Making, *supra* note 15, at 171.

[193] Türk, *supra* note 35, at 139 and footnote 101.

[194] Case C-49/88, Al-Jubail Fertilizer Company and others v Council [1991] ECR I-3187 concerned an antidumping proceeding, whereas in Case T-306/01, Yusuf and Al Barakaat International Foundation v Council and Commission [2005] ECR II-3533 the applicant's name was explicitly mentioned in the regulation, which is why the court distinguishes the reasoning from Case C–104/97 C, Atlanta and others v. Commission and Council; these cases are taken from Türk, *supra* note 35, at 130 footnote 20, who also points to the unexplained contrast between *Al-Jubail* and *Yusuf*, on the one hand, and *Pfizer*, on the other hand, because all cases refused to give the right to a fair hearing.

[195] *Pfizer* and Case T-369/03, Arizona Chemical and others v Commission [2005] ECR II-5839, para. 86 interpret the duty of diligence as an objective procedural guarantee that does not give individual rights, but can be invoked in an annulment action. *See also* Mendes, Participation in EU Rule-Making, *supra* note 15, chapter 5.

treaties. The CFR guarantees the fundamental right to sound administration in article 41. This rights-based approach might change the dominant public interest narrative by questioning the judicial restraint regarding legislative acts.[196] However, it applies most clearly to individual acts, not rules, so it remains to be seen if the EU courts will reach out to give it a broad reading that enhances the democratic legitimacy of the EU.

B. Procedure

The European Union courts recognize that their review of the procedures used by EU institutions and by Member States can be a way for the courts to police accountability and legitimacy without going so far as to evaluate substantive judgments directly, especially when complex technical material is at issue. Nevertheless, the jurisprudence seems in flux as the courts deal with many different types of challenges. The case law reflects the procedural lacunae in the treaties and, therefore, might also produce a future shift toward participation and transparency.[197]

Sometimes purely procedural challenges to the policymaking process enter almost as an afterthought. This was the case in the 2002 *Pfizer* judgment. After dismissing all of the other claims, the Court went on to dismiss the procedural complaints. *Pfizer* claimed that the European Union had failed to consult affected farmers. The Court held that the Community institutions had complied with the relevant law, which did not give farmers a right to participate. It gave a very narrow interpretation of the right to be heard and of the right of an applicant to raise objections. The holding shows the same focus on individualized harm evident in the section of *Pfizer* on standing. The substantive part of the opinion evaluates the quality of the evidence and the reasoning behind the policy, and it brings in structural concerns that implicate the proper role of science and politics. Nevertheless, when the judges turn to the role of outside participants, they are unwilling to reach out to further democratic participatory values. The Court states:

> Pfizer argues that … the Community institutions did not involve all the parties concerned, with maximum transparency, in consideration of the various possible management options once the results of the risk assessment were

196 Türk, *supra* note 35.

197 Mendes, *Participation*, *supra* note 16, at 1873–5, also makes this point. Competition policy appears to be a partial exception where the EU courts have been quite aggressive in their review of Commission procedures (Kelemen, *supra* note 13, at 159). However, the courts have especially focused on fact-finding, not broad public involvement.

> known. In particular, ... the institutions failed to consult farmers at all before adopting the contested regulation, although farmers were directly affected by the ban.
>
> ...
>
> The right to be heard in an administrative procedure taken against a *specific* person, which must be observed, even in the absence of any rules governing the procedure in question ..., cannot be transposed to a *legislative procedure* leading ... to the adoption of a measure of general application ... The fact that Pfizer – unlike the farmers in particular – is directly and individually concerned by the contested regulation does not alter that finding.... [italics added][198]

The final procedural challenge in *Pfizer* was the failure to fulfill an obligation to state reasons.[199] The Court found the reasons adequate under article 253 EC (replaced by article 296 TFEU). There is no need for an elaborate recitation of reasons, such as a cost-benefit analysis or a risk assessment would require.

> [For] measures of general application, it has consistently been held that the statement of reasons may be confined to indicating the general situation which led to its adoption, on the one hand, and the general objectives which it is intended to achieve, on the other [citations omitted].[200]

In contrast, consider the procedural issues raised by the AG in *Joined Cases C-191/09 P and C-200/09 P, Council v Interpipe Niko Tube and Interpipe* [2011] – an antidumping case – an area of law where the Court has been more willing to find a right to be heard.[201] We saw earlier how the AG uses formulaic language to limit the courts' review of both substance and procedure. However, he then outlines the content of required "relevant procedures" based on past cases. A key point, drawn from previous case law, is that:

> the undertakings concerned should have been placed in a position during the administrative procedure in which they could effectively make known their views on the correctness and relevance of the facts and circumstances

[198] *Pfizer*, paras. 485, 487. The cases that uphold the lack of transposition to a legislative process are: Case C-104/97 P Atlanta v European Community [1999] ECR I-6983, paras. 34, 37; and Case T-521/93 Atlanta and Others v European Community [1996] ECR II-1707, paras. 70–4. In Case C-150/94, United Kingdom v Council [II] ECR [1998] I-7235 para. 54, the court stated that judicial review must be less the more "the act concerned is of general application." *See* Smismans *supra* note 19 at 616–23.

[199] *Pfizer*, paras. 505–15.

[200] *Id.*, para. 510.

[201] Mendes, Participation in EU Rule-Making, *supra* note 15, Chapter 4.

> alleged and on the evidence presented by the Commission in support of its allegation concerning the existence of dumping and the resultant injury.[202]

The AG argues that the Commission erred because it did not communicate essential information to the firms at a time when the firms could have submitted their views to the Commission. However, such a procedural error does not per se constitute an infringement of the rights of the applicant. The EU courts should not order annulment unless the applicant can establish "not that the contested regulation would have had a different content, but simply that such a possibility could not be totally ruled out."[203] The AG did not think the firms had demonstrated this possibility.[204] Thus, whatever the procedural violations, the Court normally will not use them as reasons for annulment on their own. The applicant must show that the lack of process had some relation to the substance of the decision. In that respect the AG follows administrative law doctrine in Germany and France. Review does not impose anything close to the requirements of notice and comment rulemaking in the United States, where procedural violations alone can force a remand to the agency. However, it seems to exceed the U.S. judiciaries' willingness to examine the internal procedures of American legislatures.

New challenges to process are beginning to arise under the Aarhus Convention that applies to the process of making environmental decisions in the administration.[205] The Convention in article 9 requires a review procedure before a court of law (and/or another independent and impartial body established by law) to challenge both the substantive and procedural legality of any decision, act, or omission under article 6, dealing with specific decisions. Both the EU and most of its Member States have ratified the Convention. The European Union courts treat the Convention as an integral part of EU law that is binding both on the Member States and on EU institutions.[206] In a few cases, civil society plaintiffs have won

[202] Opinion of AG Mengozzi, Joined cases C-191/09 P and C-200/09 P at para. 137. This language directly quotes from Case C-49/88 Al-Jubail Fertilizer v Council [1991] ECR I-3187, para. 17, and Case C-458/98 P Industrie des poudres sphériques v Council [2000] ECR I-8147, para. 99.

[203] *Opinion of AG Mengozzi*, para. 142.

[204] *Id.* at para. 142, citing Case C-141/08 P Foshan Shunde Yongjian Housewares & Hardware v Council [2009] ECR I-9147, paras. 81 and 94.

[205] *See supra* note 87 on the Aarhus Convention.

[206] Case C-115/09, BUND, Landesverband Nordrhein-Westfalen (Friends of the Earth) v Bezirksregierung Arnsberg & Trianel Kohlekraftwerk Lünen [2011] ECR I-3673 (application to Member States); Case T-111/11, ClientEarth v European Commission [2013] (stating that international agreements are binding and prevail over EU acts, but that the Aarhus Convention gives wide discretion to the parties).

procedural victories that promote transparency against EU institutions and Member States, but they have lost others, and those decided in the GC are on appeal.[207]

A recent ECJ decision articulates a strong role for the Convention in facilitating judicial review of environmental policymaking in Member States. The case was a referral to the ECJ from a Land (state) administrative court in Germany that asked the ECJ to rule on whether the nature protection nonprofit, the BUND, could have standing in its court. The underlying issue was the adequacy of the environmental impact assessment prepared in connection with the licensing of a coal-fired power plant.[208] The municipality and the firm argued that the nature protection nonprofit organization could not bring the case under German laws of standing. The relevant laws do not confer standing unless "individual public law rights" have been infringed.[209] Because the German court considers:

> that such a restriction on access to justice could nevertheless undermine the useful effect of Directive 85/337 [the amended directive implementing the Aarhus Convention], the referring court wonders whether the action brought by Friends of the Earth ought not to be allowed.[210]

The ECJ holds EU law requires that the nonprofit organization have access to the German courts. Under the EU directive, derived from the Aarhus Convention, environmental organizations must have the same rights as individuals to access the courts, and they can do so to further the general public interest.

> If … those organisations must be able to rely on the same rights as individuals, it would be contrary to the objective of giving the public concerned wide access to justice and at odds with the principle of effectiveness if such organisations were not also allowed to rely on the impairment of rules of EU environment law solely on the ground that those rules protect the public interest. As the dispute in the main proceedings shows, that very largely deprives those organisations of the possibility of verifying compliance with the rules of that branch of law, which, for the most part address the public interest and not merely the protection of the interests of individuals as such.[211]

The public interest value under the Aarhus Convention is a procedural one – the inadequacy of the environmental impact assessment. However,

[207] For an overview of the recent cases, *see* Krämer, *supra* note 87. Some of these decisions are on appeal; so the ECJ may soon weigh in on the issue.

[208] Case C-115/09, para. 27.

[209] *Id.* para. 29.

[210] *Id.* para. 33.

[211] *Id.* para. 46.

the reasoning is potentially much more general. It could signal a broadening of standing overall. First, it could apply to cases brought in the GC against EU bodies that implement environmental policy. Second, if the ECJ sees courts as charged with "verifying compliance" with legal rules that further the public interest, then it would seem that civil society organizations ought to be able to access the GC to further public interest values, whether in EU institutions or in the Member States. It would also hear cases where individuals claim that their rights have been infringed but where the remedy they seek is a modification of policy or procedure that furthers the public interest. So far, the GC has allowed civil society groups to have standing to bring procedural challenges against EU institutions, including the Council, the Commission, and EU agencies. The groups have a mixed record in the GC, but their status of plaintiffs is not in doubt.[212]

A second ECJ case, *Marie-Noëlle Solvay and Others v. Région wallone*,[213] brought under the Aarhus Convention, required the ECJ to rule on the meaning of "legislative" under the Convention and the implementing EU Directive.[214] The Belgian Constitutional Court asked for a preliminary ruling on whether a Member State could avoid the requirements of Aarhus and the Directive by passing a statute whose only purpose was to legally approve a major project. The ECJ held that a statute, even if formally fulfilling the Member State's requirements for passage, might still be subject to the Aarhus requirements. In making this judgment the Belgian court must take

> account both of the content of the legislative act adopted and of the entire legislative process which led to its adoption, in particular the preparatory documents and parliamentary debates. In that regard, a legislative act which does no more than simply "ratify" a pre-existing administrative act, by merely referring to overriding reasons in the public interest without a substantive legislative process enabling those conditions to be fulfilled …, cannot be regarded as a specific act of legislation within the meaning of the …

[212] *See* Krämer, *supra* note 87, summarizing the case law.

[213] Case C-182/10 – Marie-Noëlle Solvay and Others v Région wallone [2012] not reported.

[214] Article 2(2) of the Aarhus Convention defines a "public authority" subject to the Convention as excluding bodies or institutions acting in a "legislative capacity." Directive 85/337/EEC, June 27, 1985, as amended by Directive 2003/35/EC, May 26, 2003, article 1(5), in turn, exempts projects "adopted by a specific act of national legislation, since the objectives of this Directive, including that of supplying information, are achieved through the legislative process." *See also* Joined Cases C-128/09 to C-131/09, C-134/09 and C-135/09 Boxus and Others [2011] ECR I-0000 and C-435/97 WWF and Others v Autonome Provinz Bozen and others [1999] ECR I-5613.

> [Convention] and is therefore not sufficient to exclude a project from the scope of that Convention and that directive as amended.[215]

In this particular case all the information on which the administration relied in reaching its decision was not before the legislature when it approved the project. As a result, passage by the Belgian parliament was not "legislative" under Aarhus. Pro forma legislative approval is not an adequate substitute for the open and participatory processes required by the Convention. The ECJ was not able to strike down the degree approving the project. It could only interpret EU law and indicate how the Belgian court should proceed by expressing strong reservations. The case is quite striking for its straightforward acceptance of the Aarhus Convention's role in furthering democratic legitimacy. It articulates in clear language the way an open administrative process can serve democratic values and recognizes that just following the forms of statutory enactment may not do much to further democracy, especially if the government in a parliamentary system uses the statutory route to supersede more accountable procedures.

EU courts' review of legislative procedures could be quite rigorous after the *Solvay* case, especially as they do not appear to distinguish between Member State and EU institutions. However, the Aarhus Convention only applies to environmental policies. Both cases were brought under EU directives that implemented the portion of the Convention dealing with specific projects (article 6). Articles 7 and 8 deal with plans and executive regulations, respectively, and are much weaker and more hortatory. Judicial (or other) review under article 9 is only required for challenges to projects under article 6(2).[216] Nevertheless, these cases might provide a background for ECJ review of administrative and legislative processes on grounds of democratic sufficiency. None of the fundamental justifications for judicial review of process is deeply tied to the Member State/EU distinction or to the environment as a substantive policy issue. Efforts to increase the democratic openness and legitimacy of EU policymaking are behind the lawsuits currently making their way through the EU courts.[217] These cases reveal the tension between the EU as a consortium of Member States grounded on expert analysis, and as a polity responsible to individual citizens.

215 Case C-182/10, ruling no. 2.

216 And review "before a court of law or another independent and impartial body" is also required for information requests under article 4 that have been "ignored, wrongfully refused, whether in part or in full, inadequately answered, or otherwise not dealt with in accordance with the provision of that article," article 9(1) of the Aarhus Convention.

217 Krämer, *supra* note 87.

IV. CONCLUSIONS

Whatever one's view of the European Union as a polity, its lawmaking procedures are unique. It draws on the experience of Member States and of the United States, but its sources of political legitimacy are more problematic and diverse. Federal states, such as the United States, South Africa, and Germany, give state governments some measure of legal autonomy and have upper houses tied to the states. Nevertheless, all three have powerful central governments supported by strong national constitutions. Even though the states guard their prerogatives and federal courts, especially in the United States, sometimes limit the central government, the legal rules passed by the federal legislature have a particularly strong claim to legitimacy. Accountability to the public through the ballot box is primary. U.S. federal courts will only hold that statutes violate the constitution if they are a threat to protected rights or federalism principles or if the procedural violations are particularly obvious. German courts seem more willing to consider the adequacy of the legislative process and the quality of the underlying information, but mainly in the interest of protecting rights. They too distinguish between statutes, on the one hand, and regulations and legal guidelines, on the other. Most crucially, statutes can only be reviewed by the Constitutional Court, whereas regulations and other executive rules can be subject to both facial and as-applied challenges before administrative courts. However, they are not treated differently in substance because the broad range of fundamental rights guaranteed in the German Basic Law mandates a strict level of proportionality review independent of the form of state activity. The German Constitutional Court has shown an inclination to engage in a thorough review of fact finding, although only so that it can make substantive judgments. Its review of executive rules generally only evaluates procedures in certain policy areas. In the EU, partly as a result of some confusion over the status of various legal norms, the EU courts tend to stress scientific and technical competence, sometimes to the detriment of public accountability. With the rise of the European Court of Human Rights and with the incorporation of a CFR into the EU treaty, the EU courts also increasingly base their judgments on violations of rights. Thus, future developments and tensions are likely to occur if legitimacy based on rights clashes with legitimacy based on expert competence. Furthermore, the democratic legitimacy of EU institutions will remain a contentious issue. Cases are now coming before the EU courts that deal with the assignment of tasks within the EU and the role of suits by private parties. So far they have not emphasized democratic legitimacy, but some aspects of the Treaty of Lisbon may make such suits likely in the near future.

Conclusion

The legitimacy of the modern state is grounded in democracy, individual rights, and the competent design and implementation of public policies. Questions of legitimacy arise as states interact with citizens, other institutions, and international actors. Our inquiry, however, is more focused. The case studies have concentrated on the legitimacy of processes that produce statutes and rules with the force of law. In particular, we consider how judicial review enhances the legitimacy of lawmaking in legislatures and executive departments and agencies. To assess the role of the courts, however, one needs to understand the behavior of political and bureaucratic actors. In our case studies, we stress the incentives of executive branch officials and legislators that arise from the polities' differing constitutional frameworks. Our conclusions depend on the expected, real-world reactions of the other branches of government to judicial review.

Judges in our three country cases and in the European Union gravitate toward the protection of individual rights and the due process values that protect these rights. Their mandate to protect rights is uncontested; other justifications for review are less secure. Yet we argue that preserving democratic legitimacy and checking competence are appropriate judicial roles, but ones that judges must exercise with restraint. Judges need to understand how government works, not just focus on abstract rights and principles. We suggest that if courts adopt that realistic posture, they can play a role in upholding democracy, not just in protecting rights. Although their review of competence will necessarily be limited by their own lack of expertise, they can help prevent abuses and encourage positive developments.

The preservation of democracy is a contested goal for courts. Judges are reluctant to become involved in "political" questions; yet they cannot avoid ruling on cases with political implications. Courts can deny standing to litigants who contest government practices on democratic or competence grounds, or they can refuse jurisdiction. However, caseload restrictions will not always be possible if the constitution and administrative law provide for judicial review of challenges outside the zone of rights. Furthermore, some cases that focus on rights will also raise unavoidable questions of democratic legitimacy or competence. Courts in our case studies differ both in the legal mandates under which they operate and in the way they interpret those mandates. As far as their jurisdiction reaches, courts can help to assure the legitimacy of the state's legislative and policymaking processes. If they do this, however, they walk a tightrope between upholding state legitimacy and undermining other public institutions by overly aggressive review.

Our analysis of judicial review of legislative and executive lawmaking rests on two sources of law – national constitutions and statutes. We take the constitutional frameworks of our cases as given. All are federated polities; the United States is a presidential system; South Africa and Germany are parliamentary democracies. The European Union is a special case whose basic structure remains in flux. We stress the way these background frameworks help determine the impact of judicial decisions on legislative and administrative processes. If the constitutional text lacks procedural detail, the incentives of legislatures and of chief executives and prime ministers are key factors that determine legal developments. Courts need to understand these dynamics even when their decisions nominally only concern rights.

In these concluding pages we summarize and reflect on the relationship between our cases and our underlying analytical framework. Section I begins with statutes that govern either executive rulemaking procedures or legislative processes and that the courts enforce through judicial review. Section II moves to the constitutional level. Constitutions do more than create an institutional framework. They also create rights and protect them through judicial review. Other aspects of the constitutional structure, such as federalism, also limit legislative action. We ask how such constitutional provisions help shape and constrain legislative and administrative processes in the United States, South Africa, and Germany. We study the impact on legislative and administrative rulemaking processes of the courts' interpretations of these often vague provisions.

Section III confronts the hybrid structure of the European Union. The Union's contested democratic legitimacy produces a distinctive set of incentives that have led the European Commission to institute procedural innovations, such as impact assessment, but not to propose judicial review of those procedures. So far, the EU courts have operated within that limitation.

We conclude in Section IV with some recommendations both for constitutional courts and for law reform. Our case studies show how judicial review sometimes fails to take account of the political realities connected to alternative constitutional structures. For example, a decision that seems only to affect rights or federalism may instead have a profound impact on the democratic accountability of the state for good or for ill. Courts should consider the broader impacts of their decisions. Even when a case ostensibly concerns rights, not the structure of government, judges ought to ask how the legislature and the executive will implement their rulings in practice. Constitutional provisions and statutes can permit courts to promote the democratic accountability of the legislative process and of executive rulemaking procedures. Giving courts a role in promoting democracy is risky, but we argue that it is a worthy and feasible goal for judges in all four polities. Thus, on the one hand, we urge the value of judicially enforceable rulemaking procedures, not just in the United States but in parliamentary systems as well, and, on the other hand, we criticize the U.S. Supreme Court for misunderstanding the nature of lawmaking in the U.S. separation-of-powers democracy.

I. PROCEDURAL STATUTES

The political incentives to constrain executive policymaking processes differ in presidential and parliamentary systems, and the statutory law illustrates these incentives in our cases. In contrast, legislators in both parliamentary and presidential systems are unlikely to support judicial review of legislative procedures. They have no interest in giving the courts authority to review their internal activities. Any procedural constraints that exist will likely be the result of constitutional texts as interpreted by the courts.

A. Executive Rulemaking in Presidential Systems

In presidential systems with powerful legislatures, such as the United States, the legislature has an incentive to impose judicially reviewable procedures on executive rulemaking if it is unable or unwilling to assert adequate control through its own internal mechanisms. These procedural constraints can become law as part of a deal with the president. Furthermore, both the president and the legislature may support legal constraints on rulemaking processes if each fears that an upcoming election could lead to a change of party control. Because legislation is difficult to enact and to repeal in presidential systems with numerous "veto gates,"[1] incumbents may try to prevent their

[1] George Tsebelis, Veto Players: How Political Institutions Work (2002).

substantive policies from being immediately undermined by a new administration. Without checks, a new presidential administration could change policymaking priorities by repealing old rules and enacting new ones, especially if it must govern with a hostile legislature. Hence, even if there is unified government, with the same party in control of both the legislature and the presidency, politicians, looking toward the future, may support statutes that mandate rulemaking procedures and permit judicial review of compliance. Judicial review of administrative policymaking processes provides a check that alerts the legislature to particularly serious problems. In the familiar terminology of Matthew McCubbins and Thomas Schwartz, judicial review acts as a "fire alarm" that relieves the legislature from costly, day-to-day monitoring activities, analogous to "police patrols."[2]

Even if judicial review saves the legislature time and trouble, it is unlikely to induce the executive to mirror legislative preferences exactly – either at the time of a statute's enactment or in the present. Judges will seldom perfectly mirror the preferences of the legislature, and, to avoid becoming too politically involved, they are likely to give the executive substantial policymaking discretion. Of course, the legislature could limit the need for oversight by writing detailed statutes or by empowering private litigants to enforce a statute, thus bypassing the bureaucracy. In many policy areas, however, these options are not realistic ways to correct market failures or to achieve social welfare goals. Statutes that delegate policymaking to the executive or to independent agencies are an inevitable aspect of policymaking in any modern state that both provides benefits and regulates the market. One cannot effectively control air pollution from automobiles or power plants through either case-by-case adjudication or detailed statutes. Relying on private lawsuits fails to resolve the collective action problems posed by broad-gauged diffuse harms. Extremely detailed statutes are impractical given both the need for technical knowledge and the potential for rapid changes in both costs and benefits over time. Hence, because delegation is functionally necessary but risky for legislators, they may empower the courts to check delegated policymaking.

But there is an alternative – enhanced legislative oversight. A statute might require that rules be submitted to the legislature for an up-or-down vote or to give the legislature time to pass a vote of disapproval. Even more intrusively, the law could permit the legislature or its relevant committees to participate directly in drafting the text. This could be a substitute for

[2] Matthew D. McCubbins & Thomas Schwartz, *Congressional Oversight Overlooked: Police Patrols versus Fire Alarms*, **28** American J. of Political Science 165 (1985).

judicial review, with the courts only checking to be sure the process was followed. Such direct involvement might violate constitutional provisions on the separation of powers, but even if it does not, the legislature may not favor such second chances. First, the enacting legislature may want to lock in future legislatures and prevent them from interfering with the implementation of a favored policy. Second, such second chances undermine many of the strongest arguments for delegation in the first place. A legislature that delegates because it lacks expertise, time, and flexibility will not want to be able to veto rules in subject areas where these reasons are salient. Of course, there are cases where other factors trump these concerns, as when the legislature acknowledges the executive's superior expertise but wants to be able to check its discretion ex post. Plans to reorganize the executive branch itself provide familiar examples in the United States.

The U.S. presidential system operates consistent with these legislative scenarios – although we, of course, cannot rule out other motivations. The Administrative Procedure Act (APA) mandates certain procedures for executive policymaking and gives the courts a monitoring role. True, the judges' views may not track the policy positions of the legislature, but the statute mandates that review should concentrate on the rulemaking process and on means/end rationality under the "arbitrary and capricious" standard. Even the seemingly stronger "substantial evidence" test concentrates on evidence, not the policy itself. The courts provide a check that does not enmesh them too deeply in policymaking. The APA requires the courts to monitor democratic values and executive competence. Of course, the ostensible policy neutrality of APA review is often violated in practice, even if judges do not explicitly take policy positions. However, the language of the APA and of procedural requirements in individual statutes does limit judicial overreaching.

The courts have gone beyond the bare bones of the APA in response to the growth in rulemaking under the range of environmental and social regulatory laws enacted after the passage of the APA. Some critique these developments for exceeding the goals of the original statute and for imposing court-like procedural models on federal regulatory agencies. This appears to us to go too far. True, one can criticize individual decisions on a range of different grounds, but it seems incorrect to claim that the courts are operating at cross purposes to congressional wishes. Congress has not responded to the courts with efforts to weaken the APA; rather, some substantive statutes go beyond its requirements and the "reforms" proposed by some members of Congress would impose more, not fewer, legal restrictions on rulemaking.

B. Executive Rulemaking in Parliamentary Systems

In parliamentary systems the legislature does not have an incentive to empower the courts to review administrative policymaking. The reasons for this are straightforward. First, the same coalition or single party controls both the cabinet and, at least, the lower house of the legislature. So long as that house has primary lawmaking authority, the governing coalition has no interest in a statute that would limit its exercise of policymaking discretion. The legislative majority might seek to provide input into rulemaking directly, but it would not want to open these processes to outsiders or to allow the courts to review the degree of openness and the reasons given. Second, in a pure parliamentary system, a statute mandating certain administrative procedures cannot lock in future governments with different priorities. If a new government dislikes existing procedural provisions, it can repeal the offending provisions. Furthermore, if the substance of a rule is inconsistent with the present administration's policy agenda, it can seek an amendment from the parliament. Of course, repeal may not be easy if the policy has support from the public, from interest groups, or from a weak upper house, but whatever pushback occurs, the legislative process is much more streamlined than in a presidential system. Absent constitutional requirements, it can follow either the procedural or the substantive route without judicial oversight. As in the German case, the government may have issued internal rules of procedure, but these are mostly prudential matters, not open to outside checks by the courts.

In contrast, parliament itself may seek to monitor and participate in rulemaking. Delegation is not a one-way street, as it is in the U.S. presidential system. Back-benchers and members of the opposition may push to include legislative oversight or approval in statutes. If party control of the legislature is strong, as it is in the South African parliament, members of the majority party itself may seek greater powers of legislative oversight to constrain the cabinet. However, these efforts will enjoy limited success if the party leadership favors a strong executive, as has tended to be the case in South Africa, and legislative control of executive rulemaking remains limited there. In coalition governments in Germany, even cabinet ministers may support the parliament's involvement in rulemaking. They might do so to limit the discretion of ministers who represent parties in the coalition other than their own. As a result of these pressures, the government might have to include such oversight as part of a deal to pass a law. However, it will seek to avoid provisions that build in considerable delay or that give legislative committees too much power. The German case is exemplary here. Several statutory delegations to the executive mandate Bundestag involvement in the drafting or the approval of executive rules, but these provisions are all relatively modest in terms of added delay and hassle, especially given the fact that the same majority controls both the executive and the lower house. Hence, in a parliamentary system, even one with a strong commitment to legislative dominance, there is only so much that the legislature can do to intervene in rulemaking once it has delegated policymaking to the executive. Of course, in principle, the majority can always entirely withdraw the delegation, or even bring down the government with a vote of no confidence, but these are both costly options that cannot be used as tools of routine oversight.

C. Statutes Governing the Legislative Process

Neither presidential nor parliamentary legislatures are likely to pass laws that provide routine judicial oversight of the legislative process. In the United States, even statutes that seek to bind the hands of Congress in the interest of a goal, such as military base closings or budget discipline, do not explicitly empower the courts to check their operation. However, such statutes raise separation of powers issues so that review is sometimes permitted to resolve constitutional doubts. In all of our cases, both presidential and parliamentary, judicial review of legislative procedures is mainly tied to constitutional provisions, especially violations of rights.

We turn next to consider the relevant constitutional provisions as interpreted by constitutional and supreme courts in our cases. As we have seen, these provisions sometimes involve the courts in quite intensive review of the operation of the legislature although usually as a side effect of review based on constitutional doctrines unrelated to legislative procedures.

II. CONSTITUTIONAL CHECKS ON LEGISLATIVE AND RULEMAKING PROCESSES

In all our cases, the protection of rights has led the courts to review some legislative procedures. In the United States such review is very exceptional, and when it does occur, the cases involve particular named individuals. In Germany the *Hartz IV* decision, an opinion written to protect individual social rights, has implications for the legislative process. It imposes standards of expertise and reason giving that can enhance both democratic legitimacy and competence, although its critics worry that it will lead the courts toward overly intrusive review. Cases involving lawmaking procedures in South Africa generally include an element of rights protection even when other values are present. The South African Court found that the public had the right to participate in political decision-making processes, thus blending the protection of rights with the maintenance of democratic values. Socioeconomic policy in South Africa is generally developed in the executive branch, not the legislature, but if such issues did arise in the legislature, judicial review of those rights could extend to legislative decision-making in ways that mimic the reasoning in *Hartz IV*.

The protection of individual rights is particularly dominant in administrative law outside the United States. Neither Germany nor South Africa has a statute like the American APA that explicitly ties judicial review of rules to democratic legitimacy and policymaking competence. Even if statutory provisions mandate certain processes, the law may not contemplate judicial review, or the courts themselves may deny review on jurisdictional or standing grounds. Even when review of rules does occur, the standards of review may be poorly tailored to the type of administrative behavior in question. Administrative law does not always recognize the fundamental difference between normative acts that make policy and individual adjudications. If review of rulemaking develops principally as judge-made law, as appears likely in South Africa, it will be very important for judges to bear in mind these differences when articulating standards.

Constitutions also empower courts to go beyond rights-based review to consider structural issues such as federalism or the separation of powers. We have shown how in South Africa, a parliamentary system, the Constitutional Court understands itself to have a duty to promote openness and participation as democratic goods in themselves, and not merely as an incident of judicial review. Hence, it engages in limited judicial oversight of lawmaking processes on that basis. The Constitution enshrines a broad conception of democracy, and the Constitutional Court has read the text to require broad participation in the legislative process. This emphasis on democratic accountability is already affecting the judicial review of procedures in substantive rights cases. It would not be a major leap for the Court to foster public participation in rulemaking processes more generally, based on the rich conception of democracy in South African constitutionalism. The Court could do this despite the uncertainties over the administrative procedure statute's application to rulemaking.

In the United States administrative rulemaking is subject to procedural constraints that improve its democratic legitimacy. But the deliberative process in the legislature is not subject to judicial control and is constrained only by electoral and other political pressures. In recent years, when the U.S. Supreme Court reviews cases that arguably violate the Commerce Clause or other aspects of federal structure, it asks if the Congress has given well-founded reasons for making inroads into state power. However, such a reason-giving requirement aims to convince the Court, not to push Congress to be more democratically accountable to the citizenry. Reason giving permits the Court to use a procedural inquiry to be sure that the substance is strongly enough anchored to survive the constitutional challenge.

In Germany abstract review of a statute can raise structural issues of constitutional law. But when an individual challenges a statute in a concrete case, the only route to review is a claimed violation of rights. However, the long list of fundamental rights guaranteed in the German Basic Law mandates a strict level of proportionality review independent of the form of state activity. This leaves a gap for statutes that only indirectly affect the general public in a way that cannot be pulled apart into a set of individualized harms – for instance, where legislative decisions concern the allocation of monetary resources or economic policy. In these cases, individuals cannot seek ex post review.

The German Constitutional Court is more willing than U.S. courts to consider the adequacy of the legislative process. It sometimes scrutinizes the quality of the information underlying a statute, but only in the interest of protecting rights.

Similarly, when German administrative courts review executive regulations, they review them through the lens of rights protection without treating process as a value in itself. Thus, they will often ignore procedural flaws if they did not affect the regulatory outcome. However, recent cases, although grounded in rights and demands for better factual justifications, suggest that German public law may be open to reconsidering established legal doctrine on administrative regulations in light of increased demands for public accountability.

III. THE EUROPEAN UNION

Whether one views the European Union as a proto-state or as a confederation of independent countries, its lawmaking procedures are unique. It draws on the experience of Member States and of the United States, but its sources of political legitimacy are more problematic and diverse. Federal states, such as the United States, South Africa, and Germany, give state governments some measure of legal autonomy and have upper houses tied to the states. Nevertheless, all three have powerful central governments supported by strong national constitutions. Even though the states guard their prerogatives and federal courts, especially in the United States, sometimes limit the central government, the legal rules with the strongest claim to legitimacy in all three countries are passed by the federal legislature. Accountability to the public through the ballot box is primary.

In contrast, the European Union courts tend to stress scientific and technical competence, sometimes to the detriment of public accountability. Nevertheless, both democratic values and rights protection are central to debates over the future of the Union. Challenges on all three dimensions come before EU courts, although an emphasis on rights is likely to increase with the EU's accession to the European Convention on Human Rights. In future, claims based on rights may clash with claims based on expert competence. Furthermore, the democratic legitimacy of European institutions will remain contentious, and the democratic status of the European Parliament has been the subject of some Member State/ EU conflicts, especially involving the German Constitutional Court.

EU courts treat agencies with the power to issue legally binding rulings the same as other bodies with that power. This conflation of all kinds of lawmaking is a distinctive feature of EU jurisprudence. Even though members of parliament are directly elected, the Council and Commission remain key sources of political power given their links to the Member States. The new agencies, which usually include representatives from each Member State, gain their political legitimacy not from their subordination to the European Parliament, but from their ability to aggregate Member State views and to claim a mantle of expertise. This contrasts sharply with our other cases where legislatures with strong democratic credentials delegate policymaking authority to agencies and executive departments. Even in the United States, where the presidency is a separate source of political authority, delegation arises from statutes passed by Congress whose claim to democratic legitimacy exceeds that of the European Parliament.

From a positive political economy perspective, the EU parliament may avoid imposing procedural requirements on the Commission or the agencies out of concern that they will end up being applied to the parliament itself. Furthermore, because all statutes must be initially drafted by the Commission, its officials are unlikely to impose judicially reviewable APA-like constraints on themselves. Although both the Commission and the separate EU agencies often express a commitment to broad participation and have created a range of consultation procedures, they have not endorsed judicial enforcement of their participatory procedures. Administrative outreach efforts are an attempt to overcome the EU's democratic deficit, but this quest for legitimacy has not led to official support of judicial enforcement.

The courts themselves have not reached out to review legislative and rulemaking procedures. Review of substance is quite aggressive, as is review of Member State judicial opinions. However, the courts may not wish to provoke an outright clash with the other EU institutions. Hence, they may defer on process. The contrasting constitutional and administrative traditions of the judges of the various Member States may reinforce this deference. Rather than exposing these differences in their opinions, they may be especially reluctant to impose views that would be a direct challenge to the existing practices of the Commission, Council, and Parliament in the name of the treaty. A move by the EU courts in that direction would be a break with established practices.

But an opening might exist. Although there are no concrete procedural duties for rulemaking, the founding principles of the Lisbon Treaty include elements based on openness, participation, and transparency. These provide a framework for judicial review. The European Union's concept of democratic legitimacy extends beyond representation. If the courts take the abstract norms of participation and transparency seriously, they may transform these principles into concrete and specific norms governing executive and legislative behavior.

The general treaty provisions on process govern all EU activity. They are not tied to the protection of rights, but seek to enhance the democratic character of the EU. Nevertheless, the courts may be reluctant to intervene. Judicial review in the name of public participation might conflict with the claim to bureaucratic competence advanced by the Commission and EU agencies.

We have seen how that tension is handled in the United States, where courts have given real meaning to the APA's demand for public participation. Given the weak democratic credentials of the European Parliament, transparency and broad public participation in rulemaking seem especially important. Despite the difficulties, this is an area that is well worth further exploration by scholars and by judges in the years ahead.

IV. REVIEW FOR DEMOCRATIC LEGITIMACY: OLD HABITS AND NEW CHALLENGES

We have stressed the interplay between constitutional frameworks, political incentives, and other constitutional factors, especially rights. Our focus has been on the contrast between presidential and parliamentary systems. Much traditional administrative law, including the distinctive U.S. pattern, flows from the different political incentives operating in these two different systems, with the European Union as a distinctive hybrid case. But, in addition, constitutional provisions, especially the content of rights, lead courts to impose de facto procedural requirements on political and bureaucratic actors that go beyond those generated by political incentives. In protecting rights, courts may well be especially concerned with process, especially when the state must take affirmative action to assure their protection. Constitutional courts have also upheld broad process standards or values, which then flow into the gaps between the more specific rules that legislatures impose both on themselves and on the executive.

If courts reach out to further procedural values, however, they should take institutional structures very seriously. Otherwise, officials in the other branches may fail to implement the courts' pronouncements effectively, and misalignments between judicial orders and political reality can create other problems. The challenge is to create judicial doctrine that harmonizes with the teachings of positive political economy.

A clear example of this kind of disjunction arose in the recent U.S. cases holding that certain statutes violate the federalism provisions of the Constitution. These cases, decided by narrow majorities, impose a strong reason-giving requirement on Congress if it seeks to legislate in areas related to federal/state power. Because many statutes can affect the states, these decisions have the potential to disrupt congressional lawmaking processes. They impose demands on drafters and committee members that are inconsistent with the inherently complex and compromise-laden procedures needed to pass statutes under American constitutional and party structures. The U.S. Supreme Court is running real risks if it expands its oversight of Congress in ways that ignore the real world of lawmaking practice in a presidential system.

Parliamentary lawmaking, in contrast, is capable of greater logic and consistency. Statutes are largely drafted inside the executive and are presented to a legislature controlled by a governing party or coalition. Of course, a grand coalition or a troublesome minor party may generate disputes, but seldom at the scale of the impasses possible in presidential systems. Hence, the German Court's decision in *Hartz IV*, with its strong demand for factual backup, represents a less serious challenge to legislative operations than would a similar decision in the United States. Similarly, although the South African court has aggressively elaborated principles of democratic participation, it applies them cautiously and scrupulously, thus preserving the ultimate right of the majority to govern.

Furthermore, where administrative procedure law tracks the incentives of political actors, the courts need to recognize that efforts to counteract these tendencies will meet with serious opposition – both overt and behind the scenes. Judicial opinions interpreting the rulemaking procedures required by the U.S. APA have produced a drumbeat of criticism that claims ossification and excess litigation. These criticisms threaten to obscure the key role of the APA in furthering the democratic legitimacy of the modern American regulatory state. Conversely, if the German Court, on its own, required notice and comment for major executive rules, such a holding would fit awkwardly with German traditions of executive branch secrecy and could produce a backlash. Nevertheless, in both countries the basic justifications for open and transparent rulemaking processes have merit as ways to further the democratic legitimacy of the state and to allow citizens to monitor the competence of executive policymaking.

Political opposition to reforms that could further public accountability means: first, that the institutions will not reform themselves, and, second, if courts try to spearhead reforms, they must be prepared to confront serious resistance. Recognizing this, courts tend to shy away from confrontations that impose a contested view of constitutional meaning on the political branches. Even the exceptions to the rule are instructive. In the United States, a deeply divided court has mustered a narrow majority for a particular interpretation of federalism. Controversial as these rulings are, they simply block congressional action – making it difficult for politicians to strike back. In contrast, the unanimous decision in *Brown v. The Board of Education* only succeeded in affirmatively reforming public education after a twenty-year struggle.[3] In *Hartz IV* the German Court's concern for social rights trumped the political risks, but the decision may have opened up a line of cases that the Court will find difficult to manage. In South Africa the workability of new standards for democratic participation is, rightly, a regular concern of the Constitutional Court, and its case law is built, to a sizeable extent, on preexisting political support for the underlying ideas.

Old habits of legal thinking sometimes interfere with the courts' response to new situations. South Africa is still working its way free from an administrative law historically focused only on individual adjudicative decisions. The German courts mainly review executive rules as applied in particular cases or if they implicate rights. In both cases the review of executive rules is a contested area. In part, this is because courts recognize that review of rules should not be based on classic notions of due process that rely on court-like procedures. If they did begin to review rules, the focus would

[3] Brown v. The Board of Education, 347 U.S. 483 (1954). On the legacy of *Brown*, *see* Bruce Ackerman, The Civil Rights Revolution, We the People, Vol. III (2014).

need to be on the strength of democratic links and the competent use of expertise, with a background check assuring the protection of rights.

The United States made this turn a long time ago, but it is caught in a different doctrinal tension. Courts sometimes immunize rulemaking from serious oversight under a standing doctrine that has little to recommend it as a logical way to manage the caseload. This is also true in Germany and the European Union. These restrictions seem arbitrary once one accepts the view that courts have an important role to play in enhancing the democratic legitimacy and competence of the administrative process.

If legal reformers seek to push the judiciary to respond to the problems of the modern state, they must recognize the courts' limited capacity for substantive review and acknowledge the value of procedure as it relates to all aspects of legitimacy – protection of rights, democratic legitimacy, and competence. Courts ought to take existing procedural duties seriously – both those expressly contained in statutes and those implied by broader principles of technocratic competence and public participation. Modern regulatory tasks make it necessary for the legislature to delegate to the executive and for the courts to defer on substance. Given this reality, the legislature, backed up by the courts, can require the executive and the agencies to consult experts and the public. Procedural reform can respond to the challenges of combining delegation with democratic accountability. Process can help manage the shift from democratic legitimacy through elections to democratically responsible policymaking that relies on both expert competence and public participation. Courts in the non-U.S. cases could take steps to improve the democratic legitimacy of executive and agency rulemaking processes, at the same time guarding against the excesses of U.S. practice.

Using the courts to enhance the democratic functioning of elected assemblies is more problematic than administrative law reform. Yet it has been responsibly carried out by the South African Court. Courts, statutes, and constitutions should distinguish between politically elected officials and decision makers who implement statutory mandates in executive ministries and regulatory agencies. If democratic values mandate strong links to the citizenry, the courts could be given the authority to be sure that they operate well in practice in the legislature, as well as in the executive. These new roles for the courts may clash with standard constitutional interpretations in some systems, but we have argued that they can be deeply consistent with democratic and republican values so long as courts exercise these roles with caution.

Courts might require legislatures to follow the bare bones of the notice and comment provisions of the U.S. APA that require notice, open-ended participation, and reason giving – without the overlay of U.S. judicial interpretations that have added procedural complexity and delay. In our cases, these procedures are, in fact, often followed for political reasons and some are incorporated in the legislative bodies' internal rules. Recall, however, our claim that the U.S. legislative process, in particular, is a locus of compromise and trade-offs, and even in parliamentary systems, partisan balancing occurs as well. Thus, courts should not require tightly reasoned "findings" but only require legislatures to articulate transparently the trade-offs made to obtain passage.

These tentative suggestions raise constitutional issues in all our cases studies, but if we take seriously the importance of democratically legitimate policymaking and if we have confidence in the restraint of the courts, a move toward more review of process is worth putting on the table for debate in the United States, South Africa, Germany, and the European Union. Maintaining the separation of powers is obviously a concern in all these polities, but independent judicial authority can help provide checks and balances as well. Modest moves could be taken toward judicial review of policymaking procedures that acknowledge the way political institutions condition legislative behavior, and that aim to enhance democratic legitimacy, not just the preservation of rights.

List of Cases

Court of Justice of the European Union

European Court of Justice

General Court [Court of First Instance]

Germany

German Constitutional Court

German High Administrative Court

Other German Courts

South Africa

United States

U.S. Supreme Court

Federal Courts of Appeal and U.S. District Courts

U.S. State Courts

Index

CPSIA information can be obtained at www.ICGtesting.com
Printed in the USA
LVOW11*1551080315

429229LV00002BA/25/P

9 781107 043671